HOW TO READ YOUR NEWSPAPER

SECOND EDITION

by Ruth B. Smith and Barbara Michalak

HARCOURT BRACE JOVANOVICH, INC.

New York Chicago San Francisco Atlanta Dallas *and* London

PHOTO CREDITS

Cover photo, Kenneth Karp; Page 1, Harbrace; 14, Harbrace, © 1969 by The New York Times Company. Reprinted by permission; 24, United Press International; 41, Eli Finer from De Wys, Inc; 56, Harbrace, in cooperation with *The New York Times*; 65, left, NASA Photo from United Press International; right, Harbrace, Snoopy Astronaut "A Peanuts Pocket Doll," © 1969 United Feature Syndicate, Inc; 79, G. Everbach from De Wys, Inc; 89, Wide World; 105 and 129, Harbrace; 144, left, Wide World; right, Harbrace Photo. Reproduced by permission from *The Christian Science Monitor* © 1968. The Christian Science Publishing Society. All Rights Reserved; © 1969 The Christian Science Publishing Society. All Rights Reserved; 159, 166, both photos, and 178, Harbrace, in cooperation with *The New York Times;* 196, Harbrace, courtesy of E. J. Korvette; 210, *The New York Times;* 226 and 238, left, Harbrace; 238, right, Harbrace Photo. Reprinted with permission of *The Wall Street Journal,* © Dow Jones & Company, Inc. 1968. All Rights Reserved; 250, © 1957 United Feature Syndicate, Inc; 258 and 266, Harbrace.

PRINTED IN THE UNITED STATES OF AMERICA

ISBN 0-15-348143-9

CONTENTS

CHAPTER 1

FINDING YOUR WAY THROUGH THE NEWSPAPER

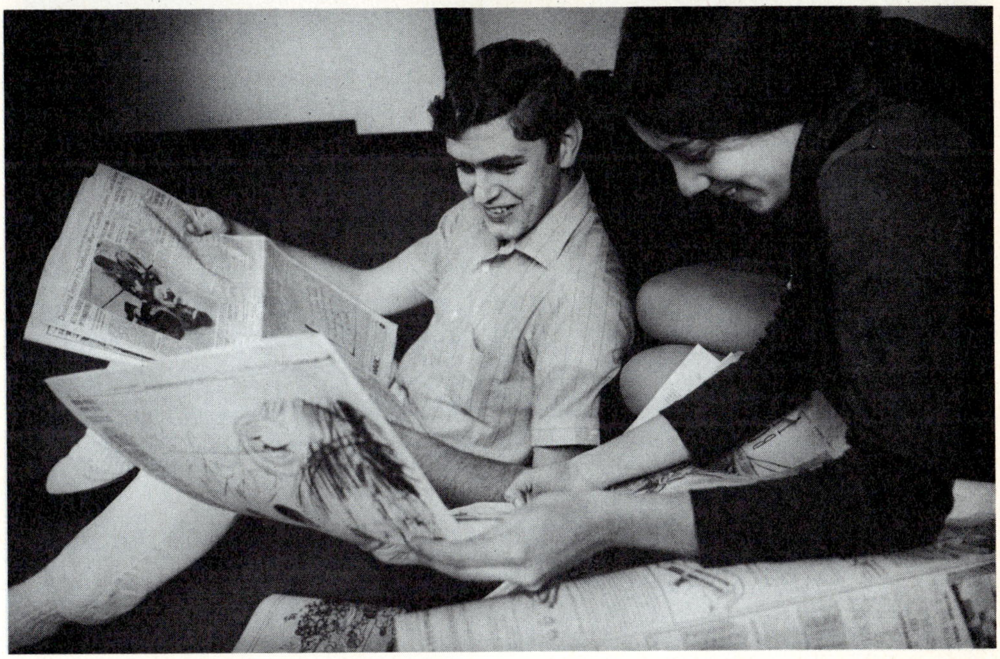

If the *ears* don't give you enough news about the storm, look over the *kickers,* scan the *decks,* and check the *cuts.* Like doctors or baseball players, newspaper people have a kind of language of their own. You should know some of these new words before you start talking about newspapers.

As you read the following list of names, with their definitions, find the parts they identify on *The Vancouver Sun* front page.

MASTHEAD

The masthead of a newspaper shouts for attention. It announces such things as

- the name of the paper
- the city it is published in
- the day of the week and the date
- the volume number
- the number of pages and sections
- the price
- the number of years the paper has been published

EDITION

Many big newspapers publish more than one version of the paper each day. Look for names such as "Suburban Edition,"

"Sports Final," "Early Bird Edition." Some papers identify editions with symbols only, such as one, two, or three dots or stars.

EARS

The boxes at each side of the paper's name are called ears. The ears are part of the masthead. One ear of *The Vancouver Sun* gives the weather, and the other gives the edition and the price. Some newspapers have only one ear, while others eliminate the boxes around the information entirely. (See *The Plain Dealer* on page 9.)

HEADLINES—MAIN, DECK, KICKER

The *main headline*—"Wide-ranging probe of food industry set"—is printed in the biggest and darkest type. It is called a banner or streamer because it stretches across the front page and leads your eye to the right-hand column where the major news story is printed.

The *deck*—"B.C. marketing boards, freeze, prices included"—is really a second headline. Decks appear between a headline and the story. Sometimes two decks are used.

The *kicker*—"2 Boys Saved"—goes before the headline. It enables the editor to present an additional aspect of the story or to supply information that makes the headline more clear to the reader. Not all headlines have kickers.

BYLINE

This line of type tells the name of the reporter who wrote the story. Not every story has a byline.

DATELINE

The dateline was originally used to tell both the *date* and *place* from which a story was sent (Example: Paris, Oct. 7). Today many papers omit the dateline, and some omit only the date. Some datelines give the news agency for which the reporter writes. For example: AP (Associated Press) or UPI (United Press International).

LEAD

The first few sentences of a news story are called the lead. The lead is usually a summary of the event being reported.

MAJOR NEWS STORY

This is the story which the editors feel is the most important at the time the edition goes to press. It gets the biggest headline and is usually found in the right hand column or columns on the page.

INDEX

Regular readers want to know where the features they like are printed. Although editors try to print features in the same sections every day, this is not always possible. An index helps you find what you want to read quickly.

FRONT PAGE

The Vancouver Sun

Focus: INSIDE

• MASSACRES: Seal hunt? What about elephants? Page Six

• MACKENZIE: A highway that leads to nowhere Page 18

• MONEY: What do do when tax shelter collapses Page 33

• BALLET: Celia Franca doesn't mince words Page 49

WEEKEND 25 CENTS

The Vancouver Sun

Tomorrow's weather: SUNNY Details page 3

SATURDAY, APRIL 2, 1977 — VANCOUVER, BRITISH COLUMBIA — ★★★★C

Wide-ranging probe of food industry set

B.C. marketing boards, freeze, prices included

Sun Victoria Bureau

VICTORIA — The provincial government Friday announced a year-long investigation of the B.C. food industry.

The comprehensive study, to be undertaken by the 10 members of the legislature's agriculture committee, will cover B.C.'s controversial marketing boards, the agricultural land reserve, food processing, future food needs and a comparison of prices with Alberta and the Pacific Northwest.

The inquiry was announced by Agriculture Minister Jim Hewett.

The investigators terms of reference give them authority to examine witnesses under oath and to hold both public and in-camera hearings throughout the province.

Hewett has also armed the committee with a research staff to ferret out facts for the four-phase inquiry.

Phase one and two — reports on the land reserve and future land needs and the look at the marketing boards — are due at the end of August.

Phase three, a report on all aspects of food merchandising in B.C. is due at the end of the year.

A final report — "a general overview of the food price situation" — will be handed down March 31 next year.

Besides Hewett, the committee includes his three predecessors in the agriculture ministers' job: MLAs Dave Stupich (NDP—Nanaimo), Cyril Shelford (Socred — Skeena), and Economic Development Minister Don Phillips, who served as agriculture minister before Hewett took over last fall.

In addition to Hewett, Phillips and Shelford there are four other Socreds on the committee: Len Bawtree (Shuswap) Harvey Schroeder (Chilliwack), Walter Davidson (Delta) and Gerry Strongman (Vancouver South).

Two of Stupich's fellow NDPers, Chris D'Arcy (Rossland-Trail) and Barbara Wallace (Cowichan-Malahat) make up the rest of the committee.

Specifically, the terms of reference direct the committee to first find out if there is enough farmland in B.C.'s agricultural land reserve to meet food requirements in B.C.

Phase one also asks the committee to decide how much land is needed for future B.C. requirements, including "economically sound" exports of food.

In the second phase the MLAs are asked

"MLAs" page 2

—Glenn Baglo Photo

AMID THE TANGLED RUINS . . . unidentiied victim receives emergency aid from two members of the fire department's rescue squad

Crane collapse kills one, injures five

"I heard big cracking noises and the whole thing was down in seconds. The big crane gave way and pulled the other one down with it."

Andy Kivinen was describing the collapse Friday of two cranes on a construction site, at the south end of Burrard Bridge which killed one man and injured five others seriously.

Kivinen was the operator of one of the cranes and had left it at the end of his shift about 3:30 p.m., seconds before it collapsed.

Witnesses said the boom and counterweight of the hammerhead crane being erected on the site toppled, causing the 230-foot boom of a mobile crane to crash into a shed and cars on adjacent National Harbors Board property.

Dead is Thomas Rudnisky, 40, of 1305 Dominion Ave., Port Coquitlam.

Garry Hamilton, 27, is in poor condition in the intensive care unit of Vancouver General Hospital with two broken legs and other injuries.

John McGowan, 35, is in serious condition with a neck injury, hospital authorities said.

John Freeman, 25, with head injuries, and Rob McDougall, 28, and Harold Hogan, 45, both with neck injuries, were all reported in satisfactory condition today.

The accident occurred as the 170-foot hammerhead crane was being prepared to begin work on the $6 million centre for the B.C. Credit Union League.

John Otterwell, project manager for the contractor, Stevenson Construction Co. Ltd., said about 25 workers were on the job when the cranes toppled.

The mobile crane, supplied by Arrow Transfer Co. Ltd., had been brought to the site to erect the hammerhead crane.

Jasco Equipment Supply Ltd. was the contractor erecting the hammerhead crane.

Jack Charles, president of Arrow Transfer, said some witnesses thought a guy wire on the hammerhead crane had snapped.

The accident prevention section of the Workers Compensation Board is investigating.

Kivinen, who has watched construction cranes being erected over the past 10 years, said he saw nothing unusual about

More pictures, pages 47

the hammerhead crane's construction or the way it was being put up.

"They were just putting the finishing touches on it," Kiniven said. Workmen were adjusting the tension of two steel pendant lines which hold the boom and counterweight in balance.

A Jasco worker at the site said he was on the hammerhead crane tower near the bottom when he felt it shudder slightly. A few minutes later, he felt another shudder.

"Crane" page 2

ANDY KIVINEN . . . heard cracking noises

Quebec language bomb shakes up non-French

By PETER HADEKEL
Special to The Sun

QUEBEC CITY — The Parti Quebecois government dropped a bombshell on Quebec's anglophone community Friday by declaring its intention that the province will not be a bilingual province after its language legislation is passed.

In releasing its long-awaited white paper on language policy, the government said it plans legislation making Quebec a massively French "state."

The recommendations in the 76-page white paper on language policy are likely to stir profound emotions as the government prepares to table its draft language bill, the Charter of French in Quebec, in two or three weeks.

The presentation of the white paper is being interpreted by some as an attempt to provoke a confrontation with Ottawa. Liberal member of the national assembly John Ciaccia called it a "de facto declaration of independence."

"The lunatics have taken over the asylum," said Ciaccia, a spokesman for Montreal's Italian community.

Several liberal MLAs warned that such legislation could lead to the death of the province's anglophone community.

The PQ's proposed language charter will go much farther than Bill 22, the Official Language Act passed by Robert Bourassa's Liberal government. Former solicitor-general Fernand Lalonde, who was responsible for Bill 22 in the Bourassa cabinet, said the PQ has substituted "incentives" for "coercion" in its attempt to make Quebec unilingual French.

Policy paper excerpts, page 12

But Cultural Development Minister Camill Laurin, who presented the white paper, called it a historic turning point in Quebec's history.

"We are no longer uncertain of ourselves," he said.

"We have come out of the winter of our oppression and into the springtime of our maturity."

The proposals to make French the only official language of the courts and the leg-

"Non-French" page 2

13 crewmen die in crashes of U.S. bomber, navy trainer

Sun News Dispatches

MARQUETTE, Mich. — Thirteen crewmen were killed late Friday and early today in the crashes of a U.S. Air Force B-52 bomber near here, and a T-39 U.S. Navy trainer in Southern California.

Searchers recovered the bodies of eight crew members killed when the B-52 crashed on a training mission in a remote area of Michigan's Upper Peninsula.

A navy spokesman said all five crew members aboard the T-39 were killed when the twin-engine trainer crashed into a mountain slope near Julian, Calif.

Officials at Sawyer air force base said the B-52 was on a training mission and was making a final approach to land at the Strategic Air Command base when it crashed.

A resident of the area said he saw a "huge flash and an explosion like ammunition was exploding" when the plane crashed.

The bomber was not carrying any weapons, an air force spokesman said.

"It just lit up like day," Colleen Womch, 21, said. "It had a real reddish tinge for 30 seconds just like broad daylight here. We heard the explosion and all sorts of little explosions from the pane for about a half hour."

Womch and her husband live about one-quarter-mile from the crash site.

"We have been out here about a year now and you get used to the sound of the planes," she said. "But this one didn't sound right. It seemed like it was too low and pretty noisy, then all of a sudden there was a big red light and we knew what had happened."

A navy spokesman in California said the T-39 was based at Pensacola, Fla., and had made a stop at Yuma in Arizona before the crash. The aircraft was used to train navigators.

Bud Getty, manager of Anza Borrego Desert State Park, said a camper saw the crash from a distance and sounded the first alarm.

Axe-swinging mob routs U.S. Nazis

Sun News Dispatches

SAN FRANCISCO — An angry mob, swinging hatchets and tire irons smashed up the Rudolph Hess Bookstore five days after the Nazi shop opened, police said.

No injuries were reported when a gang of about 50 adults attacked the store Friday night, police said. Two men were arrested and booked for assault and malicious mischief.

The presence of the Nazi store, within sight of a synagogue founded by German Jews who survived the Second World War, seemed to inflame the neat middle-class neighborhood on the city's western edge.

The store opened Monday to the sound of martial music and the sight of young men wearing Nazi stormtrooper uniforms with swastika armbands.

"We want to open the door to white people who are concerned about the future of their race," the Nazis proclaimed. "We don't let niggers in. We don't let non-whites in. This is a white people's store."

Nazi party head Alan Vincent complained earlier Friday his party was victim of "political persecution" because the store owner, a Polish Jew who survived four years in Auschwitz concentration camp where he says his entire family died, started eviction proceedings.

"We don't need people who hate other people," said Nathan Green, the 67-year-old immigrant who had not known of his new tenants' plans for the building.

Green said he consulted a lawyer, then posted an eviction notice on the bookstore which comes due April 5.

"He doesn't have any grounds to evict," Vincent said in a telephone interview. "We haven't done anything wrong. It's an obvious case of political persecution."

The attack was launched on the eve of Passover, the eight-day Jewish religious festival commemorating the biblical exodus of the Israelites from Egypt.

Earlier in the week the store's plate glass window was smashed, an attempt was made to set the building on fire and the wall was daily splattered with tomatoes.

A police spokesman, speaking of Friday night's attack, said: "Apparently there were some people in the crowd who had been attending a meeting at the Jewish Centre across the street.

"As soon as the mob began crashing in the front window the Nazis who were inside fled for their lives out the back door."

Arrested were Morris Weiss, 55, and his son, Allan, 24.

2 BOYS SAVED

Rescuer dies in park river

Special to The Sun

NANAIMO — A 65-year-old man who rescued a boy from a fast-flowing stream Friday drowned when he went to the aid of the boy's brother.

The body of Fredrick Hay was recovered from the waters of Millstone River by an RCMP diver.

The second boy was brought to safety by two municipal park board employees.

Steven Scott, 12, and brother Michael, 9 were in Bowen Park with their mother and were playing near the foot of a small waterfall when they fell into the stream shortly before 3 p.m.

RCMP said the mother heard cries, ran down the riverbank and called for help.

Hay and his wife were walking in the park and heard the screams.

Hay waded into the stream and man-

"Rescue" page 2

SCIENCE CRACKS BOILED EGG CASE

LONDON (Reuter) — A team of scientists working for 10 years, has finally solved the mystery of why modern eggs split so easily when boiled.

The reason, they said, is that eggs reach the public too quickly — before their air cell, which grows with age, has enlarged enough to accommodate the egg contents that expand when boiled.

INDEX

Bridge	66	Nesbitt	9
Business	33	Marjorie Nichols	4
Comics	53	Religion	25
Crossword	67	Sport	29
Entertainment	49	St. Pierre	47
Fotheringham	47	Theatres	42
Gardens	65	Today	50
Ann Landers	51	TV	48
Letters	5	Valley	44
Names In News	48	Wasserman	49

Classified 736-2211 — Circulation 732-2371

FOUNDED 1886 • VOL. 91 • No. [illegible]
108 PAGES

NEWS BRIEFS

These are summaries of articles or features on the inside pages. Some newspapers give these summaries on the front page. Others, like *The Vancouver Sun,* use a column on a later page.

CUT

Long ago, a woodcut was used to print pictures. Now cut means any kind of illustration, such as a photo, drawing, graph, weather map.

CUTLINE OR CAPTION

The line or lines of type that describe the cut (picture).

FOLD

Editors place the most important stories in the half of the page above the fold. This helps to sell the paper, because it is the only part of the newspaper the buyer can see when the folded paper is on the newsstand.

RULES

These lines fence off one story from another. Check where the rules are when you get confused about which story goes with which headline. Sometimes editors use rules to break up copy on a front-page story to cite pages where related stories are to be found.

CONTINUED LINE OR JUMP LINE

In order to get more stories on page one, editors print only the beginnings of most stories there. The rest of the story is printed on less valuable space on inside pages. The continued line tells you the page and the column where you will find it. It is called a jump line for short, because you have to jump across other material to get to the rest of the story.

SUBHEADS

These are put in mainly for looks. A black subhead breaks up a long gray column of type. It also may call attention to an important point in the story.

HOW TO FIND THE NEWS YOU WANT TO READ

Newspapers have signs to help you find what you want to read quickly. Each section of the paper may have a heading telling what that particular section contains. On the front page you will usually find an index which lists all of the features in alphabetical order and tells you what page each is on.

If you want the TV schedule, you look under T in the index. You don't have to keep flipping pages until you see the schedule.

B
The Seattle Times doing
Arts and entertainment
Business and Finance
Real estate
Automotive
TV-Radio
Garden
Saturday, October 9, 1976 B 1

Leisure
• Mini page • What's doin' • Amusements • Life style • Television
Houston Chronicle
Saturday, July 31, 1976
Section 2

Scene
Food
The Arts
Television
Fashion
San Francisco Examiner
Tues., Oct. 5, 1976
☆ Page 19

Top, Reprinted from the *Seattle Times;* center, the *Houston Chronicle;* bottom, *San Francisco Examiner*

Above are section heads from three newspapers. Notice that each tells you briefly what that particular section contains.

HOW NEWSPAPER SECTIONS ARE IDENTIFIED

As you can see by looking at these headings, newspapers identify sections in different ways. The three most often used are:

Letters. First section is A, second section is B, etc.

- *Example:* See section head for *The Seattle Times.*

Numbers. First section is 1, second section is 2, etc.

- *Example:* See section head for the *Houston Chronicle.*

Titles: First section is always news. The second section usually deals with editorials and analysis of the news. Sections are *not* identified by letters or numbers.

- *Example:* See section head for the *San Francisco Examiner.*

Newspapers which use letters and numbers to identify sections may also use titles for each section. For example, Section B in *The Seattle Times* is called "Doing." Section 2 in the *Houston Chronicle* is called "Leisure."

EXERCISE 1. Identifying Newspaper Sections

Directions: Look at the section heads and then answer the questions which follow by circling YES or NO.

YES NO 1. *The Seattle Times* is identified by letters and titles.
YES NO 2. The *San Francisco Examiner* is identified by letters.
YES NO 3. The *Houston Chronicle* is identified by numbers only.
YES NO 4. The *San Francisco Examiner* is identified by titles only.
YES NO 5. The *Houston Chronicle* is identified by numbers and titles.

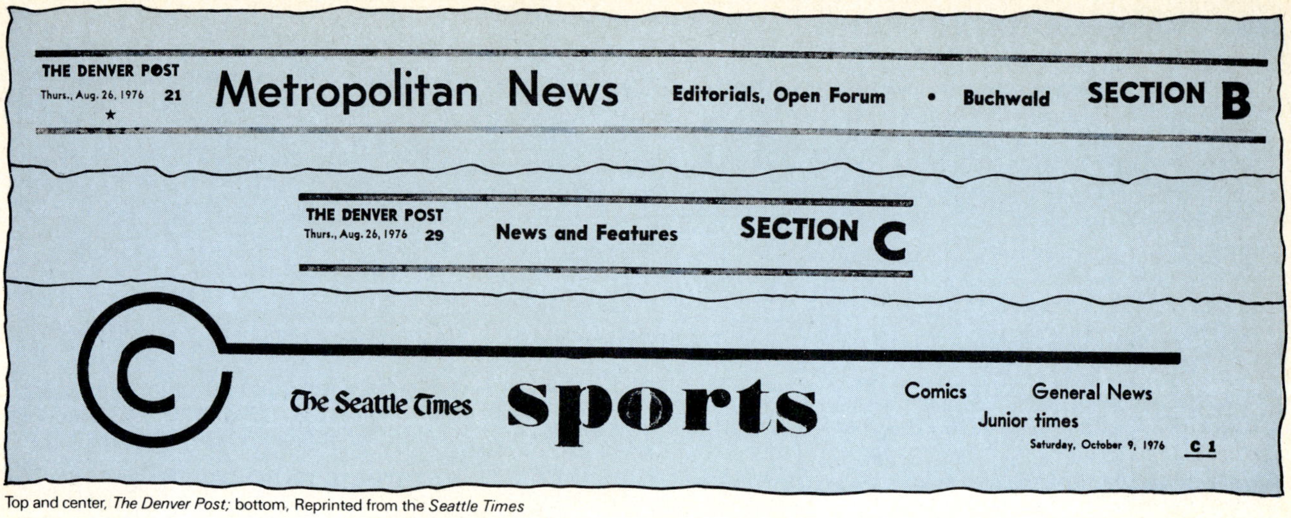

Top and center, *The Denver Post;* bottom, Reprinted from the *Seattle Times*

HOW NEWSPAPER PAGES ARE NUMBERED

Newspapers number their pages in one of two ways:

By the whole paper. Pages are numbered as in a book.

- *Example: The Denver Post.* The August 26, 1976 issue has 80 pages. The front page is page 1 and the last page is page 80.

By sections. Each section starts with page 1.

- *Example: The Seattle Times* is numbered A1–8, B1–10, C1–7, etc.

EXERCISE 2. Checking Your Newspaper's Numbering System

Directions: Look at a copy of your local paper or one assigned by your teacher and then answer the following questions.

1. (Check one): My paper is numbered by: ____ sections. ____ the whole paper.
2. Write below anything special you find about your paper's numbering system. For example, the daily *New York Times* letters its classified pages: A, B, C, etc.

____

____

____

____

____

EXERCISE 3. Identifying Sections

Directions: Look at the six sample section heads. Then read each statement below. If the statement is correct, circle YES. If the statement is wrong, circle NO. If you can't tell from the information given on the section head, circle ?.

YES NO ? 1. Section C of *The Seattle Times* has news about sports.

YES NO ? 2. Section B of *The Denver Post* contains metropolitan news and editorials.

YES NO ? 3. The comics and TV-Radio appear in the same section of *The Seattle Times.*

YES NO ? 4. Art Buchwald's column appears in the *San Francisco Examiner.*

YES NO ? 5. *The Seattle Times'* readers can get information about real estate in Section B.

YES NO ? 6. All of the papers contain information for gardeners.

YES NO ? 7. Section C of *The Denver Post* contains both News and Features.

YES NO ? 8. Food and Fashion are presented in the same section in the *San Francisco Examiner.*

MAKING A NEWSPAPER ANALYSIS SHEET

Newspapers, like people, have different personalities. You have to get acquainted before you really feel at home with them. The Newspaper Analysis Sheet helps you find out what you need to know to feel acquainted with your newspaper. On the next page is a sample of the Newspaper Analysis Sheet. You will use this later in getting to know one of your local papers. For the time being, look it over and then go on to do the exercises which follow the front page of *The Plain Dealer* on page 9. After you have practiced filling out the analysis sheet of *The Plain Dealer,* you will find it easy to combine the steps to analyze any newspaper you pick up.

NEWSPAPER ANALYSIS SHEET

1. Name of Newspaper ________________________________

2. Place of publication ________________________________

3. Day of week ____________ Date ____________ Edition ____________

4. Total number of pages __________ Total number of sections __________

5. Sections identified by letters YES NO OR by numbers YES NO
(Circle correct one.)

6. Pages in each section are numbered separately YES NO
(For example, Sports 1-15; Business 1-8.)

7. Pages in each section are numbered consecutively (like a book). YES NO
(For example, News 1-24; Editorials 25-30; Sports 31-40.)

8. Front Page -- Main headline reads ________________________________

____

9. Editorial Page -- Lead (first) editorial is about ________________

____

10. Index appears on Page __________. If there is no index, check here _____.

11. Index lists columnists by names of writers YES NO
(Circle correct one.)

	News and Features	Section	Page
12.	Business (Finance, Markets)		
13.	Comics		
14.	Crossword Puzzle		
15.	Editorials		
16.	Entertainment, movies (Amusements)		
17.	Obituaries		
18.	Religion		
19.	Sports		
20.	Travel		
21.	TV-Radio		
22.	Want Ads (Classified)		
23.	Weather		
24.	Women's Pages (Foods, Fashions)		

25. Are there sections in your paper not listed above? List those which interest you. ________________________________

____

____

____

WEATHER
Mostly sunny
High 47 (8C)
Low 30 (-1C)
See Page 10-E

THE PLAIN DEALER

OHIO'S LARGEST NEWSPAPER

STATE
*
Dow Jones
off 0.08

135TH YEAR—NO. 322 ★ CLEVELAND, WEDNESDAY, NOVEMBER 17, 1976 100 PAGES 15¢

On the inside

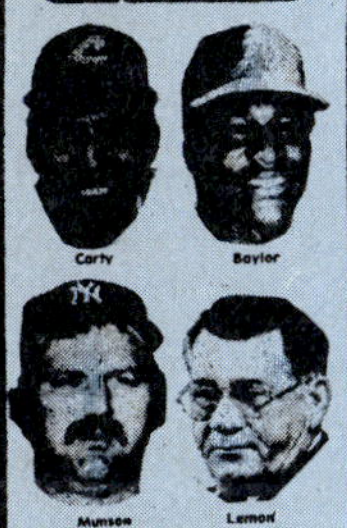

Carty Baylor Munson Lemon

Baseball

Rico Carty, sold to Toronto two weeks ago, was named the Indians' Man of the Year yesterday in a series of baseball action. New York's Thurman Munson was named the American League MVP; Indian great Bob Lemon was named Chicago White Sox manager; free agents Gene Tenace and Don Baylor signed contracts, Tenace with San Diego and Baylor with California.

Page 1-F

Movin on

Raymond L. Klauer, president and chief executive officer of the May Co. here, has been named to head May Department Stores Co. biggest division in California.

Page 7-F

Making plans

The Teamsters are planning a campaign to organize police in Ohio should the state enact a public employes collective bargaining bill next year.

Page 3-A

Summit

President-elect Carter will meet with President Ford next week and Secretary of State Henry Kissinger this weekend.

Page 18-A

OIC practices

Practices by which nearly a million dollars was illegally spent by a past Ohio Industrial Commission still continue, a report says.

Page 20-A

Page 9-F

Editorials

President-elect Carter has given some indication he may be more conservative fiscally than first believed ... Ambassador Saxbe is ending his tour of duty in characteristic fashion.

Page 24-A

581-day war futile

Lebanon faces same problems

By Stuart Auerbach
Washington Post

BEIRUT — A baker combed through the ruins of what used to be his prosperous shop in the commercial heart of Beirut yesterday, looked at the total destruction all around him and uttered what may be the best analysis of Lebanon's ugly and apparently pointless civil war.

"What fools we are," he added. "All this for nothing. Everyone lost and nobody won."

After 581 days of fighting — which saw as many of 40,000 persons killed, 160,000 others wounded, many of Beirut's major hotels, banks and business buildings destroyed by artillery fire and many towns throughout the country ravaged — all of the major political, social, economic and religious problems that led to the war remain unsolved.

The Palestinians are still in Lebanon, though under the Arab summit agreement that led to the current peace they are restricted to their camps and to "Fatahland," the rocky terrain in the southeast of the country from which they have mounted commando raids into Israel in the past.

"What fools we are ... All this for nothing. Everyone lost and nobody won."

The Palestinian presence in Lebanon was a major irritant leading to the war. Christian leaders felt the Palestinians were taking over the country by their armed presence.

The Christians, though a minority of the population, still control the political life of the country through a 34-year-old national covenant based on an outdated census.

Moreover, the fighting has worsened tensions that have existed under the surface between the Moslem majority, who feel they are being deprived of political power that should be theirs, and the Christians, who fear their way of life is threatened.

What is left of Lebanon's once-prosperous economy is still in the hands of a few, and the tax reforms and redistribution of wealth proposed by the largely Moslem leftist parties have not been achieved

This war usually is described as

Continued on Page 12-A

A war-ravaged street in Beirut. Associated Press

The Plain Dealer/William A. Wynne

Greg Burnett of Akron does a juggling act while auditioning for Clown School.

Utah killer, girlfriend take drug overdose

From Wire Reports

SALT LAKE CITY — Gary M. Gilmore, the condemned man who has tried to hasten his own execution, and his girlfriend were hospitalized yesterday after both separately took overdoses of barbiturates in what authorities called an apparent suicide pact.

Gilmore, 35, was reported in "very serious" condition at the University of Utah Medical Center after pneumonia developed in his right lung.

A hospital spokesman said gastric acid from his stomach had seeped into his lung.

The spokesman said he had swallowed about a dozen capsules of Seconal and an unknown amount of another barbiturate.

Mrs. Barrett Gilmore

In Provo, Nicole Barrett, 20, divorced mother of two who has said she would be willing to marry Gilmore before his execution by a firing squad, was hospitalized in critical condition suffering from a similar overdose. She was in a coma.

The bizarre episode came about 25 hours before Gilmore was due to appear before the State Board of Pardons to plead that his execution take place as quickly as possible.

The board had been ordered by Gov. Calvin L. Rampton to review the case over the objections of the prisoner, who had asserted that any efforts to postpone his execution constituted "cruel and inhuman" punishment.

Gilmore, who has been behind bars for 18 of the last 21 years, has indicated that he could not tolerate the prospects of more imprisonment.

It was learned that a physician had prescribed Fiornal, a barbiturate, after Gilmore had complained

Continued on Page 10-A

Canada's future clouded by Quebec separatist win

From Wire Reports

MONTREAL — Speculation about Canada's future swept the country yesterday after the separatist Parti Quebecois crushed the governing Liberals in Quebec's provincial elections.

Strong pressure was being brought by local and national federalists against any attempt by the new provincial government to break away from Canada.

Rene Levesque, who as head of Parti Quebecois is to become provincial premier in about 10 days, was warned by Prime Minister Pierre Trudeau and others that he had a mandate to govern the province but not to lead it to independence.

At a news conference yesterday afternoon, Levesque responded by saying he could not be expected to abandon his long-term goal of independence but he intended to rule as a provincial premier for the next four years within the present structures.

He said his immediate goals were financial recovery, economic development, and an honest and open administration. He acknowledged that he had been brought to power largely by an electorate protesting the previous government because it had failed in those fields.

With only 41% of the popular vote, his party captured 69 of 110 seats in the provincial legislature. The Liberal party, which had governed with 102 seats, was ousted after six years in power. Premier Robert Bourassa and 11 other ministers were defeated in their own districts. Liberals, getting 34% of the vote, won 28 seats. The National Union, Quebec's main conservative force which ruled from 1944 to 1970, was third with 18% and 11 seats. Two seats went to minor groups, with 7% of the vote.

Levesque said he wished to see Quebec "master in its own house" and in "a new and equal association with the rest of Canada." He called Monday's vote historic because it had cast off "ancestral chains" and "fear of change."

But he repeated assurances he did

Continued on Page 12-A

Clowning in the circus is a serious business

By Harry Stainer

Glen (Frosty) Little, boss clown of the red unit of Ringling Bros. and Barnum & Bailey Circus eyed 10 of his clowns and 11 novices yesterday in a ring at the Coliseum.

"Clowns talk," he yelled. "You don't have to move like a Keystone Kop. Talk and walk naturally. Remember, the gag sells the clown."

Little was auditioning the novices to see if any could qualify for the next session of the clown school operated by the circus. Next session is in September.

Little later put the clowns and the tyros through a pants-pressing routine complete with ironing board. The punchline was one clown appearing to punch another.

A clown threw a fist and a loud smack was heard as the novice fell backward to the ground. "That was done real well," Little said to the novice, because the smack was made by the novice's hands clapping as the punch missed him only by the thickness of a coat of red nose paint. He had not actually fallen, but had jumped backwards instead.

Little, 50, is the oldest clown of the red unit. But he does not perform every night. And this unit had no master clown because, Little said, few are left in the business.

Little's crew is young, and includes three women and a black male. The oldest clown in the unit is Jimmy Briscoe, 25, of San Diego who has been with the circus six years.

The circus has two units, red and blue, touring the country and each has 30 clowns. Another 12 clowns work at a Ringling Bros. amusement park in Florida.

"We conduct these auditions about 10 times a year," Little said.

Continued on Page 23-A

CWRU gets $750,000 gift to set up a professorship

Dively

A gift of $750,000 to endow a professorship of electrical engineering at Case Western Reserve University was announced yesterday by President Louis A. Toepfer. The donors are George S. Dively, honorary chairman of Harris Corp.; Richard B. Tullis, Harris chairman and chief executive officer, and Marvin Bower of McKinsey & Co. Inc.

The professorship will be named in honor of Dively, an honorary CWRU trustee. He was a trustee of Case Institute of Technology for 10 years and a CWRU trustee from 1967, when Case and Reserve united, until last year. He was chairman of the CWRU committee on long-range plans and goals of the university.

Bower was a CWRU trustee and chairman of the board for three years. He is also an honorary trustee. Tullis is a member of the board.

The Dively gift will not be used to pay the normal salary of the professor who holds the professorship. The income from the endowment will be used to supplement the salary and for other special benefits for the holder.

"I want it used to provide excellence in this department," Dively said. "A private school has got to develop excellence, and Case Western Reserve has the basics for it in engineering, the medical school and nursing."

EXERCISE 4. Using the Masthead

Directions: Look at the masthead for *The Plain Dealer*. It gives you the information you would need for the first six blanks on your Newspaper Analysis Sheet. Fill in the information requested on the blanks below:

Name of newspaper ______________________________.

Place of publication ______________________________.

Day of week ____________ Date ____________ Edition ____________.

Total number of pages ______________________________.

EXERCISE 5. Scanning Indexes

Directions: Study each sample index on page 11 to find out if

the total number of sections is given;
the sections are identified by letters or by numbers;
the pages of the sections are numbered consecutively;
columns are listed by title or by the writer's name.

Each of the sample indexes is identified with a number. Use the number to answer the questions below.

1. Sections are identified by letters in Index ____.
2. Sections are identified by numbers in Indexes ____ and ____.
3. Sections are called Parts in Index ____.
4. The newspaper is divided in two sections in Index ____.
5. The sections are not identified by letters or numbers in Index ____ and Index ____.
6. The pages in each section are numbered separately in Index ____, Index ____, and Index ____.
7. Columnists are grouped together in Index ____.
8. Telephone numbers are given in Index ____.
9. The paper has at least seven sections according to Index ____.
10. The paper has at least six sections according to Index ____.

EXERCISE 6. Finishing the Analysis Sheet

Directions: Using the model of *The Plain Dealer* on page 9 and Index 5, fill in the rest of your analysis sheet, page 12. Since no section identification is given in the index for this paper, leave the Section column blank. The first entry is done for you.

Sections identified by letters YES NO Or by numbers YES NO

①

TODAY IN THE AMERICAN

Mass murder survivor Corazon Amurao builds a new life in the Philippines.

See the Magazine

"There goes the neighborhood!"

Chicago's American

②

On Inside Pages
[In Two Sections]

Press Telephones

Home Delivery 263-1121
Want Ads — 263-1201
Other Depts. — 263-1100

Pittsburgh Press

③

IN THE PRESS

Cleveland Press

④

Today's Feature Index

THE COLUMNISTS

Milwaukee Sentinel

⑤

A Student's View

What do university students think of religion? Are clergymen fulfilling their mission today? Read one student's views in today's Ash Wednesday religion section, Page 15.

Editorials, Page 16

Unless there is a sharp change in American policy, sending of 50,000 to 100,000 more troops to Vietnam is inevitable . . . Barbers Union should make an exception for the airport shop.

Where to Find

Plain Dealer Phone Directory Page 3

The Plain Dealer

(Circle correct answers.)

Each section is numbered separately YES NO

(For example, Sports 1-15; Business 1-8.)

Page numbers run consecutively from one section to the next (like a book) YES NO

(For example, News 1-24; Editorials 25-30; Sports 31-40.)

Front Page—Main headline reads ______________________________

____

Editorial page—Lead (first) editorial is about ______________________

____

Index appears on page ____. If there is no index, check here ____.

Index lists columnists by names of writers YES NO

(Circle correct answer.)

News and Features	Section	Page
Business (Finance, Markets)		20-24
Comics		
Crossword Puzzle		
Editorials		
Entertainment, Movies (Amusements)		
Obituaries		
Religion		
Sports		
Travel		
TV—Radio		
Want Ads (Classified)		
Weather		
Women's Pages (Foods, Fashions, etc.)		

PRACTICE IN YOUR LOCAL NEWSPAPER

Now you are prepared to use the Newspaper Analysis Sheet to get acquainted with any newspaper. Your teacher may give you extra analysis sheets for each newspaper you want to analyze. Then choose one of the activities below:

PRACTICE 1. Complete an analysis sheet for Monday through Saturday for the same paper. Then compare them and answer these questions:

a. Name one special feature that appears only on a certain day of the week: ______________________________.

What day does it appear? ______________.

b. Are the crossword puzzle and comics always in the same place? ________ Where? ______________________________.

c. What day has the most information on food and the most food store ads? __________.

d. Name one columnist who has a regular place in the same section every day: ______________________________.

Tell where to look for this column: __________.

PRACTICE 2. Complete an analysis sheet for different newspapers for the same day to find out:

a. Is the headline story the same? _____.

b. Do both papers have an editorial on the same subject? ______________________.

If so, do they agree or disagree? ____________.

PRACTICE 3. Compare the front page of your local newspaper with the *Chicago Daily News* front page on page 3. Use a colored marker to circle and write on the front page the names of the important parts. Don't worry if your paper doesn't have all the parts shown on the sample.

CHAPTER 2
HEADLINES SPEED YOU ALONG

CHOOSE THE NEWS YOU WANT TO READ

Newspapers are written for everybody to read, but you only have to read what interests you. You can skip the rest. Most people finish their paper in 20 minutes. How do they do that, when the average daily paper has as much reading material as some books? The trick is in knowing ahead of time what you want to get out of the paper, and then reading *only* those things, skipping the rest.

The newspaper is set up so that you can do this quickly.

1. The editors decide what news is most important to most people, and they gather those stories together on the front page. This gives you a head start in finding the stories that are most important.

2. The editors write a headline telling the main news. You don't have to scan the whole story to find out what it is about.

3. Every reporter makes sure that he squeezes the most important elements of the story into the first paragraph or two, called the lead. So you can safely read the lead and stop, knowing you

aren't missing anything important by not sticking with the story to the end.

4. A summary of all important news is usually printed in a prominent place—the first page or two, or the first page of the second section. This digest may tell you all you want to know about most stories. If you decide you want to know more, the digest gives the number of the page where you'll find the whole story.

5. After page one, stories are usually grouped together by subject matter in their own part of the paper—all the international news is together; all the sports stories are together, and so forth. This means that if you want to read the sports news, you know exactly where to look. But, it also means that if you don't want to read the sports news, it is easy to skip over that whole page or section.

What you choose to read, and what you skip, depends on your purpose in reading the paper in the first place. Some purposes change from day to day. On Monday you may be looking for a sale on date dresses or storm coats. On Tuesday you may be looking for gift ideas for your mother or for the review of the TV special you saw the night before. But some purposes stay the same. Every day you want to know what the top news events are. Every day part of your mind is on the lookout for articles about your special interests.

For example, persons interested in photography—either as a career or as a hobby—would read an article headlined "New Sensitive Film Requires No Flash Bulbs." College-bound students would peruse "How To Meet Rising Cost of College."

Practice using headlines to identify articles that interest you, and reject articles that don't interest you.

EXERCISE 1. Reading with a Purpose

Pretend one of your purposes for reading the newspaper is to find a career. Your favorite subject in school is science. You are considering the fields of medicine and electronics.

Directions: Read the following headlines. Put M in front of those which might help you decide about becoming a medical doctor. Put E in front of those which might help you decide about a career in electronics. You may decide some articles should be marked both M and E. Remember that all headlines are not about these subjects. Keep your purpose firmly in mind and put O in front of all headlines on other subjects. Rejecting what you don't care or need to read is an important skill in reading your newspaper.

____ 1. Meet the Computer
Computers: Power Tools for Thinking
(*The Christian Science Monitor*)

____ 2. *Big Mouth Feels*
Harry Belafonte
Is 'Black Power'
(*Daily Defender*—Weekend Edition)

____ 3. Push Buttons with Your New Medic!
(*Chicago Tribune*)

____ 4. What happens when pilot
says: 'We're going to Cuba'
(*The Christian Science Monitor*)

____ 5. *Man Translates Best*
A Job Computers Can't Do!
(*Chicago Daily News*)

____ 6. *Even Boss Hit*
Computer's Impact On Firms Soars
(*Chicago Sun-Times*)

____ 7. Wheeler-Dealer at 15.
He Seeks the Stars
(*Chicago Tribune*)

____ 8. Witness Says Drug
Killed His Daughter
(*Milwaukee Journal*)

____ 9. *Opportunity Line*
TV Show for Job Hunters
(*Chicago Daily News*)

____10. Computers May Soon Direct
Car and Appliance Repairs
(Louisville *Courier-Journal*)

WHAT DO HEADLINES DO?

The main purpose of a headline is to tell the reader what the news story is about. Headlines must be short, interesting, and easy to understand. Because the space is very limited, headline writers have developed a kind of telegraphic way of writing.

You will be able to scan headlines more quickly if you understand how headlines are constructed.

LABEL HEADS

Short news stories of one or two paragraphs are usually given only a one-line or two-line headline. These are just labels. Here are two examples: *One-line label*

New York Police Height Cut

Key words are *police* and *height*. This headline will catch the eye of anyone who is interested in the height required for New York police. It is equally helpful to readers who are not interested. They can reject the story by reading just one line of type. *Two-line label*

License Fee to Rise,
Dog Owners Told

Two-line label heads like this one are widely used. The comma at the end of the line tells the reader not to read the second line as a continuation of the first.

If the headline had been written

Dog Owners Told
License Fee to Rise

no comma would be necessary. But the important idea is that the *license fee is going up* so that idea gets the top line.

"KICKER" HEADS

Here are three examples of headlines with "kickers."

Opportunity Line ("kicker")

TV Show for Job Hunters

BIG MOUTH FEELS ("kicker")

Harry Belafonte Is 'Black Power'

On the Spot ("kicker")

As Suits Rise, Firms
Scramble to Increase (main headline)
Insurance for Directors

But Liability Coverage Gets
Costlier as Plaintiffs Win (deck)
More From Managements

'Too Risky to Stay on Board' (deck)

The Wall Street Journal

You can see that the "kickers" could be removed, but each adds something. While the ideas in the "kickers" are not essential, each "kicks" the reader into paying attention to the story.

In the first example, the "kicker" is the title of the TV show. Readers who have seen the show or heard people talk about it will be more likely to read the article.

In the second headline, the "kicker" gets its appeal from the identity of the writer. Since this is a syndicated column which appears regularly, readers are interested in the opinions of Big Mouth.

The single quotation marks around 'Black Power' tell the reader that the term is defined in a special way by Big Mouth.

The third kicker—"On the Spot"—appears over a major story in *The Wall Street Journal.* It gets attention because it signals danger. Many readers will be pulled into the main headline. Executives of other firms would reason that there is a possibility their firms may also be in danger.

DECKS "LEAD OUT"

The deck headline which appears between the main headline and the story is sometimes called a "lead out" headline. In the example shown above, the first deck tells readers that insurance costs are going up as a result of court decisions against management. It tells insurance firms, lawyers, and others that plaintiffs are *winning.*

The second deck—"'Too Risky to Stay on Board'"—would surely catch the interest of any member of a Board of Directors, or any shareholder whose stock may be affected if the company's capable directors resign.

POINTERS ON PUNCTUATION

Headline writers use punctuation marks in special ways. For example, the colon (:) often indicates a quotation. For example:

Downed Balloonist:
I'm in Good Spirits

The Miami Herald

Quotations are also shown by the use of single or double quotation marks. Here are two examples:

'Stay Out,' Union Man Retorts

MRS. C. POULSEN SAYS: "Thanks to Herald-News Classified — I found my dog!"

Single quotation marks are also used to show that a word or words are used in a special way. For example, the 'Positive' in the story about the army nerve gas killing the sheep (page 21) is qualified in the article.

The comma often means *and* as in these headlines:

Mia Flies to Mexico, Divorces Frank Sinatra

Cubans to Get Gunboat Back, Release 11 Natives of Cayman

The colon and semicolon are widely used in headlines. Study the examples below to see how these punctuation marks permit the headline writer to leave out words without sacrificing the meaning.

The Auto Puzzle: Buy Now or Wait

Boston Crowds High; White Sox Gain Split

EXERCISE 2. Limiting Reading to Purpose

Directions: Practice adjusting your reading to what you want to find out. After each of the articles below you will find a set of questions. Read the questions first and then see how fast you can locate answers in the article. Underline the answer and write the number of the paragraph in which the answer appears next to the question. The first one is done for you.

Questions A

1. How much does the dog license cost now? 2
2. When will the increase go into effect?____
3. Where are licenses available?____

License Fee to Rise, Dog Owners Told

(1) If you don't get your dog license application in by Thursday, it will cost you another $1, the Wisconsin Humane society said Wednesday.

(2) The fee will increase from $2.50 to $3.50, the society said.

(3) Licenses are available at the clerk's office in the county's various municipalities.

Reprinted from *The Milwaukee Journal*

Questions B

1. How many viewers have been placed on jobs or job training programs?____
2. What kind of jobs are listed?____
3. What are the names of some of the concerns offering these jobs?____

Reprinted with permission from the *Chicago Sun-Times*

Opportunity Line

TV Show for Job Hunters

By Bob Tamarkin

Job-hunting Chicagoans can quit making that regular trip to the employment office.

(2) On Saturday afternoons they can turn to the Opportunity Line, a community-affairs program on WBBM-TV (Channel 2.)

(3) It is presented in co-operation with the Illinois State Employment Service and the Chicago Urban League.

(4) To date 1,683 viewers have been placed in jobs or job-training programs.

(5) The half-hour program features job listings available through the ISES. Viewers interested in applying for these jobs are invited to call a special phone number and talk to trained job counselors at ISES about the jobs or job-training programs.

(6) The program also features guests from employment agencies and company training programs.

THE PROGRAM which started June 10, has been successful beyond all expectations, according to its host, Bill Lowry, and the show's producer, T. M. Alderman.

(8) "Prospective employers even began calling the number we were featuring for employes. In one week we got 230 inquiries from employers alone," said Alderman.

(9) According to WBBM, 74 per cent of the job applicants were from Chicago's Near West, South and Far South areas. These areas have the "highest rates of unemployment," the station points out.

(10) Over 80 per cent of the applicants are between the ages of 16 and 44 and over 50 per cent are under 22.

(11) The program features only job listings and mentions no companies by name. Listings include watchmen, stenographers, short-order cooks, nurses aides, hospital orderlies, salesmen, draftsmen, animal caretakers and bindery workers.

(12) **AMONG** the concerns in which applicants are being placed are Harper Theater, Illinois Bell Telephone, Argonne Laboratories, Motorola, Yellow Cab, Armour & Co. and Swift & Co.

(13) Alderman says that to the best of his knowledge there is no other program like it on TV anywhere in the country.

(14) "As a result of its success, four other CBS affiliates are entertaining the possibility of having a similar show," added Alderman.

(15) The station plans to keep the show on as long "it's useful to the public and the response is kept up," said Alderman.

Questions C

1. What word in the main headline suggests a connection between the army chemical test-site and the death of the sheep? ____
2. Who said the army's proving grounds "definitely is not responsible"? ____
3. Who said the deaths "seem to be caused by some central nervous system poison"? ____
4. What have the sheep done that has aroused nerve-damage suspicion? ____
5. What is the dateline on this story? ____

Questions D

1. Who is the prober? ____
2. Who said that "no definite cause of death" has been established? ____
3. What has the army admitted? ____
4. Why did the headline writer put single quotation marks around the word *positive*? ____
5. What is the dateline on this story? ____

ARMY CHEMICAL TEST-SITE NEARBY

5,000 Sheep Die; Gas Probed

By Victor Cohn
Washington Post Special

(1) WASHINGTON—Perhaps 5,000 sheep have sickened and died in the last week in a place called Skull Valley, in Utah, 20 or 30 miles from the Army's main site for field-testing chemical and biological weapons.

(2) That center, the Army's Dugway proving grounds, "definitely is not responsible," a Dugway spokesman said Wednesday.

(3) Federal and state agricultural officials could say only that the deaths—in semidesert grazing land 50 miles west of Salt Lake City—seem to be caused by some central nervous system poison.

(4) Federal agricultural experts were just beginning their investigation. The first inspection of the animals' brains showed no obvious damage. But brain or nerve cell damage might show up only in the laboratory. The way the animals have been affected—weakening and staggering and then dying within 24 hours—helps arouse nerve-damage suspicion.

(5) Prof. Barry Commoner of Washington University in St. Louis, a member of the American Assn. for the Advancement of Science's new committee on environmental alterations, said:

(6) "The question of accidental release of nerve gases from Dugway has to be seriously examined. Nerve gases can be disseminated either by air or by contamination of surface water."

(7) Those possibilities are being examined, said Dr. E. E. Saulmon, Agriculture Department animal health chief.

Whatever the cause the case already seems to be one of history's strangest animal disasters. Saulmon said he had never heard of so many animals dying so fast, in so small an area, and of no quickly obvious cause.

(8) The sheep are still dying, and the number 5,000 was only a rough guess. The scene, said witnesses is "a sea of dead animals." A decision is due momentarily on whether to start burning or burying them.

Ken Harter © The Washington Post

Prober 'Positive' Army Nerve Gas Killed Sheep

(1) SALT LAKE CITY (AP)—The head of a special Utah investigating team said Saturday that "we are as positive as medical science can ever be" that nerve gas tests conducted at the Army's top-secret Dugway Proving Grounds killed 6,400 sheep in western Utah's Skull Valley.

(2) Dr. D. A. Osguthorpe said he feels "sufficient tests" have been made to link the deaths with Army operations March 13.

(3) An Army spokesman said the military investigation was continuing and that "no definite cause of death" has been established.

(4) Osguthorpe said: "We have narrowed the cause of death to an organic phosphate compound, the kind that is a component of nerve gas. Since the Army has admitted conducting the nerve gas tests the day before the sheep began dying, that would seem to clear the matter up."

(5) Osguthorpe, appointed Friday to head the state's investigation in conjunction with Army scientists, said "prevailing wind conditions" in the remote semi-desert Skull Valley further back his conclusion.

Associated Press

Questions E

1. At what event were the two flyers reunited? ____
2. Was Kawato ever shot down during the war? ____
3. What job does "Pappy" have now? ____
4. What did the two flyers do when they met? ____

WWII Incident

Pappy, Flier Who 'Got' Him, Chat

① LOS ANGELES (AP) — World War II fighter pilot Gregory "Pappy" Boyington, whose antics and impressive list of kills spawned a book and television series, has come face to face with the man who shot him down in the South Pacific 33 years ago.

② Amid a crescendo of applause Tuesday, the burly 64-year-old former Marine aviator and former Imperial Japanese Navy flying ace Masajiro Kawato threw their arms around each other in a hug.

③ "We were both participants in an era that is gone now and will never be repeated," said Boyington, who received the Congressional Medal of Honor.

④ The two were brought together at the annual brotherhood luncheon of the Los Angeles International Kiwanis Club.

⑤ Although it has never been established for certain that Kawato is the one who shot Boyington down, the two of them believe it.

⑥ Kawato recalls circumstances of the dogfight Jan. 3, 1944, that sent Boyington's plane down in flames over Rabaul, New Britain.

⑦ Boyington, who was credited with shooting down 28 enemy planes while he was commander of the Black Sheep Squadron, spent 20 months in a prisoner-of-war camp.

⑧ But he said he didn't run into any flak from the Japanese while he was a prisoner.

⑨ "There never was any animosity. It never existed with pilots," Boyington said. "After I was captured several Japanese pilots came to talk to me, laughing and joking."

⑩ Boyington, who lives in Fresno, retired from the Marine Corps in 1947 and 11 years later authored a best-selling book based on his experiences, entitled "Baa Baa Black Sheep." He now works as an adviser for the television series based on the book.

⑪ Kawato, 51, who was credited with downing 19 American planes, was himself shot down five times and ended the war in an Australian prisoner-of-war camp.

⑫ After the war, he returned to Japan and spent 16 more years in the reorganized military before retiring to become a pilot for Japan Air Lines.

⑬ Last year, he made a nonstop solo flight in a single-engine plane from Tokyo to Crescent City, Calif., as a personal goodwill gesture on America's bicentennial.

⑭ And, he said, it was also a personal memorial to the 7,000 American and Japanese fliers shot down in the war.

PRACTICE IN YOUR LOCAL NEWSPAPER

PRACTICE 1. See how many different headlines your newspaper uses on the front page. Look for these kinds of differences:

How many columns wide is the main headline? One, two—as wide as the whole page?

How high is the type? Measure a capital letter.

How wide is the type? Measure a wide letter—a "w" or "m." Or count the number of letters that fit in a column width.

Are the letters italic (slanted) or roman (straight up and down)?

Does the headline use all capital letters or capitals and small letters?
Does the headline have more than one line?

PRACTICE 2. Go headline hunting in several newspapers. Bring to class one or two good examples of label heads, "kicker" heads, and "leadout" decks.

PRACTICE 3. Bring in three headlines that use slang to catch the readers attention.

PRACTICE 4. Bring in three headlines that depend on pictures to help the reader understand what is meant.

PRACTICE 5. Clip out articles on subjects that always interest you. Underline words in the headline or lead that let you know the article would be of interest to you.

CHAPTER 3
HOW THE NEWS IS GATHERED

How the news is gathered depends upon *where it happens*. News that happens in the area where the paper is published is called *local news*. It is gathered by the newspaper's own staff of reporters and editors.

But what about news from the rest of the United States, and the rest of the world? Your paper may have its own special correspondent stationed in Washington to cover government news, or in New York to cover U.N. news. It may even send a reporter out of town or out of the country to cover a big story.

But most out-of-town news is covered by a press association reporter. The press association then sends the story out to your paper and to the hundreds of other papers that pay for its service. Your paper then selects the news it wishes to publish.

News about foreign countries is the responsibility of the newspaper's foreign editor. The telegraph editor is responsible for news everywhere in the United States outside of his own city. The city editor is responsible for local news.

LOCAL NEWS

The city editor must find out when and where local news may develop. He supervises a news staff which helps him cover these stories. In general, local news staffs are made up of

beat reporters
general assignment reporters
specialists

Some places produce news regularly: City Hall, the board of education, the police department, the criminal court building. So one reporter is regularly assigned to the City Hall beat; another always covers the police department, and so forth. These are *beat reporters.*

A beat reporter builds a thorough knowledge of the organization and people he contacts daily.

Other local news is covered by *general assignment reporters.* A general assignment reporter is assigned different kinds of stories each day chosen from events scheduled for that day and from "news breaks."

A news break is a news story that comes up unexpectedly. The city editor can't have advance notice about a cave-in at the local mine or a forest fire. But he does know about most newsworthy events ahead of time. One way he keeps track of them is through a *future file.* This file contains one folder for each day of the year. Editors and their assistants put reminders about future events in these folders. For example, a city editor might find notes reminding him that on this particular day

a movie star will be in town for a charity benefit
furniture buyers will arrive for their annual convention
a U.S. Senator will address the Press Association
an art exhibit will open at the museum
the City Youth Orchestra will present a concert
the Shrine Circus will hold a parade

Many of the notations in the future file result from press releases sent in by agents and organizations seeking publicity. The movie star's press agent, or the chairman of the charity benefit probably phoned or sent materials about the star's plans. The Press Association program chairman, or someone from the local political club, or someone from the Senator's staff, made sure to tell the paper about the Senator's speech.

Other future file notes come from telephone calls, mail, clippings from rival papers, and suggestions from the telegraph editor about local angles to stories coming in over the wire. Many are picked up by reporters covering other stories. The librarian may send a reminder about a special anniversary.

The *specialist* writes only about one subject that is likely to produce news continually. Most large newspapers have specialists for science, labor, politics, religion and so on. A seaport city might have a maritime (sea) news writer. The specialist becomes well acquainted with many experts in his field. He may even become an expert himself, but he must be able to report his special news in a way that can be understood by an ordinary reader.

EXERCISE 1. Naming the Reporter's Beat

Directions: Scan the headline stories on the opposite page. Each story could have been written by a reporter covering one of the beats listed in the right hand column. Match the number on each story with the beat which produced the story.

Number of Story	*Beat*
______________	Criminal Courts Building
______________	Police Station
______________	Board of Education
______________	City Hall
______________	Illinois State Building

①

Courts Plan Trials for Looters

BY JOHN OSWALD

A plan to process the 2,000 persons arrested during the

division of the court, told Judge Boyle that the Felony court will be used as an assignment court

that he will have additional deputy sheriffs and b[illegible] on duty to handle the expected large number of courtroom visitors.

The additional magistrates will be taken from their regular

computer is being used to assemble cases in various categories so that one judge may be hearing all the disorderly charges and another judge the looting charges.

Longer Dourt Day Seen

②

Sniper Surrenders: Killed Own Sister

Among the snipers on Chicago's near north side was Oscar King, 27. One of his bullets, casually fired from a

passing
and ki
She
tim to
began
corone
S
The
assass
charge
rioting
police.
by his
render
avenue
his ad
His
Walker
died in
hospita
was sh

Walker clutched her breast. "O, daddy," she gasped, before slumped in the seat.

Her father drove as fast as

④

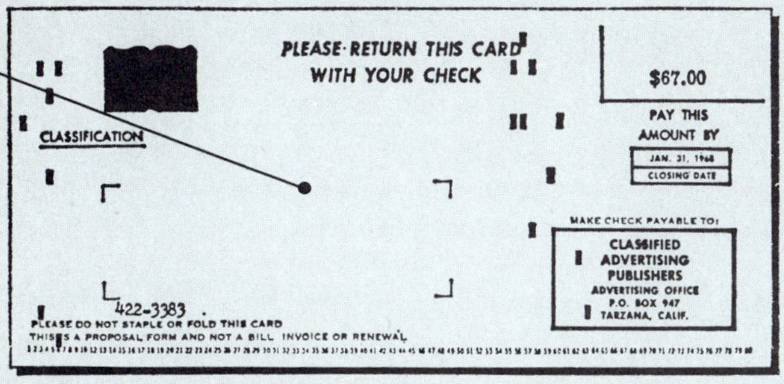

Read Fine Print

Classified Advertising Publishers form which business men often mistake for a bill, but which fine print says is a "proposal form."

The Illinois attorney general's office is investigating com-

billed for phone directory ads.

③

Mayor's Tax Plans 'Lost' in City Hall

By RUSS CONE
City Hall Writer

Hall was playing a "Button, Button, Got the Button?" to- Mayor Alioto's $38 ax program.

apparently thought t the package to the f Supervisors March a note saying it was hat it be passed be- board becomes own in details of the get April 15.

e Examiner learned at the tax legislation rrived in the Board

M. O'Connor, some 50 feet away from the supervisors' offices — and also on the second floor.

Just why, nobody knows.

The Mayor, informed of the results of The Examiner's discovery, acted promptly.

He ordered that the legislation be marched down the hall from the City Attorney's office to the Supervisors' offices right away.

O'Connor, when asked about it, explained plaintively that no legislation has

⑤

Bellevue Board Meets

Field Trip Invitation Discussed

The Bellevue School Board last night discussed the possibility of inviting a fifth-grade class from Leschi School in Seattle's central area to take part in a four-day conservation field trip on Vashon Island.

The Leschi youngsters would join a Lake Hills fifth grade class in attending Camp Sealth.

If approved, it would be the first time in the 11-year old program an outside school had participated, John Brubacher, school superintendent, said.

IN GOING over preliminary plans for its 22nd elementary school, the board last night expressed concern over the flexibility of a building with no permanent walls between classrooms and the problem of having some classrooms far removed from labatories.

Richard Smith, architect, presented preliminary plans for the proposed 16-room Spiritridge Elementary School.

The board requested more work be done on the plans. The district must submit plans to the State Board of Education this month to share in about $10 million in state matching funds.

"It seems to me we could save a considerable amount by having fixed cross walls instead of movable partitions and still retain flexibility," Donald C. Nordstrom, board chairman, said.

SMITH said the flexible partictions cost about $10 per square foot compared to $2 per square foot for static walls.

Nordstrom also expressed concern over children from two classrooms in the middle of six-room groupings having to pass through another room or outside the building to get to lavatories.

The board departed from policy in naming its seventh-junior high school the Frank Odle Junior High School. Schools previously were given American Indian names.

Frank Odle, retired last night after 55 years of teaching, 50 in Bellevue.

Top and center left, *Chicago Tribune*; center right, *The San Francisco Examiner*; center, *Chicago Tribune*; bottom, *The Seattle Times*

EXERCISE 2. Name the Specialists

Directions: Read the bylines on the articles printed on the opposite page. Then answer each of the questions by filling in the blanks.

1. The name of the science editor who writes for the *Chicago Daily News* is ______________________________
2. The name of the labor editor who writes for the *Times* (Seattle) is ______________________________
3. The name of the real estate editor who writes for the *Chicago Daily News* is ______________________________
4. The name of the political writer for the *Miami Herald* is ______________________________
5. The name of the aerospace editor who writes for the *Los Angeles Times* is ______________________________
6. The name of the education writer for the *Los Angeles Times* is ______________________________

Nun helps Lawndale home-buying p

By Albert Jedlicka
Daily News Real Estate Editor

Once a week a nun in modern religious garb comes to the loop offices of the Advance Mortgage Co. with a sheaf of loan

a month's and the pu has paid in.

Msgr. Eg tract seller of buildings

Checkless banking

Big future seen for voiceprints

By Arthur J. Snider
Daily News Science Editor

NEW YORK — Voiceprints, a visual pattern of speech

L. G. KERSTA, who developed voiceprints at Bell Laboratories in 1946, believes the error rate will become as low as 1 per 50,000 prints. In finger prints the probability of

3 Engine Failures Mar 2nd Saturn Test Fli

Early Shutdowns in Apollo Boo Necessitate 3rd Trial Before N

BY MARVIN MILES
Times Aerospace Editor

CAPE KENNEDY — Three engine failures marred the second test

the third attached A it was ellipt

Rafferty Asks Library Displays of Rejected Reading Textbook

BY JACK McCURDY
Times Education Writer

SACRAMENTO — Max Rafferty said Thursday he has requested

included in the displays. It is Lippincott, Basic Reading Series."

law says the books recommended by the Curriculum Commis st be displayed to the public adoption by the State Board ation.

Rafferty told the board, he

Phone Firm-Union Talks 'On Collision C '

By PAUL STAPLES
Labor Editor, The Times

With a nation-wide-strike deadline barely a week away, contract talks here between the Pacific Northwest Bell Telephone Co. and the Communications Workers of America were reported "on a collision course" today.

"It looks like we will be on strike with the rest of them across the nation the way things are going," Ronald Hale, union area director, said.

The negotiations in the Olympic Hotel three weeks affect 11,572 men and women in the union's Pacific Northwest Bell bargaining unit in Oregon and Washington.

also threatens to hamper telephone service here next week.

About 650 installers in Washington and Oregon assemble large switchboards and other equipment for Pacific Northwest Bell and other companies.

Hale said Pacific Northwest Bell employes in the plant, traffic and accounting departments will take a strike vote Tuesday night if a satisfactory contract offer has not been received.

Joseph Beirne, union general president, announced a strike deadline of a week from tomorrow at all Bell System companies which have not reached agreement with the union.

Kelly Delegation May Swing Votes To McCarthy Slate

By JOHN McDERMOTT
Herald Political Writer

U.S. Sen. Eugene McCarthy's bid for Florida votes got a boost Tuesday when Scott Kelly filed a third slate of delegates to oppose the "favorite son" Democrat slate for Sen. George Smathers.

With Kelly sharp-shooting at the party leaders on the Smathers slate, the McCarthy forces suddenly emerge

as a compromise between the warring factions.

At stake are Florida's 63 votes for President when the Democrats hold their National Convention at Chicago Aug. 26.

EXERCISE 3. Surveying General Assignments

Directions: Study the first few paragraphs of each of the three general assignments covered by Sara Jane Goodyear for the *Chicago Tribune.* Then circle YES or NO before each statement.

YES NO 1. She got the story about the girl mayor by telephoning Bertha Williams.

YES NO 2. She rode a bus with 50 Waller High School students to the suburbs.

YES NO 3. She probably got part of her information for the "Viet GI Dad" story by reading his letters to his wife.

PRESS RELEASES

A press release is a story the newspaper did not ask for, which someone sends in already written up in newspaper style. Almost any group might send a press release to the paper: the Department of Education, the Mayor's office, a department store, an actor's agent, a manufacturer. Papers get hundreds of press releases each day. Most get thrown out, but many get into the paper in some form.

Below is a newspaper article that is probably a word-for-word press release sent to the newspaper's food editor by the Pillsbury Company. We can guess that the company thought that if they improved this well-publicized recipe, many newspapers would judge the news to be interesting to their readers. Pillsbury was right. The *Seattle Times*—and other papers—printed the story. The Pillsbury Company got free publicity and the newspapers got an interesting story with very little effort.

The Seattle Times

Prize-Winning Cake Recipe Is Revised by Pillsbury

The Pillsbury Co. has recommended changes in the recipe for the Buttercream Pound Cake which was the $25,000 Grand Prize Winner in the Bake-Off held in February.

BUTTERCREAM POUND CAKE

2 cups butter, softened
1 package regular-size buttercream lemon or vanilla-frosting mix
6 large eggs
3 tablespoons lemon juice, if desired
3¾ cups all-purpose flour (self-rising flour is not recommended)
2 teaspoons baking powder
1 12-ounce can poppy-seed cake-and-pastry filling
Confectioners' sugar or glaze

1. In large mixer bowl, cream butter and dry frosting mix at medium speed until light and fluffy, at least 5 minutes.

2. Add eggs, 1 at a time, beating 1 minute after each. Add lemon juice. Gradually beat in flour and baking powder.

3. In small mixer bowl, combine 3 cups of the batter with poppy-seed filling. Blend well.

4. Spread half of plain batter over bottom of greased 10-inch tube pan. Then alternately add spoonfuls of poppy seed batter and remaining plain batter.

5. Bake at 325 for 1 hour and 30 to 45 minutes or until cake tests done. Cool cake in pan 15 minutes before removing. Cool completely. Sprinkle with confectioners' sugar or drizzle with glaze.

6. To make glaze, combine 1 cup confectioners' sugar and 2 tablespoons lemon juice or milk.

Girl 'Mayor for Day' Tells of Her Program

BY SARA JANE GOODYEAR

[TRIBUNE Staff Photo]

Bertha Williams

Mayor-elect Bertha Williams handled her first press confer-ence like a pro.

She calmly fielded a volley of questions from "Do you sew?" to "What are your views on the Viet Nam war?" after the announcement yesterday that she has been named "mayor for a day" of Chicago as part of the 48th annual Chicago Youth week celebration.

Miss Williams, a 16-year-old Marshall High school junior who lives at 4011 Adams st., will head 36 junior officials who will "take over" the city government on Junior Officials day, May 7.

Her Program for City

Her program if her term as mayor were a bit longer, would be a basic one.

"I would improve housing and recreation areas such as parks and beaches," she said.

Asked if she would also cut taxes, her reply was more practical than many.

"No," she said. "You can't cut taxes without cutting serv-ices and I think our services

Viet GI Dad Killed Before Seeing Child

BY SARA JANE GOODYEAR

Staff Sgt. Robert Lee Bodine couldn't wait to come home.

His letters to his wife were filled with plans for their first child who was just about to be born. His year in Viet Nam was to be completed in June, and then he could see the baby.

Diane Marie Bodine was born March 15. But her father never saw her. In fact, he never even knew.

Still in Hospital

Mrs. Rose Mary Bodine still was in Ravenswood hospital when the two sergeants came to say that her husband was missing in action. On Wednes-day they ... her

Robert L. Bodine

...many ... June he came

To Her, It's Matter of Fringe Benefits

BY SARA JANE GOODYEAR

(Pictures on back page)

The kids from the city spent a day in a suburban high school yesterday, and everyone had fun.

Fifty Waller High school stu-dents arrived at Deerfield High school by bus, admittedly ner-vous and not at all sure what they would find there.

Their appreh...

ENLARGE BUSING AREA

School officials ask par-ents in additional 12-block area of Austin community to permit busing of children.

Spokesmen for Catholic groups assail John Cardinal Cody's proposal to bus Ne-gro parochial pupils to sub-urbs. Stories on page 4.

Waller students that their ...atch ... Deer-

Many, many news stories and features start with press releases. Sometimes the newspaper prints the story exactly as it is received. Sometimes the newspaper changes it a little. Sometimes a reporter is assigned to write a story based on the press release, or even to get extra information and write his own story. So there is no sharp line between a story based on a press release and a story the newspaper originates itself.

Press releases make it easy for any newspaper to fill its columns with little work. A good, responsible newspaper will not use a great many obvious press releases. When it does use a press release, it will make it clear where the information came from—as in the case of the cake recipe—and not let the reader assume that the paper originated the story.

NON-LOCAL NEWS

Remember that news that happens *outside* of the area where the newspaper is published is classified as *non-local news*. It is gathered by (1) press associations, (2) special correspondents, and (3) regular staff members sent to cover news that is happening out of town.

The two largest press associations in the United States are the Associated Press (AP) and the United Press International (UPI). Many newspapers use the services of both of these news-gathering agencies. A separate teletype machine for each association automatically types out news releases in the newspaper office. Both associations have bureaus throughout the United States and in key news centers all over the world.

United Press International (UPI) is a profit-making organization that gathers news like a local newspaper and sells its services to any newspaper.

The Associated Press (AP) is a cooperative non-profit association made up of all the papers which use its services plus special correspondents hired by the AP. The AP has the exclusive right to select local news printed in papers published by its members. Thus a reporter may find a story he writes for his own paper going out over the AP wires for use in hundreds of other papers. Members of the AP choose the news they want to print from hundreds of thousands of words put on the teletype machines by the AP bureaus.

Editors may write different headlines, make minor changes in punctuation and grammar or add details, but they can not change facts or the sense of the story.

Another source of non-local news is the independent news services of a few great newspapers. Among these are the *Chicago Daily News, The New York Times,* and the joint service of the *Los Angeles Times* and the *Washington Post.* These papers have their own special correspondents in key spots throughout the world.

The Dow Jones News Service specializes in business and financial news and is less widely used than the AP, UPI, etc.

Many newspapers carry dispatches from the Reuters Press Association. It is a reliable source of foreign news.

Readers want to know who is responsible for the story. Study the samples given below to learn the most common way newspapers show the sources of stories.

1. Stories with bylines

Top left, *The Miami Herald;* top right, From the *St. Petersburg Times.* Permission courtesy of *The Globe and Mail,* Toronto; bottom, Associated Press

Shakedown Charged to Beach Pair

By BILL AMLONG
And MARGARET CARROLL
Herald Staff Writers

FBI agents arrested a Miami Beach attorney and a taxi company manager Wednesday on indictments by a federal grand jury probing a $50,000 shakedown charge.

100,000 may have died in China quake

China still uses ancient methods of predicting earthquakes, 2-A.

By ROSS H. MUNRO
The Globe and Mail, Toronto

PEKING — Diplomats here estimate that at least 100,000 people were killed in the two severe earthquakes that shook China on Tuesday and Wednesday.

The Chinese government has not made public any estimate of the casualties. But the diplomats made their estimate after studying the records of past earthquakes and population statistics.

Ethnic Masses Observed

By GEORGE W. CORNELL
AP Religion Writer

PHILADELPHIA — The diverse customs, languages, races and nations of Roman Catholicism unfolded here Saturday in a profusion of masses for peace in a reverential panorama of prayer, pageantry and song.

2. Stories with news service or press association identification but no bylines

GM Recalls 1.1 Million Cars for Brake Defects

DETROIT (AP) — General Motors Corp announced yesterday it is recalling 1.1 million cars, trucks and bus chassis for correction of possible defects in the braking system.

Financial-News Summary

DOW JONES NEWS SERVICE

Hammermill Paper Co. expects first 12-week sales and earnings to equal those of a year earlier and looks for "continuing strength of demand" through the first 24 weeks of the year, John H. Devitt, president, reported. In the first 12 weeks of 1967, Hammermill's net income was $2,040,000 or 49 cents a share.

Atlantic Oil would quit 'giveaways'

WASHINGTON — (AP) — The Atlantic Richfield Oil Co., reversing an earlier stand, yesterday became the first firm to ask the Federal Trade Commission to ban giveaway games used as sales promotion in gasoline retailing.

Chevvy Mails Recall Notes To 3 Million

Detroit (AP) — The first letters notifying more than three million Chevrolet owners that their cars or trucks may have defects went into the mail

Cepeda, Joe Torre In Trade

WEST PALM BEACH, Fla. (UPI) — The Atlanta Braves Monday traded Joe Torre to the St. Louis Cardinals for Orlando Cepeda.

Griffin adds warning on TV violence

WASHINGTON — (AP) — Senator Robert P. Griffin wanted the television industry yesterday it will invite government controls unless it curbs violence and sex programming.

Top left and center, Associated Press; top right, United Press International; bottom left, *The Seattle Times;* bottom center and right, Associated Press

3. Stories by special correspondents

Doctor Attacks Lack of Child Health Care

BY HARRY NELSON
Times Medical Writer

The present public policy toward children in the United States is that they are expendable, a noted pediatrician declared Tuesday.

million children living in poverty in the United States. While the majority are white, 50% of all nonwhite children live in poverty. Two-thirds of all

Marine News

Cargo Thefts Eyed at Chicago Parley

By STEPHEN A. BLOSSOM
Marine Editor

Charges of large-scale theft of cargoes on the Chicago waterfront were studied at a meeting yesterday

thefts. He said Chicago was one of the worst-hit areas, with Detroit and Milwaukee also having trouble, the Associated Press reports.

John F. Kovacic, district director of customs here,

'Their sound here to stay'

Rock bands turning 'pro,' joining Musicians Union

By Robert M. Lewin
Daily News Labor Writer

Rock bands such as The Chicago Fire and The People's Gas must be making it: They're joining the Chicago Federation of Musicians, AFL-CIO, Local 10-208.

Rock groups — composed of amplified lead, rhythm and bass guitar players, and drummers — are adding fluegel horns. They are trying to create new sounds for the monotonous, driving beat of their chords by adding a bassoon, oboe, French or English horn, violin, viola or cello, noted Garamoni.

He said the current development of rock and roll, which includes soul music, is similar to that of jazz years ago, an era that began with Dixieland and blues tunes.

Drisko contends that the first rock and roll music was the sound of protest.

Now, he said, it is the sound of fractured love.

Railroads aiming for bigger share of auto shipments

By DONALD P. O'CONNOR
Detroit News Business Writer

American railroads, presently carrying half of all automotbiles shipped across the country, are focusing in on Detroit for an even bigger share of the market.

"If we are to take our rightful place in the 21st Century, we must find ways to improve our financial stability," Goodfellow said.

"Maybe we can save on total labor costs—if reason prevails. Maybe we can save on passen-

Top left, Copyright, 1968, by the *Los Angeles Times*. Reprinted by permission; top right, *The Plain Dealer*, Cleveland; bottom left, *Chicago Daily News*; bottom right, *Detroit News*

LOCAL NEWS + WIRE SERVICE = NATIONAL STORY

A good example of cooperative news coverage is this human interest story of a 91-year-old woman who was evicted from her apartment. It first appeared in the *Chicago Daily News* on March 27, 1968. Since no other Chicago paper discovered the incident, the *News* had an exclusive story. They made sure readers noticed the story by placing it on the front page and using a second picture on the carry-over or "jump" part of the story which was continued on page 12.

It became a national story because the *News* sent it out to the ninety-plus papers which subscribe to the *Chicago Daily News* Wire Service.

People all over the United States suddenly knew about Miss Cazier and her trouble. They sent offers of help for her to the *Daily News*. This was reported in a follow-up story on March 29, by the same reporter who covered the eviction.

Aid for homeless woman, 91

Eviction tugs at U.S. heart

By Vern K. Richey

With wrinkled but steady hands, Ethel Cazier held the slips of paper.

From New York City, from San Francisco, from Miami, from the suburbs and from the heart of Chicago, the offers of help came.

Miss Cazier, 91, was evicted Tuesday from her apartment at 4878 N. Kenmore because she was behind in her rent.

Everything that had been accumulated in a lifetime was piled in the street for scavengers.

But Miss Cazier's plight, described in an exclusive Daily News story Wednesday and relayed across the nation by The Daily News Wire Service, touched the heart.

"THAT COULD be my mother out there," said Mrs. Willie B. Glover of San Francisco. Mrs. Glover, who operates a nursing home, telegraphed The Daily News and offered to pay Miss Crazier's air fare to San Francisco and take care of her for the rest of her life without charge.

Nurses House, Inc., a New York home for retired nurses, called the Montrose Urban Progress Center with an offer of help.

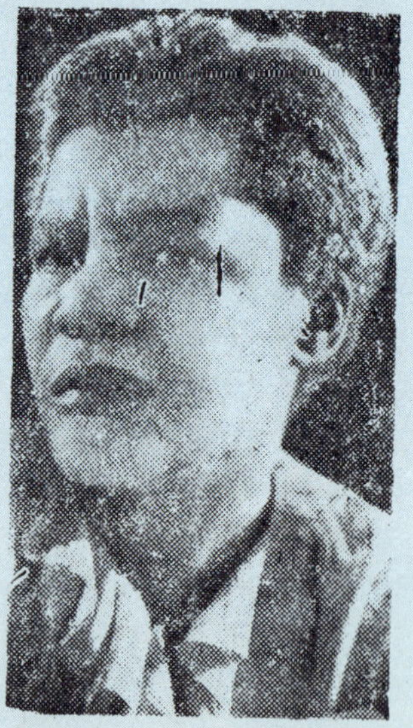

Mrs. Willie B. Glover

A retired woman doctor in Miami called the center twice to ask if Miss Cazier would be interested in coming to Florida to live with her.

THERE WERE offers of a home and help nearer the Uptown neighborhood where Miss Cazier has lived for 40 years.

"We have eight children and a summer house in Wisconsin," said a suburban housewife. "There's plenty of room for another."

A woman on the Near North side has an 11-year-old daughter who needs a grandmother.

A woman from the Jewish Family Service paid a call on Miss Cazier at her temporary home in the Wilton Hotel, 4758 N. Kenmore, and offered help.

"She said did I need money—that she had some right in her purse," Miss Crazier reported with wonder.

"These Jewish people are always helping others outside of their religion."

ALL OF THIS attention was far from what she wanted,—Miss Cazier admitted.

"I've never been one for trying to get people to notice me. Why do you suppose there are so many people interested?"

Miss Cazier has a onetime Iowa farm girl's reluctance to talk about money.

Yes, she says, she has a bit saved from the time when she was a nurse. Some was taken in a burglary recently, and the resulting confusion is what caused her to fall behind in her rent.

But whatever she has saved, it is clearly a modest amount.

Miss Cazier said she is grateful for the offers for help and just needs "some time to think about all of this—about all of the things these people have offered."

Miss Cazier leaned back on the sofa and wrinkled her forehead.

"Life's so interesting, don't you think?

"I was out eating a bite earlier and they were talking about me. I learned some things about me I'd never known."

MERRY MACKE, the specialist from the urban progress center who is working with Miss Cazier, picked up another letter and said:

"Here's another offer. George Eisenberg — he's the head of American Decal and founded the Rose Eisenberg Parkview Home for the aged—has told his administrator to make arrangements to care of you for the rest of your life. Would you like that?"

Miss Ethel Cazier looks through the mementoes of 91 years stacked on a sidewalk after eviction. (Photo by Don Bierman)

Woman, 91, evicted

Her memories pillaged

By Vern K. Richey

They put Ethel Cazier's life out on the street, under the trees with the small buds, for anybody to paw through.

Everything was there—an old doll with the left leg missing, the elegant sherry glasses, furniture, a green plant that lay crushed on the sidewalk.

Miss Cazier was evicted from her apartment Tuesday. She is 91 or 92—she doesn't remember too well—and had lived there 42 years, give or take half a decade.

THE BAILIFFS arrived at the apartment at 4878 N. Kenmore early in the morning. They moved everything onto the dirt between the sidewalk and the street.

The action was decided six miles away in a court where a landlord told a judge he wanted his overdue rent.

That was more than a month ago. The judge agreed with Ilija and Milka Kuzmanovic, the landlords. The rent was in arrears, Ethel Cazier had to move out.

MISS CAZIER says she doesn't understand what it's all about. She has the money, or would have if someone hadn't broken into her apartment and stolen some.

So she sat for a while among her belongings. Mrs. Millard Baker, a neighbor, took her in for a cup of milk. Mrs. Baker is from Kentucky and says helping people who are in trouble is what neighbors are for.

THINGS weren't always so bad, Miss Cazier explained.

"I was a nurse. But then I had a heart attack. That was 50 years ago. Since then I sewed."

The landlords were not available for comment.

Miss Cazier says she had a "fifth or sixth cousin" in California but "at 91 your friends are about all dead."

The people at the Montrose Urban Progress Center didn't hear of the eviction until midafternoon. A pretty girl named Merry Macke, who once worked with the Peace Corps in Costa Rica and now works with poor people in Uptown, came over with some other workers from the center.

OUT ON THE STREET, other people were picking Miss Cazier's life apart.

A pickup truck stopped, men dashed out, and rode off with a chest.

A station wagon pulled up, a man loaded in a table leaf and drove off as an astonished reporter watched.

One man took home a load of dishes. He came back with a supermarket shopping cart for more. There was a dresser, a bed, a broken clock. The crowd picked over them.

Miss Macke found a hotel room for Miss Crazier. Wednesday she will try to find something more permanent.

Another poverty war worker, with Miss Crazier's approval sold passerby what was left of the things set out under the trees. The sale brought $47.10.

Dear Miss Cazier,
I am 7½ Years old. I am
Sending you some dollars. I hope
you are feeling fine. I saw your
picture in the paper and you look
Verey nice. I would like to be
your friend.

Love,
Lori Somers
21 PAUL REVERE RD.
LEXINGTON, MASS.

P.S.
0 000 xxxx
(hugs) and (kisses)

Massachusetts schoolgirl's letter to evicted woman here.

1st-flight thrill

New life begins in Miami at 91

By Vern K. Richey
Staff Writer

MIAMI—Ethel Cazier, who was evicted from her Chicago apartment of 40 years last month, started a new life in Florida Saturday after the first airplane ride of her 91 years.

'What a business this airplaning is. A few years ago they didn't know anything about it—and here we are," she said Friday after arriving at the Miami airport.

She claimed her bagge—a battered suitcase, a shopping bag and two suti boxes tied together with string—from Delta Air Lines, and went on to hte city and her new life.

THE STORY of Miss Cazier's eviction on March 26 and the way passers-by plundered her belongings was carried across the nation by The Daily News/Sun-Times Wire Service.

Sympathetic readers sent in more than $1,400—enough to give the strong-willed former nurse anew start with Dr. Estella Bettencourt Helms.

Dr. Helms, a Cuban refugee and a physician with the U.S. Public Health Service, was one of sveral persons who offered Miss Cazier a place to stay. Dr. Helm's husband, Robert, a retired Army officer, agreed.

"This is just wonderful," Miss Cazer kept repeating as Helms took her arm and led her down a palm-lined street. "This is just wonderful."

She will live in a two-story home across the street from the Helms residence. Sharing the home with her will be Mrs. Helms' Cuban aunt, a peppery little woman of 80 who also speaks English.

THE LONG plane flight had been a new experience for Miss Cazier, but it hadn't shaken her.

"I'm surprised to see all this snow up here," she said after the take-off. She was told that she was looking at the Earth through a broken cloud cover. She shook her head, amazed.

"I think we're nearer heaven than Earth," she remarked later. "Don't anybody tell me how high we really are. No, tell me."

THE LETTER that had been sent to Miss Cazier before she left Chicago included one in the kind of handwriting that is taught in second grade.

It had a P.S.:
"OOOO XXXX
"(Hugs) and (kisses)."

Lori is 7½ years old and lives in Lexington, Mass. She read of Miss Cazier's plight in the Boston lobe last week.

"I hope you are feeling fine. I saw your picture in the paper and you look verey nice. I would like to be your friend," Lori wrote to Miss Cazier.

A COLLEGE student from Northern Illinois University apologized for the poor stationery he was using but said he was on the way to class.

"I realize that (the enclosed) money won't erase the memory of what happened, but perhaps it will aid Miss Cazier in getting settled in a friendlier and more humane atmosphere," he wrote.

"Somone should tell the courts that justice is futile without mercy," the youth added.

Stanley Shapiro, Hollywood producer, called and then wrote, offering to do all he could.

TO THE MONTROSE Urban Progress Center, which is assisting Miss Cazier; to The Daily News, which discovered and wrote about her plight, and to Miss Cazier the letters of sympathy and assistance flowed.

This week, Miss Cazier heeded the pleas of Merry Macke, a poverty worker at the prog ress center, and Robert Johnson an attorney with the Legal Aid Bureau of United Charities now working with the poverty program, and made a trip to the bank with her money.

At the Northern Trust Bank, Miss Cazier was met by Raymond Ott, manager of the savings department, who filled out the necessary forms. By a special arrangement with the bank, the account will be safeguarded to prevent Miss Cazier from being victimized by any confidence artists.

THE LETTERS that come from across the country expressed sympathy for Miss Cazier and indignation that such a thing could hapepn to an old woman.

"You'll have the time of your life . . . in Chicago?" wrote Robert L. Belin of San Rafael, Calif., in a sarcastic reference to the melody about the Windy City. He enclosed a donation.

"As I am sitting here in the office working I cannot hold back the tears and the lump in my throat," wrote a Chicago Heights woman.

"What kind of animals have we turned into," wrote a Chicago woman.

Signing, "In Christian Love," a housewife from Wood River, Ill., wrote to offer Miss Cazier a new home, as did a number of other people.

Miss Cazier is grateful for the letters and the financial help. But a woman who has been on her own as long as she has is not quick to give up her independence.

HOWEVER, THE THOUGHTS of a new home with a physician who could look after her and the warm sun of Florida finally won Miss Cazier over.

As Miss Cazier picked at a cheeseburger in a Loop restaurant Friday before packing for the trip, she squinted her pale blue eyes and said:

"It really will be warm there, won't it? I'll have to get some clothes. Goodness, what a bother I am."

Reprinted with permission from the *Chicago Daily News*

Staff writer Vern K. Richey stayed with the story until Miss Cazier was settled in her new home in Miami, Florida. The third story is an example of a *wrap-up* (final coverage). Millions of readers wanted to know what happened to Miss Cazier. Mr. Richey made sure they had a complete account.

This is a good example of the work of a general assignment reporter. The story was not foreseen. Mr. Richey may have simply seen Miss Cazier sitting among her belongings on his way to work one day. He saw the possibilities of a story, got an OK from the city editor, and called a staff photographer—within a few hours millions of readers knew about Miss Cazier.

EXERCISE 4. Finding Repeated Information

When a newspaper follows a story day after day like this, it can't take it for granted that every reader has read the earlier stories. So each story must include some background information for the reader who is coming to the story for the first time.

Directions: Skim the second and third articles on pages 37 and 38 to find the sections which repeat the story about Miss Cazier's eviction. Circle this information.

EXERCISE 5. Reaching Conclusions

Directions: Read the statements below. Then find three facts in the articles which could be used to prove each statement. Underline the line in which the fact appears.

____1. People are cruel and thoughtless to old people in Chicago.
____2. Many kind people are willing to help old people.
____3. The editor was right when he decided this story would interest readers all over the United States.

PRACTICE IN YOUR LOCAL NEWSPAPER

PRACTICE 1. Use a colored pencil or ink stick to mark up the front page of a newspaper. Write "L" on local stories. Write "N" on national stories—stories that come from other parts of the United States. Write "F" on stories from foreign countries.

PRACTICE 2. See how many different press association and news service credit lines you can find in your newspaper. Cut them out and fasten them on a sheet of paper. Be sure to check the business section.

PRACTICE 3. Imagine you are an assistant to the city editor. One of your jobs is to skim the rival papers to find clippings to put in the future file. See how many slips you can get from the news section of your newspaper. Circle the part that gives the future date.

PRACTICE 4. When one of your future file dates comes up, check that day's paper to see if the newspaper did actually print something on that subject.

PRACTICE 5. Look in your local newspaper for a news story or feature you think is a press release. Fasten it to a sheet of paper to bring to class. With a colored pencil, underline the words that tell what person or group probably sent the press release. Good places to look for press releases are the entertainment, business, and special feature pages.

PRACTICE 6. Check your newspaper to see how local news is covered. Clip and bring to class one example of each of the following:

> A news article written by a specialist.
> A news article written by a beat reporter.
> A news article about an event scheduled for the future. Try to find one you think comes from a press release sent by some one seeking publicity for the event.

PRACTICE 7. Not all newspapers identify their beat reporters with a line such as "Education Reporter." You can do some detective work to find out which reporter usually covers a particular subject. Choose a subject to concentrate on—for example, sports, society news, science or politics. Save the headline-lead section of each story in your subject for a week or more. Count the stories that have no bylines and fasten them together. Put all the stories by one writer together. Write a few sentences telling what you found out.

CHAPTER 4
THE NEWS STORY: WHO? WHAT? WHEN? WHERE? WHY? AND HOW?

A detective story starts with mystifying clues, and strings you along for hundreds of pages before it tells you whodunit, how, and why.

A straight news story is the opposite of a detective story. It doesn't keep you in suspense at all. You are given the most important facts in the first paragraphs, or even in the first sentence.

The rest of the information in the story is arranged in order of importance, with the least important information at the end. You can cut out at any time after the lead and be sure you are not missing anything vital.

Who? What? Where? When? Why? and How? These are the questions the reporter tries to answer for you in the *lead*—the first paragraph or two of the story. Not all of these answers are in every lead, but you will find answers to most of them. Those not answered in the lead may be given in the *body* of the story—the part that follows the lead.

Read the sample story below, keeping in mind WWWWW&H (Who, What, When, Where, Why, and How).

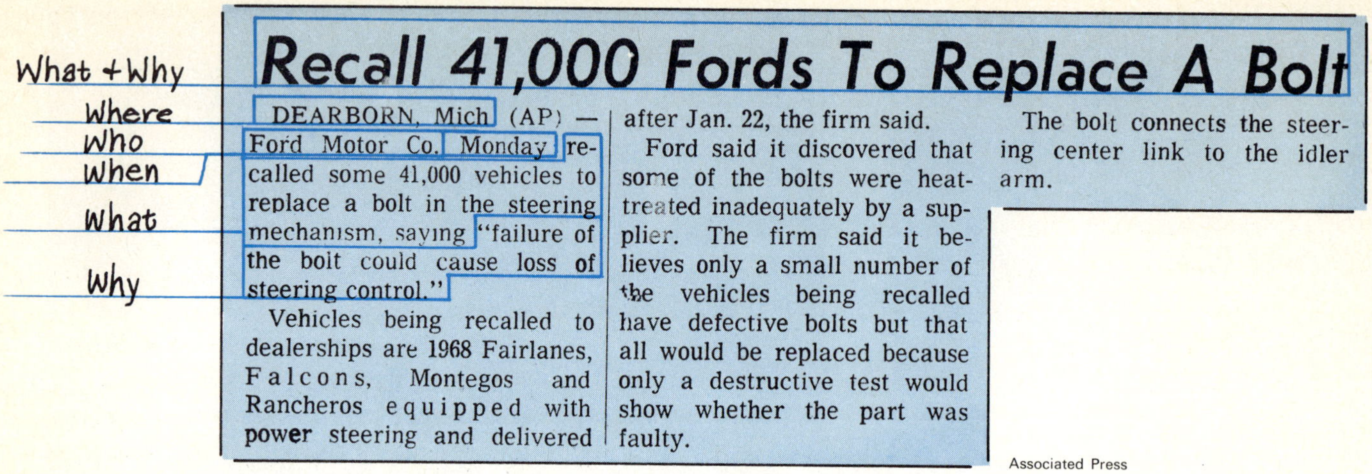

Recall 41,000 Fords To Replace A Bolt

DEARBORN, Mich (AP) — Ford Motor Co. Monday recalled some 41,000 vehicles to replace a bolt in the steering mechanism, saying "failure of the bolt could cause loss of steering control."

Vehicles being recalled to dealerships are 1968 Fairlanes, Falcons, Montegos and Rancheros equipped with power steering and delivered after Jan. 22, the firm said.

Ford said it discovered that some of the bolts were heat-treated inadequately by a supplier. The firm said it believes only a small number of the vehicles being recalled have defective bolts but that all would be replaced because only a destructive test would show whether the part was faulty.

The bolt connects the steering center link to the idler arm.

Associated Press

Look at the *headline* in terms of WWWWW&H. It tells WHAT is being done: recall 41,000 Fords. It tells WHY it is being done: to replace a bolt.

Look at the lead. The first paragraph of this story is the LEAD. If the paper printed only the headline and lead, you would still get the heart of the story:

Who or What:	the Ford Motor Co.
Did What:	recalled some 41,000 vehicles
When:	Monday
Where:	Dearborn, Michigan
Why:	. . . "to replace a bolt in the steering mechanism" that may fail and "cause loss of steering control"
How:	The story doesn't say.

The information in the lead is of interest to the public.

Look at the first paragraph of the body (paragraph 2 of the story). After the lead, the next most important information goes here.

The lead said only that "vehicles" are being recalled. This paragraph in the body tells WHAT vehicles?: "1968 Fairlanes, Falcons, Montegos and Rancheros equipped with power steering and delivered after Jan. 22." WHERE are the vehicles being recalled *to*?: to dealerships.

This paragraph is interesting mainly to Ford owners. They want to know if their car is one of those being recalled. If it is, they want to know where the repair work will be done.

Now look at paragraph 3. It answers a question that is still less important to most readers: WHY are the bolts defective?: They were "heat-treated inadequately by a supplier."

We also get some new information here that we may not have thought to ask for:

WHO? the firm

WHAT? said it believes only a small number of the vehicles being recalled have defective bolts.

WHY then are they all being replaced? " . . . because only a destructive test would show whether the part was faulty."

This paragraph is interesting, but no driver's safety would be endangered if he did not have this information.

Look at paragraph 4. Now we get down to a very detailed piece of information that would not be of interest to the general public: WHERE in the steering mechanism is the bolt? or WHAT does the bolt do?: "It connects the steering link to the idler arm."

This paragraph adds technical information which would interest such persons as car mechanics. It could be cut without hurting the story much at all.

Notice that a straight news story doesn't end with a socko finish. It just sort of dwindles away into nothing.

We have already said that one reason for this is to save the reader time. There is another reason. If it turns out that there is not enough room in the paper for the whole story, the editor knows that he can cut off as many paragraphs as necessary, starting with the last paragraph, and injure the story very little.

PRACTICE MAKING UP WWWWW&H QUESTIONS

Making up WWWWW&H questions and looking for the answers will help you with anything you read, in or out of a newspaper. You will understand the material better, because you are involved in what you are reading. In a sense, you are having a conversation with the writer. You are asking questions to which you expect answers.

Did you notice that the "Recall 41,000 Fords" story does not answer all the WWWWW&H questions you can think of? It would certainly be interesting to know HOW did Ford find out about the defective bolt? And if you own one of the defective cars, you would like to know HOW are the vehicles being recalled? Will you get a letter? Will your dealer phone you? Should you drive right over to the dealer's shop? For that matter, is it safe to drive the car at all?

Using your WWWWW&H questions will keep you alert to what a story does NOT tell, as well as what it does tell.

EXERCISE 1. How to Find WWWWW&H

Here are some more hints about picking out WWWWW&H. When you do a WWWWW&H exercise, check back to this section. After a while you will not need it.

Directions: Study each *hint.* Then underline the information requested.

(*hint*) 1. To find WHO—WHO has said something, done something or had something happen to them? WHO is not always identified by name. WHO may be described as members of a group: Boy Scouts, firemen, students, senators. WHO may be a business firm like the Ford Motor Company or a department of government such as the Interstate Commerce Commission. WHO may be an animal. There may be more than one WHO. Underline the "WHO's" in these news clippings.

Associated Press

Los Angeles (AP)—It takes more than a double dose of male chromosomes to prove a man is legally insane when he commits a violent crime, a superior court judge has ruled.

The Sun, Baltimore

Annapolis, March 7—By the closest margin possible, the State Senate gave tentative approval today to a measure to abolish the death penalty

Associated Press

MEMPHIS, Tenn.—James Earl Ray pleaded guilty today to murder in the death of Dr. Martin Luther King Jr.

Associated Press

LONDON (AP)—Two men ambushed a police bus during the morning rush hour in a tough South London district today, squirted ammonia in the faces of two unarmed prison officers and freed two robbery suspects being taken handcuffed together to court for trial.

(*hint*) 2. To find WHAT—WHAT has the WHO of the story done? WHAT has been discovered? WHAT has happened? WHAT has happened some time ago but is just now being told? WHAT has someone said? In many news stories the WHAT is a report of a statement made by an important person. Underline the "WHAT's" in these clippings.

United Press International

MOSCOW (UPI) — Thousands of Muscovites marched through a swirling snowstorm today in the second day of protests against the reported killing and mutilation of Soviet border guards by Red Chinese troops.

The Liberal Party has declared its "strong" opposition to a one per cent sales tax increase proposed by Gov. Rockefeller

Associated Press

WASHINGTON (AP) — The nation's total employment rose substantially for the the fifth straight month to 76.2 million in February, and unemployment remained at a 15-year low of 3.3 per cent, the Labor Dept said today.

United Press International

(By United Press International)

Tornadoes slashed across parts of Texas, Louisiana, Mississippi, and Arkansas yesterday and thunderstorms pummeled the south from the plains thru the cotton belt.

(*hint*) 3. To find WHEN—If the lead does not give an actual time such as the name of the week or a date, look for words like today, yesterday, this morning, etc. Then compare these with (1) the dateline before the lead, if there is one; (2) the date of the paper you are reading if no time is given in the dateline.

For example, if you are reading an October 11 paper, and there is no dateline on your story, "yesterday" in your story means October 10. But if the story has the dateline "LISBON, Oct. 10" then "yesterday" in the story means October 9.

Sometimes the WHEN is indefinite. Words like "recently" are used when the reporter does not know the exact time something was done or a statement was made, or the exact time does not matter. *The Wall Street Journal* is a paper that leaves out the dateline and phrases like "said today" unless this information is important to the story. You know the news happened "recently." Underline the "WHEN's" in these news clippings.

From *The Kansas City Star*

Dick Smith, Olympic diving coach from Phoenix, Ariz., will conduct a diving clinic at the Johnson County Y. M. C. A., 4200 West 79th street, Prairie Village, on March 22-23.

Associated Press

BECKLEY W. Va., March 9 (AP)—West Virginia's striking coal miners, only partially satisfied with a newly passed "black lung" compensation bill, voted today to remain away from work until Gov. Arch Moore Jr. signs the bill.

Reprinted with permission from the *Chicago Sun Times*

It was loud. It was laughing. It was grand. It was St. Patrick's Day, 1969.

With spectators numbering 1,000,000, according to the estimate of Deputy Police Supt. John Madl, and some 70,000 in the line of march, the St. Patrick's Day parade rolled merrily along State Street Monday.

Reprinted with permission of *The Wall Street Journal,*

By a WALL STREET JOURNAL *Staff Reporter*
JACKSONVILLE, Fla. — An outbreak of measles among 25 children here who previously had received live, attenuated measles virus vaccine (with measles immune globulin) occurred early this winter, the National Communicable Disease Center in Atlanta said.

(*hint*) 4. To find WHERE—The dateline (LONDON, Jan. 8) gives the name of the city the reporter sent the story from. This is almost always the place, or near the place, where the story happened. If there is no dateline, you know the story happened in the city where the newspaper is published.

If a more exact WHERE is important—a particular neighborhood or a street address—you will find it in the first few paragraphs of the story. Underline the "WHERE's" in these news clippings.

Winston-Salem Journal

Observers of a new computerized punch card voting system here yesterday were clearly impressed.

Associated Press

MEXICO CITY (AP)—More than 100 persons were injured yesterday in a riot that broke out during a pop music concert at Mexico's sport stadium in Magdalena Mixhuca.

From *The Kansas City Star*

The city council planning and zoning committee yesterday recommended for council passage rezoning of a residential tract at I-70 and Cypress avenue for commercial use over objections of various city agencies and area residents.

Winston-Salem Journal

RALEIGH — North Carolina public school authorities would have the right to search students for weapons under a bill proposed yesterday in the General Assembly.

(*hint*) 5. To find WHY—WHY did the WHAT happen? What is the *reason* for the action or statement? You will not find an answer to WHY in every story. Maybe there is no particular reason, or it is not important to the story. Often the answer to WHY is, "We don't know why." Then you will find statements such as, "No motive for the murder has been discovered," or "Relatives could give no reason for the sudden disappearance . . ." Underline the "WHY's" in these clippings.

Associated Press

TROY, Mich. (AP)—Faced with plunging scores in national achievement tests and increased absenteeism, Troy High School has decided to drop a controversial study program that allowed students to spend up to 40 per cent of the school day as they wished.

Winston-Salem Journal

Northwestern Bank will open two new food stamp distribution windows inside the downtown bank building as a temporary measure to eliminate the long lines outside the building every month.

© The Washington Post

Mayor Walter E. Washington asked today for an extra $25 million for the city, most of it to step up the fight against crime.

Miami Herald

Paul Pope Jr., of 2293 SW 24 Terr., says he is just an honest man trying to make a living by putting together prefabricated caskets in his back yard.

(*hint*) 6. To find HOW—When the way something was done is important, you may find it given in the lead: "Connie Dierking's two baskets in the last 45 seconds gave the Cincinnati Royals a 106–104 victory. . . ." If it is difficult to explain, it is more likely to be given in the body of the story. You will not find an answer to "HOW" in every story. Underline the "HOW's" in these clippings.

Winston-Salem Journal

SALISBURY — Three Rowan County men were killed about 7:15 p.m. yesterday when the automobile in which they were riding crashed head-on with a trailer truck in heavy rain on U.S. 601 about five miles north of here.

Chicago Tribune

A group of California table grape growers are touring the country on a mission to stimulate interest in finding a solution to the California grape boycott.

Associated Press

PASADENA, Calif. (AP) — Tidal waves in the earth's crust up to a foot high, caused by the gravitational pull of the moon and the sun, may have triggered some major earthquakes, a geophysicist said Thursday.

Chicago Tribune

The world trade opportunities listed below are specific requests for United States merchandise. Those interested in doing business with these inquirers may obtain the complete name and address from the United States department of commerce, 219 S. Dearborn st., telephone 353-4457, by referring to the code number following each inquiry.

USING ANSWER SHEETS AS GUIDELINES

The two answer sheets on the opposite page have been filled in by students who were learning how to analyze news leads by finding answers to WWWWW&H. First read the news story, "String Touches Wire, Kite Flier Killed," then study the answers Marcia and Donald have given. You will notice that some of their answers differ. Which student seems to know more about electricity than the other?

String Touches Wire, Kite Flier Killed

KANSAS CITY, Kan. (AP) — Dennis Michael Pisciotta, 22, died an hour after he was found unconscious in the back yard of his parents' home where he had been flying a kite.

Police said the kite string, containing a metallic filament, touched a 12,000-volt power line.

Associated Press

WWWWWH ANSWER SHEET FOR NEWS LEAD

Directions: Write an answer for each question. If you do not find an answer in the news article, write "not given."

The Headline Reads: "String Touches Wire, Kite Flier Killed"

1. Who? Dennis Michael Pisciotta

2. What? died

3. When? an hour after he was found unconscious

4. Where? in the back yard of his parents' home

5. Why? his kite string touched a 12,000-volt power line.

6. How? the string contained a metallic filament

My name is: Marcia Garcia Home Room # 140

My article is from Chicago Sun-Times (Give name of paper.) 3/18/69 (Date of paper)

WWWWWH ANSWER SHEET FOR NEWS LEAD

Directions: Write an answer for each question. If you do not find an answer in the news article, write "not given."

The Headline Reads: "String Touches Wire, Kite Flier Killed"

1. Who? Dennis Michael Pisciotta

2. What? died

3. When? an hour after he was found unconscious

4. Where? Does not say where he died, but he was flying kite in back yard of his parents' home.

5. Why? Electricity from 12,000 volt line electrocuted him.

6. How? His kite string contained a metallic filament which served as a conductor.

My name is: Donald Washington Home Room # 201

My article is from Chicago Sun-Times (Give name of paper.) 3/18/69 (Date of paper)

EXERCISE 2. Finding the Answers to WWWWW&H

Directions: Read the article, "Discover Rock Music Is Deafening Teens" and fill out your first answer sheet. Use *only* the information from the lead. If you can not find an answer to one of the questions, turn back to page 44 and study the hints given for finding WWWWW&H. You will also find it helpful to imagine how you would ask each question if you could talk to the reporter who wrote the news article. Remember that not every question is answered in every news lead. If you cannot find it, fill in "not given."

Discover Rock Music Is Deafening Teens

GAINESVILLE, Fla., Jan. 12 (AP) — The pounding beat of hard rock bands are blasting the eardrums of the nations teenie-boppers into old age, a University of Florida researcher said today.

In front of the bandstand at a Gainesville club for teen-agers, his team found the noise measured 120 decibels — as loud as the Saturn 5 moon rocket measured from the press site at Cape Kennedy.

40 Feet Away

Dr. Kenneth C. Pollock said his associates at the audiology laboratory were 40 feet outside the club before the sound dropped below 90 decibels, which the American Medical association says is the threshhold above which damage is caused.

In 10 youngsters examined before and after a three-hour dance session, Pollock found temporary loss of hearing acuity ranging from 1½ decibels to 35 decibels. All had ringing in their ears.

"Thirty-five decibels means they hear normal conversation as a whisper, like stuffing your fingertips into your ears," Pollock said. "Even tho most of the losses were mild, we consider them significant."

"It Embalms You"

One girl told the researcher why teens lik etheir music loud, Pollock explained: "She said, "It embalms you. It has to be that loud so that it gets inside you. Otherwise it isn't any good."

By the time they are 25 years old, the youngsters will have the problems of the aged as sounds of consonants become hard to hear.

"It's like elderly persons who complain, 'Everybody mumbles. Nobody talks plain anymore," Pollock said.

Associated Press

Prepare additional WWWWW&H answer sheet blanks on your note paper and continue your practice. Read the article, "Police 'Plants' Nab 2 Theft Suspects" and fill out one of your answer sheets.

EXERCISE 3. Finding out WHY?

Some stories are good for answering WHY questions and some don't tell us WHY. The article on page 50, "Police 'Plants' Nab 2 Theft Suspects," is a good story for WHY's. The story happened because Captain Lojacono asked himself a WHY question.

Directions: Answer the following WHY questions by underlining material in the article. Write the number of the paragraph in which the question is answered in the blank.

WWWWWH ANSWER SHEET FOR NEWS LEAD

Directions: Write an answer for each question. If you do not find an answer in the news article, write "not given."

The Headline Reads: ______________________________

____

1. Who? ______________________________

____

2. What? ______________________________

____

3. When? ______________________________

____

4. Where? ______________________________

____

5. Why? ______________________________

____

6. How? ______________________________

____

My name is: ______________________ Home Room # ______

My article is from ______________________________
(Give name of paper.) (Date of paper)

On Captain's Theory

Police 'Plants' Nab 2 Theft Suspects

①Two policemen "planted" inside the West Radio and Television Service, 368 Grant St., because of a previous burglary, captured two suspects at gunpoint after the intruders climbed in through a second-floor window early Sunday morning.

②Capt. Anthony R. Lojacono of the West Delevan Station said the two suspects who live in an apartment building next door, entered Friday morning.

③ **Charges of third-degree burglary, first-degree grand larceny and possession of burglary tools were placed against Michael David Schipani, 20, and Charles E. Herman Jr., 21, both of 354 Grant St.**

④Capt. Lojacono said the store operator, Carl Martino, of 791 Richmond Ave., reported the loss of 10 portable television sets worth $1,500 from a second-floor storage area Friday morning. The sets were removed from cartons that had been split open. The cartons then were carefully closed and piled in a stack the same way they were found.

⑤"I theorized the intruders went to all this trouble because they figured the loss would not be discovered quickly," Capt. Lojacono said. "They apparently thought that as long as there was no sign of a breakin on the lower floor the store owner would not discover the loss immediately. Therefore, I deliberately withheld releasing information about the burglary and detailed two men inside."

Take Up Vigil

⑥Patrolmen Donald L. Christopher and Robert J. Andolina took up a vigil on the second floor after the store closed Saturday night. At 12:45 Sunday morning they heard the window that had been jimmied open previously, slowly raise.

⑦They waited for the intruder to get well inside and to the storage area. There, they flashed on their flashlights, collared the suspect and placed handcuffs on him.

⑧The first suspect was Schipani. Realizing that an accomplice was necessary to carry off the television sets in the previous entry, the policemen continued their vigil. Ten minutes later Herman entered and was quickly placed under arrest.

⑨Capt. Lojacono said none of the loot in Friday's burglary has been recovered. One of the prisoners admitted the television sets were sold for a total of $255, police said.

Courier-Express,
Buffalo, N.Y.

____ 1. WHY were the policemen in the television store?

____ 2. WHY did the captain believe the thieves might come back?

____ 3. WHY did the patrolman wait after catching the first suspect?

EXERCISE 4. Unpacking the Lead

A reporter tries to pack all the important facts of a story into the first paragraph. This often makes the lead hard to understand. One way to understand a complicated lead is to "unpack" it one fact at a time.

Directions: There are some seven facts in the lead of "Police 'Plants' Nab 2 Theft Suspects." See if you can rewrite the lead in about eight sentences, with each sentence telling only one new fact. The first two sentences are done for you.

1. *Two policemen were assigned to wait inside a TV service store.*
2. *The name of the store is West Radio and Television Service.*
3. ____.
4. ____.
5. ____.
6. ____.
7. ____.

EXERCISE 5. Finding more answers to WWWWW&H

Usually the headline writer has already done the job of pulling the important parts out of a complicated lead. Remember, he wants you to get the vital information quickly and easily. Every word in the headline must count for something.

Directions: Study each of the two headlines in this story. If it answers any of the WWWWW&H questions below it, circle each question it answers *and* write out the full question. Part of number 1. is done for you as an example. Complete it, then go on to the lead paragraph and answer it in the same way. Do the same for the second paragraph.

HEADLINES

1. "Hunt Dr. King's Slayer"

Who? What? Where? When? Why? How?

Who was slain?

Who is hunted?

2. Victim of Sniper's
Bullet in Memphis

Who? What? When? Where? Why? How?

LEAD

MEMPHIS (AP) Nobel Laureate Martin Luther King, Jr., father of non-violence in the civil rights movement, was slain here Thursday night.

Hunt Dr. King's Slayer

Victim Of Sniper's Bullet In Memphis

(1) MEMPHIS (AP)—Nobel Laureate Martin Luther King Jr., father of non-violence in the civil rights movement, was slain here Thursday night.

(2) Dr. King, 39, was struck in the neck by a bullet as he stood on the balcony of his motel. He died less than an hour later in St. Joseph Hospital.

(3) Gov. Buford Ellington immediately ordered 4,000 National Guard troops back into the city. A curfew, which was clamped on Memphis after a King-led march turned into a riot a week ago, was reimposed.

(4) Police said incidents of violence, including several fire-bombings were reported after Dr. King's death.

(5) The 1964 Nobel Peace Prize winner had come to lead protests in behalf of the city's 1,300 striking garbage workers, most of them Negroes.

2 Men Arrested

(6) Two unidentified men were arrested several blocks from the motel.

(7) Police also said they found a .30-.06 rifle on Main St. about one block from the motel, but it was not confirmed whether this was the weapon that killed Dr. King.

(8) An aide who was standing nearby said the shot hit Dr. King in the neck and lower right part of his face.

(9) "Martin Luther King is dead," said Asst. Police Chief Henry Lux, in releasing the first news of the death.

(10) Assistant hospital administrator Paul Hess confirmed later that Dr King died at 7 p.m. of a bullet wound in the neck.

DR. MARTIN LUTHER KING JR.

Tells of Shooting

(11) "Dr. King was on the second floor balcony of the motel," The Rev. Mr. Jackson said. "He had just bent over. If he had been standing up, he wouldn't have been hit in the face."

(12) Dr. King had just told Ben Branch: "My man, be sure to sing 'Blessed Lord' tonight and sing it well.' "

(13) A shot then rang out, The Rev. Mr. Jackson siad.

(14) He said the only sound Dr. King uttered was: "Oh!"

(15) "It knocked him down," he said. "When I turned around, I saw police coming from everywhere. They said. 'Behind you.' The police were coming from where the shot came."

(16) Branch, another member of the King party, said, "The bullet exploded in his face. It knocked him off his feet."

(17) Solomon Jones, Dr. King's chauffeur, said he saw a "man in white clothes" running from the scene.

(18) Dr. King had returned to Memphis Wednesday to lead another massive protest march Monday in support of the garbage strikers. Sympathizers from other parts of the country had announced they would join, and as many as 10,000 or more were expected for the demonstration.

(19) A similar march on March 28 of about 6,000 erupted into the first violence in Memphis since the beginning of the civil rights movement. Police and march leaders, alike, blamed the outburst on Negro youths on the fringe of the march.

(20) One 17-year-old Negro youth was killed in the violence after the march, and his funeral Tuesday was attended by several thousand mourners.

Report Sniper Fire

(21) Violence erupted again shortly after Dr. King was shot. Police reported snipers firing on police and National Guard units and several persons were reported hit by the shots.

(22) Several fire-bombings and other acts of vandalism also were reported.

(23) Police director Frank Holloman ordered a curfew back into effect "until further notice" as youths ran rampant, many of them with fire-bombs in their hands.

(24) National Guard units, which had been deactivated only Wednesday after five days of duty here, were rushed to Memphis.

(25) A bomb threat was telephoned to Methodist Hospital and police were rushed to the scene. Armed guards were immediately posted at St. Joseph Hospital where Dr. King died.

Report on Slayer

(26) Holloman said early investigation indicated the slayer was a white male, who was "50 to 100 yards away in a flophouse."

He said police had no definite leads.

(27) Th city's garbage collectors struck Feb. 12 for union recognition, payroll deduction of dues and pay increases.

(28) Mayor Henry Loeb had declared the strike was illegal and said repeatedly he would not grant a written contract or the dues checkoff.

(29) The strike quickly took on a civil rights character.

(30) In a speech here, Dr. King had said the strike symbolized a new phase of the civil rights movement, "The Negroes' fight for economic equality."

Injunction Issued

(31) A U.S. District court judge issued an injunction against Monday's planned march after city officials said they feared it might bring more violence.

(32) A U.S. District Court judge olence. Dr. King's attorneys argued against the move, and District Court Judge Bailey Brown took the case under advisement Thursday.

(33) Dr. King had told a rally Wednesday night that the march would proceed, regardless of injunctions.

(34) That night, Dr. King had told associates that he was not disturbed about reports that he would be in danger while in Memphis.

(35) Gov. Ellington announced after the slaying that the state was taking necessary steps to prevent disorder.

(36) "For the second time in recent days, I most earnestly ask the people of Memphis and Shelby County to remain calm. I do so again tonight in the face of this most regrettable incident," the governor said.

(37) "Every possible action is being taken to apprehend the person or persons responsible for committing this act," Ellington said.

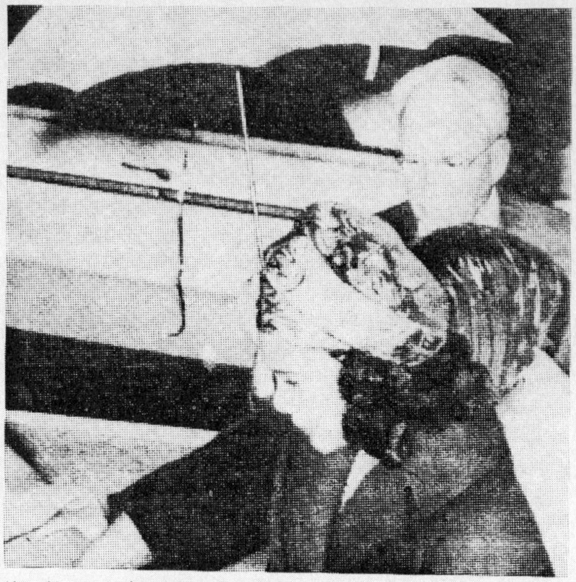

Mrs. Martin Luther King Jr. is led up the steps of her Atlanta home while Mayor Ivan Allen Jr. holds the umbrella for her. She had changed her plans to fly to Memphis when she learned Dr. King was dead. (UPI)

THE EPITAPH: 'HE DIED TO MAKE MEN FREE'

NEW YORK (AP) — Dr. Martin Luther King Jr., speaking in an Albany (Ga.) church in 1962, after shots were fired in nearby houses, said:

"It may get me crucified. I may even die. But I want it said even if I die in the struggle that 'He died to make men free.'"

An ambulance carrying Dr. Martin Luther King Jr. speeds along a Memphis street after the fatal shooting. (AP)

Who? What? When? Where? Why? How?

SECOND PARAGRAPH

Dr. King, 39, was struck in the neck by a bullet as he stood on the balcony of his motel. He died less than an hour later in St. Joseph's Hospital.

Who? What? When? Where? Why? How?

HOW TO READ THE BODY OF THE ARTICLE

There are several ways to read the body of an important news story like this. Some people will read it paragraph by paragraph to the end. Others will look at the five subheads and read the parts which they think will answer any questions they still have. Those who have heard the TV news will need to read less than those who have not. Those who have been reading the news accounts about the Memphis strike may decide they already know what is given under "Injunction Issued." They may stop when they come to that subhead.

As you read news stories, you will discover that subheads do not tell you *all* that is described in that part of the article.

ORGANIZING DETAILS

Before you start to read the details given in the body of the story, ask yourself WHY you are reading them. Do you think they will help you understand what really happened? Will they give you proof of a statement you might not accept unless you read the

◀ Reprinted with permission from Associated Press, top right photo by United Press International, bottom photo by Wide World Photos details? Will they help you recall the main idea later? Or is the event so important to you, you feel the need to read every available detail?

There are many details in the story about Dr. King's assassination. They include things that happened *before* and *after* Dr. King was shot. They include reasons for the actions of Dr. King, Gov. Ellington, Police Director Frank Holloman, and other people present at the time.

You will find it easier to read details if you practice organizing them according to *time* or *place*. For example, you might try to work out what happened in various places in the story about Dr. King:

What happened at the motel?
What happened at the hospital?
What happened on the streets during the first march?
What happened in the mayor's office?
What happened in the court room?
What happened at the Wednesday night rally?

EXERCISE 6. Seeing Details in Relation to Time

Directions: Beside each paragraph in this story, write *A* if the paragraph tells something that happened *after* Dr. King was slain or write *B* if the paragraph tells about something that happened *before* Dr. King was slain. If some person is talking after the assassination about something which happened before, write both *A* and *B*. (For an example of this, see paragraph 11.)

EXERCISE 7. Seeing Details in Relation to Place

Directions: Read the article "Motel Where King Slain in Negro Area." Also read the caption under the picture and study the picture itself. Put a check in front of each of the following statements which you think would help the reader understand the location of the scene of the crime.

____1. The Lorraine Motel-Hotel is in downtown Memphis.

____2. The motel is in a Negro neighborhood about four blocks south of historic Beale street.

____3. The motel is surrounded by warehouses.

____4. The motel is Negro-owned.

____5. Dr. King stayed at the Rivermont Holiday Inn after he was whisked away from the violence.

Dr. Martin Luther King Jr. was shot as he stood on the balcony of this motel in downtown Memphis. He was rushed to a hospital in critical condition and died an hour later. (UPI)

Motel Where King Slain In Negro Area

MEMPHIS (UPI)—The motel where Dr Martin Luther King Jr. was shot to death Thursday night is in a Negro neighborhood about four blocks south of historic Beale St.

Surrounded by warehouses, the Lorraine Motel-Hotel is a two-story structure. The motel portion was added to a smaller two-story hotel.

Dr. King and his aides choose the Lorraine because it is Negro-owned and in a Negro area

On his visit to Memphis last week, when he led a 5,000-man demonstration that erupted in violence, Dr. King stayed at the Rivermont Holiday Inn after he was whisked away from the violence.

Memphis police had no special plans for protecting Dr King.

United Press International

PRACTICE IN YOUR LOCAL NEWSPAPER

PRACTICE 1. Select a straight news story from the front page of your local paper. Paste or clip it to notebook paper. Make a WWWWW&H answer sheet like the one on page 49 and fill it out.

PRACTICE 2. Find a 5–10 paragraph news story and fasten it to notebook paper. How many paragraphs could be cut off and still leave the story so that it could be understood?
Cross out each paragraph which you think could safely be cut.

PRACTICE 3. Find a straight news story that has more than one WHERE. Paste or clip it in your notebook and circle the different places mentioned.

CHAPTER 5
"SAYS WHO?..."
WHO STANDS BEHIND THE NEWS?

As you read each piece of information in a news story, you should ask yourself, "Says who?" If it's someone you believe tells the truth and knows what he's talking about, you accept the information. But the first step is finding the answer to "Says who?" The answer is either . . .

The REPORTER SAID so. He found out it's true.

or

SOMEBODY ELSE SAID so. The reporter found out that this is what somebody else said. The reporter is *not* saying he found out what they said is true.

Once you have become aware of the difference between REPORTER SAID and SOMEBODY ELSE SAID information in one story, you can start making this important distinction in every other news story you read. We will use the news story "2 Tons of Bombs on Road" as an example. The story is almost entirely REPORTER SAID.

Read the following news story and try to get straight in your mind what happened. Then check how well you understand what happened by doing the exercise which follows the story.

TRUCKLOAD OF BOMBS OVERTURNED, BUT NOT EXPLODED
Driver and passenger escaped injury in mishap today at Port Chicago
—AP Photo

2 Tons of Bombs on Road

A truck loaded with 250-pound bombs turned over on the Port Chicago Highway early today, spilling the explosives onto the road.

The driver, Thomas Maschinot, 27, of Denver, flagged down the Highway Patrol and a patrol car crew notified the Naval Weapons Station at Concord and the Port Chicago Fire Department.

The area was blocked off while Navy men began the dangerous task of reloading the bombs into Navy trucks. CHP officer Robert Ferrero said it was a miracle the whole load did not go up.

A total of 4700 pounds of bombs were being trucked to the weapons station from Denver when, at about 3:50 a. m., Maschinot missed a sharp turn west of Willow Way.

It was a tractor and trailer rig, the trailer being of aluminum construction. One side burst and released the missiles. Firemen said the truck's fuel tank was ruptured and spilled gallons of diesel oil.

Several hours after the accident Navy men and firemen were still gingerly clearing the dangerous debris.

The San Francisco Examiner, photo by Wide World Photos

EXERCISE 1. A WWWWW&H Check

Directions: See if you understand what happened in "2 Tons of Bombs on Road." Each line begins with a question word. Circle the word in that line that answers the question best. The first line is done for you as an example.

1. who or what?	(truck)	highway	bombs
2. did what?	spilled bombs	flagged down	loaded bombs
3. when?	late yesterday	early this morning	last week
4. where?	Chicago area	Concord area	San Francisco area
5. why?	area was blocked	it turned over	explosives spilled
6. how?	gingerly clearing	trailer side burst	missed turn

Now do you know what information is in "2 Tons of Bombs on Road"? Turn the page to read the story again. This time it has been printed a special way to help you practice telling what is REPORTER SAID information and what is SOMEBODY ELSE SAID information. If you took out everything SOMEBODY ELSE SAID, the REPORTER SAID everything that is left.

Read the "Says who?" explanation next to the news story. After each part of the explanation, check back to the news story to see if the explanation makes sense to you.

"SAYS WHO" EXPLANATION

2 Tons of Bombs on Road

A truck loaded with 250-pound bombs turned over on the Port Chicago Highway early today, spilling the explosives onto the road.

The driver, Thomas Maschinot, 27, of Denver, **flagged down the Highway Patrol and a patrol car crew notified the Naval Weapons Station at Concord and the Port Chicago Fire Department.**

The area was blocked off while Navy men began the dangerous task of reloading the bombs into Navy trucks. CHP officer Robert Ferrero said

REPORTER SAID. The reporter doesn't say somebody else said it. So we know the reporter himself takes responsibility for the information.

- Some things the reporter learned for himself. Probably he got to the wreck in time to see with his own eyes the work of cleaning up.
- Some things he learned from people he was sure tell the truth and know what they're talking about. We know he talked to a highway patrol officer (paragraph 3) and some firemen (paragraph 4). Maybe he questioned the Navy men there, or telephoned the Naval Weapons station.

Notice that the reporter tells you he has satisfied himself that it is true. He does not take your time telling you how he found out, or why he believes it is true, because he does not think it is important to this part of the story.

Notice that the last words "CHP officer Robert Ferrero said," are not in heavy black letters. This is still information the reporter knows. The REPORTER SAID he knows Ferrero said the words that follow.

it was a miracle the whole load did not go up.

SOMEBODY ELSE (CHP officer Robert Ferrero) SAID. The reporter is telling us that this *is* what Ferrero said. The reporter does not say that what Ferrero says is true: the reporter does not say it is true that it was a miracle the whole load did not go up.

A total of 4700 pounds of bombs were being trucked to the weapons station from Denver when, at about 3:50 a.m., Maschinot missed a sharp turn west of Willow Way.

It was a tractor and trailer rig, the trailer being of aluminum construction. One side burst and released the missiles. Firemen said

REPORTER SAID. Again, the words 'Firemen said' are not in heavy black letters, because this is information the reporter knows. The REPORTER SAID he knows the firemen said this.

the truck's fuel tank was ruptured and spilled gallons of diesel oil.

SOMEBODY ELSE (firemen) SAID. This is what the firemen said. The reporter is not telling you what they said is true.

Several hours after the accident Navy men and firemen were still gingerly clearing the dangerous debris.

REPORTER SAID

SPOTTING SOMEBODY ELSE SAID INFORMATION

There are three different ways a reporter puts SOMEBODY ELSE SAID information in a story.

1. A WORD-FOR-WORD QUOTE

The reporter might have written paragraph 3 like this:

CHP officer Robert Ferrero said, "The angels were on that guy's side all right. If one bomb had hit just a little different than it did—well, I hate to think about it. You know, the whole shooting match could have gone up."

YOUR TIP OFF—the word "said," immediately followed by quotation marks. This is the easiest one to spot. The reporter is telling you that everything between the quotation marks is word-for-word what Ferrero said.

2. A REWORDED QUOTE

What the reporter really did write was this:

CHP officer Robert Ferrero said it was a miracle the whole load did not go up.

YOUR TIP OFF—the word "said," but no quotation marks. This is the hardest one to spot. The reporter is telling you that everything from "said" to the period is what Ferrero said. By leaving off quotation marks, the reporter tells you that hc has put what Ferrero said into different words: he has re-worded the quotation.

3. PART WORD-FOR-WORD, PART REWORDED

The reporter might have written this: CHP officer Robert Ferrero said that if a single bomb had hit the wrong way, "the whole shooting match could have exploded."

YOUR TIP OFF—the word "said" separated from quotation marks by several words. Everything from "said" to the period is what Ferrero said, and the part in quotes is word-for-word what he said. The part that is after "said" but outside quotes is generally reworded.

WORDS THAT MEAN "SAID"

Of course, "said" is not the only word reporters use to tip you off to SOMEBODY ELSE SAID information. There are many other words that mean "said." You must be on the watch for them. The next exercise gives an example.

EXERCISE 2. Finding Words that mean "said"

Here are some sentences taken from news stories. They all have SOMEBODY ELSE SAID information in them. The sentences already have a box drawn around the words that tell who said it when the speaker is named in the sentence.

Directions: Draw a circle around the words that mean "said"; draw a line under what was said. (Sometimes boxes and circles will overlap.)

Example: Ward figures the turbine will win.

1. The way Roger Ward sees it, Parnelli Jones will win Tuesday's 500-mile automobile race at Indianapolis by averaging 155 mph in his controversial, quiet, smooth jet-turbine racer.

2. Jones, it is talked, will be the next big-name driver to retire.

3. Ward admits that he saw himself slowing up last year and that's why he quit.

① ② ③ New Orleans Times—Picayune

4. The U.S. Air Force thought a defecting Soviet MIG 17 which flew deep into West Germany was an off-course allied aircraft and did not scramble any interceptors, it was learned Friday.

5. An informed military source said, "There was no scramble by American planes, no interception, nothing!"

6. A spokesman for the U.S. embassy in Bonn confirmed that the Soviet pilot "has now been turned over to American authorities at his own request."

④ ⑤ ⑥ Army Intelligence Scrambled
Morningside News

7. Wall Street may exert more influence over skirt lengths than the Paris fashion houses, according to Foy Roberson, a research analyst for Harris, Upham & Co., Inc.

8. For doubters, she contrasts today's minis with the street-sweeping skirts of 1897, and notes that the stock market has gone up 2100 percent in value since women hid their ankles.

⑦ ⑧ *Newsday*

EXERCISE 3. Finding Out Who Said What

This news story, "Army Intelligence Scrambled," is almost all SOMEBODY ELSE SAID information. ("2 Tons of Bombs on Road" was almost all REPORTER SAID.)

Directions: This news story has been reproduced in three columns on the next page. Follow the directions for each of the three parts.

① *Directions:* Draw a circle around the words that "mean said."

② *Directions:* Draw a box around the words that tell who said something.

③ *Directions:* Draw a line under what was said.

United Press International

Army Intelligence Scrambled ①

DILLIGEN, Germany (UPI)—The U.S. Air Force thought a defecting Soviet MIG17 which flew deep into West Germany was an off course allied aircraft and did not scramble any interceptors, it was learned Friday.

An informed military source said, "There was no scramble by American planes, no interception, nothing!"

"All hell has broken loose with 3-star generals fighting like cats and dogs," he said. "Army intelligence is in a turmoil."

THE SOURCE SAID the intruder was thought to be an "overflight" when it appeared on U.S. military radar screens. An "overflight" is a friendly aircraft that may have strayed over the East German border before returning to West German airspace.

The plane in fact was a MIG17 piloted by a 25-year-old Soviet Air Force first lieutenant, identified by the U.S. embassy as Vasily Ilyich Epatko. He landed Thursday in a meadow at Kicklingen, Bavaria, more than 100 miles inside West Germany.

A West German military spokesman at Dillingen, where the Soviet pilot was taken, said the defector was held in the West German army barracks there for questioning by Bundeswehr (military) intelligence.

The spokesman said it was not until five hours later that U.S. authorities were informed a Soviet plane had landed deep inside NATO's defenses.

U.S. AIR FORCE headquarters at Wiesbaden declined all comment. "All information on this is coming out of the embassy in Bonn," a spokesman said.

An embassy spokesman also refused to comment on the incident. He did confirm that the Soviet pilot "has now been turned over to American authorities at his own request." His exact whereabouts was kept secret.

West German police and a U.S. Army spokesman said the pilot requested political asylum when he reached Dillingen Thursday, but neither West German nor American government officials would confirm the request Friday.

Army Intelligence Scrambled ②

DILLIGEN, Germany (UPI)—The U.S. Air Force thought a defecting Soviet MIG17 which flew deep into West Germany was an off course allied aircraft and did not scramble any interceptors, it was learned Friday.

An informed military source said, "There was no scramble by American planes, no interception, nothing!"

"All hell has broken loose with 3-star generals fighting like cats and dogs," he said. "Army intelligence is in a turmoil."

THE SOURCE SAID the intruder was thought to be an "overflight" when it appeared on U.S. military radar screens. An "overflight" is a friendly aircraft that may have strayed over the East German border before returning to West German airspace.

The plane in fact was a MIG17 piloted by a 25-year-old Soviet Air Force first lieutenant, identified by the U.S. embassy as Vasily Ilyich Epatko. He landed Thursday in a meadow at Kicklingen, Bavaria, more than 100 miles inside West Germany.

A West German military spokesman at Dillingen, where the Soviet pilot was taken, said the defector was held in the West German army barracks there for questioning by Bundeswehr (military) intelligence.

The spokesman said it was not until five hours later that U.S. authorities were informed a Soviet plane had landed deep inside NATO's defenses.

U.S. AIR FORCE headquarters at Wiesbaden declined all comment. "All information on this is coming out of the embassy in Bonn," a spokesman said.

An embassy spokesman also refused to comment on the incident. He did confirm that the Soviet pilot "has now been turned over to American authorities at his own request." His exact whereabouts was kept secret.

West German police and a U.S. Army spokesman said the pilot requested political asylum when he reached Dillingen Thursday, but neither West German nor American government officials would confirm the request Friday.

Army Intelligence Scrambled ③

DILLIGEN, Germany (UPI)—The U.S. Air Force thought a defecting Soviet MIG17 which flew deep into West Germany was an off course allied aircraft and did not scramble any interceptors, it was learned Friday.

An informed military source said, "There was no scramble by American planes, no interception, nothing!"

"All hell has broken loose with 3-star generals fighting like cats and dogs," he said. "Army intelligence is in a turmoil."

THE SOURCE SAID the intruder was thought to be an "overflight" when it appeared on U.S. military radar screens. An "overflight" is a friendly aircraft that may have strayed over the East German border before returning to West German airspace.

The plane in fact was a MIG17 piloted by a 25-year-old Soviet Air Force first lieutenant, identified by the U.S. embassy as Vasily Ilyich Epatko. He landed Thursday in a meadow at Kicklingen, Bavaria, more than 100 miles inside West Germany.

A West German military spokesman at Dillingen, where the Soviet pilot was taken, said the defector was held in the West German army barracks there for questioning by Bundeswehr (military) intelligence.

The spokesman said it was not until five hours later that U.S. authorities were informed a Soviet plane had landed deep inside NATO's defenses.

U.S. AIR FORCE headquarters at Wiesbaden declined all comment. "All information on this is coming out of the embassy in Bonn," a spokesman said.

An embassy spokesman also refused to comment on the incident. He did confirm that the Soviet pilot "has now been turned over to American authorities at his own request." His exact whereabouts was kept secret.

West German police and a U.S. Army spokesman said the pilot requested political asylum when he reached Dillingen Thursday, but neither West German nor American government officials would confirm the request Friday.

EXERCISE 4. Acting Out A News Article

You can have more fun telling the difference between REPORTER SAID from SOMEBODY ELSE SAID information by acting it out. Some news stories read like plays—they have a setting, characters, and plot—by changing a word here and there you can act them out.

Practice this with the news story about the MIG.

Directions: When you know which SOMEBODY you are supposed to play, mark that name in the cast of characters below. Then underline only the SOMEBODY ELSE SAID information for *your* character in the article. You may have to add some of your own words to make it sound right. For example, when the Reporter reads, "An embassy spokesman also refused to comment on the incident," the student acting the spokesman for the embassy can say, "No comment!" or "We have nothing to say about it."

Reporter
Informed military source
U.S. embassy spokesman in Bonn
West German military spokesman at Dillingen
U.S. Air Force headquarters man at Wiesbaden
West German police
U.S. Army spokesman
West German government officials
American government officials

Reporter: "This is your UPI reporter (your name), reporting from Dillingen, Germany."

Russian Lands in West Germany

Army Intelligence Scrambled

DILLIGEN, Germany (UPI)—**The U.S. Air Force thought a defecting Soviet MIG17 which flew deep into West Germany was an off course allied aircraft and did not scramble any interceptors**, it was learned Friday.

An informed military source said, "There was no scramble by American planes, no interception, nothing!"

"All hell has broken loose with 3-star generals fighting like cats and dogs," he said. "Army intelligence is in a turmoil."

THE SOURCE SAID the intruder was thought to be an "overflight" when it appeared on U.S. military radar screens. An "overflight" is a friendly aircraft that may have strayed over the East German border before returning to West German airspace.

The plane in fact was a MIG17 piloted by a 25-year-old Soviet Air Force first lieutenant, **identified by the U.S. embassy as Vasily Ilyich Epatko. He landed Thursday in a meadow at Kicklingen, Bavaria, more than 100 miles inside West Germany.**

A West German military spokesman at Dillingen, where the Soviet pilot was taken, said the defector was held in the West German army barracks there for questioning by Bundeswehr (military) intelligence.

The **spokesman said** it was not until five hours later that U.S. authorities were informed **a Soviet plane had landed deep inside NATO's defenses.**

U.S. AIR FORCE headquar**ters at Wiesbaden declined all** comment. "All information on this is coming out of the embassy in Bonn," a spokesman said.

An embassy spokesman also refused to comment on the incident. He did confirm that the Soviet pilot **"has now been turned over to American authorities at his own request." His exact whereabouts was kept secret.**

West German police and a U.S. Army spokesman said the pilot requested political asylum when he reached Dillingen Thursday, but neither West German nor American government officials would confirm the request Friday.

United Press International

PRACTICE IN YOUR LOCAL NEWSPAPER

PRACTICE 1. Take one page from your newspaper that has lots of news stories.

Circle the "said" or "means said" words in the first paragraph of five stories.

PRACTICE 2. Take one page from your newspaper that has lots of news stories.

Draw a square around the words that tell "who said something," in the first paragraph of five stories.

PRACTICE 3. Take one page from your newspaper that has lots of news stories.

Draw a line under "what was said" in the first paragraph of five stories.

PRACTICE 4. Watch a TV newscast. Be on the lookout for word-for-word quotes, re-worded quotes, *Reporter said* information and so forth. Be ready to talk about how these things are different on TV, and how they are the same.

Make notes to yourself here: ______________

CHAPTER 6

THE FEATURE STORY: FUN OR FILL-IN

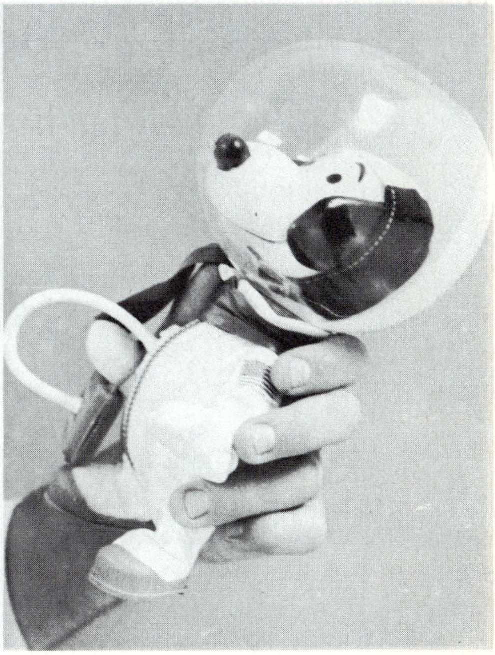

Snoopy astronaut, "A Peanuts Pocket Doll, © 1969 United Feature Syndicate, Inc.

How is a feature story different from a straight news story? One way to find out is to check the parts of a feature story—the headline, lead, and body—against what you have learned about these parts of a straight news story.

Look at the feature story, "3 Very Merry Widows." This is a true report which has probably been written more to entertain than to inform. Read it through, and then use the exercises to help you discover how the feature story differs from a straight news story.

EXERCISE 1. Making Comparisons

Directions: Read each of the statements to the left of the story. If the statement describes a way in which this story differs from a straight news story, circle *D*. If it is the same as a straight news story, circle *S*. If you cannot tell, circle ?

D S ? 1. This story has a headline.

D S ? 2. This story has a dateline.

D S ? 3. This news was gathered by a press association.

D S ? 4. This story does not explain the headline (tell why the 3 widows are merry) in the lead.

D S ? 5. This story tells why the widows are merry near the end of the story.

D S ? 6. The events of the story are arranged so that the last few paragraphs cannot be cut off without spoiling the story.

D S ? 7. This story contains news about things which have really happened.

3 Very Merry Widows: Julia, Maria, and Emma

BUDAPEST, Hungary, Aug. 5 (UPI)—The merry widows of Budapest are Julia, Maria, and Emma.

An old steelworker named Karoly E. [his fuller identity was withheld by authorities] died. A few days later Julia asked the government for her widow's pension. So did Emma. So did Maria.

All claimed Karoly E. as husband.

There was an investigation, and, sure enough, it was found that the honest, quiet steelworker had lived with the three women in three different homes for more than 40 years.

• • •

Widow No. 1, Julia, and Karoly's two children lived in Kecskemet, about 40 miles from Budapest where Karoly worked. He came home only week-ends but punctually delivered his monthly salary to his wife.

Maria, widow No. 2, provided a home for Karoly in Budapest for the first half of the week. They lived together for 43 years. And every month, Maria also was given money.

Widow No. 3, Emma, was Karoly's wife for the second half of every week for nearly 40 years. In poor health and unable to work, she relied heavily on the money Karoly regularly gave her.

Authorities discovered that Karoly, a highly qualified steelworker, gave his regular salary to Julia. Maria got his overtime or production bonuses. And Emma received money Karoly earned from inventions and making work-improvement suggestions at his factory.

• • •

Faced with three requests, the court ruled that each of the women would get an equal share of Karoly's pension.

When the decision was announced, the widows fell into each other's arms and announced they were going to live together in Maria's house as "the merry widows of Budapest."

In tribute to the hard-working man who had been a good and faithful husband to them all, each widow placed a wreath on his grave.

All three wreaths bore the same message: "To my beloved Karoly."

United Press International

ALL THE WORLD IS A STAGE

You have discovered some of the ways this feature story differs from a straight news story. When you do the exercise below you will see why some feature news stories are described as "true-to-life" dramas with real people in real situations.

EXERCISE 2. Putting the Feature Story on Stage

Directions: Imagine that you are a Hollywood scenario writer and that your studio has given you the feature story "3 Very Merry Widows" to develop into a script for a movie. Complete the outline on the opposite page to see how easily this story will make up into a movie or TV show.

1. Cast of Characters

Major: ______________________________

____

____

____

Minor: ______________________________

2. Plot

Scene 1

Place: ______________________________

Time: ______________________________

Action: (You may describe the action or write it in the form of a play with dialogue and stage directions.)

Scene 2

Place: ______________________________

Time: ______________________________

Action: ______________________________

(Hints: Use as many scenes as you need. You may want to write a complete short play in your notebook. Remember that many movies use a scene with flash-backs in time. You may add to the story and may make it comic or tragic, but do not change the facts which are given. Before you begin to write, decide the point of view—who is telling the drama?)

FEATURE STORIES VARY WIDELY

Not all feature stories are like "3 Very Merry Widows." No two are exactly alike. But they have certain common characteristics. They appeal to the emotions. You can either identify with a particular character in the story or you can recall similar experiences of your own.

Some feature stories start out like the one you have just read, but the dramatic scene is just the introduction to a straight news story. Sometimes several related news stories are interwoven. Each of these stories develops a particular thread of the main story. Each is a small part of the whole. This kind of feature story is described as a *composite story*.

Study the following example and you will be able to see how this kind of feature story is organized.

Notice that this story is also an example of a newspaper's campaign to "right a wrong" or to uncover a fraud against the public. Newspapers must be careful to have their facts in right order to avoid being sued themselves.

Surprise! State Insurance Dept. Sues Him

By Donald L. Barlett

Harold H. Woody received a subpena the other day.

It was delivered courtesy of the State Insurance Department.

And it was, says Woody, "the first time anything like this has happened to me."

Woody told The Daily News:

"I was sitting at home the other night. We live in an apartment at 6118 N. Sheridan. There was this knock at the door. I don't know how the man got in the building. It's always locked.

"There was a knock at the door and the man said, 'Mr. Woody?' and I said 'yes' and opened the door.

"He shoved this paper at me, it was a subpena, and then he ran. I never saw the man.

"This paper, it says, here, let me read it, it says:

"'The defendant has failed to pay the plaintiff the assessment sum of $174 or any part thereof, although the plaintiff has made demand for payment.'

"This $174 is for an insurance policy I had back in 1962 with Adams Mutual Insurance Co. But I don't know what they're talking about.

"I never got any bill from the Insurance Department. I didn't know I owed anyone money. They never sent me a bill. I've never had this happen before. I never received a single bill from these people."

WOODY'S STORY of a subpena and a bill for $174 he never knew he owed emerged as The Daily News continued its inquiry into the operations and practices of the State Insurance Department and the $2.5-billion-a-year industry it is charged with regulating.

At the same time, a battle is shaping up in the state Legislature over a proposal to create a legislative investigating commission.

During the next two years, the commission would investigate the activities of the State Insurance Department and problems in the insurance industry.

One of the major areas of concern is the collapse of 18 insurance companies in the last three years—more than in any other state. The wholesale failures, which usually occurred without warning, have meant millions of dollars in losses to policyholders and claimants.

During its study, The Daily News found that Woody and thousands of other persons like him are being sued by the Insurance Department.

THESE PEOPLE, who had policies with a mutual company such as Adams, are being assessed one year's premium to raise money to pay the debts of the defunct companies.

Although Adams Mutual Insurance Co. went out of business in October, 1963, it was not until last December that Insurance Director John F. Bolton Jr. moved to levy the assessment against policyholders.

But the collections are not handled by the Insurance Department.

Instead, the department has retained the services of a collection attorney, Lawrence Friedman, of 120 W. Madison.

Friedman receives 25 per cent of whatever he collects without filing suit. If he goes to court and initiates legal action, he picks up 50 per cent.

DURING joint House-Senate Insurance Study Committee hearings, held to determine the need for a state investigation, it was disclosed that Friedman's collection staff operates under fictitious names.

Peter J. Miller (R-Chicago), committee chairman, had the following exchange with William J. Dorf, special deputy in charge of liquidations for the Insurance Department:

Miller: "Do these people (Friedman's) use fictitious names in that office?"

Dorf: "I would say so."

Miller: "Why?"

Dorf: "I don't know how to answer that. I don't know."

Miller: "It would seem to me that the Insurance Department, allowing these people to do these things . . . would lose the confidence of the public. I, for one, thought it was highly irregular."

Reprinted with permission from the *Chicago Daily News*

EXERCISE 3. Breaking a Composite Story Into Parts

Directions: (1) Take a pencil or colored crayon and draw a circle around the introduction in which Harold E. Woody tells the *Chicago Daily News* what happened to him. (2) Next draw a box around the paragraphs which tell about the inquiry the *Chicago Daily News* has been conducting. (3) Underline all sentences which tell what the State Legislature is doing and may do in the future.

EXCEPTION TO THE RULE

Many human interest stories are accounts of persons doing or saying just the opposite from what the majority are doing and saying. Two good examples of this kind of news feature are printed below.

These two stories are related to a major news story—the financial crisis faced by the United States. They differ from the composite story. They deal with single incidents, but they attract our attention because they are related to important news.

A Frenchman Loves U.S., Sells His Gold

[N. Y. Times-Chicago Tribune Service]

GENEVA, Switzerland, Jan. 25—A Frenchman walked into the Geneva office of New York City's First National City bank today with a 2.2 pound gold bar tucked in the inside breast pocket of his suit.

Ten minutes later he left the bank with the receipt of an order for the purchase of a $1,128.62 United States treasury bill. He got the receipt by selling the gold bar.

"I simply wanted to express in a tangible manner that I disprove of [French President Charles] de Gaulle's anti-American policy" is the way Claude J. Despuech, 45, later explained his effort to reverse the dollar drain.

"My wife and I hit on the idea of exchanging the gold bar for United States defense or other bonds when we read newspaper stories about French purchases of gold weakening the dollar," the Paris-born Frenchman said.

Despuech recalled that in 1944 he and some companions in the French resistance organization had joined up with a United States army regiment.

"My admiration for the Americans with whom I fought until I received a machine gun bullet in the shoulder remains too great for me to be able to accept the turning of our back on the United States," the Frenchman said to explain his opposition to de Gaulle's policies.

Despuech said he had bought the gold bar here in 1965 and left it in a safe deposit box. He said that he decided to take advantage of a business visit heer to make good his desire.

Bully gesture

Briton, 71, sends U.S. $240 check in 'I'm backing America' campaign

RAMSGATE, England (UPI) — "Everywhere you go," lamented old-age pensioner Alfred Barrs, "people have it in for America—and after all they've done for us."

With that said, the 71-year-old former owner of a chain of pie-and-eel shops, launched his "I'm backing America" campaign by sending a check for $240 to the U.S. Embassy in London.

He said he came to love the Americans when he sailed with the British Fleet in World War I. "I had one or two punch-ups with the Yanks, but when it came to real trouble they were right by our sides."

United Press International

FEATURE STORIES BASED ON TIMELINESS

Some feature stories are of interest because they are related to some special day, anniversary, or happening. A good example of this is the story below:

EXERCISE 4. Locating WWWWW&H in the Feature Story

Directions: Draw a line under the parts of the story which would

FORGET THOSE TWELVE GIFTS

Your Budget Could Never Stand It!

Ft. Bragg, N. C., Dec. 7 (UPI) —The Englishman who sent his true love exotic gifts on each of the 12 days of Christmas would need the Bank of England behind him to do it at today's prices.

Sp. 4/c W. J. Chandler Jr., a lawyer and draftee from Raleigh, N. C., got to wondering about the cost of the presents while listening to the English Christmas ballad, "The 12 Days of Christmas." He used an encyclopedia and spent four days shopping by telephone to complete his list.

Five Gold Rings

On the first day of Christmas the lady received a partridge in a pear tree. Total cost from the State Wildlife commission and a local nursery: $16.25. The second day's gift, two turtle doves, runs $70 from a New York pet store. Three French hens are valued at $165. Four calling birds would be a problem. They are extinct. The last known pair was purchased by the London zoological society in 1911 at a cost of $17,230.

Five gold rings cost $175 in a local jewelry store. Six geese a-laying cost $80.10. Seven swans a-swimming would be a bit more—$315.

Eight maids a-milking, paid the daily minimum wage, total $89.60. Eight registered milk cows add up to $4,400.

Chandler went to the New York ballet for nine ladies dancing. They're worth $3,239.

Ten London Lords

Ten lords a-leaping means round-trip transportation for 10 members of the House of Lords in London. Airlines tab: $5,997.66. Eleven pipers piping would come from the New York philharmonic for $3,239.

As for 12 drummers drumming, and they would cost only $50 because Chandler can get them from the Ft. Bragg drum and bugle corps.

This totals $36,097.01. But according to the ballad, the partridge in a pear tree is sent not once, but 12 times. The two turtle doves 11 times the French hens 10, and so on. Only the drummers are sent once. Figuring it up this way, true love, are you ready? The cost is $211,758.90.

United Press International

Men-on-Moon Hoax Fools Swiss

ZURICH, Switzerland, April 1 (UPI)—A radio program, which was reminiscent of Orson Welles' 1938 broadcast about an invasion from Mars, convinced thousands of Swiss listeners today that United States spacemen had landed on the moon.

The Welles program, broadcast about a month after the Munich crisis accustomed the listeners to radio coverage of menacing situations, caused widespread panic in the United States because of its realistic use of "news bulletins" to interrupt what appeared to be an ordinary entertainment program.

The Swiss broadcast, an April fool joke, used the same technique, and thousands of listeners were taken in. Even United States authorities here were not sure the report was false.

Hurry to Hills

Hundreds of persons streamed into the hills to watch for the "return of the moonship." A railroad on Mount Uetliberg, overlooking Zurich, put on extra trains to handle the load.

Telephone exchanges were jammed for hours by callers wishing to tell relatives and friends the news or who were calling newspaper offices, radio stations, and other media for confirmation.

Consul Makes Inquiry

Belief in the story was increased because there are no week-end newspapers in Switzerland and television does not start broadcasting until 6 p. m.

The United States consul-general in Zurich called the United Press International bureau for confirmation of the landing. It was reported over all German language Swiss radio stations in an elaborate hour-long broadcast similar to Welles' historic adaptation of H. G. Wells' "War of the Worlds."

At the winter resort of Klosters, throngs of vacationing Americans staged a huge celebration. The mood sobered when the American network in Europe failed to give confirmation of the event.

Slips Add Reality

The broadcast, directed by Hans Menge of Radio Zurich, began with a "flash" interrupting a popular satirical weekly program.

It carried running reports from Swiss radio correspondents in various world capitals. There were interviews with experts and men in the street—all prerecorded. The broadcast included pre-staged "technical faults" and "slips," the slamming of doors, and the sound of newscasters running in with the latest bulletins.

A radio spokesman said that about two-thirds of the callers seemed to believe the news. Major Swiss telephone exchanges, where information on anything can be obtained by dialing 11, called in to ask the radio station for running reports on the landing so they could pass on the news to callers.

The broadcast concluded with an announcement that the moonship would take off at 7 p. m. and urged listeners to climb surrounding hills to watch its return to earth.

United Press International

be included in the lead if this story were rewritten as a straight news story. Each part should answer a WWWWW&H question.

FEATURE STORIES THAT AMUSE US

Many readers enjoy reading accounts of how others have been fooled. It makes us feel comfortable to be able to point to someone else who has had the wool pulled over his eyes and to smugly say to ourselves "I would never have fallen for that!" The story "Men-on-Moon Hoax Fools Swiss," discusses two famous radio programs which fooled thousands of people.

EXERCISE 5. Making Judgments

Directions: Imagine you are having a debate on this topic: Resolved, that using radio and TV to mislead the public should be forbidden by law. Decide whether you are for the proposal or against it. Then write down all the arguments you can think of to support your side of the question. Reread the "Hoax" article for evidence which might support your statements.

____

____

____

____

____

EXERCISE 6. Forming Opinions

Directions: On the following page is a different kind of "hoax" story. If you agree with the opinion expressed in the statements which follow it, circle *agree*. If you disagree with the opinion, circle *disagree*. If you neither agree not disagree, circle *no opinion*.

1. The audience did not know the music of Beethoven, Prokofiev, and Liszt very well.

   agree disagree no opinion

2. The audience shouted for the pianist because they accepted the publicity about his being a great Russian pianist.

   agree disagree no opinion

Swiss steals show

'Russ' pianist fools gullible Liszt-eners

ZURICH, Switzerland (UPI)—Two thousand cheering music lovers shouted for encores when the great Russian pianist Anton Sergeivitch Tartarov bowed and strode from the stage after his concert.

They were still cheering when a man stepped to the stage and told them they had been taken for a ride.

The pianist was not a Russian, the impresario said, and the selections he played were not the Beethoven, Prokofiev and Liszt compositions on the program. Even his mustache was a fake.

BUT HE WAS GREAT anyway, said impresario Kaf Heller. It's just that nobody knows it yet.

Heller told the audience they had been listening to a home-grown Swiss piano teacher named Jean-Jacques Hauser playing his own compositions.

"I invented Tartarov to give Hauser an audience free of prejudices," Keller said. "I am very pleased that you appreciated his music."

When Hauser returned to the stage the audience swallowed its pride and applauded wildly.

But the critics, whose estimate of Hauser's performance in the Tuesday concert appeared in newspapers Thursday, refused to admit they fell for the hoax. The shruggged him off as "good," but "not quite concert quality."

Hauser, with the applause still ringing in his ears, was happy anyway. "I never knew the Zurich public could be so enthusiastic" he said.

United Press International

3. The motive for inventing Tartarov was a good one.

agree disagree no opinion

4. The audience would not have responded as wildly if they had known the pianist was "a home-grown Swiss piano teacher . . . playing his own compositions."

agree disagree no opinion

5. The audience showed good sportsmanship about the hoax when Hauser returned to the stage.

agree disagree no opinion

6. The critics were poor sports.

agree disagree no opinion

7. The cirtics were more critical because they knew more about music than the audience.

agree disagree no opinion

8. The hoax will aid the career of Jean-Jacques Hauser.

agree disagree no opinion

ANIMALS— GOOD ATTENTION GETTERS

Editors know that stories about animals have wide appeal to everyone. Some people may look over their shoulders to be sure nobody is watching them, but they'll read them.

EXERCISE 7. Finding the Time Element

Directions: One of these two stories about animals has a time element in it. It should be printed right away. The other one will be just as interesting no matter when it is printed. Find the story with the time element. Underline the words that date the story.

Associated Press

When an Elephant Flies— That's Really News!

TRANG Phuc, Vietnam, June 27 (AP) — Over the jungles and into the mountains flew Cham the elephant today. That is, he flew in a helicopter.

Cham, who weighs 1,000 pounds and is 16 months old, was a gift of troops of the U.S. 4th Infantry Division at Dragon Mountain to the Jarai Montagnard tribesmen resettled in South Vietnam's central highlands.

Profits from the 4th Division's soft drink sales went toward purchasing the elephant, $250. The infantrymen got him at a village near their special forces camp.

Welcoming Committee

And so, there was Cham, walking down the road at Trang Phuc toward a CH47 helicopter. Waiting with open minds were four cargo riggers, two pilots, two door gunners, a veterinarian, and his assistant.

Cham stands four feet at the shoulder, not too big for the helicopter. He came down the road at full amble, occasionally letting out a fine trumpeting and into the helicopter he went.

Inject Tranquilizer

They gave Cham an injection of a tranquilizing drug. The riggers loosely tied each foot with a cargo strap. Cham's trunk touched everything as if he were reading Braille. As the tranquilizer took effect, his trumpeting grew lethargic, but he kept his feet.

In flight, Cham was no problem. He polished off at least three dozen 5-ounce sugar squares, a half-loaf of French bread, an da bar of milk chocolate.

Being a youngster, Cham won't be able to drag logs or do other heavy work until he is about 6 years old. After that, he can count on being on the job for about 20 years. Cham will be presented to the Jarais later this week.

An Arf Is a Wang Is a Wau

Washington, Nov. 4 (UPI) —"Hey Rover, come here, old boy," cries his proud little owner. Rover, tail wagging, runs up to his master, licks his hand, and barks, "Wang-wang."

Are you kidding? There isn't a dog in the world that barks "wang-wang."

But there is.

Rover's master is a Japanese boy and in his mind the dog is also Japanese. So in Japan, when dogs bark, they don't say "arf-arf" or "bow-wow," but "wang-wang."

• • •

Everyone in the world assumes that barnyard animals, when they moo, bark, or grunt, make that sound in the local language.

But what may be a normal "quack-quack" of a duck in English, may not be so in Czechoslovakia. The Czech embassy here, as did six other embassies, provided United Press International with the local animal sounds.

Wallowing thru the pasture, a Czech duck puts out a noise which sounds something like "taj-taj."

As the tourist wanders around the barnyard, he comes to a pig sty. Now, any red-blooded American child can tell you that a pig goes "oink-oink." But there again there is a difference of opinion between the east and the west.

• • •

"You are wrong," shouts the Czech youth. "Pigs go 'chr-chr.' "

In Thailand they have militant chickens. As they sit perched on an egg, they cackle "atak-atak."

Chickens in France are calmer, but windier. Their morning greeting is "cot-cot-cot-codi." And in Germany they say "Meck-meck-meck."

So much for the chicken.

Her mate, the rooster, is more bilingual and sounds much alike in most languages, except English. The English "cock-a-doodle-doo" turns into "kiquerique" in Spanish; "kuckeliku" in Swedish; "cocorico" in French; "kikeriki" in Czech; and "kokekoko" in Japanese.

• • •

Back to man's best friend, the dog. Pierre's Rover, running thru the French countryside, shows his happiness or anger by saying "oua-oua." But Jose's Rover in Argentina, goes "guau-guau." And Hans' German Shepherd cries out in the Bavarian Alps: "wau-wau."

Besides having militant chickens, Thailand also has talkative ducks. They "gab-gab-gab" all day. The French duck goes "coin-coin" and in Spain it's "cua-cua."

World-wide, cats make a similar noise to the English "meow." So do sheep with their "bah."

"Enof-enof" says the Swedish pig. O. K., enough.

United Press International

THE BIOGRAPHICAL FEATURE STORY

Lives of great men are a source of inspiration to many persons. Editors use many biographical feature stories. A beautiful example of this kind of news feature is the story comparing the lives and deaths of King and Gandhi.

EXERCISE 8.
Making Comparisons

Directions: After you have read the article "Martyrs of Our Time" go back and circle the paragraph that tells what Ghandi's slayer thought Ghandi was doing wrong. This supposedly was his reason for killing Ghandi. Then use the space below to write a sentence or two telling what group or groups in the United States today think the same way about non-violence as Ghandi's slayer did.

____

____

____

____

____

____

____

____

____

____

____

Martyrs of our time

King, like Gandhi, eschewed violence

"The light has gone out of our lives,
And there is darkness everywhere."
—Nehru at Gandhi's death.

By M. W. Newman

Death, like life, forever has drawn together two brown-skinned martyrs of our time.

Twenty years before Martin Luther King Jr. was slain in a Memphis hotel, the saintly Mahatma Gandhi was assassinated in a garden in India's New Delhi.

Each in his time was the world's leading apostle of non-violent resistance.

Each preached love, not hatred, and each lived close to violent death and knew it could strike at any time.

When it came, it came predictably—the sudden, senseless vengeance of some hate-filled fanatic.

Both times the world shuddered—and wondered why the man of peace must forever be crucified.

GANDHI was a skinny, funny-looking man in a loincloth who led India's 400,000,000 people to a long-cherished freedom from British rule.

He was one of the great men of the century, enduring years of prison and fasts with the strength of a prophet.

Mahatma Gandhi

His favorite weapons for rousing the masses were civil disobedience campaigns, non-violent marches and hunger strikes.

Early in his career, Dr. King visited Ghandi's tomb, now a carefully preserved national shrine in New Delhi, India.

The young Martin Luther King studied the power of this meekness greater than empire, and applied its precepts to the Negro struggle against Jim Crow.

HIS LAST march in Memphis was a reminder that 37 years ago to this day, Gandhi ended a 250-mile march to the sea that signaled the breaking of British power.

Actual freedom came in 1947—but, ironically, with it came a renewal of India's bloody old conflicts—Hindu and Sikh against Moslem.

On Jan. 30, 1948, at a prayer meeting, a Hindu fanatic named Nathuram Godse treacherously bowed before the saintly Gandhi, his hands folded reverently. Then he shot him three times.

The 78-year-old ascetic died 20 minutes later, his head cradled in his granddaughter's lap.

THE SLAYER was an extremist who considered Gandhi too easy on the Moslems and the newly formed Islamic state of Pakistan.

The police had known about the murder plot but failed to head it off. But by then Gandhi, saddened by the hatred and killing in the new India, hardly wanted to live any more.

"Have you ever seen hydrophobia?" he asked Daily News correspondent Phillips Talbot, now U.S. ambassador to Greece, not long before his death.

"This situation is analogous."

Twenty years later, hydrophobia was attacking the United States.

THE DESCRIPTIVE NEWS FEATURE

The changing of the seasons often results in news features like the one below. It creates a mood in the reader.

S'wonderful!

Indian summer fades out in gold as autumn makes pass at Chicago

By M. W. Newman

"The days dwindle down to a precious few . . . October, October."

Well, perhaps Kurt Weill's bittersweet "Spetember Song" doesn't go quite that way, but you get the idea.

Indian summer, precious Indian summer, is fading in a blaze of gold while autumn makes passes at Chicago.

WEDNESDAY was that kind of vintage day, distilled from all the best days of summer. You wanted it to go on and on, somehow stopping the calendar and the spin of Earth.

It was a day when the sun burnished the silvery Executive House on N. Wacker Dr., creating a glow so dazzling you couldn't look at it for more than a second.

Below sunbeams capered in the dark-green grime of a river flowing serenely backward—as time never does.

The day was warm and lazy and no one walked fast. Puff clouds in the sky did their best to imitate the silvery brushwork of the painter Corot, and lake and sky merged in a glentle blur.

SHIRT-SLEEVED men and bare-armed girls thronged downtown State Street. And at the 1st Ward offices at Wabash and the river, noontime lunchers dined at outdoor tables, like blooming Parisians.

A sign above them read Central Snow Office. Sureiy these were words imported from another clime, another city.

A bearded man with a pet silver gibbon on a leash turned him loose in the trees of Lincoln Park near Belmont Harbor. The ape swung joyfully from branch to branch, somersaulting in glee. Children watched and cheered.

Snorting sea Lions in Lincoln Park zoo wrestled on their water-ringed rock perch, just for the fun of it.

IN THE LOOP'S Civic Center Plaza, 15 boys form St. Damian School in Oak Forest skipped gaily around the Picasso sculpture like a chorus of sunstruck dancers.

"What is it? What is it?" they asked the Rev. William McGlynn.

He puffed on his sweet-smelling pipe and smiled wisely. What did it matter what the Picasso was on such a golden day?

Every bench in the plaza was filled, with shoppers and student artists brushing shoulders with shabby men studying scratch sheets.

NEAR A GIANT flagpole where the Stars and Stripes danced, a dozen young people stood rigidly, and a sign said: "Vigil for Peace in Vietnam."

But on this golden day, could you think about war? The busy men with the scratch sheets never even looked up.

While the mercury rose to the 80s, old men lolled on the grass in Grant Park—their shirts off, their pants rolled up to their knees.

A thousand parked cars baked in the Monroe St. lot and there was a high gleam of chrome. Only the first blushes of rust and gold coated the park's autumnal green.

AND AT WATER'S edge, the city disappeared into a dim roar of motor traffic. Boats jingled at anchor in a much-abused lake that somehow has stayed alive despite pollution and alewives.

It had been a bad summer for Lake Michigan, but here it was, doing so much more for man than man ever did for it.

The day swelled into a sun-drenched afternoon and a scattering of bathers ventured onto Oak St. beach.

At 3:07 p.m. it was 84 degrees and a stout lady cooled off by plunging her arm into the pool at the Equitable Building plaza.

Conventioneers sought the shade of the second-floor terrace at the Sheraton-Chicago Hotel. It was stuffy on CTA busses heading out of the Loop.

BUT AS YOU walked and watched your shadow ahead of you, your tie floated in a persistent breeze. Near the post office at 227 E. Ontario, brown leaves swirled.

The weatherman warned that a cooling front was knifing in, and squirrels in Lincoln Park came right up to you, on the prowl for a stockpile.

In the very fullness of the day you heard the dwindling note.

EXERCISE 9. Finding Words and Phrases That Appeal to the Senses

Directions: Some of the quotations in the left-hand column appeal to our senses. Write in one of the following senses that the quotation appeals to: Hearing, Sight, Touch, Smell and Taste.

(*Hints:* Some senses will be used more than once. Some sense appeals may be matched with more than one of your senses.)

Sense Appeals

1. Sunbeams capered in the dark-green grime of a river floating serenely backward.

2. Boats jingled at anchor.

3. The ape swung joyfully from branch to branch, somersaulting in glee.

4. Children watched and cheered.

5. Puff clouds in the sky did their best to imitate the silvery brushwork of the painter Corot.

6. The city disappeared into a dim roar of motor traffic.

7. At 3:07 p.m. it was 84 degrees and a stout lady cooled off by plunging her arm into the pool.

8. He puffed on his sweet-smelling pipe.

9. Fifteen boys . . . skipped gaily around the Picasso sculpture like a chorus of sunstruck dancers.

10. Old men lolled on the grass in Grant Park—their shirts off, their pants rolled up to their knees.

11. Only the first blushes of rust and gold coated the park's autumnal green.

12. Every bench in the plaza was filled, with shoppers and student artists brushing shoulders with shabby men studying scratch sheets.

13. Noontime lunchers dined at outdoor tables.

14. Snorting sea lions . . . wrestled on their water-ringed rock perch.

1. ______________

2. ______________

3. ______________

4. ______________

5. ______________

6. ______________

7. ______________

8. ______________

9. ______________

10. ______________

11. ______________

12. ______________

13. ______________

14. ______________

HOW THE COMEDIANS USE FEATURE NEWS

Have you ever wondered where comedians like Bob Hope and Bill Cosby get their material? One source is the newspapers. If you have watched a comedy special on TV recently, you will have noticed that much of the material pertains to news events that are happening right now. Some of these news events are made into feature stories by comic writers.

You can learn how columnists do this by reading what Art Buchwald did with the AP news feature on the next page. Read the news story first; then come back to study Buchwald's comic treatment of it in "How the Ziegenthalers Lose to Abernathys."

EXERCISE 10. Evaluating Conclusions

Directions: In the AP story, draw a line under each conclusion Dr. Weston reached. Then circle the paragraph which tells how he reached his findings.

P.S. FROM WASHINGTON

How The Ziegenthalers Lose To Abernathys

By Art Buchwald

WASHINGTON—As if there isn't enough trouble in the world, a British doctor by the name of Trevor Weston has just discovered that people are suffering from an "alphabetic neurosis." He maintains the people whose last names begin with the final eight letters of the alphabet, S through Z, have three times as many ulcers and three times as many heart attacks as those whose names begin with the letters A to R.

Dr. Weston says he believes the reason is that the people at the bottom of the alphabet are always at the bottom of the list, always waiting for their names to be called. Since they first face this in school, the S to Z children are filled with anxieties that carry through to their adult years.

I WAS VERY SKEPTICAL of Dr. Weston's theory, so I decided to see if there was any basis for it.

I went into a bar and asked a man sitting on a stool what his name was. He looked frightened. "Why me?"

"Don't be frightened, sir. I'm just taking a survey for my newspaper."

"STEVENS," HE SAID, "George Stevens."

"Can I buy you a drink, Mr. Stevens?"

"I'm only drinking milk I have a bad ulcer. It's killing me."

"That's very interesting. How did you get it?"

"Arkin and Blauvelt gave it to me. They're in my advertising agency, and they're out to get me."

"Why do you think they're out to get you?"

"They got Thomas, Unruh, Young and Vogel. I'm the only one left except for Zimbalest."

"Where's Zimbalest?" I asked.

"He had a heart attack, his third this year. God knows, I'll probably have one myself soon." He started biting his nails.

"I didn't mean to shake you up so," I said.

"It's not you. I'm trying to get the courage to go home. You see, I was up for a promotion today and I thought I'd make vice president. Carstairs made it, Douglas made it, Eberhardt made it, Franklin made it, Gregory made it, Hofstatter made it, Iselin made it, Jacoby made it, King made it, Logan made it, Mankowitz made it, Nolan made it, O'Brien made it. Potter made it, Robertson made it, and that was it. They said there were no more V. P. positions open."

"THAT'S A SHAME," I said.

"I guess I can't complain. Tait, Upjohn, Verick, Washington, Xavier, Yale and Ziegenthaler were let go."

"Were they given any reason?"

"Allenby, the president, said they couldn't stand the pressure. They were always blowing up in front of the clients. Ziegenthaler thought everyone was out to get him, and they were."

"If you're under so much pressure, why don't you quit?"

"I can't. My children are in so much trouble in school I need the job. Say, you're not a friend of Abernathy, are you?"

"No, I'm not."

"THAT'S GOOD. I think it was Abernathy who gave me my second ulcer. Either him or Donovan. They killed Zilch, you know. Say, by the way, what kind of survey are you taking?" he asked.

"I'm trying to find out if the people whose last names begin with the letters S to Z are more insecure than those whose names start with A to R."

"Why, that's ridiculous," Stevens said, as he swallowed three tranquilizers. "What will they think of next?"

So What's in a Name? Ulcers, for One Thing

BRISTOL, England, July 12 (AP)—If your last name begins with the letters between S and Z, you are twice as likely to get ulcers as are other people. And you are three times more prone to heart attacks.

A doctor whose last name begins with W reported this today to the British Medical association.

Dr. Trevor Weston said the situation is all due to the strain of waiting for your name to be called. The amount of neurosis in the S to Z group, he said, is 50 per cent higher than in the A to R group.

He said his findings are based on a 10-year survey of mortality statistics at a London teaching hospital.

"It is clear that the strain of all this waiting for your names to be reached—of always being last—renders us more liable to become morose and introspective, said Weston, who is 39 and a hospital consultant.

"And the damage begins at school age. The S to Z boys are still waiting, sick with apprehension, for their exam results while the children ahead of them in the alphabet are already congratulating each other."

Weston calls the condition "alphabetic neurosis" and says it shortens life for the group by 12 years compared with the others.

Associated Press

PRACTICE IN YOUR LOCAL NEWSPAPER

PRACTICE 1. Look through your local paper for a feature story which you think might make a good movie or TV show. Paste the story in your notebook and write a few lines to tell who the characters would be and what the main situation would be.

PRACTICE 2. Clip out a feature story that deals with a current news event. Try to find and clip out a straight news story that relates to it.

PRACTICE 3. Bring to class a funny feature story to share with your classmates. Remember to check all sections of your paper. The feature stories may be found almost anywhere.

PRACTICE 4. Bring to class a biographical feature story about some famous or interesting person.

CHAPTER 7

THINK WHILE YOU READ

Suppose that you happen to meet your friend Al just after he has watched the "fracas at fire" that is written up in the news story on the next page.

Al starts in, "Hey! Did I ever see something! This house is on fire, and some guys are waiting for the fire engine and getting madder and madder. And when the firemen finally get there, the guys start yelling at them, like, 'Hi there, enjoy your coffee break?' Then a couple of cops drive up and next thing you know they say one of the guys hit a cop, and they take him away. And the guys that were left. . . ."

Would you really keep quiet that long while Al told the story his way? Or would you break in right away with questions like, "A fire? Where? Down on 26th street? You mean the little building that has the laundry downstairs? Hey, what's the guy's name? My buddy hangs around there. . . ."

Of course you would break in with questions. It would be the natural thing to do. And your questions would help shape the way your friend tells his story—what he tells first; what he skips; what he tells in detail.

When you're reading the same story in a newspaper, you don't have the same kind of control over what goes into the story. But you can still get much more out of the story by taking part in it.

KNOW WHY YOU ARE READING THE STORY

You read the front-page headlines on faith—your faith in the judgment of the newspaper editors who choose the stories for the front page.

You must judge for yourself whether you want to read more of the story than just the headline.

Some headlines will tell you all you care to know about a story: "TRANSPLANT RECIPIENT DOING WELL" may tell you enough about the outcome of a heart transplant story you have been following.

Sometimes you will not even need to take the time to understand a headline. Take "ARABS CAUTIONED BY DAYAN ON RAIDS." A glance is enough to tell you that this story is about the Arab-Israeli border troubles. If this situation interests you only when the news reaches banner-headline size, you can skip this article.

When you do read past the headline, try to know why you are doing it. If you know "TREASURY TO ASK END OF ALL SILVER IN COINS" interests you only because you are a coin collector, you know you don't need to read the whole story. You can skip through the story until you find a paragraph about the effect on the coin collector—or until you discover that the story doesn't touch on this subject at all.

Experienced newspaper readers make these decisions in much less time than it takes to tell about it. But as a beginner, you will find it helpful to try to put into words why you are reading or not reading a particular story.

EXERCISE 1. Ask Yourself Questions

Suppose that this headline appeared in your local paper: "SAY MAN STRUCK COP DURING FRACAS AT FIRE." What could be your reason for reading into the story? What question could you ask yourself?

Directions: Complete this question:

"I am reading "SAY MAN STRUCK COP DURING FRACAS AT FIRE" because I want to find out ______________________________

____

EXERCISE 2. Find Your Answer Fast and Stop Reading

If you can find the answer to your question without reading the whole story, you're ahead of the game. But before you start skimming, the lead is worth extra attention. The reporter has a good idea of what readers want to know most, and he tries to tell those things first.

Directions: a. Read the first two paragraphs of "SAY MAN STRUCK COP," printed below.
If you find your answer, underline it and stop reading.

If you do not find your answer, go on to part b of this exercise.

Say Man Struck Cop During Fracas at Fire

By Bill McTernan and Brian Donovan

Wyandanch—One of a group of men who police said were jeering at firemen at the scene of a house fire during the weekend was arrested for allegdely punching a white policeman.

Edward Jackson, who gave his address as 30 Davidson St., Wyandanch, was accused of striking Ptl. Billy Parrish of the First Precinct about 10 PM Saturday as Parrish was trying to disperse about eight onlookers who he said were jeering the firemen as they fought the fire at 34 South 26th St. Parrish said Jackson cursed him, then punched him and struggled when he tried to lead him to a nearby patrol car. Parrish said his partner, Ptl. James Harrington, and several firemen had to help him subdue Jackson and keep the other bystanders from interfering with the arrest. Jackson, a Negro, was charged with third-degree assault, disorderly conduct and resisting arrest. Parrish is white. Jackson was arraigned before Judge Victor J. Orgera in First District Court in Commack and was released in $500 bail. A hearing on the charges was set for June 6.

b. If the lead didn't answer your question, skim through the rest of the story; look at each line, but don't really read it. When you come to some words that tell you you're getting warm, read more carefully. Underline your answer and stop reading.

If you don't find your answer, go on to part c of this exercise.

"If it hadn't been for those firemen, we would really have been in trouble," Parrish said. "I was afraid. We just got out of there as fast as we could."

Several of the bystanders and one of the firemen who helped Parrish, however, gave conflicting versions of the incident. The fireman, Merrel Hawkins of the Wyandanch company, said Jackson ran toward a group of firemen who were pulling a hose toward the house as if planning to block their way. But he said the others made no attempt to stop the arrest. "They just yelled," he said. But one of the onlookers, Ellis Freeman of 77 S. 26th St., said some of Jackson's friends were tugging on one of his arms while Parrish was pulling on the other.

Another bystander, Hector San Jurjo of 90 S. 25th St., denied that anyone in the group had touched Jackson. He said Jackson did not use obscene language but was shouting, as were others, that the firemen had taken too long to get to the "We all tried to tell the cop to let go . . . but we never touched the guy (Jackson) or the cop," he said.

Freeman said San Jurjo said it took the firemen at least 20 minutes to arrive and another neighbor. Horace Davis of 60 Jamaica Ave,. said it took 45. Davis charged that the volunteer company often arrived late at fires because the neighborhood is predominantly Negro. The company admitted its first Negro member last year after several months of demonstrations by the Congress of Racial Equality.

Fire Chief Thomas A. Brown and his first assistant, Howard Frank, said the company arrived at the fire two minutes after the alarm was turned in at 9:58 PM but they refused to comment further.

____c. NO ANSWER. If you didn't find an answer to your question anywhere in the story, put an X in the space at the beginning of this sentence.

Either you have found the answer to your question, or you have found that it isn't there. If you had read "SAY MAN STRUCK COP" in your local paper, you might go on to another story, or you might decide that reading the story has put another important question in your mind, and you want to find the answer.

Let's say that you do have more questions. Pretend that the fire was just two blocks down the street from you. Everybody in the neighborhood is talking about it, and you're trying to find out exactly what happened.

EXERCISE 3. Remember to Use Your WWWWW&H Form

You already have one basic tool for understanding a story. That is the WWWWW&H form you worked with in Chapter 4.

Directions: Fill out the WWWWW&H form on the next page for "SAY MAN STRUCK COP" using information from the whole story (not just the lead). Check back to the detailed directions on page 49 if you need help in filling out the form.

EXERCISE 4. Use the "Unpacking" Technique

Directions: You practiced unpacking a lead on page 50. Do it again here with the head and lead of "SAY MAN STRUCK COP." Identify one fact at a time, and write each down as a simple sentence in your own words. The sentences from thc hcadlinc arc done for you as an example.

"SAY MAN STRUCK COP DURING FRACAS AT FIRE"	Somebody said a man struck a cop. It happened during a fracas. The fracas happened at a fire.

One of a group . . .

> Wyandanch—One of a group of men who police said were jeering at firemen at the scene of a house fire during the weekend was arrested for allegdely punching a white policeman.

____

____

____

____

____

____

WWWWWH ANSWER SHEET FOR NEWS LEAD

Directions: Write an answer for each question. If you do not find an answer in the news article, write "not given."

The Headline Reads: ____

____

1. Who? ____

____

2. What? ____

____

3. When? ____

____

4. Where? ____

____

5. Why? ____

____

6. How? ____

____

My name is: ______________________________ Home Room # ______

My article is from ____
(Give name of paper.) (Date of paper)

EXERCISE 5. Mark up Leads for Better Understanding

Some reporters try to jam all the important information into the first sentence. The idea is to save the reader time. It may take you a short time to read that sentence, but a very long time to understand it.

Learn to use your pencil to make the important parts of the sentence stand out. Remember that newspapers are not textbooks or library books—they are cheap today, and tomorrow they will be thrown away. So mark them up fearlessly.

Directions: Several ways to mark up a lead are shown in Column A. Study them; then try these methods out on the leads in Column B.

Column A

1. Add punctuation:

One of a group of men who, police said, were jeering at firemen at the scene of a house fire during the weekend, was arrested for (allegedly) punching a white policeman.

2. Make into shorter sentences:

A group of men (police said) were jeering at firemen at the scene of a house fire during the weekend. One of the men was arrested for (allegedly) punching a white policeman.

3. Underline the main sentence. Put parentheses around less important information.

One of a group of men who (police said) were jeering at firemen (at the

Column B

1. Add punctuation:

CAIRO (UPI) — The left wing military group that seized the gov-

ernment of the Sudan installed today as premier a former chief justice

who pledged a policy more militantly pro-Arab and more anti-Western.

United Press International

2. Make into shorter sentences:

CAIRO (UPI) — The left wing military group that seized the gov-

ernment of the Sudan installed today as premier a former chief justice

who pledged a policy more militantly pro-Arab and more anti-Western.

3. Underline the main sentence. Put parentheses around less important information.

CAIRO (UPI) — The left wing military group that seized the gov-

scene of a house fire during the weekend) was arrested for (allegedly) punching a white policeman.

4. Mark off word groups:

One of a group of men / who police said were jeering / at firemen / at the scene of a house fire / during the weekend / was arrested / for allegedly punching a white policeman. /

ernment of the Sudan installed today as premier a former chief justice

who pledged a policy more militantly pro-Arab and more anti-Western.

4. Mark off word groups:

CAIRO (UPI) — The left wing military group that seized the gov-

ernment of the Sudan installed today as premier a former chief justice

who pledged a policy more militantly pro-Arab and more anti-Western.

Leads are put together in different ways. One way of marking that works well for one lead may not be the best for another. Try out different ways of marking.

EXERCISE 6. Checking Your Understanding

If you have not read all of "SAY MAN STRUCK COP," turn back to page 81 and finish it. Then work this exercise to check your understanding of the story.

Directions: There are several possible headlines for this story. Some would be better than others, but all of them should be accurate. Cross out the headlines in the following list that are not accurate.

"SAY MAN STRUCK COP
DURING FRACAS AT FIRE"

"FIREFIGHTERS SPEED
TO GHETTO FIRES"

"SAY MAN PUNCHED COP
DURING FRACAS AT FIRE"

"COP SAYS MAN STRUCK HIM
DURING FRACAS AT FIRE"

"ONLOOKERS CLASH
WITH COPS AT FIRE"

"CHARGE FIREMEN TAKE IT EASY
GETTING TO GHETTO FIRES"

"ARREST EIGHT AT FIRE;
SAID TO BLOCK FIREMEN'S WAY"

"HOUSE BURNS TO GROUND
DUE TO FRACAS AT FIRE

EXERCISE 7. Asking Questions Without Answers

News stories are not fiction with all of the loose ends neatly explained in the last chapter. They are reports on life, and therefore they leave many questions unanswered.

Directions: For each of the following questions, circle YES, NO or ? (not answered). Be prepared to tell what lines in the "SAY MAN STRUCK COP" story back up your answers.

Example:

? (YES) NO   X. Are the bystanders and onlookers the same as the group of men who were jeering?

Probably YES. San Jurjo says "we never touched the guy."

Parrish said they had to "keep the *other* bystanders from interfering with the arrest."

? YES NO   1. Did the group of men give a reason for jeering at the firemen?

? YES NO   2. Were the firemen late in arriving at the fire?

? YES NO   3. Do many of the men in the group live in the neighborhood?

? YES NO   4. Did anyone say Jackson did not strike the policeman?

? YES NO   5. Did the group try to stop the policeman from arresting Jackson?

? YES NO   6. Did Jackson use obscene language?

EXERCISE 8. Adding in *Your* Information, Opinions, and Questions

You have practiced using some tools to help you understand the information the reporter has put into the story. The reporter tells you what he knows and what others say.

But there is something else to take into account. That is what *you* know and what *you* think. Add your information to the information in the story. What do you know about fires, firemen, police, brawls, jeering, turning in fire alarms, or C.O.R.E.?

Directions: Draw on your own experience and information (as well as on information in the story) to raise additional questions about the story. Write one question on the lines below.

Example: You believe that nobody would delay a fireman if a person might be hurt by the flames. So your question is, "Did the jeering men know that no one was in the house?"

On the other hand, try not to let your experiences prejudice you in your understanding of the news. As you read the headline, "SAY MAN STRUCK COP DURING FRACAS AT FIRE," did you immediately take sides with the man or the policeman? Someone who had a bad experience with a policeman might assume the policeman was in the wrong. Someone whose father was a policeman might immediately assume that there could be no justification for the action. Try to be extra careful in making up your mind about a story when you know your prejudices are involved.

EXERCISE 9. Put Events in Time Order

A news story tells things in order of importance, and it groups related facts. In doing this, time order can get scrambled. Sometimes it helps to straighten it out in your mind.

Directions: Here are the main events of the story in the order in which they appear. Number them to show the order in which you think they actually happened. The first one is already numbered for you, as an example.

> *Hint:* First go through the list and just mark each event b, d, or a for *b*efore, *d*uring or *a*fter the fracas. Letter the b events in order, then the d's, then the a's.

A group of men were jeering at firemen

A house was on fire during the weekend (May 27–28)

A man was arrested

(Maybe) a man punched a cop at 10 p.m. Saturday

Cop tried to break up group

Firemen fought fire

"Fracas"—clash among police, Jackson, bystanders, firemen

Police arrest Jackson and leave with him

Jackson charged, arraigned, released

Hearing will be June 6

Firemen and bystanders make statements to reporters

1B C.O.R.E. demonstrates

Fire chief makes statement

Alarm turned in 9:58 p.m.

EXERCISE 10. You Be the Reporter

Directions: Write a sentence or two, to be added to paragraph 1 of "SAY MAN STRUCK COP" story, telling why the men were jeering.

___

___

___

Directions: Pretend there is room in the paper for only the first three paragraphs and three more sentences. Write three sentences that will tell the reader how other people's stories were different from the patrolman's story.

___

___

___

___

___

PRACTICE IN YOUR LOCAL NEWSPAPER

PRACTICE 1. Find two stories in your local paper that you would like to read. Write down the main question you want each story to answer. Attach the headline-lead part of the articles to your paper.

PRACTICE 2. Choose a local story from your paper. Read the story and write down one or more questions the story does *not* answer for you. Hand in your question and the story.

PRACTICE 3. Take a whole front page from your local paper. Mark up the leads of three news stories to make them easier to understand. Try to use more than one method of marking. Bring the page to class.

CHAPTER 8
THE SPORTS PAGE:
WHERE THE ACTION IS

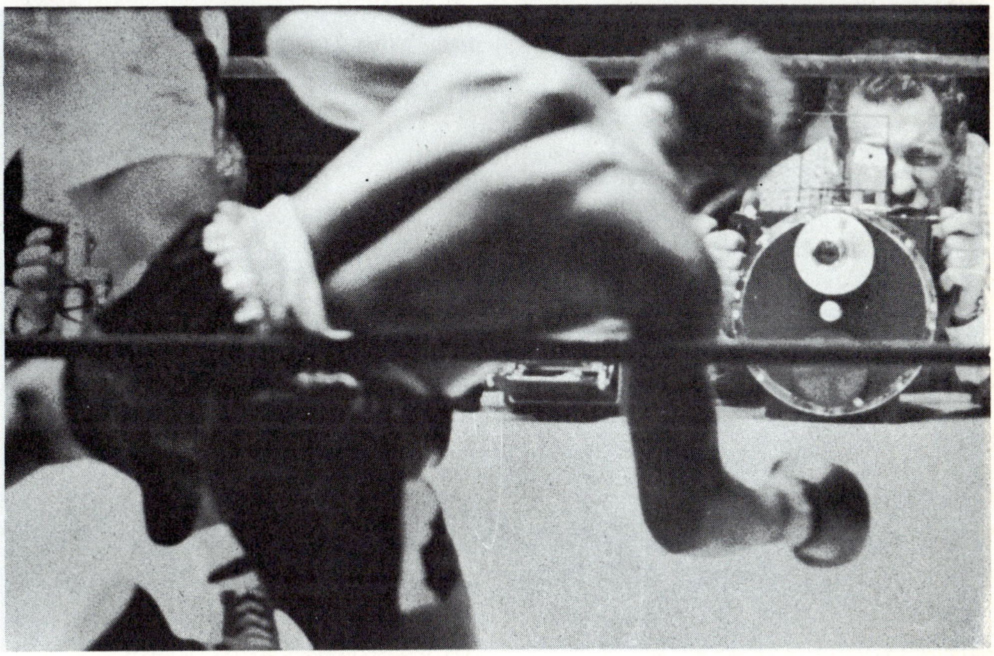

Which do you grab first—the sports page or the comics? On either page you find *action!* Nearly everyone likes to read the sports page. Who won the game? What was the final score? Has our team still got a chance to win the pennant?

Many of us read the sports page so we won't be conversational dropouts when the gang talks sports.

But have you ever thought of using the sports page

to find out how to improve your own game?
to learn about neighborhood teams you can join?
to discover sports events you can enter?

SCANNING AND SKIMMING THE SPORTS PAGE

Go headline hunting on the sports page. See how fast you can find the articles you want to read. You can practice this fast kind of reading, which is called *scanning,* by working the exercises on the next page.

EXERCISE 1. Scanning the Headlines

Directions: Each of the headlines on the opposite page has a number in front of it. Use only the numbers for your answers. Here are five questions which can be answered by one of the headline stories. Place the number of the correct headline after each question. See if you can get all the answers in 60 seconds. Ready . . . go!

1. Which article tells you about park activities?
   Headline____.

2. Which article tells you about baseball diamonds?
   Headline____.

3. Which article would help you be a better quarterback?
   Headline____.

4. Which articles would help you become a better bowler?
   Headlines____.

5. Which article tells you how much money star athletes get?
   Headlines____.

THE BIG PAY-OFF

Sports writers catch our attention with words we've never seen before. But they usually tell us the meanings a few sentences later. All we have to do is skim along. Always remember this as you read newspapers. *Read on for the big pay-off.*

Look at the headline over the article on page 92. Do you know what a *karate-ka* is? The writer doesn't count on it, so he tells you what this word means in the third paragraph.

Other words are explained in brackets. An example of this is karate "empty hand" in paragraph 4.

① ***Difference in Size of Boys Baseball Fields Explained***

② **Dick Williams—a Charlie Brown Who Wins**

Everything Gets Fouled Up, but It's O.K.

③ **YOU CRAVING ACTION? GO, GO TO PARKS!**

Half Million People Seen for Programs

④ **Mays Tells How He Plays Ball**

Willie's Advice to Kids: Keep Fit by Running

⑤ **Better bowling**

Don't steer ball on 10-pin spare

The Ol' Brawl Game ⑥

Yank-Boston Beanballs Ignite Big Free-for-All

Better bowling ⑦

1-3-9 is played from left side

Willie Signs for $125,000 ⑧

You be the QB ⑨

What's right call when motion goes to left?

EXERCISE 2. Finding New Words Defined for You

Directions: Find the places in the article where the words listed below are defined for you by the writer. Underline each definition. Then write the number of the paragraph containing the definition in the blank next to the word. The first one is done for you. Do not read. Skim along until you find the word you are looking for.

__3__ mawashi geri	____ judo-gi's
____ gedan barai	____ judo-ka's
____ koobu	____ "doomo arigato"
____ judo	____ "Hajime!"

SUBHEADS ARE SIGNS

Subheads often tell you what is in each part of an article. They are like the signs at the supermarket. Use them to save time and to pick the part that interests you.

EXERCISE 3. Reading Subheads to Find Answers

Directions: First, read all of the subheads in the article. (There are five of them.) Second, read the first question below. Now look back at the subheads. Choose the one that tells something about the question. Skim quickly to locate the answer. Write the letter of the subhead under which the question is answered in the blank. The first one is done for you. Repeat these steps for each question.

__A__ 1. What does judo teach?

____ 2. How long does it take to learn how to fall properly?

____ 3. What color of belt is worn by the beginning judo-ka?

'Y' Teaches Karate-ka's To Stay Off Their Koobus

BY EDWARD WRIGHT

(1) Any reasonably-proficient karate-ka who is faced with a mawashi geri will respond with a quick gedan barai, or he is likely to find himself flat on his koobu.

(2) The terms are Japanese, but they are becoming increasingly familiar to the many Americans who are taking up karate, the no-nonsense oriental form of self-defense.

(3) A karate-ka is one who practices karate; a mawashi geri is a roundhouse kick to the face; a gedan barai is a downward block with the forearm; and a koobu is a part of the anatomy on which no self-respecting karate-ka belongs.

(4) Both karate ["empty hand"] and its more easy-going cousin, judo ["gentle way"], are being taught at the South Shore Y. M. C. A., 1833 E. 71st st. Judo is offered to both adults and youngsters, whereas karate is taught mainly in the adults' class. About a half dozen of the Y. M. C. A.'s in Chicago offer instruction in one or the other, but South Shore is one of the few to offer both.

(A) Judo Teaches Respect

(5) Instructor in the South Shore program is Dennis Perdue, a stocky, soft-spoken 170-pounder who holds a 2d-degree black belt in judo. "Judo is good for the youngsters," he says. "In addition to teaching them how to defend themselves—which we take for granted — judo teaches them humility and respect. It develops the whole person."

(B) Color Indicates Level

(6) The various levels of attainment in judo are rigidly stratified and all presided over by the Kodokan. The symbol of the beginning judo-ka is the white belt. After moving thru the three stages of white belt proficiency, the judo practitioner is awarded the brown belt, a process which may take half a year or so.

(7) From there, the judo-ka will spend about the next 3 years mastering the 3 levels of brown belt training before he is ready to try for the black belt—the big league of judo. It is awarded only by an examining board of "high masters," all orientals, and only after demonstration of real proficiency on the part of the candidate.

(C) No Living Holders

(8) Once the judo-ka enters the world of the black belt, he is faced with a seemingly-endless series of degrees of qualification—10, to be exact, enough to command a man's attention and discipline for the rest of his life. Perdue's 2d degree black belt is no mean feat, considering few nonorientals ever get past the 5th degree, and there are no living holders of the 10th degree today.

(9) Altho karate, like judo, is also taught as a sport, this is a fairly recent development. Its basic function is injuring the adversary with explosive blows of the fist, elbow, and foot.

(D) Developed by Monks

(10) Karate was developed by Buddhist monks in Tibet to protect themselves from bandits. This form of unarmed combat spread to Okinawa, and from there to Japan where, like judo, it was taken over and institutionalized by the Japanese.

(11) A judo match at the "Y" reflects the oriental roots of the sport. Dressed in the judo-gi's [uniforms], the opponents, known as judo-ka's, perform the ceremonial kneeling bow, or za rei, say "doomo arigato" ["thank you"], and start the match at the instructor's shout of "Hajime!" ["Begin!"].

(12) "From that point, a match may run anywhere from 2 seconds — if someone is thrown quickly—to the full 3 minutes," says Perdue.

(13) The first one to be awarded one full point [ippon] by the instructor wins the match. One good, decisive throw is all that's needed for a full point. A throw with a little less authority may be good for only half a point.

(E) Must Learn to Fall

(14) Falling, says Perdue, is much of the sport. "It takes about 6 or 8 months to learn to fall properly. The important thing is to overcome both the fear of falling and the loss of pride that comes when you first fall. After that, you've got it made."

____4. How many years are spent mastering the 3 levels of brown belt?

____5. Which color belt stands for "the big league of judo"?

____6. How many living persons hold the 10th degree of black belt?

____7. Who developed karate?

> Both karate ["empty hand"] and its more easy-going cousin, judo ["gentle way"], are being taught at the South Shore Y. M. C. A., 1833 E. 71st st. Judo is offered to both adults and youngsters, whereas karate is taught mainly in the adults' class. About a half dozen of the Y. M. C. A.'s in Chicago offer instruction in one or the other, but South Shore is one of the few to offer both.

EXERCISE 4. Zig-Zag Skimming for Facts

Directions: You can locate facts quickly and more efficiently by moving your pencil, line by line, down the middle of the column. Let your eyes zig-zag from one side of the pencil to the other as above.

Your eyes should be looking for only one or two key words or numbers. Find the following key words in the article as suggested by the HINTS after each question and in this way answer the questions.

1. The name of the "Y" teaching karate is________________________

____

HINT: Look for the letters Y.M.C.A.

2. The name of the instructor is________________________

HINT: Look for capital letters. (Remember this hint when looking for the name of a person or place.)

3. The time a match lasts may run________________________.

HINT: Look for time words like minutes or seconds.

4. A full point is given for one________________________.

HINT: Look for the words *a full point.*

5. The number of degrees for each color is

white belt ________________________ degrees.

brown belt ______________________________ degrees.

black belt ______________________________ degrees.

HINT: First, find the color. Second, look only for a number. (Sometimes a number is written out as a word.)

TRIPLE PLAY REPORTING

The next sports story you will read is about the Most Valuable Player award. It uses pictures, a table, and the news article itself—a real triple play in reporting. All of this enables you to learn many details quickly.

EXERCISE 5. Getting Help from Pictures

Directions: Look at the four pictures. Then read the statements below. If the pictures show the statement to be true, circle YES. If you can't tell by looking at the pictures, circle NO.

YES NO 1. Cepeda plays for the Cardinals.

YES NO 2. Cepeda bats right handed.

YES NO 3. Cepeda has a bad knee injury.

YES NO 4. Cepeda wears a glove on his left hand while batting.

YES NO 5. Cepeda was traded by the San Francisco Giants to the Cards.

EXERCISE 6. Getting Help from Tables

Directions: Study the table carefully. See how it is set up and what it is intended to do. Now use it to fill in the blanks in the statements below.

1. First place vote is worth ______________ points.
2. Second place vote is worth ______________ points.
3. Tenth place vote is worth ______________ points.
4. Orlando Cepeda received ______________ points.
5. Pete Rose received ______________ points.

MVP Cepeda credits trainer

Orlando Cepeda . . . an over-all look at the National League's Most Valuable Player. (AP)

SAN JUAN (AP) — Puerto Rican Orlando Cepeda, named the National League's Most Valuable Player in a unanimous vote, is a very happy and proud man.

Interviewed at his Bayamon home after his selection, Cepeda gave most of the credit for his award and tremendous comeback with the world champions St. Louis Gardinals to team trainer Dr. Robert Bauman, "whose selflessness and hard work helped me greatly this year."

The Cards' big first baseman became the first player in the history of the National League to receive unanimous support from the MVP award.

HE WON WITH the highest batting average since Pittsburgh's Dick Groat won it batting .325 in 1960. Cepeda finished the season also with .325, hit 25 homers and batted in 111 runs,, top in the circuit.

"This is the most marvelous thing that could happen to a ball player," Cepeda said after receiving a telephone call from St. Louis announcing the award.

"I feel very proud, but I really don't know what to say. I want to thank all the people who helped me.

"This is so big, specially when I was so close to quitting the game because of my knee injury. Imagine, for the second year in a row a Puerto Rican player wins the award," Cepeda added.

HE WAS referring to Roberto Clemente, the Pittsburgh Pirates' outfielder winner last year and third in the voting this year. Clemente received 129 points this time and finished behind catcher Tim McCarver of the Cardinals, who got 136 points.

Ron Santo, Chicago third baseman, was fourth and Hank Aaron, Atlanta outfielder, was fifth.

Cepeda was named as the No. 1 choice on all the 20 members of the Baseball Writers Assn. of America named to pick the MVP. He received 280 points.

THE 30-YEAR-old player is in his 10th season in the majors. He was traded last year by the San Franciscó Giants to the Cards for pitcher Ray Sadecki.

The big slugger will get back in uniform around Nov. 21 with his winter league team, the island's defending champions and leaders Santurce Crabbers.

He said he is very grateful to Dr. Bauman, Dr. Sollofief of San Francisco, Dr. Ralph W. Sierra of San Juan, and former island weight lifting champion Roberto Santana, now a physical fitness expert for his recovery and eventual comeback.

Santana developed a special metal shoe for Cepeda about two years ago, when his knee injury was about to put an end to his baseball career.

MVP voting

(First place vote worth 14 points, second worth 9, third through 10th worth 8-7-6-5-4-3-2-1.)

Player, Team—	Pts.
Orlando Cepeda, Cardinals	280
Tim McCarver, Cardinals	136
Roberto Clemente, Pirates	129
Ron Santo, CUBS	103
Henry Aaron, Braves	79
Mike McCormick, Giants	73
Lou Brock, Cardinals	49
Tony Perez, Reds	43
Julian Javier, Cardinals	41
Pete Rose, Reds	40

Other Cubs—Ferguson Jenkins 12,th 26 points; Ernie Banks 14th, 22 points; Randy Hundley 23d, 5 points.

Associated Press, Wide World Photos

6. The table lists ________________ Cardinal players in the top ten.

7. Lou Brock received ________________ points less than Cepeda.

8. Ron Santo received ________________ points more than his teammate Ferguson Jenkins.

9. Ernie Banks got 22 points which put him in ________________ place.

10. Complete this table:

Cardinals ________________	Cubs ________________
Reds ________________	Braves ________________
Pirates ________________	Giants ________________

EXERCISE 7. Getting Help from the News Article

Directions: This article shows us the kind of person Cepeda really is. Read the story. Now answer the questions below. If a statement is true, circle T. If a statement is false, circle F. If no direct statement is made but you feel it can be proved by using other statements, put I for implied.

T F I 1. Cepeda received news of the award in a telephone call from St. Louis.

T F I 2. Cepeda is the first player in the National League to receive a unanimous vote for the MVP award.

T F I 3. Cepeda was the first Puerto Rican player to win the MVP award.

T F I 4. San Francisco Giants did not expect Cepeda's 10th season in the majors to be good.

T F I 5. Cepeda hit 25 homers and batted in 111 runs during the 1967 season.

T F I 6. Cepeda was traded by the Giants to the Cards for pitcher Ray Sadeski.

T F I 7. The player who won the MVP award in 1966 was not on this year's list of valuable players.

T F I 8. Cepeda plays ball all year around.

T F I 9. Cepeda wore a special metal shoe after his knee injury.

T F I 10. The St. Louis Cardinals won't have to worry about Cepeda becoming conceited.

Major League Scoreboard

AMERICAN	Chicago	Boston	Minnesota	Detroit	California	Washington	Cleveland	Baltimore	New York	Kansas City	Won	Lost	Pct.	Games Behind
Chicago	—	5	6	6	8	7	8	11	9	8	68	53	.562	—
Boston	4	—	5	9	10	8	11	6	6	10	69	54	.561	—
Minnesota	9	11	—	6	10	8	3	4	10	6	67	54	.554	1
Detroit	8	7	6	—	5	5	10	13	8	6	68	55	.553	1
California	6	8	5	5	—	5	10	7	8	9	63	61	.508	6½
WASHINGTON	5	5	7	7	10	—	5	6	3	11	59	65	.476	10½
Cleveland	3	3	7	8	3	12	—	9	7	7	59	66	.472	11
Baltimore	6	5	5	3	5	7	7	—	11	7	56	68	.452	13½
New York	4	4	5	7	7	7	8	5	—	7	54	69	.439	15
Kansas City	8	6	8	4	3	6	4	7	7	—	53	71	.427	16½
Lost	53	54	54	55	61	65	66	68	69	71				

TODAY'S GAMES

Washington (Priddy 1-5) at Boston (Santiago 7-4), 7:30 p.m.
New York (Talbot 5-5) at Chicago (Klages 1-2), night.
Minnesota (Merritt 9-3 and Perry 5-6) at Detroit (Sparma 12-6 and Wickersham 4-4), 2, twi-night.
California (Hamilton 6-3) at Cleveland (O'Donoghue 7-4), night.
Kansas City (Nash 11-12) at Baltimore (Richert 7-12), night.

RESULTS YESTERDAY

Boston 2–5, Washington 1–3.
Baltimore 2–1, Kansas City 1–6.
Detroit 7–2, Minnesota 3–1 (2nd game 11 innings).
Chicago 3–1, New York 2–2.
Cleveland 3, California 2.

GAMES TOMORROW

Washington at Boston, 1:30 p.m.
New York at Chicago.
Minnesota at Detroit.
California at Cleveland, night.
(Only Games Scheduled)

NATIONAL	St. Louis	Cincinnati	Chicago	San Fran.	Atlanta	Phila.	Pittsburgh	Los Angeles	Houston	New York	Won	Lost	Pct.	Games Behind
St. Louis	—	10	11	10	7	8	6	10	8	7	77	46	.626	—
Cincinnati	5	—	4	7	8	7	8	8	12	8	67	57	.540	10½
Chicago	5	8	—	8	5	11	11	7	6	7	68	60	.531	11½
San Francisco	6	7	4	—	5	7	7	9	9	10	64	59	.520	13
Atlanta	4	4	11	8	—	8	6	5	10	6	62	58	.517	13½
Philadelphia	4	6	7	7	3	—	3	8	11	13	62	59	.512	14
Pittsburgh	7	7	6	5	6	7	—	9	6	7	60	64	.484	17½
Los Angeles	4	8	7	3	9	3	6	—	6	9	55	66	.455	21
Houston	6	2	7	6	6	4	6	8	—	7	52	73	.416	26
New York	5	5	3	5	9	4	11	2	5	—	49	74	.398	28
Lost	46	57	60	59	58	59	64	66	73	74				

TODAY'S GAMES

Philadelphia (Ellsworth 4-5) at New York (Koonce 4-2), night.
Chicago (Nye 10-9) at Pittsburgh (McBean 3-3), night.
Cincinnati (Ellis 7-8) at Los Angeles (Osteen 14-12), night.
St. Louis (Carlton 11-6) at San Francisco (McCormick 16-6).
Atlanta (Jarvis 13-6) at Houston (Cuellar 11-9), night.

RESULTS YESTERDAY

Philadelphia 2–11, New York 0–4.
Chicago 8, Pittsburgh 1.
Houston 4, Atlanta 1.
St. Louis 9, San Francisco 0.
Cincinnati 4, Los Angeles 1.

GAMES TOMORROW

Pittsburgh at Philadelphia, night.
Cincinnati at Los Angeles, night.
St. Louis at San Francisco.
Atlanta at Houston, night.
(Only Games Scheduled)

Courtesy, *Washington* (D.C.) *Star*

HOW TO READ A SCOREBOARD

The scoreboard tells at a glance which teams lead in the pennant race. But it tells much more if you know how to read it. The exercises below will give you that know-how. Look over the Major League Scoreboard on this page and then use it to complete the exercises.

EXERCISE 8. Figuring the Games Won

Directions: Find Chicago at the top of the American Scoreboard. Read the first line of figures from left to right to answer the questions below. The first one is done for you.

1. Chicago has won ________ games from Boston.

2. Chicago has won ________ games from Minnesota.

3. Chicago has won ________ games from Detroit.

4. Chicago has won ________ games from New York.

EXERCISE 9. Figuring the Games Lost

Directions: To find out how many games Chicago has lost to each team, read down the first column of figures. Answer the following questions.

1. Chicago has lost________games to Boston.

2. Chicago has lost________games to Minnesota.

3. Chicago has lost________games to Detroit.

4. Chicago has lost________games to New York.

EXERCISE 10. Figuring Games Won *and* Lost

Directions: Use the National Scoreboard to find answers for the questions below. Remember: Games won are found by reading from left to right after the name of the team; games lost are found by reading from top to bottom.

1. St. Louis has won________games from Cincinnati.

2. St. Louis has lost________ games to San Francisco.

3. Philadelphia has won________games from Los Angeles.

4. Houston has lost________games to Pittsburgh.

5. Atlanta has won________games from Chicago.

FINDING OUT WHO'S AHEAD AND WHY

Look at the American Scoreboard again. Read from left to right and you will see that

Chicago has won 68 games
Boston has won 69 games

Chicago is listed ahead of Boston because it is .001 (1/1000) of a percent ahead.

The formula for figuring percentage is: games won ÷ by total games played. Another way to write this formula is:

$$\frac{\text{games won}}{\text{total games played}}$$

EXERCISE 11. Figuring Percentages

Directions: Study the problem at the left which is worked out for you. Then work the problem at the right the same way.

Chicago	*Boston*
68 games won	69 games won
+53 games lost	+54 games lost
121 total games played	total games played

Chicago

$$
\begin{array}{r}
.5619+ \text{ or } .562 \\
121\overline{)68.0000} \\
605 \\
\hline
750 \\
726 \\
\hline
240 \\
121 \\
\hline
1190 \\
1089 \\
\hline
101
\end{array}
$$

Boston

$$\overline{)69.0000}$$

Does your answer agree with the percentage shown in the table?

LINKING THE PAST WITH THE PRESENT

Sports pages often contain references to Greek mythology. In order to understand what the writers are saying we need to know some of the common ideas of the ancient Greeks.

The Greeks believed the earth to be flat. They thought Greece was the center of the universe. They also believed that gods controlled everything that happened. They built temples for these gods at places called *oracles.* In each temple there lived a priest or priestess who served as a spokesman for the god or godess. For example, the oracle at Delphi belonged to the god Apollo. In time, the word oracle was used to describe the priestess who served Apollo as well as the place where his temple was built.

What has all of this to do with the sports page? We are always caught up by words of history used to describe something in present-day life. This is one of the reasons for studying history and literature.

Have you ever wondered why the Olympics are called the Olympics and how these great sports contests came into being? Read the newspaper article "So That's Why . . . The Olympics Are the Olympics." When you have finished, check your understanding by answering the questions which follow it.

So That's Why ...

The Olympics Are the Olympics

BY GWEN MORGAN

[Chicago Tribune Press Service]

OLYMPIA, Greece—"What, Oracle, can save Greece from her constant civil strife?" the king of Elis asked the oracle at Delphi 29 centuries ago.

"The people of Elis, O king, must revive the gods' Olympic games," the Delphic oracle replied.

The king of Elis met with his neighbors, the king of Sparta and the king of Pisa, whose name was to travel with a colony to Italy. The trio agreed to hold games here at Olympia, then in the kingdom of Elis, and to cease hostilities during the month the games were held.

Thus Greeks began their contests here, dedicating them to Zeus, supreme among the gods, who always had prevailed in earlier times when, the Greek legends said, the gods themselves held contests in the small river valley here.

• • •

The games became so important that by 776 B. C. Greeks counted the passing of years by the every-four-year olympiad. The games were announced by heralds who proclaimed thru the Greek world the "sacred truce." The simple olive branch, made into a crown, was the victor's cherished award. Contestants flocked here.

Entrance to the stadium at Olympia.

Today the wind sighs thru the lonely pines. The once busy temples, the stadium, and the gymnasium are quiet grassy areas studded with broken stones. The ancient days seem remote, indeed, until in the museum I see a cup inscribed in classic Greek: "I belong to Phidias."

This great Athenian sculptor, whom Pericles assigned to beautify the capital, had a workshop here. His giant gold and ivory statue of Zeus, seven times human size, awed all who entered Zeus' temple here.

The games continued here for more than 12 centuries. The measure of the footrace track — 630.8 feet — is preserved in our word stadium, athletic exercise in our word gymnasium, and all athletes recall Aethlios, one of Zeus' sons, the first king of Elis and a legendary organizer of the gods' games.

In Roman times the Olympic games' standards declined. In 394 A. D. the Christian Byzantines declared the games were pagan, banned them, and transported Zeus' statue to Constantinople where the statue perished in a fire.

• • •

But the idea of peaceful competition for the joy of excellence didn't die. A French admirer of Greece, Baron Pierre de Couvertin inspired the organization of the first modern olympics in 1896 in Athens rather than in Zeus' sacred grove here in Olympia.

So that's why this week in Grenoble, France, and next autumn in Mexico City the Olympics are the Olympics.

Reprinted, courtesy of the *Chicago Tribune*

EXERCISE 12. Getting the Facts

Directions: Complete the statements below by filling in the blanks.

1. A Frenchman by the name of ________________ is responsible for our modern Olympics.

2. The victors in early Olympics were awarded crowns made from

__________.

3. The word *athlete* is derived from the Greek name__________, one of the sons of Zeus.

4. The Kings of Elis, Sparta, and Pisa agreed to __________

__________ during the month that the games were held.

5. What do you remember about the 1968 Olympics in Mexico that brought politics into the sports world? Do you think this was right or

wrong? __________

____

____

____

____

WORDS TO HELP YOU

civil strife—fighting among the natives in one country

Elis
Sparta—ancient Greek kingdoms
Pisa

cease hostilities—stop fighting

Greek legends—stories about ancient Greece

heralds—messengers

sacred truce—a promise to the gods to stop fighting for a set period of time

remote—distant

Pericles—statesman who ruled Athens during the golden age

pagan—a heathen, one who worships idols

banned—outlawed

EXERCISE 13. Separating Word Parts

Directions: There are several words in this article made up of a base word plus a suffix. Find the base word and write it in the blank at the right.

1. Delphic ____________________

2. Olympic ____________________

3. Olympiad ____________________

4. Athenian ____________________

5. legendary ____________________

EXERCISE 14. Understanding B.C./A.D. Dates

Directions: The abbreviation B.C. stands for *before Christ.* A.D. stands for the Latin words *anno Domini* meaning *in the year of our Lord.* Thus a date with A.D. following it means *since Christ was born.* From 10 B.C. to 50 A.D. would then be 60 years. Use this information to answer the questions below. Put a check mark in front of each correct answer.

1. The Olympic games began

____a. before Christ was born.

____b. after Christ was born.

____c. when Christ was born.

2. From 776 B.C. to 394 A.D. is

____a. 382 years.

____b. 1,170 years.

____c. 940 years.

3. From the time the games were banned by the Byzantines until the first modern Olympics

________a. 2,000 years passed.

________b. 1,202 years passed.

________c. 1,502 years passed.

4. The Olympic Games were held in Olympia for

________a. more than 12 years.

________b. more than 1,200 years.

________c. more than 120 years.

5. Have the modern Olympics been held every 4 years since 1896?

________a. YES

________b. NO

6. What reason do you have for your answer to the above question?

____

____

____

____

EXERCISE 15. Finding Word Origins and Word Meanings

1. Look up the words *museum* and *muse* in a dictionary. Write brief definitions below:

Museum ____

Muse ____

Now do you see why we call a museum a museum?

2. Look up *Terpsichore* in a dictionary and use this information to decide if the following statement is true or false. Circle the correct answer.

T F Zeus is to Terpsichore as
Zeus is to Aethlios

PRACTICE IN YOUR LOCAL NEWSPAPER

PRACTICE 1. Almost every day there are articles in the newspaper about baseball, football, or basketball; however, some sports such as karate are not reported every day. Watch your sports pages for one week and clip out any stories relating to unusual or seldom-reported sports.

PRACTICE IN YOUR LOCAL NEWSPAPER

PRACTICE 2. Clip out samples of graphs or tables which are used by your local newspaper to illustrate the scoring of some national or local sports event. Bring two of them to class.

PRACTICE 3. Read the sports page in your local newspaper for one week and circle all the words used which you think might have originated with the Greek games. Bring in the stories containing the circled words.

PRACTICE 4. How many different kinds of sports are reported by your local newspaper? Check it for one week and bring in one news story on each kind of sport.

PRACTICE 5. The sports page often contains stories related to sports, but not directly reporting any specific events such as biographies of the players, medical reports on injuries, or descriptions of new sports buildings. Bring to class three examples of articles that do not report a specific sports event.

CHAPTER 9
THE MORGUE: YOUR OWN NEWSPAPER CLIPPING FILE

Maybe you have a special interest in cars. Or contact lenses. Or air pollution. Or riot control.

As you read the newspaper, you pay special attention to stories on your special subjects. The more you read about them, the more you know about them.

If you cut out and save articles on your special subject, you have the beginnings of a morgue. A morgue is a place to keep dead bodies. In journalistic jargon a morgue is a place to keep clippings of "dead" stories. This does not mean that the stories will never be looked at again. They are still alive in the sense that they furnish background information when new related events occur.

When a reporter is going to write a story about riot control, for example, he looks in the morgue to see what has happened already. He puts some of this background information into his new story. The morgue stories also give him ideas on what people and facts to look for. The newspaper stories, taken together, give him the kind of complete, up-to-the-minute information he could never find in a book or an encyclopedia.

START YOUR OWN MORGUE

Let's say the subject you want to keep up-to-date on is money—especially borrowing money or buying on credit without getting into trouble.

Maybe you'll find a story on credit tomorrow, and there won't be another one for a week. But the clippings pile up. The pieces start to fit together, and after a while you have a very good idea of the entire credit picture.

This is what you do:

1. *Mark stories:* Have a bright crayon or ink stick handy when you read the paper. Mark stories right away, as you read them. Circle words in the headline or lead that tell the subject.

2. *Clip out stories:* It saves time to cut out the story right away. Try to be the last one in your family to read the newspaper, so you can do that. If you must leave the paper whole for someone else to read, mark the story and mark the page number at the top of page one. Then you can find your stories fast when the time comes to cut up the paper.

3. *Label stories:* Use a ball-point pen to label each clipping with the name (or initials) of the paper, and the date—month, day, and year. If you can recognize home-town paper clippings by the way they look, you can skip the paper name-label.

Or try this method: color-mark your article. Then tear out the whole page. The name of the paper and the date are already on at least one side of every page, so you save time writing and clipping. Fold the page so that the headline of your article shows. Later decide if the story is worth the full treatment of labeling and trimming.

4. *File stories by subject:* Decide on a place to keep each group of stories. Maybe you can find some old file folders. Or you can make a pretty good file folder out of a grocery bag.

If you started cutting out credit-loan stories, in a few months your folder might have the stories that follow. Read each story, and do the exercises to help you understand them.

EXERCISE 1. Getting the Facts

The following story is about one family out of many thousands who become victims of easy credit salesmen. In this case, the victim didn't even know he was buying anything.

Cut bag along dotted line.

Fold in three sides and tape down edges to inside of bag.

Label file bag.

Reprinted with permission from the *Chicago Daily News*

Juan: A Victim Of Credit Sharks

By Lois Wille

(1) Things were going beautifully for **Juan** Montoya and his family. The knock on the door that Thursday night only seemed **to** make them better.

(2) But, by the time the caller had left **an** hour later, Montoya's life was ruined.

(3) In the space of that hour he was sucked into the easy-credit trap—a painfully familiar story in this state.

(4) Before he can get out, he may lose his job, his home, and the self-respect he managed to build since he moved here from Puerto Rico two years ago.

(5) **HIS STORY** is one of hundreds now being gathered by the Chicago Commission on Human Relations, the Cardinal's Committee for the Spanish Speaking in Chicago, Family Financial Counseling of Greater Chicago and other agencies working for credit reform.

(6) Most of the stories begin like the Montoya case — with a house call from a salesman.

(7) Montoya, his wife and their five children live in Chicago Heights in a small home he is buying on contract for $175 a month. He earns $115 a week in an electrical plant.

(8) The salesman began by saying he wasn't a salesman. He was a bearer of wonderful news:

(9) **The Montoyas had won a magnificent gift, a full set of beautiful pots and pans.**

(10) Would Mrs. Montoya select the style she liked from this folder?

(11) "We know enough English to know we won this present," Montoya says. So we said yes, thank you, and we were very happy."

(12) Would Mr. Montoya sign this document indicating he had received the gift?

(13) Montoya took the pen and was about to sign when he noticed a figure at the bottom of the paper: $309. What did that mean?

(14) Oh, the caller explained, that was just the cash value of the gift.

(15) **SO MONTOYA** signed, and then he signed another little paper at the bottom of the big paper. Another matter of routine.

(16) The caller went to his car, brought in the pots and pans, and left.

(17) Two days later the bill arrived for $309 from a credit company that had purchased the sales contract. Montoya tried to find the company on the contract to give back the pots and pans, but no one had heard of it. There is no telephone listing, no address on his merchandise, and the credit company says it has no information, either.

(18) **BECAUSE** he budgets tightly, Montoya says he can't pay $309. The credit company is preparing to go to court to garnishee his wages — a power he gave them by signing that second little paper.

(19) When his wages are garnisheed, Montoya will lose his job. His employer, like many firms, has a strict policy of laying off garnisheed workers until their credit trouble is settled.

(20) **IF MONTOYA** loses his job, he will also lose his house and the $1,100 he already has paid toward it.

(21) Montoya, acutely embarrassed over what happened to him, now says it's all his fault.

(22) "I should know better English," he says. "And I should know not to trust people. I am so ashamed."

Directions: Read the story. Then find and underline the part of the story that answers the following questions. Write in the blank the number of the paragraph that answers the question. The first one is done for you.

__19__ 1. Why will Montoya lose his job when his wages are garnished?

______ 2. How do most easy-credit trap stories begin?

______ 3. What are the names of some Chicago agencies working for credit reform?

______ 4. Why did Montoya take the pots and pans?

EXERCISE 2. Reading for Information

Directions: Read the credit-reform story on the next page. Underline the part of the story that answers the following questions. Write in the blank the number of the paragraph that answers the question.

______ 1. What is a "schlock?"

______ 2. Why do both parties want the state to license finance companies and auto salesmen?

______ 3. If you don't pay back money you owe, can everything you own be taken and sold to pay this debt?

______ 4. How does a salesman get a buyer to sign a contract?

______ 5. What proposal would help the buyer who signs a contract with a "schlock" and then wants to get out of it?

EXERCISE 3. Looking for New Questions

A background file helps you look ahead, because it includes some questions which only the future can answer.

Directions: Write in the blank the number of the paragraph of the credit reform story which brings the following questions to your mind. The first one is done for you.

__7__ 1. Will the Credit Reform bill pass?

______ 2. Will the cooling-off period proposal pass?

Big Drama In Springfield

By Henry Hanson

Of Our Springfield Bureau

(1) SPRINGFIELD, Ill.—The players, all lawyers, stand beneath the chandeliers in the Illinois Senate. The debate is about a series of credit reform 'bills aimed at throttling the state's unscrupulous money lenders.

(2) Dialog goes like this:

Sen. Egbert Groen (R-Pekin) (indignantly):

"It will be a long, long time before these bills become law. What IS a 'schlock'? Spell it for me. Tell me what a 'schlock' is—so I can tell my people back home what you're trying to do."

(3) **Sen. Arthur Gottschalk** (R-Flossmoor) (angrily):

"You'll see some 'schlocks' when the opponents of these bills come down to testify. You'll see them face to face. And I for one am not going to be damaged by the people who fight these bills in the rotunda. I expect there will be a lot of action in that rotunda." (A dark hint of bribery.)

(4) **Sen. Thomas McGloon** (D-Chicago) (thoughtfully):

"A 'schlock', Sen. Groen, is spelled S C H L O O K. (He misspells ti.) A 'schlock' is someone who preys upon the unwary, the uneducated, the illiterate, the poor. He takes advantage of their lack of knowledge by having them sign what appears to be a local contract for goods or merchandise. But it is, in fact, a contract with usurious interest rates."

(5) **Sen. Robert Coulson** (R-Waukegan) (whimsically):

"I have a better definition. A 'schlock' is a schlemiel who puts people in hock."

(Curtain.)

Chances Are Good

(6) Acts 2 and 3 of this real-life, incredibly complicated drama of credit reform will be played out in the Legislature in weeks to come.

(7) But chances look good this year that Illinois may win some significant new laws curbing the get-rich-quick money lenders and peddlers who cheat on anything from used-car financing to fixing a furnace.

(8) It hasn't always been so. Most meaningful credit reform measures have been shot down in the hectic closing days of past sessions of the General Assembly.

(9) Rumors were rampant that wheeler-dealer lobbyists representing the money lenders were flush with greenbacks and other tokens that helped kill the bills.

(10) Everybody had a lobbyist but the victims, or so it appeared.

(11) **IN THE 1965** Legislature the Mayor's Committee on New Residents, formed by Chicago Mayor Richard J. Daley, introduced a dozen bills to deal with the problem.

(12) All of them sailed through the House, where Democrats held a 2-to-1 margin due to the orange-ballot election. When the bills arrived in the Republican-controlled Senate they lingered and died in the Judiciary Committee.

(13) In the November, 1966, election, Republicans won strong majorities in both houses.

(14) The mind of Senate GOP leader W. Russell Arrington began clicking. Most of his colleagues thought the clicks sounded like gubernatorial aspirations.

(15) But, aspirations aside, Arrington knew the Grand Old Party's future in the state depended on what kind of record Republicans could write in the Legislature.

(16) On Dec. 8, almost a month before the Legislature was to convene, Arrington and Sen. Gottschalk prefiled a dozen credit reform bills.

(17) Most of the bills sounded suspiciously like the bills filed two years earlier by the mayor's committee.

(18) Senate minority leader McGloon was not going to let this go unnoticed.

(19) "You stole them," he cried at Arrington on a panel discussion. "Comma for comma, word for word, line for line, paragraph for paragraph."

(20) "I did not," replied Arrington. "Many of them are different."

(21) **IN ANY EVENT,** the mayor's committee, chaired by Robert C. McNamara Jr., also had been at work.

(22) At 11 a.m. Jan. 17, with appropriate fanfare, the committee's 1967 credit reform proposals were displayed at a Chicago press conference. At the same time, Democratic leaders in the House were introducing the committee's bills in Springfield.

(23) The bills were quite similar, except that the Democratic proposals tended to be of more benefit to the consumer.

(24) For example, the Democratic proposal allows a five-day cooling-off period on door-to-door sales while the GOP proposal had only a 24-hour cooling-off period in which a contract could be canceled.

(25) The reasoning behind both bills is that many door-to-door salesmen prey on the unsophisticated buyer.

(26) The buyer signs complicated contracts, confession notes and wage assignments that he does not understand. The salesman often employs high-pressure techniques and promises "free" gifts.

Ceilings Proposed

(27) Democrats have suggested a ceiling of 7 per cent on new cars. This means that a buyer can be charged no more than $140 in interest on a new $2,000 car—if he pays off in one year. If it takes him two years, he pays $280 in interest; three years, $420.

(28) The Democrats want a ceiling of 9 per cent a year on cars up to two years old, and 11 per cent a year on cars over two years old.

(29) Republicans are asking 8 per cent a year on new cars, 11 per cent on cars up to two years old, 14 per cent on cars two to four years old, and 16 per cent on cars over four years old.

(30) Both parties now want the state to license finance companies and all auto salesmen.

(31) They reason that auto salesmen who defraud purchasers often skip from one used-car lot to another, changing their names or the names of their businesses. Some finance companies have become hoodlum-dominated. Banks and small loan companies are regulated by the state, but there are no similar regulations for finance companies.

(32) **ONE BILL** would increase the minimum exemption from wage attachments from $45 a week to $75. This means the first $75 of a person's wages could not be touched.

(33) Another would forbid employers from discharging employes whose wages are attached until the employe has had five wage attachments in a one-year period. Collection agencies have found involuntary allies in many employers who resent the legal and bookkeeping expenses involved in wage assignments and wage deduction orders.

(34) Another would outlaw unsoliciated credit cards. A Democratic proposal would hike the value of personal property exempt from seizure for debt from $400 to $1,400 for married persons and from $400 to $1,000 for single persons.

(35) And both parties have asked that deficiency judgments on repossessed goods either be eliminated or strictly regulated.

(36) Since leaders in both parties now wear the white hats, it will be up to the 'schlock' merchants—peddling cars, vacuum cleaners or loans—to shoot them down, using lobbyists and their lures for bullets

__________3. Will the exemption from wages be changed?

__________4. Will finance companies and auto salesmen be licensed?

__________5. Will there be a rate cap set on auto finance charges?

__________6. Will deficiency judgments be outlawed?

EXERCISE 4. Learning from Others' Mistakes

Finding out how other people get taken can help you avoid having the same thing happen to you. Read about Mr. Wilson's problems in the story at the right.

Directions: Underline the part of the story that answers the following questions. Write in the blank the number of the paragraph that answers the questions.

____1. Did Mrs. Wilson know she was buying an $895.00 freezer?

____2. What percent of Wilson's paycheck will go to the freezer company?

____3. What will happen to Wilson's job if he is garnisheed?

____4. What can he do to escape garnishment?

The Shocking Story of the Pitiful Collapse Of a Campaign to Aid the Consumer

BY LOIS WILLE

(1) A piece of yellow paper was delivered to Robert Wilson's boss one cold January morning—and with it came a shock wave that may smash Wilson's life.

(2) It was all very proper, very legal: A summons from Municipal Court ordering Wilson's employer to begin withholding 15 per cent of his $80-a-week paycheck and give it to a food freezer company.

(3) His wife, it seems, had signed an incredible sales contract that the family couldn't possibly afford. It itemized an $895 freezer, $250 membership in something called a "food discount club," $168 in canned goods and meat, and $223 "financial charges."

(4) She says now she thought the freezer would be free if she joined the "club," but what she thought doesn't matter. She signed, and the contract is legal.

(5) **NOW HER HUSBAND** is a captive of the easy-credit trap—an old and disturbingly familiar story in this city.

(6) Here's how it goes: If Wilson's wages are garnisheed, he'll be fired. His boss already has told him this, pleading "too much bookkeeping, too much time in court." (And too easy to find another laborer.)

(7) If Wilson wants to escape garnishment, he can declare bankruptcy in U.S. District Court. Then his paycheck won't be touched, but he'll probably have to give up the house he just bought—again, on too-easy credit.

(8) His wife told the story last week to attorney Mark J. Satter, who has heard it a thousand times but still gets boiling mad.

(9) "He's in a deadly spot," Satter says. "He loses his home if he goes bankrupt, he loses his job if he doesn't. He has a wife and four children. Jobs can't be found. The end of the line usually is relief rolls."

EXERCISE 5. Saving Money with Simple Math

Directions: Learning some easy arithmetic will save you a lot of money and trouble. Here is an easy place to start practicing.

Wilson's employer is ordered to give 15% of Wilson's $80.00 paycheck to a food freezer company. Wilson wants to know what that is in dollars, so he needs to figure 15% of $80.00.

Here's how he does it. 15% means 15 parts out of every 100 parts. There are 100 cents in a dollar, so the employer takes 15 cents out of every dollar Wilson earns. He earns $80.00. So the company gets 15 cents 80 times. Wilson would multiply 15 cents by 80 to get the answer:

    15 cents out of every dollar
  ×80 dollars
1200 cents = $12.00 out of every week's paycheck

Credit Reform...

ONE MILLION UNDERDOGS
How Pitchmen Bilk New Bankrupts Here

The Tragedy of William Rodriguez

Mortgage Credit Refusals Squeeze Minorities Here

ONE MILLION UNDERDOGS
Greedy Vultures Find Easy Prey In Chicago's Installment Jungle

Fast-Talking Pitchmen Stalk ... Wage Assignments

Leaders Map War Against Credit Traps

Court Begins Crackdown On Shady Credit Operators

VICTIM OF 'LIFE ON THE CUFF'
Death of a Nobody Spurs Move To Reform Time Payment Laws

Mayor's Committee to Ask Legislature To Eliminate Shoddy Credit Practices

MILLION CHICAGO VICTIMS
How Sharpies Bilk Unfortunates Here

...Fanfare and Flop

The Shocking Story of the Pitiful Collapse Of a Campaign to Aid the Consumer

BY LOIS WILLE

A piece of yellow paper was delivered to Robert Wilson's boss one cold January morning—and with it came a shock wave that may smash Wilson's life.

It was all very proper, very legal: A summons from Municipal Court ordering Wilson's employer to begin withholding 15 per cent of his $80-a-week paycheck and give it to a food freezer company.

His wife, it seems, had signed an incredible sales contract that the family couldn't possibly afford. It itemized an $895 freezer, $250 membership in something called a "food discount club," $168 in canned goods and meat, and $223 "financial charges."

She says now she thought the freezer would be free if she joined the "club," but what she thought doesn't matter. She signed, and the contract is legal.

NOW HER HUSBAND is a captive of the easy-credit trap—an old and disturbingly familiar story in this city.

Here's how it goes: If Wilson's wages are garnisheed, he'll be fired. His boss already has told him this, pleading "too much bookkeeping, too much time in court." (And too easy to find another laborer.)

If Wilson wants to escape garnishment, he can declare bankruptcy in U.S. District Court. Then his paycheck won't be touched, but he'll probably have to give up the house he just bought—again, on too-easy credit.

His wife told the story last week to attorney Mark J. Satter, who has heard it a thousand times but still gets boiling mad.

"He's in a deadly spot," Satter says. "He loses his home if he goes bankrupt, he loses his job if he doesn't. He has a wife and four children. Jobs can't be found. The end of the line usually is relief rolls."

IF YOU THINK you've heard all this before—you have. The easy credit trap that sucks in the unsuspecting was first described by Daily News reporters four years ago, after a young debt-ridden Puerto Rican named William Rodriguez killed himself by drinking rat poison.

If you think the great reform wave that swept the city and state after that suicide gave the story a happy ending—you're wrong.

The beginning was grand enough: Cries for crackdown from the Mayor's Committee on New Residents and civic and welfare agencies, promises of a relentless war from Municipal Court, rounds of meetings between attorneys and legislators and illustrious civic leaders.

But this was reform Illinois-style, one that got twisted around in Springfield and emerged giving greater benefits to money lenders and less protection to the poor.

IN A WAY, reform never had a chance. The odds were stacked against it from the day in August, 1962, when Gov. Otto Kerner appointed a 64-member Credit Study Commission to recommend new laws.

A year before the Legislature had passed a few bills limiting garnishment to 15 per cent of gross pay and requiring the creditor to give the employe notice of garnishment. It wasn't much—but it triggered panic in the credit industry.

"The credit interests were so upset by this reform—not that it hurt them—but they felt it was a preview of things to come," says Dorothy Lascoe, staff assistant in charge of garnishment procedures at Inland Steel Co. and active in credit reform.

"They banded together—the banks, loan companies, finance companies—to make sure 1963 wouldn't hurt them."

They demanded and got heavy representation on Kerner's committee. One committee member, State Rep. Abner J. Mikva, says of that group: "It had no consumer extremists but a great many credit extremists. So the compromise that was reached was between the middle-of-the-roaders and the credit extremists."

The bills that emerged went to the Legislature late in the 1963 session, when birth control and public aid ceilings grabbed all the public attention. What happened to them happened quietly, almost without notice: Of 10 bills, only five passed—the five not opposed by the money lenders.

HOW DID IT happen? "The credit companies are the single most powerful and influential lobby in Springfield," says Mikva.

For example, Household Finance Co. alone had two registered lobbyists. More came from other finance companies, auto dealers, retail merchants, banks, loan companies.

Now, speaking of the great "reform," Mikva says: "We tried to solve burglary problems by legalizing burglary."

Satter adds, "Reform? It was betrayal. A clear case of violent betrayal."

Not all see it like that, of course. Fred Goerlitz, president and lobbyist for the Illinois Retail Merchants Assn., says he just can't understand what happened to the reform bills.

"It's one of those mysteries that you find down in Springfield," he says. Then he adds:

"You've got to remember you have crooks on both sides. Crooks buying and crooks selling. I think the laws now strike a balance between the two."

A HEARING in City Council chambers on Monday may prove otherwise.

The Mayor's Committee on New Residents,

WILLIAM RODRIGUEZ
A forgotten death

alarmed by growing reports of credit abuse, will sponsor public hearings to determine whether new legislation is needed. They'll hear an ugly set of facts.

In 1960, before credit "reform" began, Municipal Court heard 49,131 garnishment cases. In 1964, after reform, it heard 73,363.

"Look around the courtroom," says Satter. "You don't see anyone from lily-white suburbs. No, this is a black man's court. The Negro isolated in his ghetto isn't conditioned to treachery. He's the prey."

Robert Wilson's wife, who paid a total of $1,536 for a freezer and a little food, is a typical example.

The mayor's committee will hear others, all drawn from the city's million gullible underdogs: Puerto Rican, Mexican, Negro, Japanese, Southern white.

JACK GABRIEL, manager of the Pilsen Neighbors Council credit union, will tell about Maria S., who works in a factory to support her three children and speaks little English. Just enough for her to sign a sales contract for a $1,623 color television set.

"She says the door-to-door salesman told her she would get it free if she sold 10 others," Gabriel says. "He told her that would be easy."

In U.S. District Court there are still nearly 1,000 bankruptcy cases a month, as many as before "reform." About 90 per cent are wage earners seeking relief from garnishment. This is a per capita rate nearly 20 times as high as in the New York City area.

ONE OF THEM is Charles K., a Japanese-American salesman who asked Satter to file his bankruptcy petition.

Deeply in debt with six loans for a house, medical bills, a car and furniture, Charles answered a classified ad for part-time vending machine salesmen. When he read over the application blank he signed at his job interview, he discovered he had bought an $800 coffee vending machine.

"That did it," Satter says. "Now he has to go bankrupt."

Once he does, the credit hounds know he can't go bankrupt again for six years—so they've got a sure sucker for garnishment. Look through newspaper classified ads and you'll see their lures:

"Bankrupt? Call us. You're OK. We can help."

Or he'll get one of the letters sent to all new bankrupts, who are coveniently listed in the Daily Law Bulletin:

"Dear Sir:

"This is to tell you how sorry we were to hear about your bankruptcy. . . . You and I both know how important good credit is to live. I and my staff will be at your service. I am enclosing a credit card I send to all my special accounts. . . . I have already set up your account for $200. . . ."

We're just beginning to feel the effects of our staggering bankruptcy rates, according to Mikva. He says:

"The Negro who wants to buy a home but once was bankrupt and climbed back up now can't get legitimate credit. We've established problems that will haunt us for years to come."

Curbing credit abuses—See editorial on next page.

REFORM TOOK ANOTHER beating two years ago when Municipal Court abolished the job of credit commissioner, held by attorney John J. King.

"He provided instant justice," says Mrs. Lascoe. She processes the 60 to 70 new garnishment cases Inland Steel gets each month.

"When a man comes into court with a fistful of money orders showing he had paid bills and shouldn't be garnished, who takes time to look at them now? He gets growled at."

Mrs. Lascoe thinks re-establishment of the commissioner is essential in any true credit reform.

OTHERS ACTIVE in the fight agree—but would take additional, more radical steps.

Satter, for one, is convinced that the only way to halt credit abuse is to abolish garnishment of wages.

"If the shlockmeisters didn't have the power to go after a man's wages, they wouldn't push their fraudulent deals," he says.

But he's virtually alone in his position.

"I sympathize with him emotionally," Mikva says. "But prohibiting garnishment might cut off legitimate credit to legitimate borrowers. If every state abolished it, this conceivably could bring on a drastic reduction of time sales—and a tremendous recession."

Instead, Mikva would like to kill off the loan sharks by attacking from another angle. Offering sound, cheap credit to the poor. The kind of low-interest credit the rich can get easily from banks.

"If you had to make all your purchases on credit and were forced to pay 25 per cent interest on them, you couldn't do it either," he says. "I couldn't."

"This is what happens to the average underpaid, overfamilied Negro working man."

CREDIT UNIONS do offer low-interest loans, but they can be chartered only as arms of some organization such as a labor union or a business firm. Most low-income families have no access to them.

"Why couldn't they be permitted just on a geographic basis?" Mikva asks. "And I'd like to see depositor insurance for credit unions—your money is insured when you deposit, the way it is in a bank.

"Maybe what we need is federal government insurance for small loans, the way the Federal Housing Administration guarantees housing loans. It's a wild idea—getting the federal machinery operating for a $100 loan—but something like that is needed."

What is also needed is the support of legitimate credit interests for credit reform.

"It's our constant hope there will be enough of them that will look beyond their noses," Mikva says.

"A far-sighted bank should be as much for credit reform as any trade union. When they see the danger signs—the startling increase in garnishments, the high bankruptcy rate—they ought to be concerned, too.

"These are not signs of a healthy economy."

Section Two
CHICAGO DAILY NEWS
Saturday, Jan. 23, 1965 Page 13

Success Takes a Licking

One of the casualties of the credit reform collapse has a special mystery about it.

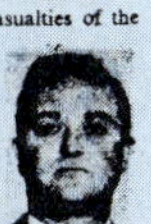

JOHN J. KING

The Municipal Court credit commissioner and the two police detectives assigned to him got nothing but praise for their work. Yet the team was abolished in February, 1963, about two years after it was formed.

The former commissioner, attorney John J. King, says credit gouging was so blatant when he stepped in that "your name on a blank sheet of paper was enough to get a garnishment."

His tough law enforcement program and his crackdown on sloppy procedures of collection attorneys soon was reflected in a drop in garnishments.

In the two years since the team was abolished, garnishments soared from 58,991 to 73,363.

KING GIVES all the credit for the team's success to the two detectives, Sylvester Rehm and Aurelio Garcia.

"They're magnificent actors," he said. "They could be anything a salesman wanted them to be—dumb, drunk, anything.

"They got convictions because they had the evidence and were articulate witnesses.

"Without witnesses like that, you can't get a case to stand up in court," King says.

SUDDENLY, one winter day in 1963, King got a phone call from an aide to Police Supt. O. W. Wilson's office. The two detectives were being transferred—immediately.

"I tried to find out why," King said, "and was told there are 12,000 rapes a year in this city."

King resigned a month later "because the job no longer had teeth in it."

WHY HASN'T the job been restored?

Judge Augustine J. Bowe, chief justice of the Municipal Court division, gives this explanation:

"We've kept our eyes open for the right person but haven't found him. King was exactly right for the job."

But in two years no one has been found.

The Springfield Twist

The Credit Study Commission appointed in 1962 by Gov. Otto Kerner to reform bad credit practices produced 10 bills. Then came the Springfield twist — and reform came out backwards.

Six of the 10 would have given some protection to consumers. The credit industry and its swarm of Springfield lobbyists opposed five of these. None passed.

The sixth, which limits miscellaneous credit fees, was considered harmless enough by the industry and permitted to pass. The four other bills benefitted the credit industry. All four passed.

FOUR OF the pro-consumer bills that failed were killed by the Senate Banking Committee. The fifth, which would have put a ceiling of 28 per cent interest on installment sales, somehow slipped by and went to the Senate floor.

But every time Lt. Gov. Samuel Shapiro was about to call for a vote on it, something funny happened. The bill's sponsor, former State Sen. Dwight Friedrich (R-Centralia), signaled for Shapiro to pass it by. Shapiro did, and the vote never came.

There is an epilog: Friedrich, defeated for re-election last fall, operates a small loan company. "With legislators like him," say one veteran Springfield observer, "the credit industry didn't need lobbyists."

HERE IS the before-and-after story of the 1963 credit reform in Springfield:

- Before: Interest on small loans (from $800 to $5,000) was limited to 7 per cent add-on, or about 13 per cent a year.

After: Interest ceilings on small loans was raised to a whopping 19.56 per cent a year. (New York and Pennsylvania have about 12 per cent. Michigan and Ohio about 13 per cent.)

"We need these rates because with some loans the risk is so great," said Morton I. Goldman, head of a loan company and president of the Independent Finance Assn.

Attorney Marvin Mindes, who argued this point with Goldman when both were members of the governor's credit committee answers: "If the risk is that great, the man shouldn't be borrowing in the first place. Some credit should not be given."

But Goldman replies: "I would say that's his business. If a man wants a loan, who is to judge whether or not he should have it?"

- Before: Small loan companies were prohibited from taking a home as security.

After: The prohibition was removed. Loan companies can now hold second mortgages and foreclose if the borrower defaults.

- Before: Loan companies were permitted to sell life insurance with their loans. This often meant requiring the borrower to take out a "credit life" policy at fat fees.

After: Loan companies now are permitted to sell life, health and accident and property insurance. The low-income man in a firetrap building, a favored mark for the loan industry, thus will pay huge insurance fees to get his loan.

- Before: There was no limit to interest charges on installment sales. A used car dealer could charge 200 per cent interest, as long as the charge appeared somewhere on the contract.

After: Two bills to set 28 per cent interest ceilings on autos and other goods died. Illinois still has no limit on installment interest.

- Before: Dealers who repossessed cars or appliances when payments fell behind could demand and collect further payments, claiming "depreciation." This is called "deficiency judgment."

"The dealer says, 'In the month you had the car you got it in such bad shape that it's now worth only $200 instead of $1,500,'" explaines Dorothy Lascoe, staff assistant in charge of garnishment cases at Inland Steel Co.

"So he garnishees the man's pay for $1,300, on a wreck of a car that was worth nothing in the first place. Then he finds another gullible buyer and sells it for $1,500 again.

After: This still happens. A bill to abolish deficiency judgments died.

"Even the legitimate parts of the credit industry wouldn't support this bill," said State Rep. Abner J. Mikva (D-Chicago).

"I'll introduce it again. It would remove the largest single source of bankruptcy and garnishment. It would mean that sellers would have to insist on a much bigger down payment to cover depreciation—so it would prevent sales to people who couldn't afford them in the first place.

"A dealer would think twice before selling. Now, he has nothing to lose."

Three other pro-consumer bills killed by the Senate Banking Committee would have tightened auto dealers license requirements, broadened the attorney general's powers of credit-abuse law enforcement, and licensed and regulated sales finance companies.

'We Tried to Solve Burglary Problems by Legalizing Burglary' --- State Rep. Abner J. Mikva

What is the total amount Wilson owes? Add these figures to find out:

$895.00	freezer
250.00	membership
168.00	canned goods and meat
+223.00	"finance charges"
______	Total amount Wilson owes.

At $12.00 a week, how long will it take Wilson to pay off his debt?

______ = Number of weeks it will take

$12(= Total amount Wilson owes

Here is another one to try. Al buys something he doesn't want, because he doesn't understand what he is signing. He refuses to pay, so the company orders his employer to garnish his wages for 20% of his $100.00 weekly paycheck. Al owes the company $220.00. How much will Al's boss take out every week (if he doesn't fire him)? How long will it take Al to pay off the debt?

EXERCISE 6. Getting the Whole Story

The Credit Reform story on page 111 is a good example of what a newspaper can do to expose people who make a lot of money from cheating the poor and uneducated. The newspaper points out that we need better laws to control this exploitation. It takes pressure from the press and the people (you) to force our lawmakers to pass these laws.

Directions: Underline part of the Credit Reform story that answers the following questions.

1. How often can you go bankrupt?

2. Why would "credit hounds" want to give credit to a bankrupt?

3. Charles signed a contract for an $800.00 coffee vending machine. What did he think he was signing?

AD A

The Atlanta Constitution

AD B

The Oregonian

EXERCISE 7. Figuring Finance Charges

Directions: Compare advertisements A and B on page 112 to answer the following questions. The answers for Ad A are given. Use a calculator if you can. In the column headed *A to B*, write the difference between the amount in Ad A and the amount in Ad B.

	Ad A	Ad B	A to B
1. Cash Sale Price.	$2850.00	________	________
2. Down Payment. If you finance the car, you must still pay this amount of cash (or trade in a car worth this).	$ 200.00	________	________
3. Amount You Are Financing (Borrowing). Subtract Down Payment from Cash Price—you are financing what's left.	$2650.00	________	________
4. Monthly Payment.	$ 61.83	________	________
5. Number of Monthly Payments.	60	________	________
6. Total Monthly Payments. Multiply Monthly Payment by Number of Monthly Payments.	$3709.80	________	________
7. Deferred Payment Price. The total price you will pay if you finance the car. Add Down Payment to Total Monthly Payments.	$ 200.00	________	
Deferred Payment Price:	$3909.80	________	________
8. The Dollar Amount of Interest. This is the extra amount you pay to finance and pay back over time. Subtract the Cash Sale Price from the Deferred Payment Price.	$2850.00	________	
Dollar Amount of Interest:	$1059.80	________	________
9. Annual Percentage Rate (APR). Also known as the True Annual Interest or True Interest. The higher the rate, the more money you pay for each dollar you borrow. The APR is difficult to calculate, so lenders must state it.	14.12%	________	________

YOUR MORGUE GROWS AND CHANGES

If you have your picture taken once a year for five years, those five pictures will show something different than five pictures of you taken all on the same day.

The pictures taken over five years show you growing and changing. Your morgue file on credit is like that. It shows a story that is constantly growing and changing.

When reporter Marjorie Hunter wrote the next story, we can guess that she went to the morgue to check on background. And the story she wrote then went in the morgue to provide background for some future story.

You need some background to understand a story. It's like coming in in the middle of a movie. You see what's going on, but you can't understand it. You have to whisper to the person next to you, "What happened before this?"

EXERCISE 8. Separating the Parts of the Story

Directions: The story has been broken into parts. Some parts have a list next to them:

Underline one label in each list to tell what kind of information is in that part of the story. Some are marked for you as examples.

Underline BACKGROUND if the part tells "what happened before this."
Underline TRUTH IN LENDING if the part tells you what is and is not in the bill, or what it would and would not do.
Underline WHY NEEDED if the part tells you why the bill is needed.
Underline WHAT NEXT? if the part tells you something to look for in the future.

EXERCISE 9. Following Up on the Credit Reform Story

Remember all the questions you had after you read the earlier story, "Credit Reform Crisis" on page 109? On page 116 is a story written eight months later that should answer those questions. Underline the part of the story that answers the following questions.

Directions: Write in the blank the number of the paragraph that answers the question.

____________1. Will the Credit Reform Bill pass? Will the governor sign it?

____________2. Will the cooling-off period be passed? Will it be 3 days or 1?

Truth in Lending Bill Voted by Senate, 92-0

By MARJORIE HUNTER
Special to The New York Times

WASHINGTON, July 11—Breaking a seven-year stalemate, the Senate unanimously passed today a so-called truth-in-lending bill to help American consumers shop for the best bargains in credit.

Long sought by both the Kennedy and Johnson Administrations, the landmark bill would require that consumers be told the approximate cost of much of the $92.5-billion in goods bought on credit each year in this country.

BACKGROUND
TRUTH IN LENDING
WHY NEEDED
WHAT NEXT?

Despite unanimous approval by the Senate, 92 to 0, the bill is expected to encounter some hostility in the House. However, chances for final passage this year now appear bright.

Big Savings Forecast

Senator William Proxmire, Democrat of Wisconsin, predicted that the bill could save consumers millions of dollars in credit costs, now estimated at about $12.5-billion a year.

BACKGROUND
TRUTH IN LENDING
WHY NEEDED
WHAT NEXT?

Sellers would be required to disclose total costs—both in terms of annual interest rates and dollar amounts—of installment buying.

Full disclosure would apply to some $30-billion in automobile sales, $20-billion in personal loans, $19-billion in large credit purchases, such as television sets, refrigerators, furniture and other appliances and furnishings, second mortgage loans and various other credit payments.

Not covered would be first mortgage loans, items with interest charges of $10 or less a year, and ordinary revolving credit accounts, on which a minimum monthly payment is required but to which new purchases may be added before the old balance is paid off.

BACKGROUND
TRUTH IN LENDING
WHY NEEDED
WHAT NEXT?

Senate passage of the bill was the climax to a fight begun seven years ago by Paul H. Douglas, Democratic Senator from Illinois until his defeat last year. Until this year, the bill had been blocked by a conservative majority on the Senate Banking Committee.

Two factors led to the breakthrough:

First, a shift in committee membership gave supporters a clear majority.

Second, Senator Proxmire, who took up the fight where Senator Douglas left off, agreed to compromises that Senator Douglas had rejected.

These compromises included exclusion of ordinary revolving credit accounts, first mortgages and small accounts involving $10 or less in annual credit charges.

Another major compromise permits "approximate" disclosure of interest rates, allowing a tolerance of about 1 per cent, instead of the "precise" disclosing on which Senator Douglas had insisted.

BACKGROUND
TRUTH IN LENDING
WHY NEEDED
WHAT NEXT?

Senate Banking Committee hearings disclosed some instances in which interest rates of 289 per cent or higher were charged on used automobiles and up to 285 per cent on television sets.

Senator Proxmire noted that a recent survey of 800 families showed that they estimated they were paying about 8.3 per cent on consumer debts. The actual figure, he said, was 24 per cent.

The bill would not regulate the amount of interest charges, but would help consumers choose the best terms.

BACKGROUND
TRUTH IN LENDING
WHY NEEDED
WHAT NEXT?

Senate passage was termed "a great victory" for the American consumer by Betty Furness, special assistant to the President for consumer affairs.

Predicting its final passage by the House, Miss Furness said the bill would enable the consumer to "shop for credit as wisely as he has been able to shop for merchandise."

Representative Leonor K. Sullivan, Democrat of Missouri, whose House subcommittee on consumers will handle the bill, described it as "a mere skeleton of what it should be." She said she would offer a far stronger bill and hold extensive hearings next month.

BACKGROUND
TRUTH IN LENDING
WHY NEEDED
WHAT NEXT?

Signs 10 Bills

Kerner OKs Credit-Buyer Protection

By Lois Wille

(1) Gov. Otto Kerner signed 10 credit reform bills into law in his Springfield office Wednesday, ending a seven-year campaign to protect buyers from cheat-and-sell artists.

(2) With his signature, he also wrote "finis" to the life and death of a young Puerto Rican named William Rodriguez.

(3) Rodriguez was a victim of an overdose of credit.

(4) Seven years ago he left his $60-a-week job as an order filler for Sears, Roebuck and Co., bought a bottle of rat poison at a drug store, and gulped it down.

(5) He died a few hours later, whispering to police that he was "hounded" by bills.

(6) He died, and the death was noted by only a few — his wife, his four children and The Daily News. His obituary was a story of life-on-the-cuff: $200 for a used and faulty television set, when he thought he was buying a new one; $117 for jewelry from a fast-talking door-to-door salesman; $34 for a bedspread left in his house 'on trial" by another salesman, who never came back but sent the bill; and on and on.

(7) **THE RODRIGUEZ** case touched the public conscience. More and more stories unfolded of the easy-credit trap that annually sucked in thousands of the illiterate and the gullible. "One Million Underdogs," a series by Daily News reporter Nicholas Shuman, exposed the state's backward credit practices and laws, which gave virtually no protection to the buyer.

(8) With great fanfare, a reform campaign was born. Committees were formed and petitions signed. Bills were prepared and introduced in the Legislature.

(9) And there it all withered away.

(10) The block, according to the handful of legislators who fought for credit reform, was the credit lobby.

(11) "The credit companies are the single most powerful and influential lobby in Springfield," says Abner J. Mikva, former Democratic representative from Chicago and author of dozens of credit bills that died.

(12) **AFTER THE FUROR** over the Rodriguez death, the credit lobby grew even stronger.

(13) "The companies were afraid of what might happen to them," said an officer of a big manufacturing firm that has long been concerned about its employes' debt problems.

(14) "They all banded together—the responsible elements and the unscrupulous ones, the banks, the loan companies, the auto dealers, the finance companies—to make sure they wouldn't be hurt."

(15) They weren't. In 1961 minor changes in wage garnishment procedure were passed. But other bills setting limits on installment charges, licensing sales finance agencies and requiring buyers to spell out interest charges on contracts were killed.

(16) **SOME OF THE BILLS** the Democrats had wanted were killed in committees, but the final package was still strong:

(17) • After purchase of merchandise of $50 or more from a door-to-door salesman, the buyer has three days to change his mind and get a full refund.

(18) • Sellers must spell out interest, insurance and other fees in dollar terms on contracts.

(19) • Maximum interest rates are set, for the first time in Illinois. On new cars, the ceiling is 15 per cent a year, or $300 for a $2,000 car. For cars less than two years old, the ceiling is 21.8 per cent. For cars between two and four years old, the ceiling is 27.5 per cent. On older cars, the ceiling is 31.5 per cent.

(20) On other merchandise, maximum interest for items under $500 is $16 a year for each $100. If the item costs $300, the ceiling is $48 a year. For items between $500 and $800, the ceiling is $14 a year for each $100. For items more than $800, it is $12 a year for each $100.

(21) • Sales finance agencies will be licensed by the state, and applicants must give proof of character. This was suggested by Charles Siragusa, executive director of the Illinois Crime Commission, as a means of weeding out hoodlums.

(22) • The portion of wages exempt from garnishment was raised from $45 a week to $65 a week for heads of families, and $50 for single persons.

(23) Democrats had hoped for more. They wanted to outlaw deficiency judgments, which permits a seller to reclaim merchandise when payments fall behind—and then sue to collect the full purchase price. This, they hope, will come in the next legislative session.

(24) In 1963 and 1965, reform packages sponsored by Democrats and pushed by Mayor Richard J. Daley were killed by Senate Republicans.

(25) But in 1967, after three Legislative failures, the reform bills finally passed.

(26) **THERE WERE THREE** big reasons for the switch, and the chief one was named W. Russell Arrington.

(27) Last December the Senate Republican leader astonished Democrats and conservative members of his own party by filing credit reform bills.

(28) Most of them were nearly identical to Daley's 1965 bills.

(29) "You stole them," cried Sen. Thomas McGloon (D-Chicago), Senate minority leader. "Comma for comma, word for word, line for line, paragraph for paragraph."

(30) Many of Arrington's colleagues thought he filed the bills because he wanted to be governor, and he wanted support of the little people.

(31) Arrington himself said he always has been a champion of the "little people," and is really a lot more liberal than his image.

(32) **McGLOON AND** other Democrats were the second big factor in the success of credit reform.

(33) They had a set of bills similar to Arrington's, but when their bills were killed they supported the Republican package. And, every time it looked as though Republicans might drop credit reform, the Democrats needled and nagged.

(34) When House majority leader William E. Pollack (R-Chicago) tried to shunt the bills to a subcommittee, minority leader John P. Touhy (D-Chicago) shouted:

(35) "This subcommittee is going to be the depository for the death of these bills."

(36) McGloon added, "Credit reform down here is strictly phony. It will be annihilated and emasculated and buried to the deep six, because it offends certain industries that produce Republican campaign contributions."

(37) **BUT SOME OF** those industries were the third reason for the success.

(38) The old coalition of credit firms broke apart, and—for the first time — responsible credit and sales agencies sat down with legislative leaders and worked out compromises. The changes were minor.

(39) But some collection agencies, door-to-door firms and sales finance agencies continued to lobby against the bills. At one point, Sen. Arthur Gottschalk (R-Flossmoor), chief sponsor of the bills, said he had been subjected to "unusual economic pressure."

(40) "There were surprising lengths to which some groups went to reach me, with regard to my livelihood," said Gottschalk, an executive for Reuben H. Donnelley Corp. "But I can assure you they didn't succeed."

(41) When the bills finally reached the Senate floor late last month, the vote was 55 to 0 for passage.

____________3. Will the confession clause be abolished?

____________4. Will finance companies and auto salesmen be licensed?

____________5. Will there be a rate cap on auto finance charges? Will it be 7% or 9%?

____________6. Will deficiency judgments be outlawed?

EXERCISE 10. Reading for Details

Directions: Underline the part of the story that answers the following questions. Write in the blank the number of the paragraph that answers the question.

____________1. Did any state senators vote against the ten credit reform bills?

____________2. What is a deficiency judgment?

____________3. What part of his weekly paycheck will a single man in Illinois now be allowed to keep when his wages are garnished?

◀ Reprinted with permission from the *Chicago Daily News*

EXERCISE 11. More Simple Math to Save Money

First, you need to know what "true interest" or "true annual interest" is.

You borrow $100.00 on January 1. One year later, on December 31, you pay back the $100.00 plus $6.00 in interest. You have had the use of the whole $100.00 for the whole year. You haven't given any of it back to the bank until the year was up. The credit cost was $6.00. $6.00 is 6% of $100.00. You have paid 6% true annual interest. (Annual means "yearly.")

Now, interest and credit charges are quoted in many different ways. Trying to compare them is like comparing apples and oranges. But if you know what they equal in *true annual interest,* then you can compare them and choose the best. That's what *truth in lending* is all about.

Directions: Study Mary Feeley's story. Then check the phrase that best completes the statement.

1. A 12-month loan is quoted to you at a discount rate of 6%. You are to pay it back in twelve equal monthly installments. The true annual interest rate on this loan is about:

____________ a. 12%

____________ b. 6%

____________ c. 4%

2. When you borrow $100.00 at a discount rate of 6% you get:

____________ a. $94.00

____________ b. $100.00

____________ c. $106.00

3. When you borrow $100.00 at an add-on rate of 6%, you pay:

____________ a. $6.00 to borrow $100.00

____________ b. $6.00 to borrow $94.00

____________ c. $11.77 to borrow $100.00

Associated Press

Truth in Lending Bill Will Tell Credit Cost

BY MARY FEELEY

[Money Management Consultant]

NO TRUTH IN lending bill could actually prevent an individual from getting into debt over his head if he's irresponsible to begin with.

But statistics show that many consumers, especially young marrieds, borrow too much for too long a period of time because they don't realize what it's going to cost them. Maybe if this new truth in lending bill, which passed the Senate and is now in the House, becomes law, it will help the public to understand more clearly the actual cost involved in using credit.

Some questions that naturally occur to the consumer at this point:

Q. Why does the consumer need a truth in lending law?

A. Because the consumer's financial stability depends in large part on his getting a fair return for his money. He should know the cost of borrowing so he can estimate his ability to repay.

Q. If borrowing can cause so much confusion for the consumer, why hasn't there been a truth in lending law before this?

A. Many economists have been concerned about this situation for years, but clarifying credit costs on a national scale is no simple matter. Many states have their own truth in lending laws. And previous bills in Congress have gotten nowhere. It has taken years of work by the National Conference of Commissioners on Uniform State Laws and others to shape one that might have any real chance of acceptance. The effort to arrive at more clarification of credit costs has involved bankers, retailers, consumer finance and small loan companies, all of whom had to be concerned not only with their own organizational structures but with varying state laws already existing.

Q. How did the cost of borrowing money get so complicated?

A. Because of the many different ways in which credit costs are set up. Financial historians point out that in the past when conservative lenders declined to accept what they thought were undue risks, other lending institutions were created to accept such risks, at a higher cost to borrowers.

Q. What will the bill as it now stands mean to the consumer?

A. If it becomes law, it will require that both the annual true interest and the dollar cost of credit be stated in the contract, in addition to the interest generally quoted. Any other charges such as service and delivery must also be clearly stated.

Q. What's so confusing about a loan that's quoted at, say, 6 per cent interest per annum?

A. Confusion can result from the fact that different types of loans, even tho quoted at the same rate, produce different true interest rates. Also, there can be confusion as to what "6 per cent" really means. A 6 per cent "add-on" loan costing $6 for $100 will amount to 11.1 per cent in true interest for 12 months. This is because the $6 [6 per cent of $100] is added to the $100 at the time you get your loan—and over a 12-month period you are actually paying interest on the full $106. You will owe about $50 at the end of six months, but you'll still paying interest on the full $106 when you make the final payment. On a 6 per cent "discount" loan costing $6 for $100, you will not receive $100 but $94. Here the true interest rate will be 11.8 per cent for a 12-month period. This is because, while you received $94, you pay interest on the full $100. With this type of loan, you have the use of less money even tho the rate quoted is the same.

Q. Are revolving credit arrangements affected by this bill?

A. No, because it would be difficult accurately to state in advance the dollar cost of revolving credit. The very fact that it's revolving means that the true cost will depend on how the monthly unpaid balance fluctuates — whether the consumer makes additional purchases from time to time during the year.

[For Mary Feeley's helpful booklet, send $1 to "Make Every Dollar Count," in care of The Tribune.]

THE NEW YORK TIMES, TUESDAY, NOVEMBER 28, 1967

City Consumers Complain About the High Cost of Credit Buying

By C. GERALD FRASER

(1) A mother of six told a consumer credit hearing yesterday that an encyclopedia set she had purchased for $400 would eventually cost her $1,400—and the company has repossessed the books.

(2) The woman, Mrs. Florence Kennely, 38 years old, wore her hat and overcoat and clutched her handbag as she sat in the witness's chair before the state Attorney General, Louis J. Lefkowitz, and described her plight.

(3) She was one of 25 witnesses at the day-long hearing out of which the Attorney General hopes to develop a truth-in-lending bill to present to the 1968 Legislature.

(4) Mrs. Kennely observed Mr. Lefkowitz' request to witnesses not to mention companies by name.

(5) A salesman came to the door of her apartment in the Abraham Lincoln Houses at 2101 Madison Avenue, she said.

(6) "He told me the school sent him," Mrs. Kennely said.

(7) "The books would cost about $400," Mrs. Kennely said, "and the salesman said I could pay for them on credit—$16.50 a month.

(8) "I paid for almost a year and stoppe dwhen I had to take a leave of absence from my job. I was out from 1963 to 1966. When I went back to work they had a garnishee on my salary.

(9) "They take out $16.30 every two weeks," she said.

(10) Mrs. Kennely, a nurse's aide at Bellevue hospital said the company used to write her letters but never sent a summons.

(11) The book company sent a man who asked her to pay $50 on her account or he would take the books.

(12) "I told him to take them," she said.

(13) When she returned to her city job and had her wages garnished, Mrs. Kennely said she went to a "lawyer in the Municipal Building" for advice.

(14) He told her, she said, that the garnishes would extend for four years and cost her about $1,400 for the balance due on the books, interest and other charges.

(15) The company told her if she wanted, she could "buy another set again."

(16) Mr. Lefkowitz punctuated Mrs. Kennely's testimony by saying: "A classic case."

(17) "There is a glaring lack of knowledge on the part of most consumers of the actual cost of credit to them.

(18) "Few families know how much interest they are paying and, tragically, the binge of borrowing has emboldened loan sharks and slippery salesmen to take advantage of an often too-trusting public."

(19) Hearings were held in the state office building at 80 Centre Street. The audience was made up of witnesses and reporters.

(20) Several witnesses told of the spiraling cost of credit for low-income families who purchase food freezer plans, furniture and "no-downpayment" automobiles.

EXERCISE 12. Reading for Information

Directions: Read the article above and write in the blank the number of the paragraph that answers the question.

__________ 1. Why were the hearings being held?

__________ 2. Why didn't Mrs. Kennely tell the name of the book company?

__________ 3. Who did the salesman say sent him?

__________ 4. At $16.50 every two weeks, how long will it take to pay the $1,400 balance?

__________ 5. Is Mrs. Kennely's case unusual?

EXERCISE 13. Reading for Information

This story on page 120 shows that even if you keep up your payments, you may not be able to get what you paid for. The carpeting company went out of business. Mrs. Hill must continue making payments, but no one is responsible if she has a complaint about her carpeting.

Directions: Underline the part of the story that answers the following questions. Write in the blank the number of the paragraph that answers the question.

__________ 1. What is the LDF?

___________ 2. How did the credit company get Mrs. Hill's contract?

___________ 3. What do the LDF attorneys want the court to decide?

___________ 4. What does LDF think credit companies will do, if they know that they will take over a seller's responsibilities when a seller goes out of business?

Credit Dealings In City's Ghettos Come Under Fire

①A major attack on consumer frauds was launched last week by attorneys of the NAACP Legal Defence and Educational Fund, Inc. (LDF) with a suit against the Coburn Credit Co., a major interstate financing company.

② The Coburn Credit Co. is charged with buying a contract from a "fly-by-night" carpeting firm, which sold wall-to-wall carpeting to poor tenants in low income housing projects at prices "so high in relation to the carpet as to render the contract unconscionable within the meaning of the Uniform Commercial Code.'

③According to the LDF attorneys, on September 9, 1965 a salesman representing himself as an agent of the Great Northern Carpet Corp. came to Marcel Hill, a tenant in a low rent public housing in Bronx county, and persuaded her to buy wall-to-wall carpeting for three small rooms of her apartment.

④"The salesman persuaded the plaintiff to sign a contract to purchase this carpeting at a price of $920.00 plus $237.57 service charge, plus $13.35 credit life insurance, plus $31.76 property insurance, for a total of $1,202.68, to be in euqal monthly installments," said the attorneys.

Not $3,000 A Year

⑤Mrs. Hill lives with her daughter and has a yearly income of about $2,281.00.

⑥"The salesman," continued the attorneys, "assured Mrs. Hill that as a term of this contract, the company would service her carpet for twenty-five years."

⑦However, the attorneys claim that within a year from the date of sale the carpeting company went out of business.

⑧Immediately after the sale to Mrs. Hill the carpet company assigned the contract to the Coburn Credit Co. This situation, argues LDF attorney Leroy Clark, leaves the credit company in a position of "enjoying all the privileges and none of the responsibilities that go with the contract."

Specific Charges

⑨Specific charges include:

Before buying the contract the credit company did not ascertain that the seller was reputable, honest, and sufficiently capitalized, and that it sold goods only on conscionable terms.

⑩The contract contained an insufficient description of goods sold.

⑪Not all the printed portion of the contract was in eight-point type.

⑫The contract did not contain all of the terms agreed to, in that it omitted the service warranty.

⑬Because of the close working relationship between the seller and the credit company with respect to this contract, the LDF attorneys argue that the defendant is responsible for the seller's contractual obligations now that the seller has gone out of business.

⑭"If we win this case on the merits," asserts attorney Clark, "credit companies will no longer be able to hide behind a mask of innocence, but will be required to investigate the companies they do business with and ascertain that those companies are dealing fairly with the public."

From the New York *AMSTERDAM NEWS*

EXERCISE 14. Using Your Own Common Sense

Directions: Write a short answer to this question: "How can borrowing from a loan shark push a person into crime?" Don't write more than four sentences. The answer is started for you.

"If you don't pay back a loan shark, he might ________________

____

____

____

Few Loan Sharks Are Hooked by New and Stricter Laws

By SYLVAN FOX

Law enforcement officials said yesterday that they were virtually helpless to deal with the spreading problem of loan-sharking despite recently enacted stricter laws designed to stamp out the racket.

Alfred J. Scotti, chief assistant district attorney of New York County, said there were fewer than a dozen loan-sharking prosecutions a year in Manhattan, one of the racket's most fruitful feeding grounds.

In Brooklyn, another section of the city where loan sharks operate actively, there are relatively few arrests for the crime, according to Elliott Golden, that borough's chief assistant district attorney.

The two officials, and other law enforcement authorities who supported them, made their observations in interviews after the Joint Legislative Committee on Crime focused new attention on loan-sharking last week at a hearing at which Michael Metzger, a New York County assistant district attorney, called it the "principal vehicle by which the underworld may infiltrate otherwise legitimate areas."

Loan-sharking, authorities have said, is an element in the charges against James L. Marcus, the former city Water Commissioner, who is accused of accepting part of a $40,000 kickback on an $835,000 reservoir cleaning contract. These authorities have said that Mr. Marcus was forced into the kickback scheme after he fell into debt to loan sharks.

The problem faced by law enforcement officials in combating the loan shark racket is not that they do not know who the loan sharks are.

"We are quite familiar with the identities of those involved," Mr. Scotti said with a faint smile.

Nor is the problem the law itself, which investigators and prosecutors agree is now adequate to deal with the challenge of usury, the statutory name for loan-sharking. The law, passed in 1965 after an inquiry into loan-sharking by the State Commission of Investigation, made it illegal to charge more than 25 per cent interest a year on loans.

The problem, the law enforcement experts said, is to collect evidence of loan-sharking that will stand up in court and win convictions. At the present time, the officials said, this is virtually impossible.

Loan-sharking seldom comes to the attention of the police, as most other crimes do. This is because loan-sharking involves a transaction in which two adults—the lender and the borrower—participate willingly, unlike a robbery, a rape or an assault in which the victim is an unwilling participant.

In this respect, loan-sharking is somewhat similar to the sale and purchase of narcotics. And like the narcotics trade, neither party to a loan-sharking transaction wants anyone else to know it has taken place.

As a result, Mr. Scotti explained, "people who borrow from loan sharks rarely come forward on their own."

The key to the control of loan-sharking, according to most investigators and prosecutors, is the wider use of wiretap and other eavesdropping devices.

"Court-ordered eavesdropping should be made available to law enforcement officials," Mr. Scotti said. "That is indispensable. It is imperative."

Telephone wiretapping is authorized by New York State law, and the Supreme Court ruled last December that the Constitution did not forbid electronic bugging by law enforcement officers if they first obtained warrants authorizing the bugging.

"If we had that, we could get them," Mr. Scotti, a small, animated, white-haired man said, snapping his fingers, "like that."

Mr. Scotti ranks loan-sharking second only to gambling as the prime source of underworld revenue, and he said the racket, which exacts interest rates up to 700 per cent and in which the Mafia is estimated to get at least $30,000 a year on every $10,000 it lends, is growing.

Law enforcement authorities have detected not only a growing level of loan-sharking activity but also some significant changes in its character.

Years ago, they noted, loan sharks preyed primarily on poor people unable to borrow from banks or other legitimate lending organizations because of a lack of collateral.

Loan-sharking then, the officials said, was strictly a financial operation backed by terror. Money was loaned, usually at the traditional six-for-five rate (paying back $6 for a $5 loan). If it were not repaid promptly, the delinquent borrower was threatened, beaten or even killed to provide an example to other borrowers.

Such strongarm tactics are still common. In Brooklyn recently, a delinquent borrower was stripped of his clothing, taken out in a boat and threatened with being thrown overboard unless he agreed to pay the money he owed the loan sharks.

But new tactics have been added to the loan shark's repertory of terror, the law enforcement officials said.

Alternatives to Payment

Today, one official said, the loan sharks and their Mafia bosses adopt the position that if a man cannot repay his loan promptly, "what use can we get from him?"

Instead of beating the victim or threatening his family, the loan shark's strongarm men persuade him to help them. If the victim is in the meat business, for example, they force him to buy a load of stolen or tainted meat. If he is in the trucking business, they make him agree to point out a shipment of valuable goods for easy hijacking.

"Once he's in that far," said one assistant district attorney, "he's in for good. He does their bidding. It's a kind of financial blackmail that results in a moral slavery."

The result is that a man who had no intention of becoming a criminal when he borrowed a few hundred or a few thousand dollars from a loan shark begins an irreversible plunge into a series of criminal activities dictated by his loan-shark masters, the official said.

"I think," he commented, 'this can happen to a public official. It can happen to anyone."

Law enforcement officials said yesterday that they were virtually helpless to deal with the spreading problem of loan-sharking despite recently enacted stricter laws designed to stamp out the racket.

Alfred J. Scotti, chief assistant district attorney of New York County, said there were fewer than a dozen loan-sharking prosecutions a year in Manhattan, one of the racket's most fruitful feeding grounds.

Nor is the problem the law itself, which investigators and prosecutors agree is now adequate to deal with the challenge of usury, the statutory name for loan-sharking. The law, passed in 1965 after an inquiry into loan-sharking by the State Commission of Investigation, made it illegal to charge more than 25 per cent interest a year on loans.

Law enforcement authorities have detected not only a growing level of loan-sharking activity but also some significant changes in its character.

Years ago, they noted, loan sharks preyed primarily on poor people unable to borrow from banks or other legitimate lending organizations because of a lack of collateral.

Loan-sharking then, the officials said, was strictly a financial operation backed by terror. Money was loaned, usually at the traditional six-for-five rate (paying back $6 for a $5 loan). If it were not repaid promptly, the delinquent borrower was threatened, beaten or even killed to provide an example to other borrowers.

Mr. Scotti ranks loan-sharking second only to gambling as the prime source of underworld revenue, and he said the racket, which exacts interest rates up to 700 per cent and in which the Mafia is estimated to get at least $30,000 a year on every $10,000 it lends, is growing.

Alternatives to Payment

Today, one official said, the loan sharks and their Mafia bosses adopt the position that if a man cannot repay his loan promptly, "what use can we get from him?"

Instead of beating the victim or threatening his family, the loan shark's strongarm men persuade him to help them. If the victim is in the meat business, for example, they force him to buy a load of stolen or tainted meat. If he is in the trucking business, they make him agree to point out a shipment of valuable goods for easy hijacking.

EXERCISE 15. Filling In the Answers

Directions: Fill in the following statements by writing in the missing word or number.

1. Usury is the statutory (legal) name for ________________.

2. In New York State, a loan-shark is someone who charges more than ____________ percent interest a year on loans.

3. The loan-sharking racket exacts interest rates up to ___________ percent.

4. The traditional loan-sharking rate was $___________ for $___________.

EXERCISE 16. Reading Newspaper Opinions

You're getting some action on the Federal Truth in Lending bill now. This *New York Times* editorial tells you about three amendments to the bill. It would like to see two dropped, but it would like to keep the third.

Directions: The three amendments are marked. Write DROP next to the two amendments the *Times* is against. Write KEEP next to the amendment the *Times* is for.

EXERCISE 17. Completing the Morgue on Credit Reform

Now the House has passed a Federal Truth in Lending bill. Reporter John D. Morris has been looking in his background file. He says, "The Senate . . . passed a less comprehensive bill."

Directions: Make a box score to compare the Senate bill and the House bill. Score them 1 for each area their bill covers. Score them 0 if they don't cover that area. The first one is done for you as an example.

Truth in Lending

As the House of Representatives takes up the long-stalemated truth-in-lending bill, the need for a strong, comprehensive law is heightened by the steady growth in the volume of consumer credit. Buyers and borrowers must have the protection of a law requiring full disclosure of the true cost of obtaining credit. These safeguards are particularly necessary for the least educated and the poorest, who can ill afford mistakes in managing their money.

The bill as it comes to the House floor would be improved if the members strike out two amendments adopted in the Banking Committee. The first would ① **exempt retail stores and mail-order houses from telling their customers the interest rate on an annual basis for so-called revolving charge accounts. An interest charge of 1.5 per cent a month on the unpaid balance sounds rather low. Yet, on an annual basis, this is 18 per cent.**

Equally objectionable is an exemption in the bill ② **providing that credit terms do not have to be detailed if the interest charge is less than $10 per transaction. As a practical matter, such a provision would exempt most loans and purchases of less than $100. This is exactly the size of transaction in which persons with the smallest incomes need protection.**

On the plus side, an amendment successfully offered in committee by Representative Halpern, Republican of New York, strengthens the bill by ③ **restricting the garnishment of wages. The first $30 of a worker's wages would be exempt from attachment by a private creditor, and no attachment could exceed 10 per cent of his remaining wages. No one would be harmed by such a modest restraint except those dubious merchants who prey upon the poor by selling shoddy merchandise on "easy" credit.**

HOUSE, 382-4, VOTES HELP TO CONSUMER

'Truth-in-Lending' Measure Now Goes to Conferees

By JOHN D. MORRIS
Special to The New York Times

(1) WASHINGTON, Feb. 1—The House passed today a comprehensive "truth-in-lending" bill designed to give consumers full and clear information on how much they pay in interest and other finance charges on loans and credit purchases.

(2) The bill, which its supporters call an unusually strong consumer protection measure, was approved on a roll-call vote of 382 to 4.

(3) The Senate unanimously passed a less comprehensive bill last year. A Senate-House conference committee will try to work out a compromise version.

(4) President Johnson issued a statement praising the House for bringing "every American consumer another step closer to knowing the cost of the money he borrows."

(5) "I urge the House and Senate to resolve their differences promptly and to give the American consumer a strong truth-in-lending bill," he added. "I hope this will be the first of many measures that will mark this Congress as the consumers' Congress."

(6) The four votes against the bill today were cast by Representatives Thomas G. Abernethy and G. V. Montgomery, Democrats of Mississippi; Robert G. Stephens Jr., Democrat of Georgia, and James A. McClure, Republican of Idaho.

(7) The House bill would require banks, finance companies, other lenders and retailers to inform borrowers and credit customers of finance charges in terms of annual percentages as well as in dollars and cents.

(8) The bill would also prescribe advertising rules for consumer loans and other consumer credit plans.

(9) Advertisements mentioning any credit terms would have to provide detailed information on annual interest rates, cash prices, incidental charges and other conditions.

(10) The Senate version does not cover advertising.

(11) Also included in the House bill but omitted from the Senate text were provisions to limit the garnishment of debtor's wages and to require the statement of credit charges on revolving charge accounts in terms of annual rather than monthly interest rates.

Revolving Accounts

(12) Revolving charge accounts are those on which interest, usually 1½ per cent, is charged on the unpaid balance at the end of each month. An interest rate of 1½ per cent a month is equivalent to one of 18 per cent a year.

(13) First-mortgage loans, exempted from the Senate bill's disclosure requirements, were included in those of the House bill.

(14) The Senate bill would exempt finance charges of $10 or less from the disclosure requirements. The House version would include them.

(15) House passage of the bill marked a high point in a seven-year battle for "truth-in-lending" legislation. Senator Paul H. Douglas, Democrat of Illinois, led the fight until his defeat for re-election in 1966.

(16) Senator William Proxmire, Democrat of Wisconsin, took over the task last year while Representative Leonor K. Sullivan, Democrat of Missouri, led the successful House fight.

(17) With "truth in lending" carrying a high priority rating in President Johnson's legislative program, the Administration actively supported the House version sponsored by Mrs. Sullivan.

	Senate bill	House bill
Advertising	0	1
Limit garnishment	____	____
Revolving charge	____	____
1st Mortgage	____	____
Interest under $10.00	____	____
Score:	____ to	____

EXERCISE 18. Reading for More Information

Directions: Underline the part of the story that answers the following questions. Write in the blank the number of the paragraph which answers the question.

____________ 1. Who voted against the House bill?

____________ 2. What is the next step to be taken in making a Truth in Lending bill into law?

____________ 3. What name would President Johnson like to see this Congress earn?

____________ 4. What is the usual yearly interest on revolving charge accounts?

____________ 5. Did the Administration support the Senate version or the House version?

CONGRESS PASSES 'TRUTH IN LENDING'

Requires Consumers Be Told Exact Charge for Loans

By JOHN D. MORRIS
Special to The New York Times

① WASHINGTON, May 22—Congress sent to the White House today a comprehensive "truth in lending" bill regarded by supporters as one of the strongest consumer protection measures in recent history.

② The measure is designed to give consumers full and clear information on how much they pay in interest and other charges on loans and credit purchases.

③ Finance companies, banks, other lenders and retailers would be required to inform borrowers and credit customers of credit charges in terms of annual percentage rates on the declining balance of obligations, with few exceptions. They would also have to inform borrowers of the dollars-and-cents cost of financing loans and purchases.

④ The measure would also impose restrictions on the garnishment of wages to satisfy debts, make extortion by loan sharks a Federal crime and seek to protect homeowners from unknowingly signing second mortgages to finance home repairs.

⑤ The final text of the bill was agreed on last Wednesday by a Senate-House conference committee after a long battle over differences between versions passed earlier by the two chambers. At the time, President Johnson acclaimed the action as "a great victory for the American consumer."

⑥ Betty Furness, the President's special assistant for consumer affairs, said tonight she was "overjoyed that the truth-in-lending bill so ardently supported by the President" had cleared Congress.

⑦ The conference agreement was approved by the House and a few hours later by the Senate on voice votes.

⑧ Disclosure provisions of the measure, officially titled the Consumer Credit Protection Act, generally apply to loans and installment purchases up to $25,000 and to mortgages of any amount for home buying. Credit for business or commercial purposes is not covered.

Special Exemptions

⑨ A special exemption is provided for installment purchases on items costing $25 or less. Items costing $25 to $75 would be exempt if the finance charge was less than $5. Up to $7.50 in finance charges would be allowed on purchases of more than $75 without requiring disclosure of the interest rate and other credit charges.

⑩ Advertisements mentioning any figures for credit would have to provide detailed information on annual interest rates, cash prices, incidental charges and other conditions.

⑪ The bill includes a special rule for "revolving" charge accounts used by many department stores and some other retailers. These accounts usually call for payment of 1½ per cent monthly on the unpaid balance. This is equivalent to 18 per cent a year.

⑫ Both monthly and annual interest rates on revolving accounts would have to be stated unless they amounted to less than 50 cents a month and were billed as service charges.

⑬ In addition, the retailer could state the "effective" annual interest rate on revolving accounts if he wished. This would take into account any free time allowed to customers, usually a brief period during which no interest is charged.

⑭ The bill's disclosure provisions and most other features would take effect July 1, 1969. Garnishment restrictions would become effective a year later.

Garnishee Exemptions

⑮ At least $48 in weekly take-home pay would be exempted from any garnishment. In any case, no more than 25 per cent of an employe's weekly take-home pay—total pay less legal deductions—could be garnisheed.

⑯ Employers would be prohibited from discharging employes because of a single garnishment.

⑰ Under the provision designed to protect homeowners from inadvertently signing second mortgages for home repairs, the bill would allow a three-day period for the owner to cancel the transaction.

⑱ The bill would make "extortionate extensions of credit," or loan sharking, subject to a maximum penalty of $10,000 and 20 years' imprisonment. It would cover attempts to collect illegal loans by "extortionate means" and apply when the interest charge was 45 per cent or more.

EXERCISE 19. Finding the End to the Truth in Lending Story

Here's the end of the Truth in Lending story. The House and Senate passed different bills. Then they had to compromise on a single, final bill to send to the President.

Directions: Circle the paragraph of the story above that answers question 1. Check the correct answer to question 2.

1. What machinery do the House and Senate have for reaching a compromise when they have passed different versions of a bill?

2. Look back at the earlier stories. Then answer this question:

The final Truth in Lending bill is closest to:

____________ a. The House version.

____________ b. The Senate version.

The Augusta Chronicle 5B

More than 36 month term

The long term loan for a car is becoming a growing trend

By HAROLD REAMES

1 Three and a half or four years is a long time to make car payments, especially when the car depreciates faster than the buyer can pay for it.

2 But 25 per cent of American car buyers are doing it these days, according to the Federal Reserve Bank.

3 Although financers encourage quick payment for cars, increasing prices are forcing more people to buy on extended term loans.

4 Last year, 16 per cent of cars financed through General Motors Acceptance Corporation were bought on loans to be paid back in more than the average 36 months. During the first three months of this year, 23 per cent of the firm's financing was done on extended term loans of 37-48 months.

5 Johnny Gray, sales manager at Walker Ford, said 25 per cent of the cars sold there are financed for 37 months or more. But only about 5 per cent of those are financed for 48 months, he said.

6 Banks are stricter in granting loans for more than 36 months, he said. "If they're going to stretch it for 48 months they want to make sure they're not going to get the car back."

7 Extended term loans are based on the stability of the applicant and his ability to pay, Jimmy Turner, vice president of retail banking for Citizens and Southern National Bank in Augusta, said.

8 When extended term loans are granted "you're increasing the number of months where you don't have value in your collateral," he said. "If a guy has been around here 15 years we don't much worry about it.

9 Less than 10 per cent of the automobile loans granted by the bank are extended term loans for new cars, Robert Swearingen, assistant manager for sales finance, said.

10 A new car's value depreciates 40 per cent during the first year after it is sold, Bill Evans of Motor Contract Co. of Augusta said.

11 Motor Contract Co. will not finance a car for more than 36 months because to do so would not be "sound business," Evans said.

12 Banks have become lenient in granting car loans because "the prices of cars are getting out of this world," he said. "Long terms and low down payments result in a lot of repossessions. Then when you repossess the car it isn't worth the balance.

13 "If you take 42-48 months to pay for an automobile you have to pay on it for three years before you have equity to trade it," he said.

14 Cars should not be financed for more than 36 months, and a 36-month loan should require 25 per cent down payment, Evans said. "It used to be you couldn't buy a vehicle for less than one-third down."

15 Walt Haskins, sales manager at Southside Datsun, said Southside's customers prefer not to buy on long term loans because the banks usually require 20 per cent or more down payment.

16 "You can offer it to them, but they would rather pay $10 or $15 more and keep it down to 36 months, he said.

17 "Banks are more aggressive" on extended term loans, Bob Richards of Bob Richards Chevrolet said. Richards said less than 5 per cent of the cars he sells are financed for 48 months

The Augusta (Ga.) *Chronicle*

EXERCISE 20. Auto Loan Vocabulary

1. "Extended term loan" is another name for a long-term loan. It is a loan that is extended, or stretched, beyond the usual 36 months. A paragraph in the article above that explains why lenders don't like to make extended term loans is number ____.

2. "Collateral" is something of value that you agree the lender can take if you don't keep up your cash payments. In an auto loan, it is usually the auto. Collateral is mentioned in paragraph number ____.

3. When a car "depreciates," it goes *down* in value. Sometimes a buyer still owes money on a loan contract even after the lender has repossessed the car. A paragraph that helps you understand how this can happen is number ____.

EXERCISE 21. Comprehension

The article on page 125 quotes five local dealers and lenders. Which ones grant loans of more than 36 months? More than 48 months?

Directions: In the table below, fill in the per cent of loans each dealer or lender makes in the two categories. Put a question mark when the article doesn't tell you for sure. And remember that "over 36" includes "over 48."

	Over 36	*Over 48*
Walker Ford	________	________
Citizens and Southern Nat. Bank	________	________
Motor Contract Co.	________	________
Southside Datsun	________	________
Bob Richards Chevrolet	________	________

EXERCISE 22. Classifying Stories in Your Morgue

You know a lot about credit now. You have more than a dozen clippings in your folder marked Credit/Loans. They are printed in this chapter in the order in which they were published—the oldest one first. But remember that you should file clippings with the oldest one on the bottom. Each new clipping is put on top.

You have so many clippings, it's hard to find just the one you want. This is the time to break the file down into narrower subjects.

Directions: The titles of clippings in this chapter have been repeated here with a number. Read the questions that follow this list and then look back over the stories. Circle the numbers of the stories that fit the description in the question. The first one is done for you as an example.

1. Juan: A Victim of Credit Sharks

2. Big Drama in Springfield

3. The Shocking Story . . . (Mrs. Wilson)

4. Credit Reform . . . Fanfare and Flop

5. New '76 Pinto Pony

6. Truth in Lending Bill Voted by Senate, 92–0

7. Kerner OKs Credit-Buyer Protection

8. Truth in Lending Bill Will Tell Credit Costs

9. City Consumers Complain . . .
10. Credit Dealings in City's Ghettos Come Under Fire
11. Few Loan Sharks Are Hooked . . .
12. Truth in Lending (Editorial)
13. House, 383–4, Votes Help to Consumer
14. Congress Passes "Truth in Lending"
15. The long term loan for a car . . .

1. Find three clippings that tell how a racket works. They will go into a file labeled, Credit Racket Examples.

(1) (2) 3 (4) 5 6 7 8 9 10 11 12 13 14

2. Find one clipping that tells about borrowing money—rather than about getting credit when you buy something.

1 2 3 4 5 6 7 8 9 10 11 12 13 14

3. Find two clippings that tell about the Federal Truth in Lending Law.

1 2 3 4 5 6 7 8 9 10 11 12 13 14

4. Find one clipping about a credit company's rights and responsibilities.

1 2 3 4 5 6 7 8 9 10 11 12 13 14

5. Find one clipping that advertises cars sold on credit.

1 2 3 4 5 6 7 8 9 10 11 12 13 14

6. Find two clippings that tell about state-level action on credit reform.

1 2 3 4 5 6 7 8 9 10 11 12 13 14

EXERCISE 23. Thinking About Credit

Get ready for a class discussion of credit sharks and loan sharks. Look back at clipping 1 and clipping 2. How are credit sharks and loan sharks alike? How are they different?

You need to know this extra fact: The courts say credit service charges are not interest. So they are not covered by loan-shark laws.

PRACTICE IN YOUR LOCAL NEWSPAPER

PRACTICE 1. Find a story in your local paper with a couple of paragraphs of background information. For example, the paragraphs on the background of the fight for Truth in Lending legislation in clipping, "Bill on Truth in Lending is Voted by Senate." Mark the background paragraphs.

PRACTICE 2. Find and bring in ads for bank or finance company loans. What methods do they use to persuade you to borrow?

PRACTICE 3. Ask someone else in the class to work with you in a skit to act out in front of the class. One of you will be a "schlock merchant." The other will be a tenant who is determined not to get stuck with a credit contract. Look at clippings 1, 2 and 3 for ideas for your skit.

PRACTICE 4. Start your own clipping file. Choose a subject (like credit, job ideas, party food recipes); or a person (like Barbra Streisand, O.J. Simpson, Chris Evert); or a place (Antarctica, Puerto Rico, your section of the city). Make a file folder for your subject and bring it to class with your first clipping in it. Keep this file in school where you and other students can use it and watch it grow.

CHAPTER 10
USING THE NEWSPAPER TO FIND JOBS AND CAREERS

Many students find jobs by reading news articles like the one on the next page. They don't wait until the last minute to look for work. Notice that this article about summer jobs appeared in March.

You can tell that another article has appeared by the phrase "Second in a series." Since more articles may be published, an interested reader would check tomorrow's paper by scanning headlines and looking for the byline by Marjorie Brahms.

EXERCISE 1. Skimming for an Overview

Directions: Skim the following story by reading *only* the first sentence in each paragraph. Then answer the questions which follow it by going back and finding the information requested. (If you skimmed well, you will know just about where the information for each question is given.)

For job-hunting students: an important telephone number

By Marjorie Brahms

(Second in a series)

Starting in April, one of the most important things a job-hunting student will need to know is this telephone number: WE 9-1968.

That will be the central number at the Illinois State Employment Service for high school and college students seeking summer jobs.

It is also the number for employers who want to place job orders with the statewide service.

Job seekers are advised to ask for "Mr. Summers" and to state that they are looking for summer work. They will then be told to come into the ISES office at 608 S. Dearborn, where, according to present plans, about 25 staff members will be on hand to interview them.

Last summer the ISES sought jobs for some 20,000 young people, about one-third of those in the Chicago area who were looking for work.

This summer, ISES youth officials expect the number of job-seeking young people to increase.

For "early birds" who want to get started before the central telephone number and listings officially go into effect in April, the ISES suggests registering now at one of its offices, listed in the telephone directory.

Most ISES jobs in previous summers have been in service industries. Among them have been:

Gas station attendant, fountain clerk, car washer, countergirl, user, busboy, carhop, waiter, concession attendant, babysitter, delivery boy, window washer, caddie and orderly.

Other jobs the ISES expects to have available include cook, guide, tutor, typist, receptionist, office clerk, library aide, sales clerk, survey worker, lifeguard and laboratory assistant.

ISES "job development teams," which work year-round, are now asking employers to list jobs for students.

Mayor Daley's summer jobs for youth committee, meanwhile, is also trying to encourage employers to hire vacationing students. These jobs will be listed with the ISES, as will jobs with federal agencies and some union jobs.

The major thrust of the ISES "Summer Jobs for Youth" program is to provide jobs for students from low-income families. The ISES encourages students who are able to use "connections" with family and friends to obtain jobs in that way. It also asks that some of these students, who want to work for experience and personal satisfaction rather than because of financial need, consider volunteer work. Jobs in hospitals social service agencies, nursery schools, camps, settlement houses and the like, ISES officials said, might prove more rewarding than a paid job and would help to provide work for students who need money to return to school.

1. Write the central number at the Illinois State Employment Service for high school and college students seeking summer jobs. ________________

____

2. Give the name of the man you are told to ask for when seeking summer work. ________________________________

3. Does the article suggest that preference may be given to youth from "low-income families?" Circle: YES or NO

4. When can you start calling WE 9-1968 to get job listings? ____________

____

5. Where can an "early bird" register? ____________

____

6. How can an "early bird" locate the street address for an office of the Illinois State Employment Service? ____________

____

7. Name two jobs listed last summer which a boy interested in cars could apply for. ____________

____

8. List one job which an assistant in the school library would have a good chance to get. ____________

EXERCISE 2. Understanding Implied Meanings

Directions: Reading between the lines and using common sense will help anyone get a job more easily. Take out job insurance by looking ahead. Read the situations described below. From what you have read and what you know from common sense, circle YES or NO to show your answers.

Would your chances of finding work through the ISES office be better if . . .

YES NO 1. you had a reference from your gym instructor stating you had passed your senior lifeguard test and had experience as a pool guard?

YES NO 2. you could furnish written references from mothers for whom you had done babysitting?

YES NO 3. you had held a part-time car-washing job at a neighborhood gas station.

YES NO 4. you admitted you had never done any kind of work but wanted to earn spending money?

FINDING JOBS IN ADS

Another place to look for jobs is in the Classified Ad Section. Not all Want Ads are about jobs. First, study any Index you are using to see how it is organized. For example, do the subheads use symbols (such as a graduate's cap for Schools) to help you? Are ads for Employment separated from those offering Instruction? Is the number following an entry a page number or the number appearing at the top of a column containing ads for jobs of that kind?

EXERCISE 3. Using the Ad Index

Directions: Study the Classified Index and Information Guide reproduced here. Show that you know how to use it by writing the number you would find at the top of the column for each entry in the classified section. The first one is done for you.

230 1. Help Wanted, Part time

______ 2. Correspondence Schools

______ 3. Employment Agencies

______ 4. Household Help

______ 5. Tutoring

______ 6. Trade Schools

______ 7. Employment Services, Counseling

______ 8. Help Wanted, (not part time)

______ 9. Positions Wanted, Men*

______ 10. Positions Wanted, Women*

* *Note:* Never apply for jobs described in ads under Positions (or Situations) Wanted. These are ads placed by people who are looking for jobs.

526-8892
Want Ad Direct Line
7:30 A.M.-6 P.M. Daily
10 A.M.-2 P.M. Sunday

Check the Want Ads now for autos, houses, apartments, jobs, furnishings, appliances, pets, merchandise, business opportunities, industrial, leisure, etc.

CLASSIFIED INDEX AND INFORMATION GUIDE

Designed for easy, fast reference to All CLASSIFIED ADS!

ANNOUNCEMENTS

Dine Out 110
Personals 115
Car Pools 118
Insurance 120
Income Tax Service 125
Special Notices 130
Day Care, Baby Sitter
Service 140
Cars Furnished,
Travel, Tours 145
Lost 150
Found 151

DIRECTORY OF SERVICES

BUSINESS SERVICES OF ALL KINDS
Over 40 numbered classifications; arranged alphabetically by type of service offered. A classification for every need.

INSTRUCTION

College Level Instruction . . 155
Vocational, Trade Schools . 160
Business Schools 165
Correspondence Schools . . . 170
Private Instruction,
Tutoring 175
Kindergarten 180

EMPLOYMENT

Employment Agencies 210
Employment Services,
Counseling 215
Household Help 220
Help Wanted 225
Help Wanted, Part time . . 230
Postitions Wanted, Men . . . 240
Positions Wanted 242
Positions Wanted, Women. 245

FINANCIAL

Franchises, Distributorships,
Investments 250
Business Opportunities 258
Business For Sale 260
Bids Wanted 265
Stocks, Bonds, Royalties . . 270
Wanted to Borrow 275
Money To Loan 280

PETS, LIVESTOCK, AGRICULTURE

Dogs, Puppies, Supplies . . . 305
Cats, Misc, Pets,
Supplies 307
Livestock Supplies 310
Poultry, Eggs, Supplies . . . 315
Grain, Hay, Feed,
Seed, Plants 320
Fertilizers, Chemicals,
Sprays 325
Farm Imp., Tractors,
Misc 330

MERCHANDISE

Auctions 400
Heavy Equipment,
Machines 405
Shop Tools, Machines,
Engines 410
Logs, Sawmills,
Equipment 415
Building Materials 420
Buildings For Sale 425
Office Equip., Supplies . . . 430
Store, Restaurant Equip . . 435
Miscellaneous 440
Air Conditioning, Heating . 445
Swaps 450
Gift Suggestions 455
Good Things To Eat 460
Wearing Apparel 465
Diamonds, Watches,
Jewelry 470
Musical Merchandise 475
TV, Stereo, Radio,
Recording 480
Garage Sale 484
Household Goods 485
Sewing Machines 487
Antiques 490
Wanted To Buy 495

LEISURE ACTIVITIES

Boats, Motors, Supplies . . . 505
Hunting, Fishing Needs . . . 510
Sporting, Goods,
Games, Hobbies 515
Campers, Trailers,
Motor Homes 520
Recreation Vehicles 525
Coins, Stamps,
Collectors Items 520
Movies, Cameras, Film . . . 540
Lawn, Garden 545

REAL ESTATE, RENT

Resort, Recreation Prop . . 605
Room and Board 610
Nursing Homes, Care 612
Rooms 615
Wanted To Rent 620
Rentals to Share 625
Apartments, Furnished . . . 630
Apartments, Unfurnished . . 640
Renters, Services, Mgmt . . 642
Duplexes, Townhouses,
Condominiums,
Furnished 645
Duplexes, Townhouses,
Condominiums,
Unfurnished 650
Homes, Furnished 655
Homes, Unfurnished 660
Rentals, Suburban 665

COMMERCIAL, INDUSTRIAL PROPERTY

Office, Desk Space, Rent . . 705
Warehouse Space, Rent . . . 710
Commercial Prop, Rent . . . 715
Industrial Prop., Rent 720
Wanted To Rent 725
Property Management 730
Commercial,
Industrial Services 735
Commercial Prop., Sale . . . 740
Industrial Prop., Sale 745
Investment Prop., Sale . . . 750
Wanted To Buy 755

REAL ESTATE, SALE

REFER TO WANT ADS MAP, POSITIONED IN REAL ESTATE CLASSIFICATIONS, TO PINPOINT LOCATION OF ADVERTISED PROPERTY.
Out of Town Realty 805
Mississippi Real Estate . . . 807
Farm Lands, Sale,
Rent, Wanted 810
Cemetery Lots 815
Lots, Subdivisions 820
Suburban Acreage 825
Homes, Suburban 827
Realty Wanted 830
Realty Exchange 835
Realty Loans, Insurance,
Notices 837
Resort, Recreation Prop . . 840
Homes, Area 1 845
Homes, Area 2 850
Homes, Area 3 855
Homes, Area 4 860
Homes, Area 5 865
Homes, Area 6 870
Homes, Area 7 875
Homes, Area 8 880
Homes, Area 9 885
Homes, Area 10 887
Mobile Home Living 895
Mobile Home Lots
Rent, Sale 897

TRANSPORTATION

Motorcycles, Bikes 905
Airplanes, Services 910
Auto Trailers 915
Auto Parts, Services 920
Trucks, Trailers, Buses . . . 925
Auto, Truck Lease, Rent . . 930
Auto, Trucks Wanted 935
Import, Sports Cars 940
Antiques, Classic Cars,
Parts 945
Automobile Notices 950
Automobiles for Sale 960

The Commercial Appeal

FINDING JOB OPPORTUNITIES THROUGH READING ADS

Don't wait until you need a job to study want ads. Get a head start by checking ads now to see just what kinds of jobs employers are trying to fill. This is one way to find answers to questions like these:

1. What qualifications are required for jobs which interest you?

2. Which firms give on-the-job training?

3. Are you taking the right kind of courses for the job you hope to get?

4. Do you have a special ability that employers are looking for?

You can practice using ads in this way by doing the following exercise.

EXERCISE 4. Getting Information for Future Jobs

Directions: Look over the group of ads reproduced on these pages. Answer the questions for each ad by circling YES or NO. Each ad is numbered. Study only that ad for the questions asked about it.

Ad 1

YES NO 1. Are Keypunch Operators offered a full-time permanent job?

YES NO 2. Are there openings in more than one shift?

YES NO 3. Can you tell the machines on which you must have had recent experience?

YES NO 4. Does the company offer Profit Sharing?

YES NO 5. Is Discount Shopping a benefit?

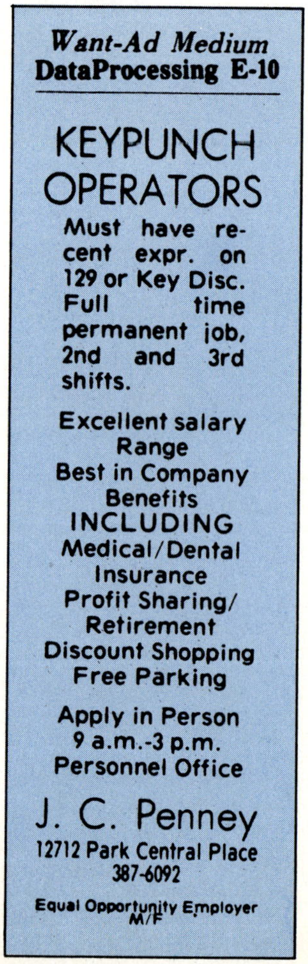
Want-Ad Medium
DataProcessing E-10

KEYPUNCH OPERATORS

Must have recent expr. on 129 or Key Disc. Full time permanent job, 2nd and 3rd shifts.

Excellent salary Range
Best in Company Benefits
INCLUDING
Medical/Dental Insurance
Profit Sharing/ Retirement
Discount Shopping
Free Parking

Apply in Person
9 a.m.-3 p.m.
Personnel Office

J. C. Penney
12712 Park Central Place
387-6092

Equal Opportunity Employer M/F

Dallas Morning News

BEAUTY
Operators

NEW TO AREA OK

Compare our salon look. Quality products and paid benefit plan, high commission, paid vacation and holidays, medical and dental available, profit sharing and no supply costs.

APPLY IN PERSON

JCPenney

Southcenter
Retail Store

An Equal Opportunity Employer

Reprinted from the *Seattle Times*

Ad 2

YES NO 1. Can a person who has just moved to Seattle get the job?

YES NO 2. Does an operator qualify for paid vacation and holidays?

YES NO 3. Can you tell if an operator is paid a salary?

YES NO 4. Can you tell if the company pays for medical and dental insurance?

YES NO 5. Can an operator participate in Profit Sharing?

SECRETARY

Perform standard secretarial and clerical duties. Some shorthand required. Also, basic accounting skills and statistical typing involved.

We offer salary commensurate with experience plus liberal fringes, such as: 37½ hour work week, free dental, medical, life insurance, sick leave, etc.

Apply in person between 8:30 am-11 am and 1 pm-4pm; call 213/549-7600 ext. 227

TOYOTA

Industrial Trucks, U.S.A. Inc.
1041 East 230th St.
Carson, California 90745
An Equal Opportunity Employer M/F

From the *Los Angeles Times*. Permission courtesy of Toyota Industrial Trucks, U.S.A., Inc.

Ad 3

YES NO 1. Would 3 years experience as a bookkeeper help a person get this job?

YES NO 2. Would a portfolio of statistical charts typed for a thesis be a good thing to present to the interviewer?

YES NO 3. Would the hours enable a person to attend evening school?

YES NO 4. Does the company pay for dental, medical, and life insurance?

YES NO 5. Is this job in Los Angeles?

FILE CLERK TRAINEE

$400-475/MO.

File forms, records, and letters. Also handle mail and lite typing of forms. Benefits include 80% college tuition refund. For your interview call 281-6263. INTERNATIONAL BUSINESS ASSOCIATES, INC., 1301 Chamber of Commerce Bldg., Empl. Agcy.

The Pittsburgh Press

Ad 4

YES NO 1. Does this job require experience?

YES NO 2. Does this job require a person to be able to type 50 WPM?

YES NO 3. Would this job be a good one for someone who wants to go to college?

YES NO 4. Is this job offered by an employment agency?

YES NO 5. Does this job require an interview?

EXERCISE 5. Using the Telephone

Learning to get information by phone can save you time and effort. You may find out from a phone call that you don't have all the qualifications required for the job or that there are things about it you don't like. In either case you will have saved yourself an unnecessary trip.

Directions: Here is an ad that gives you a telephone number to call. On the lines next to it, write four or more questions you might want to ask when you phone.

STUDENTS
8th, 9th, 10th, Grade
Maryland Area
GAITHERSBURG
ROCKVILLE
ONLY
WHO CAN WORK
AFTER SCHOOL AND
ALL DAY SAT.
For Major Newspaper
Circulation Campaign
IF YOU WANT TO EARN
$30 TO $50 WK.
COMMISSION +
PRIZES
AND OUT OF TOWN
TRIPS, CALL
JOHN GREEN
MON. THRU FRI.
Hrs: 11 A.M. to 3 P.M.
656-4114

Look back over your questions. Are there any you should or could answer yourself before you phone? Cross out such questions.

WATCH OUT FOR COME-ON ADS

When you read Help Wanted ads, remember that the newspaper staff has not written the ads. The newspaper sells the space to the advertiser, and the advertiser supplies the words.

Most Help Wanted ads you find in the newspaper will be legitimate, but some of them will not. Learn to be sharp in reading between the lines, so that you can at least avoid the more obvious of the ads that aim to trick you.

Some advertisers have ways of getting young people to work for very little money just by holding out the promise of lots of money to be made later. Don't be taken in!

Ad #1.

TEL. Sales—Comm. Ofc. supplies

★

CLEAR

$500 PER WEEK

Yes it's possible!

EARN WHILE YOU LEARN.

Call for immediate appt!
MR. NELSON

213/828-5633

U.S. Toner Corp.

Ad #2.

TRAVEL

MEN-WOMEN

Can place 10 over 18. Free to travel major U.S. Cities. No exp. necessary. On the job training. Job transportation furn. Cash advanced. Good potential earnings. For appt. apply Holiday Inn, 2247 E. Van Buren or Phone 244-9347.

Arizona Republic

Ad #3.

EARN

$400. Per Mo.

While In Training

If you have a High School diploma and havn''t been able to find a good job—call us—We offer practical training and counselling—we teach resume writing—we have a full time placement counselor to help you. Call 329-1000. Ask about "Job Readiness Training."

Arizona Republic

Ad #4.

I AM A SUCCESS!

I get a monthly clothing allowance.
I get a monthly car allowance.
I get free hospitalization, including $10,000 Life Insurance.
I also get a 2-week all expense paid vacation.

If you are a man or woman and not earning a least $1000 per month and receiving all the above benefits then you ARE only cheating yourself.

You Can Have The Good Life!

We Have The Formula!

Personal interview only.
MON. NOV. 8th 1976
1 PM SHARP
NO OTHER TIME
Saddleback Inn
24th St. & Camelback

Absolutely No Phone Calls
Master Mfg. Co.

Reprinted from the *Seattle Times*

Look at Ad #1. Does "Clear $500 Per Week" seem a likely amount to "earn while you learn"? Does the ad give the name of the company? What does the small print at the top of the ad tell you?

Now look at Ad #2. Does the ad say that the "on the job training" and "job transportation" are free? Why would the company be willing to give "cash advances"? Does the ad give the name of the product or service being sold? What does "good potential earnings" really mean?

Read Ad #3. Does the ad guarantee you a job, or is the "Earn $400 Per Mo" a come-on? Does placement of this ad under "360 Training for Jobs" tell you that this is probably only an offer of instruction which may or may not help you get a job?

Study Ad #4. Does it give any job description? Why does the ad say "Absolutely No Phone Calls"? Does the ad say that you will get the benefits that the "I" in the ad enjoys, or does it just imply this?

There is nothing illegal about these ads. It is up to you to be smart enough to follow certain hints when you read the Classified Ads in your paper:

1. Read the ads carefully and ask yourself some questions as we did above. Use common sense!

2. Never sign anything without reading it over carefully for yourself, and understanding it for yourself. Don't accept someone else's explanation of what it means. One man was told he was signing an agreement to sell a new coffee maker to restaurants, and then found out that the contract required him to buy one of the $1,200 coffee makers on time as a "sample."

3. Try to find out if the company you consider working for is reliable. Ask older people you trust if they know anything about it. How many employees does it have? How long has it been operating?

CHICAGO TRIBUNE, SUNDAY, APRIL 14, 1968

Answering a Want Ad in the Chicago Tribune's MID AMERICA JOB-GUIDE?

Improve your chances for employment. SUBMIT A RESUME to the employer or employment agency. Here's how to do it.

LIST THE FOLLOWING FACTS IN YOUR RESUME:

YOUR NAME Address:	Home phone number Business phone
Personal:	Age, height, weight, marital status, number of dependents.
Education:	School name, grade attained; high school, college diplomas, special schools, honors received. Extracurricular activities. Offices held.
Business Experience:	List present or last position first. Give date of joining and leaving companies, kind of business, addresses, positions held. Be explicit. Describe your exact duties, progress, accomplishments. Give reason for leaving each position. List your supervisor or other references for each job.
In a supplementary paragraph:	List any other information that may interest the employer and help him fit you into a job. Include a photograph of yourself. Be brief and factual. Be informative and neat. Be complete—use a second page, if necessary. For the largest selection of jobs in Mid America, make it a habit to see offers below this heading:

Reprinted, courtesy of the *Chicago Tribune*

POINTERS FOR EFFECTIVE JOB INTERVIEWS

1. DO be prompt for your appointment. This indicates to the employer he may expect the same consideration from you when he is paying you for your time.
2. RELAX! Be gracious and courteous.
3. DO fill out your application completely and neatly.
4. DO show an interest—ask questions about the company and the job.
5. DO speak clearly and to the interviewer. Direct eye contact is very important.
6. DON'T chew gum.
7. DON'T make slighting references about previous employers, friends, school, etc.
8. DON'T boast. Confidence is fine, but be sure your interviewer knows you have the ability to merit his confidence, too.
9. DO sell the employer if you feel you really want the job. DON'T be afraid to let him know how you feel.
10. DO be responsive to any sign that the interview is over. Thank the interviewer for his time and consideration.

Tho you cannot practice for an interview, keeping these basic do's and don'ts in mind will enable you to make a better impression on your prospective employer.

To hire help quickly, dial 222-4242

Reprinted, courtesy of the *Chicago Tribune*

OTHER WAYS NEWSPAPERS HELP YOU GET WORK

Newspapers want you to find a job that they are advertising. Because of this they sometimes give advice on how to apply. Study the suggestions about preparing a résumé and the pointers for effective job interviews. Knowing what to do and what not to do at the job interview can mean the difference between working and not working.

Perhaps your teacher will set aside some time for acting out some practice interviews.

LEARNING FROM THE EXPERTS

Newspapers contain many articles about careers written by experts. Study carefully what each has to say. But don't stop there! Check things out for yourself. The article below refers you to valuable resources you can find at your school or public library. Always keep in mind that predictions about careers can change, and that you need to be constantly updating your information.

Some good guides for career advice

A lot of free advice on career choices is close at hand at your local public library. Here's some valuable resources you may want to consult:

● If you're looking for the addresses and names of persons to write at potential employers, reach for Moody's Industrial Index, Standard & Poor's Index, and Thomas' Register. The College Placement Annual also lists 1,400 businesses and government agencies, along with persons to contact.

● If you want to write for a variety of career and guidance material, consult the Educators Guide to Free Guidance Material. If you want to read such material compiled into a single volume, look for the Occupational Outlook Handbook, the Dictionary of Occupational Titles, and the Encyclopedia of Careers and Vocational Guidance. You may also consult general encyclopedias under the subject headings, vocation or careers.

● If you want to read magazines on the subject of careers, look for such publications as Manpower, Occupational Outlook Quarterly, Career World, Today's Secretary, and Vocations for Social Change.

● If you seek schools offering preparation for careers, consult Barron's Guide to Two-Year Colleges, Vol. 2 — Occupational Program Selector. The Guide to College and Career Planning also may be helpful.

Several books on the subject of careers also have been published, especially in recent months. Ask your librarian for help in finding them.

A number of magazine articles on the subject also have been written. You may locate them by consulting A Reader's Guide to Periodical Literature.

Reprint, courtesy of *Chicago Tribune*

PLANNING FOR YOUR CAREER

Your career will be a very important part of your life. We spend most of our waking hours at our jobs, so we should be happy in the work we chose to do. Newspapers often carry stories about people who have achieved success. The stories tell how they got started, what things helped them to succeed, and which obstacles almost defeated them.

You can learn many things about careers and get some ideas of your own by reading these biographical stories. Often the person admits riding a hobby into a successful career. They counsel young people to find something they really enjoy doing.

If you have a hobby you enjoy, you may want to look for careers which require similar skills. Suppose you enjoy taking pictures. You might find a career in photography the life work you would most enjoy.

EXERCISE 6. Getting Career Ideas from the Newspaper

Directions: Read each of these articles to see how newspapers might help you become a professional photographer. After each article you will find a question. Write a one-sentence answer in the space provided.

Model 1.

Life in Wisconsin Pond Spawns Photo Exhibit

BY ERWIN BACH

A 20-year career with Life magazine took Photographer Wallace Kirkland, 224 S. East av., Oak Park, to such faraway places as India to meet and work with such personalities as Gandhi, but it's the assignment back home he treasures.

Recently he took hundreds of pictures of life in a Wisconsin pond, but he claims his most satisfying picture assignment was the time he spent photographing an Indiana poorhouse.

Kirkland will talk on "Photographing the Little Things in Life" at 12:15 p. m. next Thursday in the main public library's second-floor assembly hall at Randolph street and Michigan avenue. Admission is free to the show.

Worked with Walt Disney

Well known for his picture story of an otter, Kirkland also worked as cameraman on the Walt Disney film about an otter.

Altho he retired from the magazine's staff in 1957, he continued to travel and has written two books, "Recollections of a Life Photographer"; and "Shenshoo, the Moose." He is just completing a third called "The Pond."

His talk, illustrated with 100 color slides, highlights the tiny creatures living in his "pond" [which is an imaginary composite of several ponds]. There are dragonflies, firebugs, mosquitoes, and the Cecropia moth shown in their complete life cycles.

Born in Jamaica

"I get a little philosophical about such things in nature," said Kirkland, who was born in Jamaica and came to this country when he was 14.

"It suddenly dawned on me the other day when I was drying milkpod seeds that they resembled caterpillars twisting in their cocoons [Cecropia caterpillars feed on milkweed]," he said.

Worked with Jane Addams

Apart from discovering such parallels in nature, Kirkland also conducted a summer workshop in photography at the Peninsular School of Arts, Fish Creek, Wis., and recently filmed a safari in Mozambique.

Kirkland came to Chicago in 1914 to study sociology at George Williams college, then in the city. He lived at Hull House working with the late Jane Addams as a Y. M. C. A. secretary.

"Jane Addams, like Gandhi, was one of the 'greats' in this world," he said. "She had empathy—not sympathy, that's only feeling sorry for someone from the outside—actually getting inside a person and feeling the way they do."

Q. If this article were in your paper today, what could you do to get first hand information about a career in magazine photography? ____________

____

____

____

____

High Schools' State Photo Contest Begins

BY ERWIN BACH

A search for the state's outstanding high school photographer is again being sponsored this year by the Illinois Press Photographer association. Last year's winner was Mike Polillo of St. Teresa High school, Decatur.

To enter the contest you must be an Illinois high school student and submit five to 10 unmounted black and white pictures [the longest side must be 10 inches], postmarked no later than March 31.

Entries may be sent to T. Jan Wiseman, Glenbrook North High school, 2300 Shermer rd., Northbrook, 60062. Final judging will be held on April 13 at Forest View Hgh school, 2121 S. Goebbert st., Arlington Heights.

Name Contest Judges

This year's judges are Hallie Hamilton, photojournalism teacher at Northern Illinois university, De Kalb; Robert Strawn, Rolling Meadows, who was named suburban photographer of 1967 [he works for Paddock Publications, Inc. of Arlington Heights]; and Clifford Rowe, Elk Grove Village, an associate editor for Paddock Publications.

Awards are made in three categories: photographer of the year; best print of the show; and best high school newspaper. Each young photographer is judged on the basis of his portfolio of pictures entered.

Last year's contest drew 39 portfolios totaling 353 prints from high school photographers, said Wiseman. Finishing second in the outstanding photographer of the year category was Robert Johnson of Wheeling High school, Wheeling. William Burlingham of New Trier East, Winnetka, came in third.

Wins 1967 Award

Neil Krey of Forest View High school,Arlington Heights, won the 1967 best print of show award with his still-life of a glass pear reflecting sunlight from a window.

Photographs are judged on the basis of versatility and originality of style, as well as technical excellence.

The winning photographer of the year receives a free photography course, a trophy, a subscription to National Press Photographers magazine, and free registration in the Illinois Press photographer association.

Reprinted, courtesy of the *Chicago Tribune*

Model 2.

Q. What teacher in your high school might have more information about this contest? ________

____

____

____

Camera Club Notes

Fort Dearborn-Chicago Camera club again will hold its 8-week Evening School of Photography starting at 7 p. m. March 26 in the club's third floor quarters at 30 S. Michigan av. The Tuesday evening sessions will run thru May 14.

Loren Root, school director, said the course will cost $20 and will cover such topics as film development and processing, color films, printing and enlarging, lighting, protraiture, and how to see pictures. For application blanks, write to Miss Mary Gray, secretary, Fort Dearborn Evening School of Photography, 30 S. Michigan av.

A panel program, "Ask An Expert," will be held at 8 p. m. tomorrow by the **Fort Dearborn Camera Club**, 30 S. Michigan av. Come with questions for panelists Mrs. Mary Root, Miss Carol Rice, Tom Pake, and others. Club operation, and printing are among the topics.

Works of two young photographers, **Barry Burlison** 4457 N. Drake av.; and **Barry Koral**, 3036 Princeton av., now are on display for 20 weeks at the Hull House [Jane Addams center] - theater gallery, 3212 Broadway. The 30 pictures concern the human figure primarily treated in multiple image combinations. Both men are graduate students in Illinois Institute of Technology's institute of design and are working for their master's degrees in photography.

Moviemakers with a taste for the experimental are invited to enter the **Seventh Annual Independent Film Makers festival** sponsored by Foothill college, Los Altos Hills, Cal.

For entry forms, write to Gary Hair, student coordinator, Independent Film Makers festival, Foothill college, 12345 El Monte rd., Los Altos Hills, Cal. 94022

Reprinted, courtesy of the *Chicago Tribune*

Model 3.

Q. How could you find out if the camera you own could be used in the photography course?

____

____

____

____

Model 4.

Q. Why should you call the Picture Editor from as close to the scene of news as possible?

Chicago's American

PRACTICE IN YOUR LOCAL NEWSPAPER

PRACTICE 1. Bring in the classified advertising section from your local paper. Mark three or four jobs which interest you and which you think you would qualify for now.

PRACTICE 2. Clip out any special features from your newspaper which would help you get a job or plan for a career.

PRACTICE 3. Cut out three job ads that interest you and fasten them to a sheet of paper. Underline the names and addresses of the agencies or companies. Using street maps and transportation maps, find out how you would reach each address from your school. Write brief directions next to each ad. Tell about how long the trip would take and how much it would cost.

PRACTICE 4. Have you or one of your friends ever been "burned" in a job search? Did you learn about a job-offer "con game" from a newspaper story or television program? Use a notebook page to jot down a few sentences explaining the trick so that others will recognize it and avoid it. If you don't know of any tricks, use the space to put in your own words some of the advice given in this chapter. The teacher may call on you to read what you have written. Read it over to yourself a few times so that you can speak without stumbling.

PRACTICE 5. Your teacher will group you into committees. Study the Help Wanted ads and choose three ads to investigate. Discuss what the ads say, and what they might mean. Write a group report with about five sentences of comment on each ad. Be sure to tell what you know about the company or agency, or where you would turn to find out.

PRACTICE 6. Get ready to write a résumé. Take a page from the job ads section. Circle in color five words or phrases that give you an idea for information to include in a résumé. For example, if the ad says "Your typing speed should be 40 wpm or better," that is a reminder to include your typing speed in your résumé. So underline typing speed. Write your usual heading on a sheet of notebook paper; fold the newspaper page to about the same size and attach the notebook sheet to it.

PRACTICE 7. Write a résumé of about ten lines that you could leave with employment agencies or prospective employers. Use the suggestions from Practice 6, and from the résumé outline on page 138.

PRACTICE 8. Salaries in the want ads of your local paper can be quoted per hour, per week, per month, and per year. You know that $240 a month is less than $60 a week, but it is hard to make comparisons. Your teacher may assign you to a committee to work out a chart to make it easy to compare one figure with another, in the salary ranges a high school student is likely to be offered for summer work. A line on the chart would look like this:

per hour	40 hr. wk.	per month	per year
$1.50	$60	about $260	$3,120

(To get the monthly figure, multiply the weekly figure by 52 weeks, then divide by 12 months.)

CHAPTER 11

AN EDITORIAL IS AN ARGUMENT

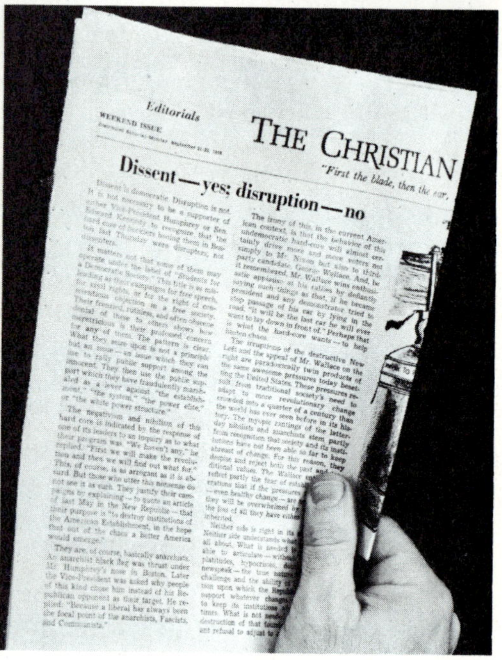

A news story gives you information. It lets you decide what *you* think about it.

An editorial gives you an argument, in the sense that "to argue" means "to give reasons for or against." The editorial comes right out and tells you what the newspaper owners and managers think. It gives reasons why you should think the same way.

There are good arguments and there are arguments that just sound good. It is your responsibility to be able to tell the difference. Don't accept an opinion in an editorial unless it really convinces you fair and square.

This Pogo comic strip is a good example of bad reasoning. Read it through just for fun and then check your own ability to spot bad reasoning by answering the questions in the exercise that follows.

Study the comments next to the comic strip panels below.

Panel 1
Pogo uses "rare" to mean "wonderful." Porky takes "rare" to mean "happening rarely."

Panel 2
Now Pogo acts as though "rare" means "small in amount." And he takes it for granted that all months are equal.

Panel 3
Porky says all months are not equal. And an August day is worth more because it comes from a bigger month.

Pogo stands by his argument that all months are equal, so one twenty-eighth of a month is more than one thirty-first of a month.

Panel 6
Porky takes it for granted that a hand with more fingers is more powerful. And he thinks it follows that a month with more days is "more."

Pogo takes it for granted that all hands are equally powerful, no matter how many fingers.

Panel 7
Pogo and Porky: This experiment will prove whether or not all hands are equal.

EXERCISE 1. Spotting Bad Reasoning

Each of the statements that follow explains some kind of bad reasoning. Put a check in front of the letter of the phrase that best answers the question.

1. If an *army* is strong, it does not follow that every *man* in it is strong. It is bad reasoning to say that what is true for a whole thing must be true for all parts of it. There are other examples of this in the Pogo–Porky conversation in:

____a. Panels 3 and 6

____b. Panels 1 and 5

____c. Panels 1 and 2

2. Pogo doesn't put it into words, but in Panel 2 he takes it for granted that all months are equal. This kind of reasoning is called false assumption. Porky makes a false assumption in

____a. Panel 6

____b. Panel 4

____c. Panel 5

3. Saying there is a logical connection between two things does not make it so. If Porky wins the Indian wrestling in Panel 7, that proves

____a. thirty-one fingers are stronger than twenty-eight fingers.

____b. A day in February comes along less often than a day in August.

____c. Porky is stronger than Pogo.

4. Most words have more than one meaning. Taking the wrong meaning of a word can cause trouble. Porky does this in

____a. Panel 2

____b. Panel 1

____c. Panel 4

FOLLOWING AN ARGUMENT IN AN EDITORIAL

You have seen how poor reasoning led to problems between Pogo and Porky. Now see if you can follow the steps in a more sensible argument. The editorial that follows has been cut apart to show the steps.

First read the editorial as it appeared in the Long Island, New York newspaper, *Newsday*. Then go back and read the "translation" printed at the side.

Translation of
"Parking and Profit at the Nassau Coliseum"

It costs $1 to park your car at the Nassau Coliseum. The coliseum management wants to charge $2. The coliseum is losing money now. The management says the coliseum would probably start showing a profit if it got the extra money from the $2 parking fee.

Nassau County owns the coliseum, so the county supervisors have to give their approval before coliseum management can raise the parking fee. We think that before the county supervisors approve the $2 parking fee, they should consider two important points:

FIRST, the reason the coliseum is so close to making money is that attendance has been growing steadily. We're certain that attendance would have grown faster if the coliseum had free parking.

Long Islanders are used to the free parking they get at places like shopping malls.

Parking and Profit at the Nassau Coliseum

The management of the Nassau Coliseum claims that doubling the existing $1 parking fee would probably put the county-owned arena in the black next year.

That's an attractive argument, but the county supervisors shouldn't approve the increase without weighing a couple of important considerations.

First, the arena is approaching the break-even point because its management is well along in the process of building an audience for coliseum events. The existing parking fee undoubtedly retarded that process.

Long Islanders are accustomed to what they regard as "free" parking, even though the cost of providing the massive parking areas surrounding the Island's many shopping malls is ultimately paid by consumers. There would be considerable resistance to shopping at any mall that asked customers to pay for parking.

Newsday

If the coliseum management wants to accelerate the movement into the black, it would be more canny psychologically to abolish the parking fee altogether and increase ticket prices proportionately.

The coliseum management should do what the parking malls do—have free parking, and raise prices enough to cover the costs of the parking areas.

The second consideration is the lack of alternatives to traveling by car to get to coliseum events. In attempting to justify its request for a 100 per cent increase in the parking charge, the coliseum management argues that its parking fee is the lowest in the nation. Among other examples, the management cites the $1.75 charged at Yankee and Shea stadiums.

SECOND, the only way people can get to Nassau Coliseum is by car. The coliseum management points out that every other sports arena in the country charges more than $1, and that there is a $1.75 parking fee at New York City's Yankee Stadium and Shea Stadium, right in our own area. Nassau Coliseum management is saying that a high parking fee hasn't hurt profits at Yankee and Shea, so it won't hurt profits at the coliseum.

But to get to them a fan can easily leave his car at home and take the subway or even, in the case of Shea, the Long Island Railroad. There is some public transportation serving the Nassau Coliseum, but a few buses hardly represent an alternative to auto travel.

But that is not good logic, because the coliseum is different from Yankee and Shea in a very important way: a Yankee or Shea fan can leave his car at home and easily get to the stadium by subway. Shea is also served by the Long Island Railroad. A few buses serve Nassau Coliseum, but basically, the only way to get there is by car.

A public purpose might be served by increasing the fees at the city stadiums. This would encourage the use of the readily available public transport.

Maybe raising parking fees at Yankee and Shea stadiums would benefit the public. The higher fees would encourage fans to get to the stadiums by subway or train. There would be less auto traffic, less air pollution, and higher income for the public transportation system.

Increasing the fee at the coliseum, however, would only encourage people to stay home. And when the taxpayers have to absorb the coliseum's deficit, that serves no public purpose at all.

Newsday

But higher parking fees at the coliseum would only encourage people to stay home. Ticket sales could drop so much that the coliseum would lose more money than it does now. Extra public money—taxpayer money—would be used to cover the loss, and the public would get no benefit at all.

EXERCISE 2. Finding the News that Triggers an Editorial

Directions: An editorial is usually written in response to a news event. Reread "Parking and Profit at the Nassau Coliseum" and underline the sentence that mentions the news event it is responding to.

EXERCISE 3. Finding the Main Opinion

An editorial is written when a newspaper has an opinion it wants to make known to the public. It is very often a call for some kind of action by the government.

The editorial doesn't always start off with this main idea, the way a news story does. The main opinion may be stated at the beginning, the end, in the middle of the editorial, or in all three places.

Directions: Check the phrase you think gives the main opinion of the editorial you have just read.

____a. ". . . doubling the existing $1 parking fee would probably put the county-owned arena in the black next year."

____b. ". . . the county supervisors shouldn't approve the increase without weighing a couple of important considerations."

____c. ". . . abolish the parking fee altogether and increase ticket prices proportionately."

EXERCISE 4. Understanding Background

If you don't know the background of an issue, you can't understand the editorial. Usually some background information is included in the beginning of an editorial. Use this exercise to check your understanding of the background of "Parking and Profit at the Nassau Coliseum."

Directions: Put a check mark in front of the phrase that best completes each statement.

1. When they drive to Nassau Coliseum events, fans

____a. pay $1 to park.

____b. pay $2 to park.

____c. park free at a shopping mall.

2. Coliseum management wants to increase the parking fee because

____a. the existing fee encourages people to attend other stadiums.

____b. that would probably put the arena in the black next year.

____c. this would encourage the use of the bus and subway systems.

3. The coliseum parking fee is

____a. the lowest in the nation.

____b. 100% higher than at Yankee Stadium.

____c. free, but ultimately paid by consumers.

4. Fans can reach the coliseum by

____a. car, subway, or Long Island Railroad.

____b. bus mainly—parking is limited.

____c. car mainly—there are few buses.

Food stamp reform closer?

Another step toward food stamp reform came with House Agriculture Committee approval of a bill that would tighten stamp eligibility regulations, cutting down on the number of recipients but increasing benefits for many of those still eligible.

Something certainly needs to be done. As presently administered, the food stamp program is a mess. Whether reform can be instituted any time soon remains to be seen. Reforms implemented by the Department of Agriculture have been held up in court, and the Congress has been moving slowly. The Senate passed a bill last spring. The House bill likely won't pass all the hurdles before Congress adjourns in October.

Meanwhile, the errors are costing American taxpayers dearly and are working a hardship on many families that depend on food stamps. For instance, a recent audit showed Texas far below the national average in amounts paid out erroneously for food stamps, yet the errors account for about one out of every eight federal dollars spent on food stamps in Texas.

The House bill would cut down on the number of people who have taken unfair advantage of the food stamp program. For instance, strikers and most students would not be eligible for stamps.

Among the attractive features of the House bill are the cost and the way deductions to determine eligibility are handled.

The revised program would cost about $6 billion a year, about the same as the present program, yet would, in many cases, increase benefits for those deemed truly needy under the new guidelines. And the plethora of individual deductions would be replaced by standard deductions, based on marital status, number of children and so on.

Whatever course is taken, food stamp reform is long overdue. For the sake of taxpayers and those who need the stamps, we hope something can be done this year.

The *Houston Chronicle*

EXERCISE 5. Spotting Opinions

A fact gives you definite information. An opinion tells you what someone thinks or feels. People who write news stories have to be careful not to let their opinions show. Editorials, on the other hand, exist to show the newspaper's opinions on various issues.

Directions: Here is a list of sentences and phrases taken from the *Houston Chronicle* editorial "Food stamp reform closer?" Read them over to determine which quotations are facts and which are opinions. Put a check next to each quotation that gives the newspaper's opinion about something, and underline the word or words that show opinion. The first one is done for you as an example.

✓ a. "Something <u>certainly</u> needs to be done."

____b. "As presently administered, the food stamp program is a mess."

____c. "Reforms implemented by the Department of Agriculture have been held up in court . . ."

____d. ". . . the errors are costing American taxpayers dearly . . ."

____e. ". . . a recent audit showed Texas far below the national average . . ."

____f. "The House bill would cut down on the number of people who have taken unfair advantage of the food stamp program."

____g. "Among the attractive features of the House bill . . ."

____h. "The revised program would cost about $6 billion a year . . ."

____ i. ". . . food stamp reform is long overdue."

EXERCISE 6. Connecting Opinions and Reasons

A newspaper doesn't just tell its main opinion. It tries to convince you by giving reasons and examples, as do Pogo and Porky in the comic strip.

Directions: The following statement was used in the editorial "Parking and Profit at the Nassau Coliseum" as a reason to support *Newsday's* opinion. Write the opinion that this statement supports on the lines below.

> "Long Islanders are accustomed to what they regard as "free" parking even though the cost of . . . the parking areas . . . is ultimately paid by consumers."

____

____

EXERCISE 7. Finding the Other Side of the Argument

It takes two to argue. In the cartoon strip at the beginning of this chapter, you can see Pogo arguing with Porky. An editorial is arguing with you. The editorial writer knows what questions or objections readers might have, and answers them ahead of time. By reading the editorial carefully, you can often guess what objections were expected.

This quotation from "Parking and Profit . . ." is an example:

"There is some public transportation serving Nassau Coliseum, but a few buses hardly represent an alternative to auto travel."

The editorial writer has anticipated a possible argument, and has explained why it is not valid.

Directions: Read the marked paragraph of "Puerto Rico Stays Put." On the lines that follow write the objections you think this paragraph is answering ahead of time.

____

____

____

____

____

____

Reprinted with permission from the *Chicago Daily News,* July 26, 1967

Puerto Rico Stays Put

In rejecting statehood for their island commonwealth, Puerto Rican voters went the way their pocketbooks beckoned. The outcome of Sunday's plebiscite, solidly endorsing commonwealth status, also refuted the Castro-Communist line that Puerto Rico remains aligned with the United States under duress. Only a scattering of votes were for independence, as against 60 per cent for the status quo and 39 for statehood.

Though extremist independence groups boycotted the plebiscite, as did some advocates of statehood, the size of the turnout —some 66 per cent of the eligible voters—made it clear that full participation in the balloting would not have altered the results appreciably.

Those who did plump for statehood sought to appeal to pride: "Don't you want to be first-class citizens?" The emotional tug wasn't enough to overcome the realization that commonwealth has brought unparalleled prosperity and the highest per capita income in Latin America.

Per capita income in Puerto Rico has soared from $120 in 1940 to the present level of $1,149—still considerably behind the lowest in the United States (Mississippi's $1,751) but well ahead of Latin America's highest, some $900 in Venezuela. It has brought the once impoverished Puerto Ricans many of the good things of life, including a sense of dignity and achievement.

Ex-Gov. Luis Munoz Marin's thesis that Yankee standards of democracy and efficiency can be adapted to Latin America without destroying the Latin personality has been proven. The plebiscite was an overwhelming vote of confidence in this thesis and in Puerto Rico's voluntary association with the United States.

Directions: Look at the marked paragraph of "Banning Sonic Booms." Underline an objection to Senator Case's bill that this paragraph answers in advance.

Banning Sonic Booms

Senator Clifford Case introduced an important little bill the other day to ban sonic booms by aircraft flying over the United States pending further study of their effects. While technical and budgetary difficulties have slowed development of an American supersonic aircraft, the British and French are progressing with their joint-venture model. It is important to have some protection on the law books before the booms come crashing down on the nation's ears.

Sonic booms are conceded to be highly disruptive sounds, more annoying to some people than to others. They follow an aircraft as waves follow an ocean steamer, in a wide, rippling wake. Continuing tests reveal that booms might crack plaster, break windows and have harmful effects on people with certain physical ailments. Extensive testing in Oklahoma City some years ago showed that a significant portion of the population could not tolerate multiple booms.

Developers of the American S.S.T. say they "assume" it will fly at supersonic speed only over water but this is too important an issue to be left to anyone's assumption. Senator Case's bill deserves public hearings and positive Congressional action.

EDITORIAL CARTOONS

Editorial cartoons are editorials in pictures. They try to use few words or even no words at all. The opinion expressed should be clear. In this cartoon from the *N.Y. Amsterdam News* you would know what the cartoonist thinks of the new constitution even without the caption printed above it.

Not Enough Protection

From the *New York AMSTERDAM NEWS*

Spending Money

Hungerford in the *Pittsburgh Post Gazette*

Editorial cartoons use many caricatures and symbols to help you understand the message. There are three examples in this one cartoon.

(1) a caricature of President Johnson; (2) a combination piggy bank and barrel symbolizing Congressional "pork barrel" projects; and (3) a fat man in a string tie symbolizing Congress.

"I'm Not Smoking, Ma—I'm Just Breathing"

EXERCISE 8. Interpreting Editorial Cartoons

Directions: Here is a Mauldin cartoon from the *Chicago-Sun Times.* What point do you think the cartoonist is trying to make here? Use the lines below to write what you think Mauldin is trying to say.

____

____

____

____

____

____

____

Editorial cartoons may say more than one thing at a time. One thing the Haynie cartoon on gun control below says is, "The gun lobby shot down the arms control legislation." Can you see something else it is saying? Write the other message in the space below.

____

____

____

____

____

____

Think about this: Would the effect of the cartoon be different if the man labeled "Gun Lobby" were slim and good-looking, and the dead man looked like a fat thief?

Louisville Courier-Journal

PRACTICE IN YOUR LOCAL NEWSPAPER

PRACTICE 1. Choose a news story from your local newspaper, or use one of the stories that follow. Get ready to tell the class about your opinion on the issue in the news story. Back up your opinion with reasons and examples.

Mark up the news story, and make notes in the space that follows it, to remind yourself of what you want to say.

PRACTICE 2. Choose a news story from your local paper or use one of the news stories that follow. Write a short editorial giving your opinion. Or choose an editorial from your local paper, and write a short editorial disagreeing with it.

____

____

Training Fund Lack Trips Student Drivers

LOS ANGELES — (AP) — **An estimated 100,000 California high school students may be prevented from obtaining driver instruction permits for which they are eligible .according to Verne Orr, Department of Motor Vehicles director.**

The confusion stems from the public school system's inability to train as many prospective drivesr as required under a new state law, Orr said.

"We're immobilized," he said. "The matter is strictly between the Legislature and the schools."

The law, effective July 1, requires students to wait until they are 17½ to apply for an instruction permit unless they have completed driver education and "behind the wheel" training courses offered in the state schools. Previously students could apply for the certificates at age 15½ without the courses.

In Los Angeles, 32,000 students will receive the required behind-the-wheel training, a city school official said. But there are not enough funds to train another 18,000 prospective drivers.

Associated Press

____

____

____

____

____

____

____

____

____

Reprinted from *The Newark News*

City Says No to K-9 Corps

By LADLEY K. PEARSON

The Newark City Council, perhaps once and for all, decided not to establish a K-9 (police dog) Corps in the city.

The council by a vote of 7 to 2 concurred with a recommendation of a five-man committee that the corps not be established in Newark because "it's disadvantages by far outweigh its advantages."

The controversial and emotional issue has been raised by the council four times since last summer's riots. It was defeated initially, then approved, and then defeated again and turned over to the study committee.

Angry Debates

Over the past few months, the K-9 Corps formed the basis of at times long and angry debates between proponents and opponents. Despite the fact that the issue has been raised at every council meeting since December, it has long been considered dead.

Councilmen Lee Bernstein, who served on the committee but did not sign its recommendation, and Frank Addonizio voted no when the council was asked to concur with the committee's report.

Those signing the committee's recommendation were Councilmen James Callaghan, Calvin West, Joseph Melillo and Philip Gordon.

West Comment

West said the K-9 Corps issue "is more than the simple matter of six or eight dogs, it is the matter of people and how they are stacking up, one group against another." He added, "this issue would only result in further polarization of these groups."

Melillo said, "At normal times, it might be advisable to add such dogs to the police department, but these are not normal times. The disadvantages by far outweigh the advantages."

Bernstein said he favored the establishment of the K-9 Corps because "if this be one tool that can keep potential criminals out of our community, let it be this way."

Intimidations Cited

He said that the rising crime rate in Newark necessitated the corps. "There are many, many persons who favor the K-9 Corps," he said, "but because of threats and intimidations are afraid to speak up for it."

When the decision was reached by the council, most of the audience of 300, many of them from the militant North Ward Citizens Committee, broke into a loud "boo."

Talk Interrupted

Anthony Imperiale, president of the citizens committee, later condemned the action by the council and predicted the council members "will live to regret it."

Imperiale spoke more than 10 minutes before the council and on some 15 occasions was interrupted by the loud cheers, whistles, and foot stompings of his supporters, most of them teen-agers.

Several times during the 3½-hour council meeting, Imperiale's supporters, a dozen of them wearing Army fatigue uniforms with the initials "NWCC inked on tape over the left shirt pocket, succeeded in creating an atmosphere of bedlam in the council chambers.

The group was most vocal when Councilmen Philip E. Gordon, who has been appointed the city's new corporation counsel, tried to read into the record his letter of resignation.

Several councilmen commented after the meeting that in their years on the council they had not seen such rudeness, discourtesy and disrespect before.

In Passing, Glass Coffins

ATLANTA (AP)—An Atlanta mortician has adopted the drive-in approach for busy persons who want to drive by and view a deceased friend.

Hirschel Thornton is building five windows in a row as an extension on his funeral home. Each window is six feet long and will contain a body in its coffin. The display will face a driveway at the side of the home located on a busy street.

"So many people want to come by and see the remains of a relative or friend," Thornton said, "but they just don't have the time. This way, they can drive by and just keep on going."

"The deceased will be lying in a lighted window, sort of tilted to the front so they can conveniently be seen," he added.

Where did he get the idea for the drive-in window?

"It's purely imagination," he said. "I dreamed it one night." Thornton said a surprising number of persons like to view a body in the late hours—midnight and 1 a.m.—for reasons of their own.

"Perhaps it's because they work late. But this habit keeps attendants at the funeral home answering the phone at all hours. And the drive-in window will elminate these interruptions," he said.

"Another thing," Thorton added. "The people won't have to dress up to view the remains."

What about curiosity seekers? Isn't he afraid of traffic jams from these?

"We expect these," said Mrs. Thornton, who works at the mortuary, "but we think curiosity seekers will eventually tire."

Families must give their permission for the drive-in viewings, Thornton said.

Each window will contain a name plaque and each will have wall-to-wall carpeting and drapes.

Associated Press

PRACTICE IN YOUR LOCAL NEWSPAPER

PRACTICE 3. Find an editorial in your local newspaper that asks for Government action. Underline the main opinion. Bring the editorial to class.

PRACTICE 4. Choose any editorial from your local paper, or use "Soaking Commuters." Circle all the opinion words and phrases. Bring the editorial to class.

Soaking Commuters

New York's City Council has decided unanimously that the way to ease its fiscal problems is to soak the commuter. Though this is hardly a new idea, the council has topped previous proposals by asking the Legislature to raise the city's commuter income tax to resident levels.

Fortunately, the City Council is rarely taken seriously at Albany, and its proposal is given scant chance of approval by the Legislature. Even Mayor Lindsay, who has long advocated a higher commuter tax, has never gone so far as to say commuters should pay the full resident rate.

In February, City Finance Administrator Goodman asked that the commuter tax be doubled "as a matter of simple equity." But he didn't go into the equity of taxing outsiders who receive few of the services their money helps sustain.

Reprinted from *The Newark News*

CHAPTER 12

LETTERS TO THE EDITOR

Editorials tell you what the paper thinks.

Columnists tell you what the experts think.

News stories pass along what people like presidents, movie stars, and world leaders think.

But . . . to find out what just plain people think, read *Letters to the Editor*. If the paper plays fair in choosing letters to print, you get a good idea of . . .

How the public feels about news events and about editorial stands.

How many different people and interest groups are part of the life of your city.

How many different sides there may be to a story.

You are the public. You can write a letter to the editor, too. Maybe you will explain why a traffic light is needed on your corner. The editor could choose your letter to say, "I think . . ." to the whole city.

Your letter is not wasted if it is not printed. It can help make the pile of letters on traffic lights so big that the editor decides to print one.

What information should you put in your letter to give it a better chance of being printed? The important elements that you will find in most published letters are noted below, using examples from "The Big Noise at the L.A. Airport."

WHAT IS THE WRITER *REACTING TO?* News reports of ". . . the big talk about insulating buildings in the approach path at the L.A. Airport." Most letters are reactions to something printed in the paper a few days before.

WHAT IS HIS MAIN *OPINION?* "I think one of the phoniest attempted whitewashes of a dirty, sticky problem is the big talk about insulating buildings in the approach path at the L.A. Airport."

Letter writers don't have to be as careful as the paper.

The Big Noise at The L.A. Airport

I think one of the phoniest attempted whitewashes of a dirty, sticky problem is the big talk about insulating buildings in the approach path at the L.A. Airport.

I live close to the path (about one block) in a well-insulated building. The sound comes right through closed windows and since you have to keep the windows open all summer, it is just as bad as standing outside. The insulation doesn't do a bit of good.

Living here, it is necessary to keep TV and radio volume approximately double what would be considered comfortable listening. At this level the program is drowned out for about 15 seconds each time one of the screaming meemies goes through. This happens 15-20 times in a 30-minute program and always takes out the punchlines to the jokes, items of interest, clues, etc.

All the insulation talk is good for is to try to insulate those responsible from the dirty mess.

I have an ideal solution. Build a short, narrow landing strip out into the ocean.

DONALD SISSEL, Inglewood

Los Angeles Herald Examiner

DOES HE BACK IT UP WITH *REASONS AND FACTS?* Reason: ". . . insulation doesn't do a bit of good." Facts: "TV . . . is drowned out for about 15 seconds . . . 15–20 times in a 30-minute program . . ."

DOES HE HAVE SPECIAL *QUALIFICATIONS* FOR WRITING ON THIS SUBJECT? "I live close to the path (about one block) in a well-insulated building."

DOES HE GIVE *IDENTIFICATION?* Donald Sissel, Inglewood.

EXERCISE 1. Picking Out Important Elements

Look out for these elements when you are reading letters as well as when you are writing them. It is another way to help you understand what you are reading—like looking for WWWWW&H in news stories. You will read many more letters than you will write!

Directions: Not all letters have all the elements. Use the check lists at the right to mark the elements you find in these three letters. Cross out missing elements. The "Play Street" one is done for you.

Creative Society?

Editor of The Bee — Sir: I think it is time we considered recognizing one of the most important facets of our economy, one of the things which gives the economy its cohesiveness and thus keeps our nation strong. For too many years we as a people have ignored its meaning to our lives.

Think about it. Where would our country be without garbage?

It is the backbone of the nation. Not only does it enable industries to stay in business, maintaining a demand for goods, and encourage the flow of goods from producer to consumer to dump, but it keeps the dumps in business, and our maintenance men in jobs.

Each household has at least one shrine of plastic, rubber or metal in almost every room for garbage, and yet the conscious awareness of its pervading significance is very little. People do not stop to appraise a can of trash in its true light, with the awe of how much they contribute to it.

No one should pass by a car graveyard without being inspired by all the work that has gone into it. It is time that we set aside at least one day to pay tribute to trash. People could drive out and put wreaths around the dump, garbage bins and rusty cars, and burn incense before litter cans.

Our citizens should be made aware that "Waste is our most important product."

I hope a legislator will propose such a day soon, because rubbish is all around us needing recognition.

A LOCAL HOMEMAKER.
Sacramento.

The Sacramento Bee

Reacting to . . .

Opinion

Reasons

Facts

Qualifications

Identification

'No Parking'

It is a constant source of aggravation for me to see a green 1966 four-door Chrysler parked illegally in a "No Parking" zone directly in front of a fire hydrant on the circle in front of Faneuil Hall in Dock sq. The car is parked there from at least 8:30 a.m. until 5:00 p.m. each day.

It is apparently protected by a card on the dashboard which reads "City of Boston, Public Facilities Department, Official—1967."

I pay $1.75 each day to park my car in the city in a lot only about 100 yards from the Dock sq. circle. If I were able to devote my parking expenses toward instalment loan payments, I would probably be able to drive a Chrysler, too.

PETER S. DAMON
Needham

Courtesy of *The Boston Globe*

Reacting to . . .

Opinion

Reasons

Facts

Qualifications

Identification

$3,000 Play Streets

To the Editor:

In your June 29 printing, you mention that it costs $3,000 to open a city play street. Was this a misprint? If not please tell the people where our money goes and to whom?

Joann Budwig

Courtesy of *The Boston Globe*

Reacting to . . .

Opinion

~~Reasons~~

~~Facts~~

Qualifications

Identification

EXERCISE 2. Finding the Main Opinion

Directions: The letter-writer doesn't always state his feelings directly. You have to learn to read between the lines. Read these three letters again and try to determine what the writer wants you to think. Then check the phrase that best completes the sentence in each example.

$3,000 Play Streets

To the Editor:

In your June 29 printing, you mention that it costs $3,000 to open a city play street. Was this a misprint? If not please tell the people where our money goes and to whom?

Joann Budwig

1. Miss Budwig wants you to think that

____a. $3,000 is very cheap for a play street.

____b. this newspaper makes many mistakes.

____c. a $3,000 play street probably means waste and graft.

2. Mr. Damon wants you to think that

____a. officials should pay $1.75 to park on the streets.

____b. it is wrong for the official's Chrysler to block a fire hydrant.

____c. the city parking rules should be enforced for all citizens.

'No Parking'

It is a constant source of aggravation for me to see a green 1966 four-door Chrysler parked illegally in a "No Parking" zone directly in front of a fire hydrant on the circle in front of Faneuil Hall in Dock sq. The car is parked there from at least 8:30 a.m. until 5:00 p.m. each day.

It is apparently protected by a card on the dashboard which reads "City of Boston, Public Facilities Department, Official—1967."

I pay $1.75 each day to park my car in the city in a lot only about 100 yards from the Dock sq. circle. If I were able to devote my parking expenses toward instalment loan payments, I would probably be able to drive a Chrysler, too.

PETER S. DAMON
Needham

3. A local homemaker wants you to think that:

____a. garbage is a necessary evil.

____b. the public ignores the real tragedy of the new society—we are being surrounded and consumed by the increasing problem of waste disposal.

____c. trash of all types might actually be artistically interesting and attractive if we learned to look at it in the right manner.

Creative Society?

Editor of The Bee — Sir: I think it is time we considered recognizing one of the most important facets of our economy, one of the things which gives the economy its cohesiveness and thus keeps our nation strong. For too many years we as a people have ignored its meaning to our lives.

Think about it. Where would our country be without garbage?

It is the backbone of the nation. Not only does it enable industries to stay in business, maintaining a demand for goods, and encourage the flow of goods from producer to consumer to dump, but it keeps the dumps in business, and our maintenance men in jobs.

Each household has at least one shrine of plastic, rubber or metal in almost every room for garbage, and yet the conscious awareness of its pervading significance is very little. People do not stop to appraise a can of trash in its true light, with the awe of how much they contribute to it.

No one should pass by a car graveyard without being inspired by all the work that has gone into it. It is time that we set aside at least one day to pay tribute to trash. People could drive out and put wreaths around the dump, garbage bins and rusty cars, and burn incense before litter cans.

Our citizens should be made aware that "Waste is our most important product."

I hope a legislator will propose such a day soon, because rubbish is all around us needing recognition.

A LOCAL HOMEMAKER.
Sacramento.

READ DIRECTIONS TO GET YOUR LETTER PUBLISHED

Along with their *Letters to the Editor*, many papers print a paragraph of the information they want people to keep in mind when preparing their letters to the editor.

Here are the directions from three newspapers:

The Amsterdam News welcomes letters on either side of any subject. It is preferred that letters not exceed 250 words and they must be signed. Names will be withheld on request. No letters can be returned. All must be addressed to the Editor.

From the New York *AMSTERDAM NEWS*

Letters to the editor must be signed, and address given. Names will be withheld for good reasons. Letters should be kept brief. They are subject to editing and condensation. Letters cannot be returned.

Pittsburgh Post Gazette—Letters to the Editor

Letters from readers are welcome. All are subject to condensation. We assume no responsibility for statements made.

EXERCISE 3. Class Discussion

Get ready for a class discussion of *Letters to the Editor* by thinking and making notes about the questions that follow.

1. What does "We assume no responsibility for statements made" mean?

____

____

2. What does it mean to you when someone signs his letter, "A Reader," instead of giving his name? ______________________________

____

____

3. If the paper agrees not to print a person's name and address with his letter, why do they want to know it? What could happen if the paper accepted and printed anonymous (unsigned) letters? ______________________________

____

____

4. Pretend that you are going to write a letter to the editor. The paper you are going to write to prints only short letters, but you know the editor is willing to trim your letter down to size. Is it better for you to write a long letter or a short letter? Why? ______________________________

____

____

____

5. Pretend that you are a newspaper editor. How will you choose a fair sample of the hundreds of letters that are received every day? How could your power to choose and edit letters be used to give readers an unfair picture of public opinion on an issue? ______________________________

____

____

EXERCISE 4. Writing a Letter to the Editor

Directions: When you read, you don't just take in information. You *react* to it,

When you react very strongly, you might want to write a letter to the editor. Practice by writing a short letter to the editor now. Choose a subject that makes you react.

Use one of the letters in this chapter.

Or choose something in your local paper—a news story, letter, editorial, editorial cartoon, feature column, or a situation you know about, such as the one in the 'No Parking' letter.

Then use the outline below to organize a first draft of your letter.

Tell what you are *reacting* to: ______________________________

____

____

____

Give your main *opinion:* ______________________________

____

____

____

Support your opinion with *reasons* and *facts:* ______________

____

____

____

Identify yourself by including your name, address, and group membership, if relevant: ______________________________

____

Do you want your name and address withheld? Explain why to the editor: ______________________________

____

PRACTICE IN YOUR LOCAL NEWSPAPER

PRACTICE 1. Bring in a letter from your local paper that is like one of these:

a. a letter that criticizes something in the paper
"I found the column biased . . . unfair . . . historically inaccurate . . .

b. a letter from an expert
". . . the Social Security tax is a regressive element falling relatively more heavily on lower income groups . . ."

Eli Schwartz
Professor of Economics

c. a letter that praises the paper
"My congratulations, in addition to thousands of others, who appreciate the clarity and courage of your editorial policies . . ."

d. a letter from a group representative
"The lack of patriotic enthusiasm . . . was clearly shown by the fact that only about 1000 persons took part in the Veterans Parade on Saturday . . ."

Phil Jones
Asst. Public Relations Chairman
Veterans of World War I

e. a letter praising a specific piece of writing
"I wish to commend education reporter Robert L. Levey for his objective treatment of the pros and cons of an urban site for U Mass-Boston . . ."

PRACTICE 2. Cut out the directions for writing letters to the editor in any paper and bring it to class for discussion.

PRACTICE 3. Cut out something in a paper that you want to answer. It could be a news item, a feature column, a movie review—almost anything. Write a sentence telling why you might want to write a letter to the editor about it.

CHAPTER 13
THE COLUMNISTS: FASHION, FOOD, FIGURE, HEART, HOME, HEALTH

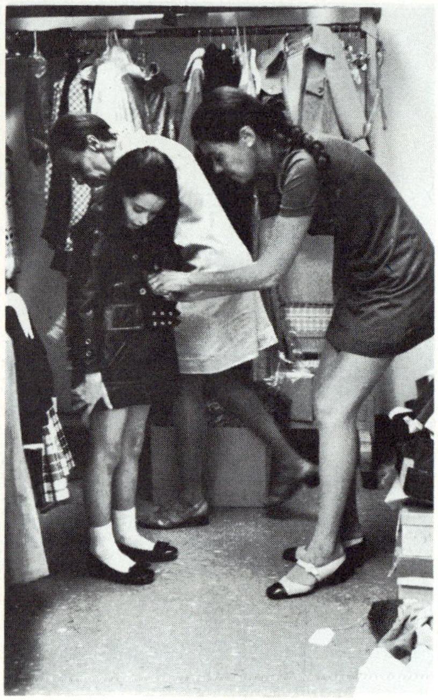

A giant oil slick is threatening the beaches of the French Riviera, and melted butter from corn-on-the-cob just dripped on your new suit.

Today's newspaper includes these two articles: "Oil Slick Reaches French Beaches; See $2 Million Loss in Tourist Trade" and "Oily Clothing Stains: What to Do Until the Dry-cleaner Comes." Which one will you read first? Which one will you tear out and keep for future reference?

A small problem that is very close to you matters more than a big problem that is far away. Newspaper editors know this very well. Your newspaper writes about how to treat dry hair, as well as how forest rangers deal with drought-dried forest lands. It tells you how Dionne Warwick feels about clothes, and how a Senator feels about emerging nations.

The newspaper gives a lot of information and advice on your everyday problems and interests. You just need to learn where to look.

And then you need to learn what to skip. Not all interests are your interests. For example, you can probably skip the "Senior Citizens" column for the next thirty-five years or so.

EXERCISE 1. Finding What Interests *You*

The headlines and first few lines of fifteen stories are printed on the next page. Scan them as quickly as possible; then answer each question by circling one or more headline numbers.

Example: John has ulcers. The doctor told him to drink lots of milk. John wants to read:

(1) 2 3 4 5 6 7 8 9 10 11 12 13 14 15

1. Sharon wears glasses and hates them. She would like to make money baby-sitting. Sharon wants to read:

1 2 3 4 5 6 7 8 9 10 11 12 13 14 15

2. Phil has a complaint about the city bus schedule. Phil wants to read:

1 2 3 4 5 6 7 8 9 10 11 12 13 14 15

3. Salvador wants to lose 10 pounds. He wants to read:

1 2 3 4 5 6 7 8 9 10 11 12 13 14 15

4. Louis is a newsboy. He wants to read:

1 2 3 4 5 6 7 8 9 10 11 12 13 14 15

5. Vincent is steamed up because a policeman told him he couldn't be out alone at midnight. He wants to read:

1 2 3 4 5 6 7 8 9 10 11 12 13 14 15

6. Wanda does all the food shopping and cooking for her family. She wants to read:

1 2 3 4 5 6 7 8 9 10 11 12 13 14 15

7. Manuela worries about her waistline. And she is tired of going out with the same boy. She wants to read:

1 2 3 4 5 6 7 8 9 10 11 12 13 14 15

8. Claudia is mad about clothes. She and her girl friend like to wear matching outfits. Claudia wants to read:

1 2 3 4 5 6 7 8 9 10 11 12 13 14 15

(1) **Milk Tablet**

(Reprinted from Rodale's Health Bulletin)

An innovation has been made available to ulcer patients who are urged to drink plenty of milk but find it impractical. Known as PMT

(2) **The Salt Lake Tribune**

Food and Women's News

First Section — Monday Morning, April 1, 1968 — Page 13

Dear Ann Landers: My son has a 13-year-old daughter who is quite mature for her age, but still she is only 13. Her mother allows her to accept Friday and Saturday night sitting jobs in the apartment building. Last night she had full charge of three youngsters. Please tell me what you think about this. —CONCERNED

Dear Concerned: It is up to the girl's mother to decide whether or not she is capable of handling the responsibility. Some 13-year-olds are extremely reliable, others at 13 need someone to sit with THEM. M.Y.O.B., Granny.

(3) **HINTS FROM HELOISE**

By Heloise

Cleans Shoes

Dear Heloise: To keep my little boy's blue denim tennis shoes looking nice between washings, I clean the white rubber part with rubbing alcohol

(4) **The Way You Look**

By Malinda Wiesner

(The Register's Fashion Editor)

A light streak down the center of the nose will tend to make a broad nose look narrower, and a dark spot on the tip of a long nose

(5) **Play It Cool**

Break It Off

Dear Mrs. Ricker: I will be 15 in two months and I am fairly popular. My problem is my steady boy friend, Harold, who is 15. When we're alone he acts okay but when we're

(6) **Newsboys Don't Have Easy Job**

DEAR ELEANOR HART:

I am a widow and my son has had a route two and a half years. Delivering The Herald is like a small business to the newsboy. He has to have the money early Saturday at 5 or 6 a.m. to pay for the papers he delivered all week. Regardless of

(7) **MEDICARE MAILBOX**

By WENDELL COLTIN

NO REFUNDS IF HEALTH GOOD

"When you have been in Social Security Medicare a year and don't have to be hospitalized, do

(8) **Rude Move To Buy Same Dress**

DEAR MRS. POST:

As a birthday present I received a lovely dress. When I wore it to school everyone loved it. Well, the next day my girl friend told me she bought the exact same dress but in a different color. Though I didn't make a fuss, I wasn't too happy about it. Do you think it was right of her to buy the same dress on purpose?

Lucille

(9) **Lucy Lincoln Talks**

Registered U. S. Patent Office

Teen Would Reduce Contours

DEAR LUCY LINCOLN: I am 15 years old and 5 feet, 9 inches tall, with a 38-inch bustline. I'm way overweight and am on a diet now. Will losing weight reduce my bust as well as my waist and hips? Wearing a size 16 dress now, is

of your height and it seems unlikely that a short-waisted junior size would fit you properly regardless of your weight.

Guest List

(10) **NEWS Power**

A Buffalo Evening News Reader Service

NEWSpower is a forum for solving problems, getting action on complaints, cutting red tape, insuring your rights. Send your question in writing to NEWSpower, Buffalo Evening News, 218 Main St., Buffalo, N. Y. 14240. Letters must be signed. Do not send records or documents. Answers will be given only as they are printed in

(11) **Ask The JOURNAL**

This column will help any citizen in his dealings with government agencies and officials and on other questions of general interest. Obviously we can't answer or even acknowledge every inquiry. Only those of broadest public interest can be published.

Write: Ask The Journal, The Milwaukee Journal, Journal Square, Milwaukee, Wis. 53201. Please give name or initials.

Details of City Curfew Law

Please tell us what the curfew law is in the city of Milwaukee. Are there any exceptions? What are the penalties?

D. P.

(12) **Pick of the Crop**

Here is a roundup of foods that are currently being featured on Long Island at budget prices, compiled by Newsday Food Editor Barbara Rader.

MEAT, POULTRY: If you haven't gotten a turkey for tomorrow, then look around for a steak, either porterhouse or

(13) **MR. FIXIT**

Q. ARE CONTACT LENSES widely used? Does their price indicate their quality? Does a company usually make replacements of contact lenses that they have sold to a particular customer at a discount in case of loss, breakage, or different prescription? On the average, how often does replacement occur? Is it true that contact lenses can be worn only a limited time before they

(14) **HINTS FROM HELOISE**

By Heloise

Removes Iron's Rust

Dear Heloise: Here's an idea for you from three guys at Purdue university who have to iron their own shirts. It's a great way to remove rust and burned fragments from the bottom of irons.

(15) **Arlene Dahl**

Trim The Waist Saddled to a Desk

"I have a great job as an executive secretary, and I make pretty good money. But I'm beginning to wonder if it's worth it. In the two years that I've had this job, my lower posterior measurement has increased 3 inches! I'm NOT eating more, but (after my recent tape measure experiment) I'm enjoying it less. In fact, from the waist down, I've gone to pot.

back of the chair. Take a deep breath, pull in your abdominal muscles, and hold this position as you exhale slowly to the count of five. Relax, and repeat 10 times. Do this at least twice a day.

While you work, guard against slumping shoulders and keep your chin off your chest to prevent doubling it! Keep your knees together, too, whether

Arlene Dahl

Trim The Waist Saddled to a Desk

"I have a great job as an executive secretary, and I make pretty good money. But I'm beginning to wonder if it's worth it. In the two years that I've had this job, my lower posterior measurement has increased 3 inches! I'm NOT eating more, but (after my recent tape measure experiment) I'm enjoying it less. In fact, from the waist down, I've gone to pot. I know that constant sitting is the cause, but there's no cure for that unless I switch my profession to a lady softball player. Can you please help a sedentary secretary from San Francisco?"

Dear S. S.: There's no doubt that a secretary's job is broadening both intellectually and physically. Ever-widening hips are considered the occupational hazards of stenography. But there IS a remedy!

1. Join an evening gym class and concentrate on spot reducing twice a week.
2. Buy a good girdle and wear it.
3. Practice tension—relax exercises daily while sitting at your desk.

TO FIRM and trim the posterior: Sit very straight in your chair and contract your buttocks muscles. Clench them tightly as you would a fist. Hold for a few seconds, then relax. Repeat up to 20 times at every opportunity.

To correct a sagging abdomen: Sit very straight, shoulders back, and hips against the back of the chair. Take a deep breath, pull in your abdominal muscles, and hold this position as you exhale slowly to the count of five. Relax, and repeat 10 times. Do this at least twice a day.

While you work, guard against slumping shoulders and keep your chin off your chest to prevent doubling it! Keep your knees together, too, whether they show or not.

During your lunch hour, take a brisk walk in the fresh air, even if it's just around the block. And breathe deeply. Make at least one posture check before returning to your desk.

Your best figure protection, of course, is in getting as much exercise as you can during your off-hours. Do your "spot reducing" gym exercises either morning or evening, and try to plan at least one outdoor activity for each weekend. Good luck!

EXERCISE 2. Following Directions

Many life-help features are set up like the following one. First, a letter from the reader explains the problem, then the expert answers with comments and advice.

It's fun to read the reader's letter. But to save time, try this: Skip the reader's letter and go straight to the answer. If it is a long answer (like this one), read the first few words of each paragraph until you spot the part that matters to you. In this example, it is probably the marked exercise directions. Read this part carefully.

Directions: Let's say you decide to do the "sagging abdomen" exercise. Read the directions again, a step at a time, and follow the directions in your mind. Then check your understanding of the directions by answering these questions. Read the statement and then circle T or F.

T F 1. Find a comfortable position in the chair.

T F 2. Hips must touch the back of the chair.

T F 3. Take a deep breath, then pull in your abdominal muscles.

T F 4. Relax slowly as you exhale to the count of five.

T F 5. Keep your knees together while you do this exercise.

EXERCISE 3. Sorting Out Information You Need

The following column has short questions and answers. You have to read the question to understand the answer. You can't save much time by skipping. But you can save your brain some work by concentrating hard only on those parts of the question-and-answer that help *you.*

Directions: There are many bits of information in this question-and-answer advice that are interesting to G.N., the welfare department, and the repair service. But there is only one sentence other people on welfare in Buffalo need to remember. It is one of the three that follow. Put a check mark in front of it.

____1. "No money was paid the second time."

____2. "You should not pay a company doing work for welfare, as the department pays direct."

____3. "He suggests you call so an appointment can be made when you are at home."

NEWS *Power*

A Buffalo Evening News Reader Service

NEWSpower is a forum for solving problems, getting action on complaints, cutting red tape, insuring your rights. Send your question in writing to NEWSpower, Buffalo Evening News, 218 Main St., Buffalo, N. Y. 14240. Letters must be signed. Do not send records or documents. Answers will be given only as they are printed in this column. Initials will be used on request of the writer.

Q—A repair service made two calls to my home to fix our washer. The first time my daughter paid them $37.44. As I am on welfare, the repairman told me to submit a bill to the department and I would get a refund when it paid the company. I have not received the money. No money was paid the second time. The machine is out of order again, and I have been trying for two months to get the repair service to examine . , but with no success. I have even left a key for them. G. N., Buffalo.

A—This has turned into quite a complicated situation, G. N. The Social Services Department says the repair service told them your daughter paid $27.50 cash for the first repair. After the second job the repairmen said he submitted a bill for $37.44 to welfare and they reimbursed him.

The department is trying to examine the records of the repair service. This should show how much money you are owed. You should not pay a company doing work for welfare, as the department pays direct.

As for your current problem, the owner of the repair service told NEWSpower that he had been to your home several times, but you were away and he would like you to be there when he looks at the machine. He suggests you call so an appointment can be made when you are at home.

From *The Buffalo Evening News*

EXERCISE 4. Understanding What You Read

When you find information that matters to you, stop skimming and read carefully. Make sure you understand what you are reading. A slight mistake in reading can sometimes change the meaning completely.

Directions: Read "Details of City Curfew Law" and then circle the following statements either T or F.

T F 1. All children under 17 must be off the streets from 11 p.m. to 5 a.m.

T F 2. All children under 17 out after 11 p.m. must be with an adult.

T F 3. A child who breaks the curfew law can be fined from $10.00 to $200.00.

Ask The JOURNAL

This column will help any citizen in his dealings with government agencies and officials and on other questions of general interest. Obviously we can't answer or even acknowledge every inquiry. Only those of broadest public interest can be published.

Write: Ask The Journal, The Milwaukee Journal, Journal Square, Milwaukee, Wis. 53201. Please give name or initials.

Details of City Curfew Law

Please tell us what the curfew law is in the city of Milwaukee. Are there any exceptions? What are the penalties?
D. P.

Under the city ordinance, the curfew applies to any person under 17. The curfew is in effect from 11 p.m. to 5 a.m. The ordinance lists no exceptions, and an officer may stop any youngster during those hours if the child is not with his parents, guardian or an adult responsible for him. However, circumstances determine what further action — if any — is taken. Often, no further formal steps are taken. No penalty is provided for the child. However, if the situation is an aggravated one, the parents, guardian or adult responsible for the child can be fined from $10 to $200.

Reprinted from *The Milwaukee Journal*

Pick of the Crop

Here is a roundup of foods that are currently being featured on Long Island at budget prices, compiled by Newsday Food Editor Barbara Rader.

MEAT, POULTRY: If you haven't gotten a turkey for tomorrow, then look around for a steak, either porterhouse or sirloin, priced at 80 and 90 cents a pound in some supermarkets. Or select a chuck shoulder steak for London broil. Remember to slice on the bias for tender eating.
FISH: Mackerel, porgies, whiting, cod, flounder in fin fish; crabmeat and hard-shelled crabs are in good supply.
EGGS. They're still low priced. Be sure to pick up a dozen or so, hard cook them for deviled eggs, which are simple to make. Just cut egg in half lengthwise, mash yolk with mayonnaise, dry mustard, salt, pepper and spoon back into white.
VEGETABLES, FRUIT: Expect them to be high priced, because of cold weather in producing areas, but best buys are potatoes, carrots, scallions, cucumbers in vegetables; grapefruit, bananas, pineapple in fresh fruit.

EXERCISE 5. Food Editors Show You the Bargains

Egg prices go up and down, depending on how hard the hens are working that week, and how much people want eggs. When the price is low, you get more eggs for your money. Newspaper food editors keep track of changing prices, so that you can take advantage of bargains.

Directions: The foods in this story are listed by groups. When you look at the story to check an answer, save time by looking in the right group. Circle T or F in front of these statements.

T F 1. Some supermarkets have sirloin steak for 90¢ a pound or less.

T F 2. Vegetables and fruits are low-priced now.

T F 3. Carrots are a best buy in vegetables.

T F 4. Eggs are still low-priced.

T F 5. Oysters are a best buy.

T F 6. Codfish are offered at budget prices.

EXERCISE 6. Getting Advice on Health

The dentist wants to X-ray your teeth. The school nurse thinks you should go to the clinic for a chest X-ray. The doctor wants to X-ray your broken arm to see how it's healing. What should you do? Work this exercise to see if you got the point of the health column on X-rays on the next page.

Directions: Circle T or F in front of each statement.

T F 1. There is a big difference between diagnostic X-rays and X-rays for treatment.

T F 2. There is no reason to fear diagnostic X-rays.

T F 3. X-ray treatment has no harmful effects.

Health Column

Concerning Fear About X-Rays

By JOSEPH G. MOLNER, M.D.

Dear Dr. Molner: I am terribly concerned that I have done my 14-year-old daughter great harm. She was the picture of health until she was 12 and began having trouble with her stomach. Until then she never had an X-ray.

A series of gastro-intestinal X-rays was inconclusive. She was hospitalized for another series, and six months later, over my protests, for some more. In all, four series in 18 months.

The head of the laboratory tried to reassure me by saying they had the newest equipment, and four or five series would cause less exposure than one series five years ago. Also they took my daughter's age into consideration when doing each series.

Now comes the part that frightens me. She is going to Boston for a complete gastroenterology workup. They said they would take new X-rays only when absolutely necessary and that even if she has another series there was nothing to worry about. Oh, Dr. Molner, I disagree.

I am so worried that I have thought of calling off the trip. She also has had three bite-wing X-rays at the dentist's this year. Have I let the child be harmed for the future? Will her reproductive organs be damaged?—Mrs. N. B.

I don't think you should hesitate for a minute about going ahead with the new examination.

It is true that we all should avoid any needless exposure to X-rays. We know that the effect can be cumulative, and that too much can (or may) be harmful. Being careful makes sence.

But fearing the use of X-ray for any diagnostic need is carrying carefulness beyond the point of reasonableness.

Think of it this way. Sometimes X-ray treatments are given in series of exposures which may be measured in minutes, and at full power. And of course some harmful effects must be expected.

Now how does that compare with diagnostic X-ray? the exposure, per film, is about 1/10th of a SECOND, and you must remember that much less intensity is required—with use of image-intensifiers and such devices, only a small fraction of the radiation formerly required is needed now. Thus the total exposure your daughter has had amounts to only a couple of seconds.

There is no reason to be fearful over such X-ray as may be required for diagnostic purposes.

There are great masses of statistics and studies, but it boils down to this: **There is no reason to be fearful over such X-ray as may be required for diagnostic purposes.**

EXERCISE 7. Reading to Eat

Most newspapers print at least one recipe a day. Before you spend time studying a recipe, check it against these questions:

Does it sound like something we'd like to eat?
Are any of the ingredients too expensive or difficult to get?
Does it call for equipment we don't have—blender, oven, special pan?
Does it take more time or work than I want to give?

Recipes use some words that are new to you, too. And here you have to know exactly what the word means. It's no good guessing. What if you are making this recipe, and you guess that simmer means to cook over high heat? You'll have a pan of crisp, black applesauce.

Many cookbooks have a section that explains words used in cooking. And of course, the words are in a regular dictionary.

Directions: Here are the meanings of five words from the recipe on page 173. Study them. Then see if you can write the right word in the blanks in the paragraph below the recipe.

simmer: To keep just below the bubbling point.
saute (pronounced saw-tay): To fry quickly in a little fat.
shortening: a "hard" cooking fat, such as margarine, butter, or lard. Recipe writers say "liquid shortening" when you are to use a cooking oil such as Wesson oil.

Different Ham Sandwich

WELCOME FOR BREAKFAST OR SUPPER
Big, light, tender pancake sandwiches

Ever make sandwiches with pancakes? They're great for breakfast or supper, especially when they are put together this way.

Light, tender cakes, big ones, have a "filling" of gently frizzled ham slices. Over the top goes spicy, fragrant apple sauce that's been simmered with butter, cinnamon, allspice and lemon.

HOT APPLE AND HAM PANCAKE SANDWICHES

2 cups canned apple sauce
½ cup light brown sugar
½ tsp. cinnamon
¼ tsp. allspice
2 tbsps. butter
½ tsp. grated lemon rind
1 tbsp. lemon juice
1½ to 2 cups pancake mix
Boiled ham slices
Shortening

Combine apple sauce, sugar, cinnamon, allspice, butter, lemon rind and juice. Simmer five minutes; keep hot until ready to serve. Saute ham slices in shortening; keep warm in oven.

Follow directions on package for making pancakes. Place ham slices between each two cakes; top with the apple sauce. Serve immediately. Six to eight servings.

San Francisco Examiner

grate: To break into tiny bits by rubbing against the rough surface of a grater. You are expected to know that when a recipe calls for grated lemon rind, that means only the thin, shiny yellow surface of the lemon skin.
serving: A helping; a portion.

Prepare the __________ lemon rind. Measure the first seven ingredients into a saucepan. Put the applesauce mixture on the stove and __________ for five minutes. Put a few tablespoons of __________ in a frying pan. __________ the ham slices one at a time. Follow the directions on the pancake mix box to make the pancakes. Then put your ham and pancake sandwiches together and top with the hot, spicy applesauce mixture. Everyone will want more than one __________!

EXERCISE 8. Breaking a Job into Parts

A job is easier if you can see that it breaks down into different parts. Follow this recipe in your mind. You will find that you prepare three separate things, and then put them together to make the pancake sandwich.

Directions: Write in the blank the letter of the list that best completes the sentence.

1. There are three main steps in preparing this recipe. They are:_____.

a. Make applesauce topping, fry ham slices, make pancakes.
b. Open canned applesauce, grate lemon rind, boil ham slices.
c. Make applesauce topping, add spices, make pancakes.

EXERCISE 9. Putting Yourself into the Article

Everyone has to wake up in the morning. Some of us bounce out of bed, but some of us have to be pulled out.

Read this selection, then get ready to give a 1-minute talk to the class about waking up on school days. Perhaps you can relate it to other ideas you have heard about the process of waking up.

Here are some ideas on what to include in your talk:

What does Dr. Ginott say that you especially agree with?
What does he say that you especially disagree with?
Do you have to get your brother or sister up? How do you do it?
Do you have trouble waking up?
How do you like to be waked up?
Do you think it's silly to worry about the right way to wake up a child?

Between Parent and Child

Don't Overplay Role of Policeman

Editor's Note: In the serialization of his book, "Between Parent and Child," Dr. Haim Ginott, internationally known specialist in child psychotherapy and parent guidance, offers an effective approach to the day-to-day dealings parents have with their children and their problems in such areas as discipline, sex education and anxieties.

By Dr. Haim Ginott

Civilization has cast parents in the role of "killjoys" who must "no" many of the small child's pleasures. Some restrictions are inevitable if the child is to become a social being. However, parents should not overplay their role of policemen for civilization, lest they invite avoidable resentment and hostility.

Dr. Ginott

The 'Good Morning'

Mother should not be the one to wake up her schoolage child every morning. The child resents a mother who disturbs his sleep and disrupts his dreams. It is better for all concerned if the child is awakened by an alarm clock.

A child who cannot wake up easily should not be called lazy; and he who does not rise and shine instantly should not be labeled "sour puss." Rather than engage with them in a battle, it is best to let them enjoy another ten golden minutes of sleep or daydreams. This can be accomplished by setting the alarm clock to ring earlier. Our statements should convey empathy rather than anger or scorn or alarm over health:

"It is hard to get up this morning."

"It is such a pleasure to lie in bed and dream."

"Take another fives minutes."

Make Morning Bright

Such statements make the morning bright; they create a climate of warmth and intimacy.

Dr. Haim Ginott, Professor of Psychology at New York University and Adelphi University, is the author of the best selling books: BETWEEN PARENT AND CHILD, Macmillan, 1965, BETWEEN PARENT AND TEENAGER, Macmillan, 1969 and TEACHER AND CHILD, Macmillan, 1972.

EXERCISE 10. Picking Out Interesting Facts

You are a bug about Dionne Warwick. So are your sister and your mother. You are going to cut out this article to show to them.

Directions: First underline some of the most interesting bits of information, so that you can find them fast when you talk about the article. Write the number of the paragraph in which the following questions are answered. The first one is done for you as an example.

_8_ 1. What size dress does Dionne Warwick take?

____ 2. How much do her clothes cost? (Hint: Look for dollar signs—$)

____ 3. How tall is she and how much does she weigh? (Hint: Look for numbers and foot-inch-pound words or symbols: ', ", lbs., #)

____ 4. How old is she?

____ 5. What is her favorite dress?

A Singer With No Wardrobe Blues

By JUDY KLEMESRUD
Special to The New York Times

(1) MAPLEWOOD, N. J. — Dionne Warwick likes to tell about the time when, early in her singing career, she was visiting Italy and a shopkeeper who obviously was a fan insisted on giving her a "pretty little dress." It wasn't until Miss Warwick returned to her home in New Jersey that she learned the dress was a $185 Pucci.

(2) Times have changed.

Miss Warwick was recently named "best dressed singer" by the Paris Couturier Association, an organization of young French designers. She now has so many clothes that it takes three houses to hold them, and she can tick off the labels as readily as if they were the names of the songs she has recorded.

List of Luminaries

(3) Her wardrobe — both private and professional — includes fashions by such luminaries as Valentino, Galanos, Chanel, Oscar de la Renta, Chester Weinberg, Cardin, Sarmi, Saint Laurent, Dior, Geoffrey Beene and Louis Feraud.

(4) Does she prefer the European or the American designers?

(5) "I prefer clothes, period," she said diplomatically, even though she is a personal friend of both Feraud and Saint Laurent, whom she met during singing engagements in Paris. Then, after a moment's thought, she added:

(6) "But my favorite dress is one that I bought for $60 in Arizona. It has a multicolored chiffon shell over culottes, and I haven't the faintest idea who designed it."

(7) The 27-year-old singer looked like the chic, high-cheeked model she used to be during an interview the other day in her three-bedroom brick home here, where she lives with her husband, Bill Elliott, an actor.

(8) The curviness of her 5-foot-5-inch, 118 pound figure was emphasized by a pair of snug black and white checked slacks and a white ruffled blouse ("I love to get as much femininity out of pants as I can"), and when she changed into a dress she opted for femininity again — a white ruffled number (size 7) by Chester Weinberg.

(9) "I love all the current fashions — except for the midiskirt," she said firmly. "I just *hate* that. I mean, that was 20 years ago. This is 1968. I don't understand why they'd even think of such a horrible thing."

(10) If Miss Warwick had been born tone deaf, she probably would be in the fashion business today. As a child, she sewed many of her own clothes ("I had good home economics teachers") and later was a teen-age model at Bamberger's in Newark. At one time she thought seriously about going into the boutique business with a girl friend, who had attended the Fashion Institute of Technology.

(11) "It's a lucky thing I didn't," she said. "The boutique was burned down during the Newark riots."

(12) Miss Warwick buys most of her clothes at either Martha Inc. of New York on Park Avenue or at the designers' dress houses. She often pays wholesale prices, but the cost really doesn't matter to her.

(13) "I can deduct most of my clothes from my income tax because I need them for my career," she said, grinning broadly.

A Movable Wardrobe

(14) The pop - jazz - gospel - rhythm - and - blues singer keeps the overflow of her daytime clothes and accessories in the home of her parents, who live 10 blocks away in Orange. (Her father, Mancel, is a chef at the Masters School in Dobbs Ferry, N.Y.) Most of her gowns are stored in the home of her valet, Willie Dixon, who lives in Brooklyn.

(15) Two of her proudest possessions are a gold Balmain gown that Marlene Dietrich gave to her after a performance in Paris in 1962 ("I guess she liked my singing," Miss Warwick said), and a mink-lined raincoat that she had custom-made after she saw a similar coat in a Doris Day movie, "Touch of Mink."

(16) For just puttering around the house, she sometimes throws on a mink miniskirt, a ruffled blouse and black patent stretch boots. (She thinks her boot and shoe wardrobe is probably more extensive than her clothes wardrobe — but she can't be sure because she hasn't had time to count her shoes.)

(17) Perhaps her most unusual costume is a daisy-covered white organdy blouse with matching short shorts by Oscar de la Renta. She wore it recently at a performance in Constitution Hall in Washington, which is owned by the ultraconservative Daughters of the American Revolution.

(18) "I didn't do it purposely to shock anyone," the singer said. "It's no shorter than a lot of miniskirts you see."

(19) Miss Warwick recorded her first song, "Don't Make Me Over," in 1962, while she was a scholarship student at the Hartt College of Music in Hartford, Conn. Since then her soulful recordings have sold more than 5 million LP's and 6.5 million singles. Her best-known singles are "Anyone Who Had a Heart," "Alfie," and "Valley of the Dolls."

(20) Despite her new affluence, there's still one thing that Miss Warwick hasn't gotten around to buying.

(21) "I want a sable," she said, "and when I have that, I'll have everything I want."

The Salt Lake Tribune

Food and Women's News

First Section — Monday Morning, April 1, 1968 — Page 13

Ann Landers, Field Newspaper Syndicate from the *Salt Lake Tribune*.

Dear Ann Landers: My son has a 13-year-old daughter who is quite mature for her age, but still she is only 13. Her mother allows her to accept Friday and Saturday night sitting jobs in the apartment building. Last night she had full charge of three youngsters. Please tell me what you think about this. —CONCERNED

____6. Is she married?

____7. Where does she live?

____8. Where does she buy most of her clothes?

EXERCISE 11. Using Your Own Judgment

It can be fun to read some of the letters from readers who are asking for advice. Do you like to give advice? Here's your chance.

Directions: Pretend that this letter was sent to you. Write two or three sentences answering "Concerned." Use the space below.

Dear Concerned: ____

____

____

____

____

PRACTICE IN YOUR LOCAL NEWSPAPER

PRACTICE 1. Find out what kind of help your local newspaper offers in the areas listed below. Your teacher will assign you to one or more of the groups. Check mark your groups and for the next week or so, keep an eye out for features that fall in your group's subject area. Cut them out and bring them to class. Maybe your paper has features that don't seem to fit any of these groups. Bring those in, too.

Advice on relationships with people (Ann Landers, etc.)

Advice for teen-agers (Dorothy Ricker's Teenage Mail, etc.)

Household Hints (Hints from Heloise, etc.)

Etiquette (Doing the Right Thing by Elizabeth Post, etc.)

Newspaper gets answers and action for you (News Power; Ask the Journal, etc.)

Health (Dr. Molner; Medicare Mailbox, etc.)

Beauty (Arlene Dahl, Ida Jean Kain, etc.)

Recipes and Menus

Child Care (Points for Parents, etc.)

Fashion (The Way You Look, etc.)

Best Buys in Food

Hobbies and special interests (stamp column, gardening, fishing, and hunting, daily dress patterns, etc.)

PRACTICE 2. Your teacher will divide the class into groups of three. Each of you will prepare to give a one-minute talk before the class. Use the class clipping file of features and columns (above) to find a subject and information. You might describe a menu for a teenage party, give a forecast of fashion trends, or demonstrate an exercise. (Write your name and subject on a bulletin board list, so that someone else will not choose the same subject.) Try out your talk on your other two group members. Use their comments to guide you in changing your talk before you give it before the whole class.

PRACTICE 3. Does your local newspaper have a reader service like the *Buffalo Evening News* "News Power," that gets action on reader problems? Save five or more columns. Color mark the lines that tell what person or agency the paper turned to in order to get the information or action the reader wanted. On an attached sheet of paper, write four or more sentences telling what ideas this gives you about steps you yourself could take to get action on problems.

CHAPTER 14
THE BIG NEWS STORY

Some news events are so fascinating, readers just can't read too much about them. The first successful transplant of a human heart is an example of this.

One news article a day is not enough to tell readers all they want to know about such a big news event. The story explodes into a constellation of stories.

It all began when headlines announced:

TRANSPLANT HUMAN HEART!
A HISTORIC FIRST, MAN DOING WELL

All over the world readers began to follow the story. There were hundreds of questions they wanted to have answered. Will

Where to Find It:

Comics	18	TV, Radio	17
Editorials	10	Weather	13
Wilson	4-8	Women	15

★★★★

THE WEATHER — Variable cloudiness and slightly warmer today; high in the 50s. Little change Tuesday. Sunrise 7:24, sunset 4:45.

The Des Moines Register

The Newspaper Iowa Depends Upon

Des Moines, Iowa, Monday Morning, December 4, 1967—26 Pages—Two Sections

Price 10 Cents

TRANSPLANT HUMAN HEART!

A HISTORIC FIRST, MAN DOING WELL

Auto Crash Victim Used as Donor

Louis Washkansky
The Recipient

Denise Ann Darvall
Her Heart Used

CAPE TOWN, SOUTH AFRICA (AP) — A South African hospital claimed Sunday the world's first successful human heart transplant.

Surgeons removed the heart of a young woman who died after an automobile crash and placed it in the chest of a 55-year-old man dying because his own heart was damaged, the announcement said.

When the transplanted heart was in place, it was started beating by an electric shock. Dr. Jan H. Louw, the hospital's chief surgeon, said, "It was like turning the ignition switch of a car."

Groote Schuur Hospital said the man was doing well late Sunday but that the next few days would be a critical period.

The heart was removed from the body of Denise Ann Darvall, 24, an accounting-machine operator at a bank, and transferred to Louis Washkansky, a businessman, the hospital said.

Five-Hour Operation

Washkansky, described as of medium build, was reported fully conscious and in very satisfactory condition after the five-hour operation that ended at 6 a.m. The announcement said his blood pressure was normal by Sunday afternoon.

In the first stage of the heart transplant operation, both Washkansky and the body of Miss Darvall were put on heart-lung machines, each manned by a team of technicians.

In the second stage, the donor's heart was removed and the circulation of her heart, once it was taken out, was kept going by a pump.

The third stage was the removal of Washkansky's heart.

The fourth and most intricate stage of the operation was the placing of the donor's heart in Washkansky's body. When the transplant was completed, electrodes were placed against the heart walls, and a high current was switched on for a fraction of a second.

The heart started beating immediately, said Louw.

Surgeons at California's Stanford Medical Center have been reported by the Journal of the American Medical Association to be ready for a heart transplant whenever the ideal donor and ideal recipient appear there at the same time. Animal heart transplants have been successful at that center.

Sources at Groote Schuur Hospital said the transplant for Washkansky nearly took place last Wednesday with another donor but was canceled at the last moment because the donor died too soon.

Kidneys Also Used

Miss Darvall's kidneys also were removed and taken to Cape Town's Karl Bremer Hospital for a successful kidney transplant to Jonathan Van Wyk,10.

The announcement of the transplant to Washkansky came from Dr. Jacobus G. Burger, medical supervisor of the Groote Schuur Hospital.

"The operation was his only chance," Burger said. "Washkansky was dying and wouldn't have lived longer than a few days otherwise." Burger said the next two or three days would be the critical postoperative period.

"The longer Washkansky goes on, the better," he said, "although that does not mean the heart will not be rejected later. The body could decide in 5 or 10 years' time that it doesn't want this heart."

Washkansky has a tracheotomy — a tube inserted in his throat through which he is breathing — and is unable to speak, said Burger. He is being kept absolutely quiet in a special room.

"Even the nurses don't speak to him," he added. "They are doing everything for him and keeping him quiet."

Clotting Peril

Dr. Burger said apart from the body's natural tendency to reject the heart, the main danger could come from blood clotting and resultant heart failure. Washkansky is being fed anti-clotting drugs to counter this.

"We are also using steroids to prevent the heart being thrown out (rejected)," Burger said.

He said Washkansky had been kept alive by using pumps to assist his heart, but this could not have gone on indefinitely.

"The heart muscle was fibrosed, which means that all the muscle was gone and there was only fibrous tissue there," the doctor said. "It wouldn't pump the blood any more, and his condition was deteriorating."

"We thought he was dying a week ago, and he would have died immediately if we had taken the pumps away.

"Washkansky knew what he was going into, but it was his only chance."

Heading the team of five cardiac surgeons was Prof. Chris Barnard, father of South African women's water ski champion Deirdre Barnard.

In addition to the cardiac surgeons, there were two neurosurgeons and two anesthetists. Altogether there were about 20 in the theater, including five or six theater nurses, said Burger. All the surgeons were South Africans.

Injured Saturday

The woman donor was injured fatally in an auto accident Saturday afternoon. Neurosurgeons, with an electro-encephalogram to measure her brain waves, alerted the cardiac surgeons the instant she died and the operation began immediately.

Consent earlier had been obtained from her father to use her heart.

"The operation had to begin within half an hour of her death," Burger said. The woman's mother was killed instantly in the same auto accident.

Dr. Norman E. Shumway, the Stanford surgeon who 13 days ago announced plans for transplanting a human heart, said Sunday the operation at Cape Town was "pretty exciting." Shumway, head of Stanford's division of cardiovascular surgery, said he worked with Professor Barnard at the University of Minnesota about 10 years ago.

After hearing of the heart transplant at Cape Town, Shumway said, "It sounds to me like a damn good job — scientifically valid."

Shumway said he and his surgical team are still awaiting the required combination of patient and heart donor at Stanford.

"Definite Chance"

In Washington, D.C., a Navy researcher in the field of organ transplants said, "There is quite a definite chance" that the recipient of the Cape Town transplant might survive "at least two years or more."

Dr. Kenneth Sell of the U.S. Naval Medical Research Institute said several dogs which had received heart transplants from other dogs still are alive two years after the surgical transfer.

But he cautioned that prospects for such long-term success in the case of the human patient could only begin to be evaluated some 10 to 11 days from now.

This is when he said the "next critical period in this case would take place" —that is, the time when the first signs of immunological rejection of the implanted heart might ordinarily be expected to show up.

One known unsuccessful heart transplant has been made in the U.S. In 1964, University of Mississippi kept a patient alive despite his failing heart in a long wait for a human donor. When his heart could wait no longer, they hurriedly transplanted the heart of a chimpanzee, which failed after one hour.

ociated Press

the man live? Who is he? Why was he chosen for the first transplant? If he lives, will more hearts be transplanted? What are the chances of his living? When will he be out of danger? Who donated the new heart? How was it done?

EXERCISE 1. Digging Out the WWWWW&H

Directions: Read the story on page 179 and fill in the blanks by finding answers to the questions below.

1. (Where?) What is the name of the town and country given in the dateline? ________________

2. (Where?) What is the name of the hospital where the transplant was made? ________________

3. (When?) On which day of the week was the transplant made? ________________

4. (Who?) Who received the transplanted heart? ________________

5. (Who?) What was the name of the woman whose heart was used? ________________

6. (How?) What caused the death of the woman whose heart was transplanted? ________________

7. (Why?) Why was the transplant necessary? ________________

8. (Who?) What is the name of the professor who headed the team of five cardiac surgeons performing the transplant operation? ________________

9. (How?) How was the transplant done? Mark your answer on the article by circling each of the paragraphs describing the four stages.

____

____

____

____

EXERCISE 2. Verifying Sources of Information

Directions: Skim through the story to find the paragraphs which give information gathered from sources in the United States. Write *USA* in the margin beside each of these paragraphs. The first one is done for you.

EXERCISE 3. Anticipating the Reader's Questions

Directions: The story contains answers to several questions which most readers would want answered. Read each question below. Then put a check in the blank in front of the answer which is given in the article.

1. Has the patient regained consciousness?

a. ____ The patient is still unconscious.

b. ____ The patient is fully conscious.

2. What was the blood pressure of the patient on Sunday afternoon?

a. ____ High.

b. ____ Low.

c. ____ Normal.

3. Has the patient spoken to anyone since the transplant?

a. ____ To Dr. Barnard.

b. ____ To the nurses.

c. ____ To no one.

4. How long does Dr. Burger estimate it may take to be certain Washkansky's body will not reject the transplant?

a. ____ Two or three days.

b. ____ Five or ten years.

5. After the danger of reject, what is the other danger?

a. ____ Heart failure caused by a blood clot.

b. ____ High blood pressure.

6. Has any hospital in the United States announced that it is ready to transplant a heart?

a. ____ California's Stanford Medical Center

b. ____ U.S. Naval Medical Research Institute

7. How soon after death of the donor did the operation have to begin?

a. ____ One day.

b. ____ Half an hour.

8. What event occurred to prevent an earlier transplant scheduled for Wednesday?

a. ____ The blood type of the donor was wrong.

b. ____ The donor died too soon.

EXERCISE 4. Applying the Cut-off Test

Directions: Remember, a news story is often written so that it can be cut and still retain the important facts the reader needs to know. Imagine that this story must be made twenty-seven lines shorter for the final edition of the paper. Put a check in front of the statement which describes material that could be left out with least damage to the main story.

____1. The last paragraph.

____2. The subhead "Definite Chance" and all paragraphs which follow.

____3. The five paragraphs following the subhead, "Five-Hour Operation."

____4. The four paragraphs following "Kidneys Also Used."

EXERCISE 5. Finding Out There Is "More to Come."

For eighteen days readers followed the story of Mr. Washkansky's struggle for life. Newspapers carried detailed accounts of his operation, his day-to-day condition, what he said, what he ate, and how he slept.

Then readers learned the answer to their question of how the story of the first human heart transplant would end. As you read the account of "Mr. Washkansky's 18 Days," notice that the story of heart transplants is *not ending.*

Directions: Underline the statement which shows that there will be more transplants.

Mr. Washkansky's 18 Days

Drugs That Helped Keep Him Alive Also Made Heart Patient Vulnerable

Four days after the Dec. 3 operation, Ann Washkansky was allowed a four-minute reunion with her husband, Louis. They were not allowed to kiss because the 53-year-old Cape Town grocer was still dangerously vulnerable to infection. Over the radio Mr. Washkansky told South Africa, "I'm feeling fine." Medicine's first heart-transplant patient was inching back toward full health and a normal life.

But Mr. Washkansky lived under a fateful shadow. No doctor had solved the problem of rejection—the ability of the body to reject foreign protein intruders, whether those intruders be infectious germs or new livers or hearts. (1) To reduce the immunizing process in Mr. Washkansky's body, his doctors fed him special drugs. (2) (Not fully explained) But in doing so their patient became particularly susceptible to infection. In other words, in a maneuver to keep the new heart, (3) (Not fully explained) Mr. Washkansky was stripped of his normal defenses against disease.

Thirteen days after the operation, Mr. Washkansky developed a mild form of pneumonia. Despite heavy doses of penicillin his condition deteriorated. (4) He was placed in an iron lung, and then on Dec. 21 his wife was taken to his bedside to say good-by. Three hours later Louis Washkansky was dead.

According to an autopsy, the cause of death was a severe localized infection of the lungs. Mr. Washkansky's new heart, transplanted from the body of Denise Darvall, a 25-year-old traffic-accident victim, pumped well until the end. (4) Less than eight hours after the patient died, Dr. Christian N. Barnard, head of the 30-man transplant team, called a press conference to announce: "As soon as the occasion arises we will do the next heart transplant."

Dr. Barnard also said he saw no evidence that Mr. Washkansky's body had rejected the transplanted heart of the young woman. (5) Asked if the death meant that his experiment had failed, the South African surgeon replied: "Firstly, I would not consider it an experiment. It was a treatment for a sick patient. The problem of infection was loaded against the surgical team." (5)

Mr. Washkansky's death had a special meaning for the heart donor's father, Edward Darvall. Said Mr. Darvall, whose wife also perished in the accident that killed his daughter: "I feel completely empty. After the operation there was at least part of my daughter alive in Mr. Washkansky. But now she is completely dead."

The National Observer

EXERCISE 6. Problem-Solving as You Read

Directions: Sometimes when you read a news item it will help you to understand it if you visualize methods and conclusions. Study the diagram on page 184. Then look at the step-by-step diagram of the scientific method used in the article "Drugs That Helped Keep Him Alive . . . " Notice that each step has a number. The article does not give complete details, but you can follow the method. Pretend you are the doctor who has to figure out a new working hypothesis before the next heart transplant. On the basis of what you learn from this article, what might you try next time to avoid stripping the patient of "his normal defenses against disease"? ______________________________

____

____

EXERCISE 7. Knowing Your Vocabulary

Directions: Often people do not agree on word meanings and often both sides are justified in their interpretations. Look up the words *experiment* and *treatment* in a dictionary. Before you do so, write your own definitions to see how close you come. Write the dictionary definitions in the spaces provided below. Then decide whether you think the first heart transplant was an experiment or a treatment. Check the one you choose and write why.

Experiment means ______________________________

____

____

Treatment means ______________________________

____

____

Conclusion: I believe the first human heart transplant was ____ an experiment because ____

____

________________________ a treatment because ____________________

____

____

I think Dr. Barnard objected to the use of the word *experiment* because

____

____

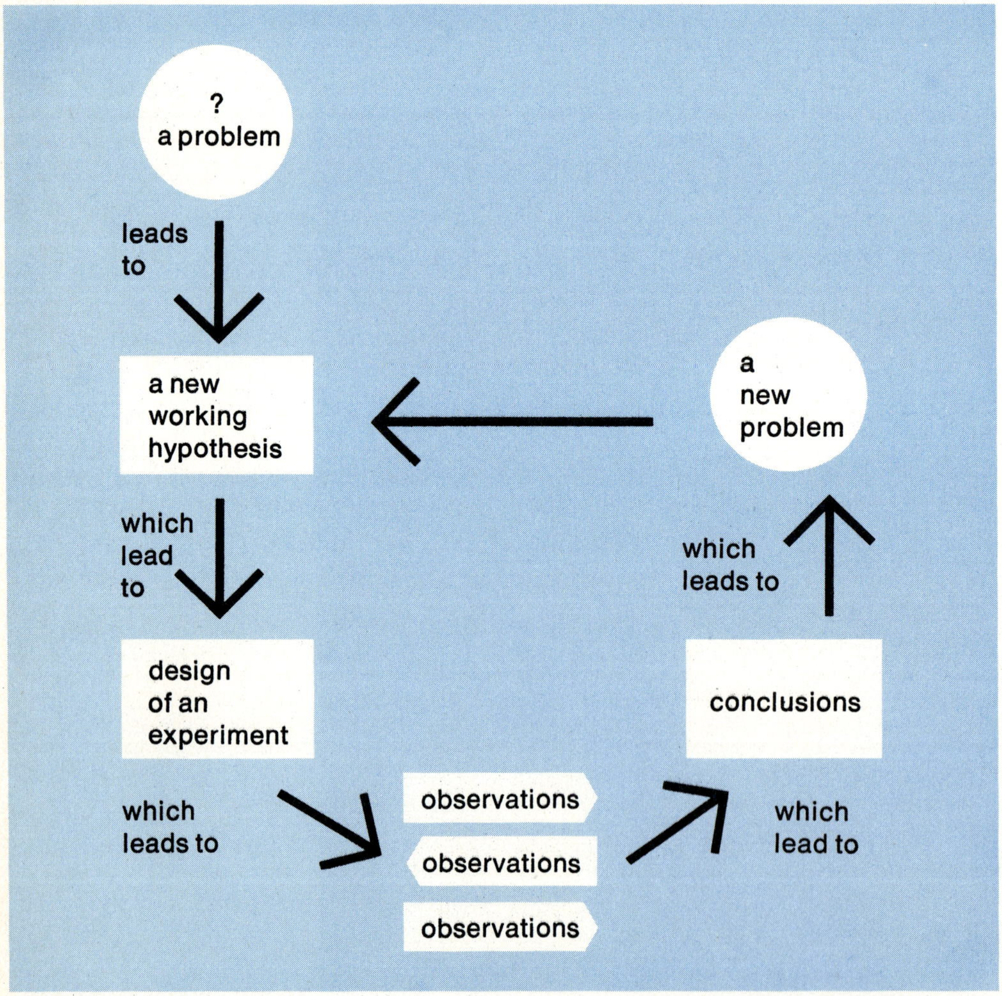

Redrawn from YOU AND SCIENCE by Paul Brandwein et al., copyright © 1960 by Harcourt Brace Jovanovich, Inc. and reproduced with their permission.

THE STORY OF HEART TRANSPLANTS GOES ON

Three days after Dr. Barnard's first human transplant on Louis Washkansky, the second human heart transplant was performed in Brooklyn, New York. Dr. Adrian Kantrowitz implanted the heart of a two-day-old infant in a two and a half week-old child, but the baby died six and a half hours after the operation at Maimonides Hospital.

On January 2, just eight days after the death of Louis Washkansky, Dr. Barnard performed his second heart transplant at Groote Schuur Hospital. By now the public had read millions of words about Dr. Barnard and heart transplants. They were ready for more technical information like that contained in the article by Arthur J. Snider, Science Editor for the *Chicago Daily News*.

As with any technical subject, the reporters will do what they can to make the subject easy to understand. This cannot always be done. In this case, you might want to look over the words and phrases defined in the box before reading the article.

WORDS TO HELP YOU

"biological kinship of his tissues and that of his mulatto benefactor" means that tissues from the two men belong to one of the families (groups) of tissues.

incompatability—condition in which two tissues can't exist when combined in one person.

immune—protected from a disease or the like, as by inoculation. For example, children are given Salk vaccine to make them immune to polio.

immunity—state of being immune to a disease; a condition in which persons won't become ill from the disease.

immunology—that branch of medical science which deals with immunity to diseases and the production of such immunity.

immunologist—a person who practices immunology.

antigens—substances carried in certain cells of transplanted tissue.

antigen-typing—classifying antigens, putting several similar antigens into groups.

COMPARING THE KNOWN WITH THE UNKNOWN

Scientists search for answers to the mysteries of life. Each new discovery is used to help find answers to other unknowns.

This news story compares the use of the scientific method to find the answers required to match blood types with the present attack on the problem of matching types of tissue.

When you have finished reading the article see if you can complete the parallel outlines. This is a good way to trigger a scientific guess which scientists call an *hypothesis*. As you have learned from the diagram on page 184, after a scientist works out an hypothesis, he designs one or more experiments to check his guess. He makes many observations. Then he draws conclusions. These conclusions often show him more problems which must be solved. For these new problems, the scientist must figure out more hypotheses and repeat the other steps. Little by little, answers are found.

Reprinted with permission from the *Chicago Daily News*

6 CHICAGO DAILY NEWS, Wednesday, Jan. 3, 1968

2d transplant in S. Africa

Matched tissue aids heart patient

By Arthur J. Snider
Daily News Science Editor

A plus factor going for dentist Philip Blaiberg in Cape Town's second heart transplant is the biological kinship of his tissue and that of his mulatto benefactor.

It has been demonstrated in kidney grafts that the closer the tissue ties, the less vigorously the body seeks to reject the transplant.

Tissue is now matched in much the same way as blood. As in the case of blood transfusions, there is likely to be a violent reaction in the event of incompatability.

Dr. John S. Thompson, immunology specialist in the University of Chicago department of medicine, says considerable progress has been made in tissue-matching in recent years. This boosts chances for the Cape Town transplant.

"The odds still are very much against them out there," he said in an interview, "but the odds were very much against the first kidney transplants at the time they were done."

TISSUE - MATCHING .tests were developed for kidney transplants after it was observed that people have antigens in their tissues distinctive to the individual. As in the case of blood, antigens have no relationship to race.

Antigens are substances carried on certain cells of transplanted tissue. They provoke the recipient to form resisting antibodies.

Antigen-typing is more complex than blood-typing as there are many more tissue antigens, Dr. Thompson said. But, like blood, it is hoped that many antigens will turn out to have similarities that will permit classifying them in groups.

"In the case of blood, there are at least 26 blood cell types and one could find anywhere from 40 to 90 antigens, depending on how hard he wanted to work at it," Dr. Thompson continued.

"However, blood types can be grouped and we find clinically we need only pay attention most of the time to the A-B-O and Rh blood types and to only about eight antigens."

A HOSPITAL spokesman in Cape Town said tissues of Blaiberg and his doner, Clive Haupt, 24, a son of white and Negro parents, were "not perfect, but satisfactory."

The tissue typing took almost four hours. Tests developed by Dr. Paul Terasaki, immunologist at the University of California, Los Angeles, were used.

Dr. Thompson's laboratory has developed a two-hour test, soon to be reported in the medical literature.

A rapid test will enable physicians to proceed much quicker in transplant situations where time is urgent.

EXERCISE 8. Making Comparisons

Directions: Read and compare statement 1 of the "Blood Transfusion Outline" with statement 1 of the "Tissue Transplant Outline." Then read 2 of the "Blood Transfusion Outline." Can you complete 2 of the "Tissue Transplant Outline" with material that compares with that in the 2 of the "Blood Transfusion Outline"?

(*Hint:* Try to imagine that you are a scientist lining up what was done to make matching blood possible. This may suggest ways to attack the problem of matching tissue.)

BLOOD TRANSFUSION OUTLINE	TISSUE TRANSPLANT OUTLINE
1. During early blood transfusions many violent reactions occurred because scientists did not know how to match the type of blood being transferred with the type of blood in the patient.	1. During early organ transplants, many rejections have occurred because scientists do not know how to match the type of tissue in the transplant with that of the patient.
2. Scientists studied the blood and discovered at least 26 blood types.	2. Scientists are studying the tissues and have discovered that ______________________ ______________________ ______________________
3. Scientists discovered that blood types have similarities that permit classifying them in groups.	3. Scientists hope that __________ ______________________ ______________________ ______________________
4. Scientists discovered that most of the time they need pay attention only to the A, B, O, and Rh blood types.	4. Scientists may discover that most of the time they need to pay attention only to __________ ______________________ ______________________ ______________________

EXERCISE 9. Following up Leads

Directions: Imagine you plan to become a medical technician. You are interested in learning more about antigen-typing. Underline the paragraph in the article which tells where you will be able to learn about a new two-hour test for tissue typing.

SEEING ALL SIDES OF THE STORY

As the news of the first heart transplant hit the front pages of newspapers all over the world, the story was that it could be done. A few weeks later, newspapers printed stories stating that many persons thought heart transplants should not be done.

Arguments about the ethical, moral, and legal implications of transplant surgery sprang up everywhere. People began to debate how the moment of death was to be decided. The beating of the heart did not seem to apply any longer. Some doctors argued that a person was dead when the brain stopped functioning.

8 CHICAGO DAILY NEWS, Tuesday, March 12, 1968

Barnard bars moratorium

Barnard plans third transplant

By Arthur J. Snider
Daily News Science Editor

Dr. Christiaan Barnard, admittedly taken aback by the professional criticism surrounding his pioneering heart transplant work, rejects any suggestion of a moratorium on further operations.

The lean South African surgeon said every doctor must decide the question for himself and that he intends to proceed with preparations for a third transplant on his return Thursday to Cape Town.

Since the death of his first patient, Louis Washkansky, who lived 18 days with a transplanted heart last December, Dr. Barnard has been the target of increasing criticism.

THE 44-YEAR-OLD trailblazer has been accused in medical journal editorials of promoting publicity, raising hopes that may not be fulfilled and pushing ahead on a new frontier without full knowledge of the hazards and consequences.

Individual cardiologists have suggested a moratorium until transplants already done can be fully evaluated.

The National Academy of Sciences has recommended only a relatively small number of careful investigations involving cardiac transplantation need be done at this time."

IN A FORTHRIGHT defense of his ethical, legal and moral position, Dr. Barnard told 750 members and guests of the Chicago Press Club Monday that he and his associates have fulfilled every standard of the World Medical Assn." governing clinical operations of this sort.

Barnard

Responds to heart transplant critics

He explained the serious illnesses, of Washkansky and Dr. Philip Blaiberg, his second patient and, outlined the procedure for obtaining the donor hearts. He concluded his talk by saying:

Now I leave it to you to decide whether we have been immoral and have done anything outside the law."

DR. BARNARD said later in an interview he was "surprised" by the criticism the operation evoked from doctors, adding:

"I was surprised because there was no criticism of liver transplants, for example. The liver, like the heart, is not a paired organ. If the liver transplant fails, the patient also is lost."

Criticism in England has been even more severe than in the United States, he said.

The American Heart Assn., and the American College of Cardiologists have established committees to set up guidelines for transplant operations, but Dr. Barnard said he cannot necessarily be bound by their recommendations.

A doctor has the right to determine whether he will proceed with a heart transplant operation just as he makes other life and death decisions," he said.

CITING THE CASE of Dr. Blaiberg, whom he expects to discharge this weekend, about 2½ months after the operation, the surgeon said:

I feel that Dr. Blaiberg will be able to go back home and live a normal life. I don't know how long he can live. No one can say that. He may have trouble with his transplanted heart.

But one thing I do know. Any time he lives from now on will be more than he would have lived if he did not have the transplanted heart. And more important, the time he lives will be a much happier time, free of the agony of severe heart failure."

EXERCISE 10. What Do You Think?

The articles on these two pages give Dr. Barnard's and patient Blaiberg's reaction to this criticism. Read the articles and try to decide how you would answer the question: Should doctors transplant hearts?

Directions: Write your three to four sentence answer on the lines below.

'My heart: a gift'

In conclusion, a salvo at Barnard critics

Eileen and Dr. Philip Blaiberg drink a toast to their future, something that seemed an impossibility last December. In the last article in his series, Blaiberg salutes Dr. Christiaan Barnard and his heart-transplant team and rebukes their critics.

By Dr. Philip Blaiberg

This is my last column in this series and I want to make use of it by saying something special in reply to a doctor who has criticized Prof. Chris Barnard and his heart-transplant team.

I have been stimulated to write this after reading a clipping from a news magazine. According to that, several cardiologists, headed by the arch-critic Dr. William Dempster of Hammersmith Hospital in London, said they doubted I would recover.

Dr. Dempster said I was still breathless. "You could see this on TV," he said.

In the same article, Dr. M. C. Botha, the immunologist on Prof. Barnard's team is asked: "Are heart-transplant procedures premature?"

Dr. Botha replied: "This question should be put to Dr. Blaiberg."

SO, HERE I come with my reply. And I am going to be frank. First, that suggestion of breathlessness is absolute nonsense.

The TV picture to which Dr. Dempster referred was taken long before I was discharged from the hospital on March 16.

At that time I walked around the two rooms of the transplant unit 10 times on five occasions each day—without any signs of breathlessness.

The conclusion of a series by the world's first heart-transplant survivor and his wife, Eileen.

Now I stride up and down the balcony outside my flat. I cover a distance of about 250 yards twice daily. I am not left panting for breath.

I also do exercises to strengthen my thigh muscles, which became weak when I was in bed for so long. This is a symptom with which every doctor is familiar, even when a man is in bed for a week with influenza.

Now my legs are less than 5 per cent short of normal.

What is more, yesterday I went out and drove my own car for the first time since the operation. I did so with the greatest of ease.

I will challenge Dr. Dempster any day to a walk several times up and down my balcony and to my leg exercises, which are pretty strenuous. Let's see how breathless he gets.

SECONDLY, about the suggestion that this operation was premature.

When I went into the hospital on Dec. 14 last year, I did not think I would live every succeeding 24 hours.

Then I was certainly struggling for breath. I had what is medically called apnoeia—or great difficulty with breathing.

I felt thoroughly miserable and would have welcomed death as a merciful release.

Now I feel better than I have felt for years. I enjoy every minute that has been given to me.

Premature? I should say not.

What is more, I enjoy all the pleasures of life.

I am doing what I like and liking what I am doing for the first time in my life. You see, I love reading and writing, but there was never time for it before.

Premature? Do you begrudge me this time to enjoy myself, good doctor?

I SUGGEST you salute Dr. Barnard and his gallant team for having courage to undertake an unprecedented operation.

If your promise proves to be right, you can then say "I told you so." If not, let your statement fade into oblivion.

One more thing: Why put a damper on my happiness and optimism?

It certainly does not inspire confidence in aspiring heart-transplant patients.

I suggest you look optimistically toward the future.

That is what I am doing.

Reprinted with permission from the *Chicago Daily News*

WORDS TO HELP YOU

criticism—act of passing judgment.

professional criticism—criticism by persons belonging to a profession, in this case the medical profession.

moratorium—a period of delay ordered by an authority.

cardiologist—a heart specialist.

evaluate—judge, in this case a study to see whether a transplant is of value.

ethical—dealing with right or wrong in conduct. Members of the medical profession have special rules of conduct (standards) which all doctors are expected to observe.

READING FOR DIFFERENT POINTS OF VIEW

When Dr. Philip Blaiberg wrote "My heart is a gift," he was the only man alive who could describe the feelings of a person with a transplanted heart. This article is the first of a series which appeared in many newspapers. People not only wanted to know what the doctors and other professional people thought—they wanted to know what a person felt like who had another person's heart.

Read about Dr. Blaiberg's own feelings in the news report on the next page.

A BACKWARD LOOK

When a big breakthrough like the heart transplant is achieved, readers want to see it in relation to the place it will occupy in history. This is possible when writers supply background information like that in "A History of Transplants."

EXERCISE 11. Supplying Background Information

Directions: Pretend that you are a reporter writing the first big heart transplant story. You want to include a paragraph on the history of human

'My heart is a gift'

By Dr. Philip Blaiberg

When I woke up this morning it seemed just like the old days again. I was so happy. I felt as if I had never ever been in the hospital. The operation, and the miserable months of sickness that preceded it, seemed nothing more than a dream.

All I longed for during those lazy moments of waking and dressing was the warm touch of soft sunshine on my face, and the smell of fresh air.

I love the outdoor life. I suppose this stems from my childhood, and my days playing rugby as a student.

That is why, during my confinement to our flat, the little balcony outside will mean so much to me. There I can stand and breathe deeply.

Dr. Philip Blaiberg: "The little balcony will mean so much. There I can stand and breathe deeply."

I WILL NEVER FORGET the excitement of leaving Groote Schuur Hospital—just three months after I was admitted with my failing heart.

At that time I never ever thought I would leave the hospital alive. Death, then, would have been a happy release.

But as I left the hospital, it was wonderful to find so many people waiting to wish me well. When some of the nurses and staff applauded as I passed I could have wept with joy.

Even so, I still cannot understand why people should wish to treat me as a hero. What have I done to deserve it?

The truth is that when I entered the hospital last December I was on the edge of death.

And when Professor Christiaan Barnard offered me the chance of a new heart, I took it because there was no other alternative. It was a case of Hobson's choice.

By that time I had become indifferent to life, and my indifference was a source of strength to me at that time.

I was lucky. The operation snatched me from the jaws of death. And those terrible days of suffering when I had to fight for breath were over.

Prof. Barnard, of course, is a brilliant surgeon. There can be no doubt about that.

AFTER THE OPERATION he showed me my old heart, preserved in a plastic case, and we examined it. The bulk of the tissue was badly damaged, just as if it were hanging together by a thread.

In fact, the pathologist said he could have sworn it had been removed from a corpse.

When it was all over, I accepted the success of the operation immediately. Yet I also accepted the danger of my own tissues rejecting those of the new heart. I used to think to myself, "At least I will die in comfort."

THE TROUBLE WAS, of course, that there were no means of establishing how the rejection would manifest itself. These are all situations one has to face during a period when heart transplantation is still in its infancy.

Yet, I believe they can be faced, if you give the team your confidence and co-operation. The most important thing is your determination to help yourself.

The way I kept going was to set myself weekly targets, from Saturday to Saturday, and I used to get quite a kick out of reaching the target.

For nine months before the operation I had been like a fish kept alive by being plunged in and out of water. That is exactly how I felt. I kept gasping for air.

It was only when Prof. Barnard gave me the plastic container, and I became the first man to literally hold his own heart in his hand, that I saw how bad it really was.

As a dentist I have had some basic grounding in medicine, and now I think I also know quite a bit about cardiology. But I realize that I have entered that no-man's land where there is no precedent and where everyone has to feel his way.

The physiotherapist would give me exercises to get my leg muscles working. At first it was terribly difficult, and I would spur myself on with the thought that the sooner I get over this the sooner I get out of here.

But I let myself down one day. I had just started walking around the ward when Dr. Barnard walked in. He stared at me in surprise and said, "Marvelous!"

THEN I PUT UP my fists, pretending to challenge him to a fight. It was then that my legs gave way and I fell.

The nurses were dumbfounded, but as a rugby player I learned how to fall softly. I just got up and carried on my walk around the room.

Now I am home again with Eileen, surrounded by all my own familiar belongings. What more could I wish for?

Certainly I would like to take Eileen abroad at some time—perhaps to revisit all my old haunts. I'd love to see London again and sail up the Rhine as I did in my student days.

But even if this is impossible, I will be happy to end my days here in this flat, with all its peace and calm.

One day soon I hope to go for a drive around the Cape Peninsula, and gaze again at the sea.

This is my next target.

A History of Transplants

Human Renewal

TRANSPLANTS began long before the birth of Christ. Hindu surgeons used "flap-grafts" of forehead skin to repair amputated noses in the B.C. era. Historians also believe they may have used free skin grafts, in which skin is completely removed from one part of the body and grown on another portion of the same body.

IN 1665 in London, Richard Lower cross-transfused blood between two dogs. Two years later he transfused the blood of a lamb into a man with apparent success. But not until 1818 was the first human-to-human blood transfusion believed to have been successfully performed. The first record of such a transfusion in the United States was dated 1832. During the early 1800s John Hunter, also in London, transplanted the spur of a rooster into a chicken's comb.

VEGETATIVE fusion was performed successfully as early as 1743, when scientists grafted one hydra to another. The hydra is a fresh-water polyp, a form of invertebrate, that grows as long as one-half inch. Experiments at the beginning of the Twentieth Century, now routine in high-school biology laboratories, proved that earthworms could be fused together and that extra limbs could be grafted to frogs.

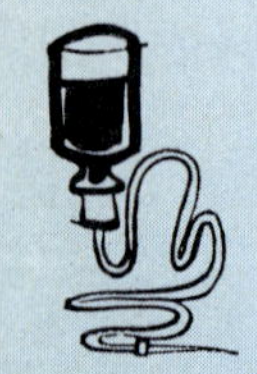

DURING the first few years of this century, scientists made the first of two major advances in blood transfusion: blood typing. Once doctors learned the process of typing, blood transfusions became a practical therapeutic method. But not until 1937 was an efficient method of blood preservation, involving plasma, developed. Plasma came into routine use in World War II.

IN THE early 1920s successful kidney transplants from the same type of animal were under way in dogs. Scientists also transplanted the heart of a puppy into the neck of an adult dog. In Russia in 1941, scientists transplanted hearts in frogs. Early this month, Russians transplanted the head and forelegs of a puppy onto the lower neck of a four-year-old dog.

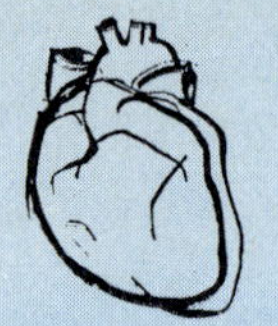

IN DECEMBER 1954 Dr. Joseph Murray at the Peter Bent Brigham Hospital in Boston performed the first enduring kidney transplant, placing a kidney from Ronald Herrick into his identical twin brother, Richard. Richard, then 23, died eight years later of a heart attack; Ronald is still living. Since 1954 more than 1,500 kidney transplants have been performed.

A LUNG transplant was successfully performed on a dog in 1950. The "auto-transplant"—meaning that the lung was taken out of the dog's body and then replaced in the same cavity—was considered a major breakthrough in vital-organ salvage. The first human-lung transplant was performed by Dr. James Hardy at the University of Mississippi's medical center in Jackson in June 1963. John Richard Russell, 58, an inmate at the state prison, lived 18 days after the transplant. An autopsy showed that death resulted from causes other than the transplant. In January 1964 a team of doctors headed by Dr. Hardy transplanted the heart of a chimpanzee into a 68-year-old man. The recipient lived 90 minutes.

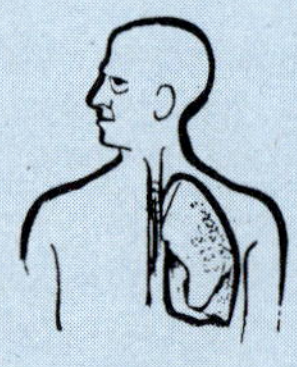

IN 1963 the first liver transplants from man to man were performed in Denver and Boston. The patients died after durations of up to 22 days. Since July 1967 Dr. Thomas E. Starzl has performed five liver transplants at the University of Colorado's medical center. Three of the patients, all 2-year-old girls, have survived. They are in "fair" condition at the hospital.

THEN on Dec. 3, 1967, at Cape Town, South Africa, the world's first human-to-human heart transplant was performed. Dr. Christiaan Barnard transplanted the heart of a 25-year-old woman into Louis Washkansky. Mr. Washkansky, 53, died 18 days later of a lung infection. A month later Dr. Barnard transplanted the heart of a 24-year-old man into Dr. Philip Blaiberg, 58, a Cape Town dentist. Dr. Blaiberg is still living. Three other transplant recipients, all in the United States, have died.

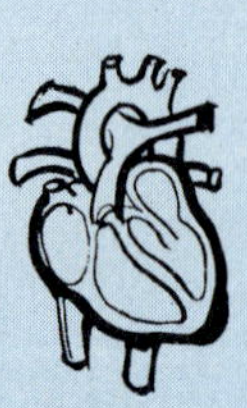

transplants. You are using "A History of Transplants" as your research source. Check the statements that best fill in some blanks in your paragraph:

1. The Louis Washkansky transplant is the first human-to-human heart transplant. An animal-to-human transplant took place

____a. before Christ.

____b. in the early 1800's.

____c. in January 1964.

2. The largest number of human-organ transplants have been done with:

____a. kidneys.

____b. livers.

____c. lungs.

3. High school biology students now routinely transplant

____a. worm segments and frog legs.

____b. frog hearts.

____c. dog legs.

A FORWARD LOOK

Will the next development be an artificial heart? Read the article on the next page to learn about another direction in which heart transplant research is headed. The sentence that relates to the current interest in heart transplants is underlined.

Directions: Pretend you have just heard a TV news flash announcing that three days ago the type of artificial heart described above was successfully implanted in a seventeen-year-old Chicago boy. Write a list of five or more questions that come to your mind:

____

____

____

____

____

CHICAGO DAILY NEWS, Tuesday, April 2, 1968 11

Totally implantable

New artificial heart near

WASHINGTON (AP)—A high-ranking government heart researcher forecasts development by 1973 of a totally implantable artificial heart based on a new concept of energy-supply: Use of the body's own digested food and inhaled oxygen.

Electrical energy to pump the robot heart would come from a fuel cell that would burn oxygen from the blood stream and also glucose, a form of sugar produced by food digested in the normal fashion.

Dr. Frank Hastings, chief of the artificial heart research program of the National Heart Institute, said promising results have been achieved at the laboratory level in developing the fuel-cell concept.

HE SAID IT looks like the best prospect yet for ultimately making completely implantable artificial hearts available to hundreds of thousands of cardiac patients newly stricken each year. He indicated it would eliminate the need for human heart transplants.

The idea would be to graft the fuel cell—consisting of a porous but tough, jelly-like plastic material—into the aorta, the body's major artery, beginning at the point where the blood vessel normally connects with the natural heart. The cell would employ a thin sheet of gold-alloy fibers which would act as a catalyst in promoting energy-producing chemical reactions.

Electrical energy, produced by the fuel cell, would flow to the "muscles" of the nearby implanted artificial heart, enabling it to pump blood in and out of itself.

The robot heart itself would consist of a tough but flexible rubbery material, which would be covered with a thin envelope of living tissue fashioned from a vein in the patient's leg.

Associated Press

PRACTICE IN YOUR LOCAL NEWSPAPER

PRACTICE 1. Keep your eyes open for a breaking news story that "explodes" into a constellation of stories. Save these stories over a period of days or weeks. Make a rough sketch for a bulletin board display showing the spin-off stories surrounding the basic news story. Label the spin-off stories. In the case of the heart transplant story, for example, stories might have been labeled historical background, biographical background, first-person accounts, comments from experts, related scientific developments, and so on.

PRACTICE 2. Bring this heart transplant story up-to-date by finding articles in your local paper or other papers which refer to developments in heart transplants.

PRACTICE 3. In even the smallest news story, WWWWW&H questions can go on endlessly. Every answer raises more questions. Find a news story that interests you in your local newspaper. List all the WWWWW&H questions you can think of. For example: What is the name of the man who did the heart transplant? What is his background? What is his moral position on heart transplants? Does he have a family? What kind of personality does he have? What does he look like? Is he old? Does he have a heart condition?

PRACTICE 4. Here is a kind of puzzle for you. Below are a few paragraphs from a story on a fifteen-year-old scientist. Just for fun, write on a sheet of paper some of your thoughts about the situation. (*Hint:* How long can an animal live without oxygen?)

Reprinted, courtesy of the *Chicago Tribune*

Big League Scientist at 15

BY RONALD KOTULAK

A 15-year-old sophomore at Brother Rice high school isn't letting his first brush with big league science bother him, even tho he just narrowly lost a race for medical fame.

What started out for Richard P. Regan of 4636 99th st., Oak Lawn, as a project for the high school science fair has mushroomed into a high-level basic research program that may eventually result in new life-saving procedures for man.

Barely Misses Out

Richard got an idea for developing a synthetic blood and he missed out by only a few months on being the first person to report on the promising liquid that has been used to replace blood in animal experiments.

While the Oak Lawn youngster was working in a sparsely-furnished laboratory in the Brother Rice high school, a Harvard university researcher was working on the same project in a modern laboratory with assistants.

Neither of them knew the other was working wtih fluorocarbons, the material that is used to coat nonstick frying pans and other utensils.

Vein Is Target

Richard became interested in the biologically inert material after he saw a report about a Duke university scientist who immersed rats in a tank of liquid fluorocarbons. The animals remained alive for up to 18 hours altho they were completely submerged.

Richard thought that the liquid must have some ability to carry oxygen to the lungs, and he got the idea that if the rats were able to survive in a tank of fluorocarbons they might also be able to live with the liquid injected into their veins.

But Dr. Robert P. Geyer, associate professor of nutrition at Harvard's school of public health, had the same idea and he began to work on it full-time.

Being a newcomer to medical research, Richard, who is an "A" student, progressed slowly. He had only one well-used hypodermic needle and at first had trouble locating the target for his injections — the small vein in the tails of the rats.

But he overcame these problems and was able to show that the fluorocarbons could carry three times as much oxygen as natural blood, and that the material was tolerated by the animals. His work won him the top award in his high school's science fair.

He sent a report of his findings to Dr. S. Frederick Rabiner, director of hematology at Michael Reese hospital, who described Richard's work as "remarkable."

Doctor Offers Help

"It is amazing that he was able to do what he did — develop the idea for the experiment and carry it out in a preliminary phase," Dr. Rabiner said. Dr. Rabiner has offered to help Richard to improve his experimental methods and continue his research.

Meanwhile Dr. Geyer also had found that the fluorocarbons were nonpoisonous to the rats. He went two steps further. He replaced 80 per cent of the animals' blood, and finally all of it with the material.

The animals that had only liquid fluorocarbons flowing thru their veins were able to live up to eight hours.

The blood substitute was able to take over the job of the red blood cells. It carried oxygen from the lungs to the body tissue and it took the carbon dioxide wastes and brought them back to the lungs, where they were expelled.

With this evidence in the bag, Dr. Geyer reported his findings at the meeting of the Federation of American Societies for Experimental Biology last month in Atlantic City.

"I was kind of sad that he beat me to it, but I was awfully happy to find that I was on the right track," Richard said.

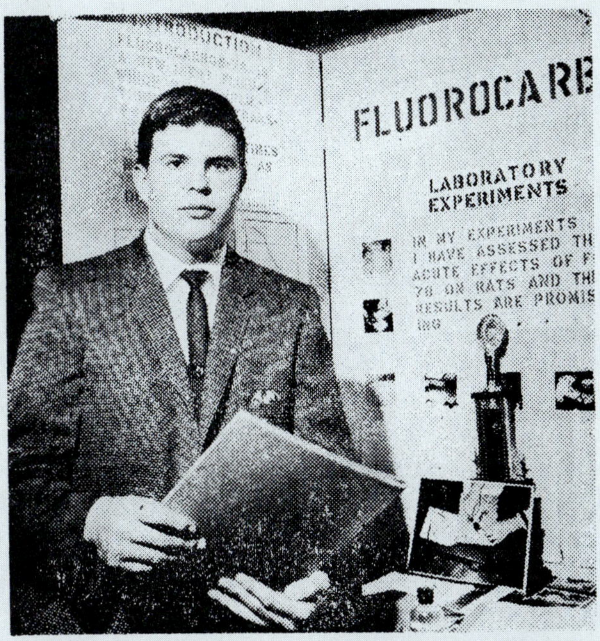

[TRIBUNE Staff Photo]

Richard Regan, the youth who narrowly missed being the first to develop an idea for synthetic blood.

CHAPTER 15
ADVERTISEMENTS:
READ WITH CARE

Say you live in Philadelphia. If you and twenty-five friends organize a committee to work for lowering the voting age to sixteen, you can tell the *Philadelphia Inquirer* about it. The editors might decide to write a story about it and on the other hand they might decide not to. It would depend upon what other stories they had to print and how interesting yours was.

No amount of money would make them put the story in for sure. But, if you collect 10¢ apiece and send $2.60 to the Classified Advertising Department of the *Inquirer,* a half million readers will have the chance to look in the Personals column and find this ad:

> Lower Voting Age to 16! To help, call 433-9979 4–6 p.m.

The editors of the newspaper decide what will be in the editorial space—what news, what columnists, what comics.

Anybody can decide what will be in the advertising space, if he has the money to pay for it.

Most advertising tries to get you to do something. And what most ads want you to do is buy what they're selling.

It can be fun to window-shop through the ads even when you are not planning to buy something. And when you are ready to buy something, reading the ads carefully is a good first step in making a choice.

ADS TELL YOU WHAT THE POSSIBILITIES ARE

Suppose that it is May or June and you are looking for some new clothes to wear to the beach. By thumbing through the pages of your newspaper you will find all sorts of beach-wear suggestions advertised by the different department stores. If you are a girl you might have set your heart on getting a really daring bikini, but one of the ads might show a one-piece suit in an unusual design that makes you change your mind. If you are a boy, you might have decided to buy a pair of sandals like your best friend bought at a certain store for $6.95. When you look through the newspaper for the name of the store, you might see the same sandals advertised on a special at another store for $5.95.

Ads not only show you the many possibilities in styles, colors, materials and varieties of things you want to buy, they also show you that a little comparison shopping can save you money.

CAN YOU TRUST WHAT THE ADS SAY?

An advertisement is just like a Somebody Else Says quotation in a news story. The newspaper does not say that what the advertiser says is true. All the newspaper says is, "This is what the advertiser says." To find out whether it is true or not is up to you. All the statements in the ads are the advertiser's statements, not the paper's.

Some of the statements give a piece of definite information. Suppose that the bathing suit ad said "These suits are available in many colors, plain or striped." Striped is a piece of definite information. It could mean wide printed stripes, or narrow woven stripes, but it definitely means stripes—not flowers, polka dots, or stars.

Some of these statements are opinions you can squeeze a little information out of. Suppose the ad also says "color-fast, long wearing material." You know that color-fast means it isn't going to fade in the sun or bleach out in the laundry, but "long wearing" could mean anything. They don't tell you what the fabric is which would be some sort of guide. All they say is "long wearing." The advertiser might think one year is long wearing, but you may expect three summers of wear out of the suit. "Long wearing" is an opinion you can't be sure you would share.

Some words in ads are just window dressing words, scattered around to give things a sparkle and put you in a mood to buy. Here are some window-dressing words from a perfume ad:

How many of these window-dressing words really make sense?

Do girls really treasure a gift of fragrance most?

Will any fragrance really win the heart of any woman?

Can a scent have an intoxicating, haunting note?

The Plain Dealer

EXERCISE 1. What Do Ads Really Mean?

Directions: What do you think each of these statements from ads really means? Put a check in front of the statement that comes closest to what you think.

1. "Quantities are limited. Don't wait," probably means:

____a. the store is definitely going to sell out before you have a chance to get there.

____b. the store wants you to think that you have to hurry.

____c. the store is worried that you will be disappointed.

2. "Never before such a low price," probably means:

____a. the advertiser has checked all other sales of this product and knows that he is selling it for the lowest price ever.

____b. the advertiser is selling this product at the lowest price he could possibly sell it for and not lose money.

____c. the advertiser is selling this product at the lowest price he has ever sold it for, not necessarily what someone else has sold it for.

3. "Compare to $125.00," probably means:

____a. this same product is selling all over town for up to $125.00.

____b. this is as good a buy as you will find under $125.00.

____c. you would have to pay over $125.00 to get more for your money.

4. "Your credit is good with us," probably means:

____a. if you have good credit references with other places and the necessary references, this company will be glad to give you credit.

____b. this company will give you a credit card with no questions asked just to get your business.

____c. the company prefers that you charge your purchases.

EXERCISE 2. Writing Your Own Ad

Many newspapers have ad space for individuals who have things they want to sell. These ads are usually small and are divided into categories, so that the reader can quickly scan the ad section looking for the headings under which he might find things of interest to him. On the next page is an example of this kind of ad section.

Directions: Suppose that you have a hi-fi set you want to sell, so that you can buy a stereo. You want the ad to be as short as possible (four lines), but you want to be sure that the buyer will be interested enough to call. Read the following facts about your hi-fi set, and then write a four line ad to put in the newspaper. Remember that some information is more important than other information. You don't have to tell about everything that is listed here.

floor model
good looking cabinet
26″ high
36″ wide
AM/FM radio
3 years old
needle just replaced
cost $120.00 new
you want to sell it in order to buy a stereo

the cat scratched one side
brown wood cabinet
50 pounds weight
good tone
4 foot cord

Your ad: ____________________

____

____

____

____

____

13. Schools — Lessons

THE House Of Sunshine Kindergarten. Bilingual instruction. Child will be picked up at home. Reg.-now open. The Best CARE. 764-4420.

SWIMMING Lessons Children & Adults. Day & Eves. Pvt. Pool. Reasonably priced. Melba: 789-3252

KARATE & Self defense for men & women in the comfort of your home or office. 725-1975 after 1 PM.

HARRY & CAROLL HAUCK
Previously 4 yrs. at Caribe Hilton: Individual swim lessons. Condado hotel 723-0010 Cab. 11

SUMMER ART CLASSES
Drawing & Painting
Children's Classes
PHONE 765-5092

SWIMMING — Guaranteed to learn in 5 Lessons. Ages 6 — 106: Free analysis for children under age 6. Contact Joe Baker's Water Sports. Ent. Sheraton Hotel. 724-3817. Home of the famous water baby John-John Baker.

SUMMER SCHOOL with tours. OPEN FOR ENROLLMENT. 783-3145; 782-9545; 767-4494. Ave. J. Pinero 1000, altos, Pto. Nuevo.

13-A Music Lessons

DRUMS, GUITAR, PIANO, ORGAN Your home or our Studio. Music Teachers' Assoc. 764-2504; 785-0867

BEGIN GUITAR lessons now! A good summer activity for Students. Cost $3. Call Nick Shaw, evenings 725-6986.

13C Summer Camps

WE NEED 4 or 5 more children ages 8-10 to complete our small group for SUMMER EXCURSIONS & FUN. Call for registration slips and literature 724-3013 ext. 256. Registration deadline June 6.

14. Language Classes

PRIVATE SPANISH LESSONS in ... HOME Concentrated conversation. Very reasonable. Call ... Tel. 782-0975.

SPANISH in small groups by Dept. of Education instructor.
723-1794, Vieques St. 1110
Apt. 5 Condado

CONVERSATIONAL FRENCH & lessons by French teacher.
Madame Lefevre,
764-2145,

CONVERSATIONAL SPANISH, Grammar, by UPR graduate, long experienced teacher, all levels.
724-3087

FINANCIAL

15. Business Opportunity

"FOR SALE"
San Juan finest ladies Boutique Shop on top of Ocean Front Hotel. Approx. 1,500 SQ. FT. Owner leaving country must sell! Long lease.
Write to San Juan Star
Box F-41, San Juan, P. R.

FOR SALE
Tax exempt Hotel
For information
Call
767-1722

15. Business Opportunity

RESTAURANT for lease in Santurce business section. Well established. Capacity 70 persons, best clientele. 723-1690.

FOR SALE: FULLY Equipped Ladies Underwear Store (Merci) in Edificio Ferramar, 1060 Ashford, Condado, P.R. 725-1915, 722-4496.

SHOE STORE: Mid-town Santurce, 9 years established. SPEC. Men's leading brands, children, women, retiring from business. Good opportunity for right party. 724-6660.

EXCEPTIONAL OPPORTUNITY. Rest. & Cocktail Lounge established clientele. Potential growth possible. Nice location. Call: Vittorio. 765-2720.

8 BEDROOM BEACHFRONT (Ocean Park) Guest House. For sale, no cash required. Income $20,000. Value $180,000. Required: securities or real estate collateral to secure $80,000 note. Call 724-8657 after 10 AM.

FOR RENT OR SALE Pizzeria-Restaurant, fully equipped. Going business in best location on the Golden Mile. Priced for quick sale. Stop 27 & Munoz Rivera Ave. Call after 10 AM 724-2587; eve. 766-2070.

HOTELS with Casino license, hotel sites approved, restaurants, bars, stores, guest houses, shopping centers, beauty parlors, theaters, for sale or trade. All areas. Down from $3,000-up. Specializing in buying, trading & selling business.
CONDADO REALTY
723-4897, 725-2566, 725-9584

Due to illness. Must sell. Store centrally located Lady Casual in Plaza de Mercado Shopping Center (De Diego St.). Fully equipped, ladies & children's apparel. 1,500 sq. ft. completely remodeled, with merchandise. Terms Mr. Rios.

ATTENTION ALL CARIBBEAN ISLANDS:
WHATEVER YOU MAY NEED, WE HAVE IT!
Let us be your purchasing agent in Puerto Rico. Save trips, time and money. Only $10 charge per service. We take care of anything. We ship within 24 hours if available, if not, we'll find it for you. Be another SATISFIED client of: RAMROD SALES COMPANY, GPO Box 3171, San Juan; P.R. 00936.

CAFETERIA FLORENCE, 163 Calle San Andres, eq. Fdez. Juncos, Puerta de Tierra. 63 seating capacity. 725-9987. Must see.

FOR SALE: BEACH FRONT GUEST HOUSE with above average income return. For more information CANSO REALTY 767-0507.

HARDWARE STORE in Ponce de Leon Ave. for sale. Best location in Santurce. Priced by inventory. Payment facilities. Unique Opportunity!
ESPINDOLA-DELLA-TORRE INC.
725-9023

FOR SALE Laundromat in Country Club, Rio Piedras-Carolina area. Very good investment.
Inq. 722-3871

COMMERCIAL LOCATION: Yabucoa, Main St. Munoz Rivera corner of Catalina Morales. $20,000. Unbelievable financing arrangements.
Taylor Realty
725-7021

HOTEL SITE with beachfront, close to airport. Also well known established Hotel with 17 years Tax Exempt. Information only by personal appointment. Canso Realty 767-0507.

COMMERCIAL Space, 2,000 square feet. Tourst area. $700 per month, or will sub-divide 6 rooms. 259 Calle Cristo, San Juan, 725-7127.

FOR SALE OR RENT: Beauty Shop equipped with aircond., telephone. Will sell equipment separately. Location proper for other commercial purposes. For inf. 725-8689, or 724-0353.

15. Business Opportunity

Chance of a lifetime. For small amount invested will sell my interest in profitable Boutique-Gift Shop. At superb location in Old San Juan. Excellent inventory. Books available. Principals only. Box F-46-San Juan Star, 00936.

CEMENT BLOCK FACTORY for sale, full production, for Inf. Km 20, H-1 Carr. No.2, Candelaria Arena. Toa Baja. Call 785-5331.

BOX LUNCH—Fried Chickan French Fires, Cake; fully prepared: 75 cents. Other Specials. Ten minimum order. 769-8925

17. Mortgages

BUILDERS. Money available for land loans. Up to 5 million per project for the interin without limit for the permanent. Speed action, insured and conventionals. Refinancing available for existing buildings up to $100,000, 20 years to pay. Manhattan Investment Corp., 630 Fomento Bldg. Phone 767-8800.

NEED FINANCING FOR YOUR F.H.A. OR V.A. first MORTGAGES & CALL IMMEDIATELY Mr. Ramos 765-0545

ANIMALS

18. Pets, Supplies, Services

When I see a boy who hasn't a dog,
Or a dog that hasn't a boy,
I think of the lot they are missing
Of frolic and genuine joy.

Some parents think dogs are a nuisance,
Just something to bark and annoy,
They can't know how badly a boy needs a dog,
Or how sadly a dog needs a boy.

HUMANE SOCIETY of P.R.
GPO Box 3472, San Juan 00936
767-5300 K 6.8 Road 176

"WILDANE KENNELS"
Boarding, dogs & cats. Obedience. Crates, shipping. Visiting hours 10 to 4. Closed Wed. & Sun. Rio grande, 797-3205.

UNCLE SAM CLIPS
POODLES BEST
765-2037—765-2028
Calle Hatillo No.6, Hato Rey

TESSIE'S POODLES
BEAUTICIAN-725-1111
Complete grooming, free pick up & delivery.

No. 1
- In Dog Training
- All Phases of
- Obedience & Guard
- Importer of Fine
- German Dogs
- At Stud Droll V.D.
- Rodheimer Pforte

"World Champion Youth Class"
HARRIS & WITHERSPOON
S.T.D., Inc.
786-3110 Rd. 2 Km. 19.6
P.O. Box 845 Bayamon

LABRADOR PUPPIES
Black, 6 weeks old,
AKC, registered.
722-1808

DALMATIAN puppies
AKC Reg. 7 weeks
Wormed. Only 2 females left.
Vi-Mar Kennels 789-5989

DOG SHOW-THE PUERTO RICO KENNEL CLUB announces ALL BREED DOG SHOW AT DORADO BEACH HOTEL, Sunday June 8, from 10 AM to 6:30 PM. For information and entry blanks call 767-4504, 764-2701 and 783-7571.

18. Pets, Supplies, Services

GERMAN SHEPHERD, puppies AKC registered, show quality, 7 wks. old, parents on premises. Call 765-7936.

POODLE. Female min. Registered 3 yrs old. loves children, $30 call after 4:30 783-9366

SCHNAUZERS, miniature, (2) females. Pure Bred, 6 weeks old. El Ferrol, Ave., F.D.R. 119, Apt. 1002, 723-5058.

GERMAN Shepherd male 8 months, old, black & silver, AKC reg. $125 Call Rodriguez 725-3030 ext. 314 8-5PM.

BOXER PUPPIES: Females only. 4 weeks old. No papers but purebred. $50. 782-1162 Mrs. Gomez, office hrs.

DOBERMAN PUPPIES
Cut tail,
Black.
Inq. 782-0328.

GERMAN SHEPHERDS: 6 weeks, male $90; female $75. Squirrel monkeys $24.95; Capuchin $50; Maranossetes $28. Boas $8. Gerbills $375. Red squirrel $19. Chuckers $25. La Casa del Agricultor, Plaza de Mercado, Rio Piedras. Tel. 765-4887.

... TRIMMING &
... ALL BREEDS
... RWELL
...
... Las Marias

WANTED Adult Person who will take care of my Chihuahua dog, old and friendly. Call Gypsy Markoff 724-8276. leave message.

TINY POODLES, Scottish Terriers, Miniature Schnauzers & Pekingnese Top quality, wormed & shots, AKC. 724-5290

SIAMESE KITTEN
FEMALE,
$20.
789-5201

BEAUTIFUL TINY TOY POODLE female, for sale. Lower prices on account of owner's accident. By appointment only. 785-9570.

FOR SALE-MALE & FEMALE Seal Point Siamese Kittens, 2 mos. old, $25. Call 842-5844 (Ponce).

KENNELS — BOARDING
791 2259
Pick-up & Delivery
German Shepherd Stud Svce

GERMAN SHEPHERD puppies with pedigree, sons of Champions. $75 ea. Calle 12, esq 13, Fairview, Cupey, R.P. 767-1779 Eves.

IDEAL GIFT FOR Father's Day Dachshund puppies. Miniature. AKC reg. $100. each.
722-0468

SIAMESE KITTEN
Female, 3 months old
$20 each
788-1417

PEKINGNESE MALE & FEMALE TOY POODLE; MALE & FEMALE AKC REG.
782-8388

GERMAN Shepherd puppies, pure bred, male $85, female $75. Frontera M-21, Villa Andalucia. R P Call 767-0638

WE WILL PURCHASE OLDER DOGS
1½ to 3 year old Shepherds, Dobermans, Danes, others.
HARRIS & WITHERSPOON
SENTRY TRAINED DOGS
785-8575 786-3110

NEWER ANTIQUES

To qualify as as antique to enter the country duty free an article had to be made prior to 1830. A revision in the law now defines any object 100 years old as a bonafide antique.

You may have antiques you don't care to use but are what someone else wants. You can trade them for cash with a San Juan Star Classified Ad. For quick results dial 782-4200 Ext. 55 & 56 for a courteous Ad Writer now!

MERCHANDISE FOR SALE

... STAR will not ... accept ads from ... firms who do not in ... ads the name of th... the word "Dealer" ... an ad that seems ... a private party ... dealer please notify ... San Juan STAR Classified ... ext. 55 & 56.

20 Miscellaneous for Sale

BEAT THE HEAT! Installing a ceiling fan (with or without lamps: All sizes. Height no problem. 3 mos to pay 766-5609. Arzuaga 200, Rio Piedras.

REELS 24 to 60 inches. Original cost $60 selling for $5 each. British Ropes Corp ... Ind Mario Julia, Calle A Blk. 12. 782-7373.

PIECEGOODS: Manufacturerladies dresses has surplus goods in Avril and cotton prints. Large quantities at close-out prices. Also steady supply remnants. Sophia Fashions. Box 931, Rio Grande, 00745. Call 797-2680.

BOY'S formica top desk $25; archery set, bow & 12 arrows, 41 lb. pull, $100; play pen $8. 783-2424 ext. 788.

ANTIQUES: 3 King set $50; Santos, Spanish Painting $200; Small Lamp $25; Wood Motar $6; Pre-Colombian Stone $25; Iron $8. Call 766-2332.

FABULOUS SALE of Antiques at Fabulous Finds. Da Vinci Hotel-South. Pre-inventory Sale. Everything goes, greatly reduced.

CORPUS JURIS
SECUNDUM
101 volume $300.
Information 724-8484.

GO CAR
2½ HP motor, 1 hr. used,
$220.
765-0568

CLOSE OUT Warehouse sale Danish teak & canvas chairs $22 Sealy mattress or box spring $16 each Porch aluminum chairs $2. Desks $10 to $18 Rattan arm chairs $1... June 8,4-6 PM in front of Volunteer Library, 118 Pomarosa St. Santurce. 725-8300.

COMPLETE Classroom equipment, primary and elementary grades for sale. Little used, modern functional equipment at reasonable price. Call Mr. Otero, office hours and also from 9:PM. 783-4440 Ext. 53; 783-8916, all day

21" GE console TV $100, kerosene stove $15, antique clock $15, blender $15, thermos $5, toaster $15, Toshiba radio $15, antique radio phonograph RCA $25, tape recorder solid state $50 723-8680.

COMPLETE Living room set, 1 sofa, 2 chairs, 1 swivel chair, 1 coffee table, 2 end tables. $300. Mrs. Rivera 767-8484 Ext. 283 8-5.

SELLING, 10 gallon aquarium & accessories, Piano, Sears & Suzuki motorcycles, portable TV, games & books. Call 722-1825.

BABY FURNITURE for sale, various arts. Under $100, ea. 791-0124

FOR SALE APPROXIMATELY 2000 wooden pallets, different sizes, in the same condition they are. Inf. Mr. Jaun Cogan Distribution Center, Pueblo Supermarket, 769-8383 Ext. 394.

GE refrig, frost-free, coppertone, like new; 2 aircond units; 6 chairs; dining table. All like new.
724-3269

21. HOUSEHOLD GOODS

DISCOUNT. All brand new articles w factory warranties. Serta box spring & mattress set, reg. sizes. $48; living room set 3 pieces $69; 19" T.V. all channels $110. Furn. & other household items at factory prices. San Francisco Discount 302 San Fco St. Old San Juan. Tel. 725-4661.

ANTIQUE FURNISHINGS & Accessories. A complete collection of finest imported period pieces from the World's finest markets & private estates. Collectors items. Fashions In Furniture, 402 Ponce de Leon, Puerta de Tierra. 722-1858.

RUG: 100 per cent Acrylan, 12x20 ft. Beige. Good buy $100. 724-1036.

SOFA WITH MATCHING CHAIRS and marble tables, all Victorian antique reproductions. Perfect cond. Sacrifice at less than half original price. Call 765-1834.

MUST SELL 3 piece Danish living room set $150, Chest of drawers $45; both like new.
725-3629

RATTAN 7 piece BR. set, sofa, table & 4 chairs, bar & stools, tables. Also twin mattresses, stereo, folding bed, Chinese chest, Oriental & modern lamps, drapes. 767-6659.

COUCH, NAUGAHYDE, green, $90. Naugahyde armchair $70, walnut din. table, 6 chairs, buffet $150. Call 723-5821.

FOR family room, Teakwood Girard sectional sofa with end & coffee table. $350. See at: H-53, Palmar Sur, Isla Verde. 791-0154.

INTERESTING VALUES
LAMPS, CHAIRS, sofas, beds, small appliances. 68 Refrigerator, slat bench, sewing machine, custom curtains and complete braun music center, recently purchased. 724-7092 for details.

COMPLETE HOUSEHOLD: Hide-a-bed, $75; Bedroom set, $50; Refrig. $45; Washer $75; Chevelle Malibu 1964 $875 with 4 new tires. 767-9698.

ANTIQUE, two-armed glass chandeliers from Ponce. Also large Spanish clay urn (tinaja). Tel. 723-0425.

FOAM bed $75, single $25, cabinet $15, dishwasher $45. Bargain. 30 Venus St. Atlantic View.

DOUBLE BED, SINGLE BED, dresser, 3 piece liv. room set, kitchen table, chairs. 2234 Amapola, Levittown.

TWO BLACK MAHOGANY and nylon chairs $15 ea., 723-3939.

21-A Carpeting

EXERCISE 3. Getting Information from an Ad

Directions: Congratulations! You sold the hi-fi for $50.00 cash. Now you have decided to buy the stereo second-hand through the want ads. You want to ask for the most important information first, so you won't waste a lot of time on the phone. In the following list of questions, cross out those that don't matter to you. Then put numbers next to each of the remaining questions to show which you think you should ask first, second, and so forth.

____How many speakers does it have?

____Does it have AM/FM radio?

____What kind of wood is it made of?

____What color is it?

____Is it a cabinet model or portable?

____Does it have any scratches or other marks?

____How old is it?

____How much does it weigh?

____Will you deliver it?

____What brand is it?

____How can I get to your place from here?

____How much have you used it?

____Does it have a new needle?

____Will it look good with modern furniture?

____Have you ever had it repaired?

____Have children been using it?

____How much money are you asking for it?

EXERCISE 4. Giving or Getting Information by Telephone

The class is going to practice getting information over the telephone. The teacher will tell you if you are a buyer or a seller.

Directions: Are you a buyer? Take another look at the questions for Exercise 3, above.

What will you say when they answer the phone?
What will you say if they don't give a straight answer to a question?
What will you say when you know that you don't want to buy the stereo and you want to end the conversation?

Are you a seller? Make up answers for the questions in Exercise 3. Be thinking of how you will talk to the buyer who phones you.

What will you say when you pick up the phone? Remember, you don't know if it is a friend or someone calling about your ad.

What will you say if they just say, "Please tell me about the stereo you have for sale?"

What will you say if they say something rude, like, "Man, you've got a lot of nerve asking $50.00 for a beat-up stereo!"

EXERCISE 5. Preparing to Buy

Suppose you want to buy a car. Just by studying newspaper ads, you can learn many of the factors you need to consider in making your choice of car and dealer. For example, the circled ad copy on this page suggests these questions: How long is the warranty period? How many miles per gallon does the EPA (Federal Environmental Protection Agency) say it gets? Does the price include the charges for freight and dealer preparation?

Directions: Look through the auto purchase ads on this page and circle five parts of ads that suggest useful questions. Then use the space below to write out two of your questions.

1. ______________________________

____

2. ______________________________

____

All five advertisements from *The Miami Herald*

> REPOSSESSIONS FOR SALE
> ALLEN-PARKER CO.
> N.W. 36 St. Corner 12th Ave.

> BANK CARS
> MIAMI'S largest selection of clean repossessions priced hundreds below regular dealer prices low down payments with bank financing available. You do not assume or take over anyone else's payments Open till 9 PM
> METRO AUTO SALES
> 2940 NW 36 St. 633-0636

EXERCISE 6. Inferences: Reading Between the Lines

When you read these two ads, you find out where to look for used cars. The advertiser also wants you to figure that these cars can be cheaper because the dealer already got some money from the last owner.

If you take one more step and say to yourself, "Boy, a lot of guys must guess wrong about how long they can keep up payments," you have made an *inference*. An inference is a pretty good guess based on a little evidence.

Directions: See if you can make some more inferences. Read each ad. Look at the statements under it. Then put a check in front of the statement that is a reasonable inference from the evidence in the ad.

> BANK CARS
> MIAMI'S largest selection of clean repossessions priced hundreds below regular dealer prices low down payments with bank financing available. You do not assume or take over anyone else's payments Open till 9 PM
> METRO AUTO SALES
> 2940 NW 36 st. 633-0636

1. I can infer from this ad that:

____a. Metro has Miami's largest selection of clean repossessed cars.

____b. A lot of people guess wrong about how long they can make payments.

____c. Metro charges regular dealer prices.

> NO CASH
> BANK FINANCING
> NEW car dealer must sell 50 trade-ins. Even if you have been turned down before, we will finance you with no money down if qualified. Widows, divorcees, young married couples. Call Ben Roberts, credit Mgr. Sunshine Pontiac, 667-7501. Credit by phone.

2. I can infer from this ad that:

____a. Widows, divorcees, and young married couples are often considered poor credit risks.

____b. Sunshine Pontiac will finance anyone with no money down.

____c. Widows, divorcees, and young married couples automatically qualify for credit.

> NO
> MONEY
> DOWN
>
> Financing No Problem
> 1st payment 45 Days
>
> FINEST USED CARS IN SO. FLA.
> ALL MAKES AND MODELS
>
> YOU DO NOT ASSUME OR TAKE OVER ANYONE ELSES PAYMENTS. WE ESTABLISH CREDIT FOR YOU. ALL WE ASK! BE 21 OR OVER. AND HAVE A STEADY JOB. CONTACT CREDIT MANAGER AT 635-0491.
>
> MUNICIPAL

3. I can infer from this ad that:

____a. It is a good idea to take over someone else's payments.

____b. It is not a good idea to take over someone else's payments.

____c. Municipal is sorry it can't let you take over someone else's payments.

EXERCISE 7. Comparing Costs

Directions: Study the ads on this page. Fill in the blanks in the questions, and be prepared to talk about the money advantages and disadvantages of buying a used car or a new car; financing it through the dealer or directly with a bank; buying a car or leasing it.

1. "APR" means Annual Percentage Rate. A higher APR means you are paying more for each dollar you borrow. In Ad #1, the APR for the new '76 Pinto is ______%. For the '72 Pinto, the APR is ______%.

2. In Ad #2, "OEL" means "On Equity Lease." "OAC" means "On Approved Credit." Leasing is renting instead of buying—like a 3-year lease on an apartment. In an auto *equity* lease, you can just return the car at the end of the lease, *or* you can pay an extra amount and own the car. In this ad, you can figure the amount of money that goes for finance charges: ______ months times $______ per month gives you $______, the total amount paid during the lease. If you then buy the car, you add the balance ("bal") of $______, for a total of $______. Now subtract the "Cap Cost" (Capital Cost—same as Cash Price) of $______. The difference, $______, is the additional cost of buying by lease-purchase instead of paying cash.

3. Choosing a car and choosing a way to finance it are two separate actions. You don't have to do both at the same place. If you qualify for credit at the bank in Ad #3, the APR you pay would be ______%.

4. Ad #4 is a regular "closed end" lease. You lease the car for two or three months or more. There is no buy-back option and no build-up of equity. The rental figure in Ad #4 includes two expenses that anyone who buys or leases a car must consider: ________ and ________.

Ad #1, *The Oregonian;* Ad #2, From *The Los Angeles Times.* Permission courtesy of Holmes Tuttle Leasing; Ad #3, From *The Los Angeles Times.* Permission courtesy of Independence Bank; Ad #4, From *The Los Angeles Times.* Permission courtesy of Olins Rent-A-Car.

Ad #1.

Ad #2.

Ad #3.

Ad #4.

Average auto insurance in county to cost $337

New automobile insurance rates approved by the State Board of Insurance will increase the average Harris County premium payment to $337 from the current $325.

The board also adopted a new deductible plan for comprehensive and collision rates. Beginning Oct. 1, there will be an automatic $50 deductible on comprehensive coverage and $200 deductible on collision.

There is a current miminum of full comprehensive coverage and $100 deductible for collision.

Owners still will be able to get the old, lower deductibles, but the rates for such policies will be much higher than the $50/$200 automobile deductible policy.

Here are the average new premiums, effective Oct. 1, for private passenger auto coverage in Harris County compared with those of last Jan. 1:

	1-1-76	10-1-76		
Class	Rate	Rate	increase	Defensive driving graduate
1-A	$290	$297	$ 7	$274
1-B	$325	$337	$12	$310
2A-1	$564	$596	$32	$543
2A-2	$475	$451	$24	$412
2C-1	$800	$835	$35	$758
2C-2	$668	$633	$35	$576
2D	$444	$486	$42	$444
3	$431	$440	$ 9	$402
6A	$290	$297	$ 7	$274
6B	$325	$337	$12	$310
8	$431	$440	$ 9	$402

Class definitions:

1-A — No male operator under 25 years of age; no unmarried female operator under 21; no operator 65 or over; auto not used for business or driven to or from work.

1B — No male operator under 25; no unmarried female operator under 21; no operator 65 or over; auto not used for business but driven to or from work.

2A-1 — One or more male operators under 21 and each is either married or not an owner or principal operator.

2A-2 — One or more male operators 21 or more but less than 25, and each such operator is married or not an owner or principal operator.

2C-1 — An unmarried male operator under 21 who is an owner or principal operator.

2C-2 — An unmarried male operator 21 or more but less than 25 who is owner or principal operator.

2D — No male operator under 25; but there is an unmarried female operator under 21, and the auto is not used for business.

3 — No male operator under 25; no unmarried operator; no operator 65 or over, and the auto is used for business.

6A — No male operator under 25; no unmarried female operator under 21 but there is an operator 65 or over and the auto is not used for business or driven to or from work.

6B — No male operator under 25; no unmarried female operator under 21, but there is an operator 65 or over and auto is not used for business but is driven to or from work.

8 — No male operator under 25 but there is an operator 65 or over and the auto is used for business.

The *Houston Chronicle*

EXERCISE 8. Reading an Insurance Table

Auto insurance is a major cost of owning an automobile. It can cost as much as the car payments. The Carson family of Harris County, Texas, wants to know how much they have to pay. Mrs. Carson is 45 years old and drives to work. Carl is 16 and does not use the car very much. Both are defensive driving graduates.

Directions: Skim the article above, then study the premium table. The last column of the table gives the rates for Defensive Driving Graduates.

1. Circle the lowest rate and the highest rate in the Defensive Driving Graduate column. You know that the Carsons' rate will be no less than $_____ and no more than $_____.

2. Some rates are the same. For example, $274 appears for both Class 1-A and Class 6-A. $310 is the rate for both Class _____ and Class _____. There are 11 classes, but only _____ different rates.

3. The many class definitions are made up with different combinations of just a few categories. Compare the definitions for the two classes that have the $274 rate. Notice that the first category is the same for both: "No male operator under 25 years of age." In fact, all the categories are the same except one. Write here the one category that is different: __________.

4. You are ready to find Mrs. Carson's rate. Remember that she is 45 and drives to work. Mrs. Carson is in Class _____; the rate is $_____. But if Carl operates the car at all, then the Carsons are in Class _____ and the rate is $_____.

EXERCISE 9. Getting Meaning from Word Parts

Directions: Below are groups of words from car ads. The words in each group start with the same prefix. Put a check in front of the answer that best tells what you think the "Word Parts" means.

Example: predict prepare prepay

Pre- means

✓ a. before or in front of

____ b. after or in back of

____ c. having to do with money

1. defroster depreciate decelerate

In these words, *de-* means

____ a. to do the opposite of

____ b. to increase

____ c. to do again

2. repair replacement repossess

In these words, *re* means

____ a. to come before

____ b. again

____ c. away from

3. automobile automatic automation

In these words, *auto-* means

____ a. self-propelling

____ b. mechanical

____ c. having to do with gasoline

4. contest contact compare

In these words, *con-* or *com-* means

____ a. full of

____ b. not

____ c. with or together

5. transportation transmission transformer

In these words, *trans-* means

____ a. with or together

____ b. across, through, or changing

____ c. carry or pull

PRACTICE IN YOUR LOCAL NEWSPAPER

PRACTICE 1. Find two or three ads in your local paper selling the same kind of thing—men's winter coats, for example, or diamond rings, or bath towels. Then circle all the words that *give* you information, and underline all the words that show you need more information.

EXAMPLE: On stadium jackets, you might circle "pile-lined." If you find it hard to locate two usable ads on one subject, use the two wig ads that follow.

Chicago Tribune

Chicago Daily Defender

PRACTICE IN YOUR LOCAL NEWSPAPER

PRACTICE 2. Find examples of different kinds of ads in your local paper. See if you can find three of these:

a. An ad that gives the store's name, but is not selling anything.

Example: Stern's . . . Closed Washington's Birthday . . . Open Tuesday.

b. An ad that sells something, but says "No mail or phone orders."

c. An ad that sells something, but does not give the price.

d. An "on sale" ad that gives a reason for the lower-than-usual price.

Example: "close-out" . . . . "seconds" . . . . "Father's day"

e. An ad that is selling ideas.

Example: An ad calling on readers to support a redwood national park to save the redwood trees.

f. An ad with a play on words.

Example: "It's no fare (almost!). . . . with low Canadian National Railway fares."

PRACTICE 3. Find out the advertising rate in your local newspaper. Write an ad to sell something you no longer need which you think someone else would like to buy. Try to keep your ad short enough to take advantage of the lowest advertising rate. This may be difficult because you want to be sure to include all necessary information and to make your ad appealing.

____

____

____

____

PRACTICE 4. Circle three of the ads on page 200 that particularly appeal to you. Explain what it is that attracts you to each one. Is it the item being sold? the way the item is described? the price? ______________________________

____

____

____

____

PRACTICE 5. Circle one of the ads on page 200 that doesn't appeal to you. Rewrite it in a way which you think would make it more appealing to the reader. ______________________________

____

____

____

____

CHAPTER 16
NEWS OF GOVERNMENT AND POLITICS

How can government at all levels—local, state, and federal—best serve the people? Many individuals and groups seek to improve the quality of life by a more active participation in politics and government.

Since America is blessed with a free press, a careful reader can find information on all sides of controversial questions. But you, and you alone, are responsible for forming the opinions which will decide how you vote and what issues you will support.

EXERCISE 1. What Do You Think?

Directions: Read the article "Press freedom vs. judges." Then pretend that a representative of the Gallup Poll has come to your classroom and asked you to answer the following questions. Circle one of the three choices. If you feel that you don't know enough about it to form an opinion, circle "NO OPINION."

Jailing of California newsmen raises questions

Press freedom vs. judges

By Brad Knickerbocker
Staff correspondent of The Christian Science Monitor
San Francisco

The jailing of four California newsmen on contempt of court charges again raises two key questions:

- Should reporters have a blanket "shield" from prosecution for withholding identification of their news sources?
- Can the contempt power of the judiciary supersede legislation?

Following a 20-month court battle, two reporters, the managing editor, and former city editor of the Fresno Bee newspaper last week began serving indefinite terms for refusing to reveal the source of a 1975 story which included grand jury transcripts involving local corruption and a Fresno city counselor.

The four hold that the states' liberal "shield" law permits them to publish grand jury information even though it has been ordered sealed by the court. The judge in the case sees it otherwise and has ordered the four to reveal the source of their information. "Coercive" indefinite sentences were meted out in an attempt to force the newsmen to talk.

California law states simply that journalists "cannot be adjudged in contempt . . . by a court for refusing to disclose the source of any information procured for publication."

But California courts in the case of "the Bee four," as they now are called here, have ruled that the state Legislature cannot tell a judge what to do. The lawyer for the quartet appealed to the United States Supreme Court, citing First Amendment press freedom guarantees in the U.S. Constitution. But so far this has been to no avail.

In a telephone interview from a county prison farm 20 miles west of the central California city, Fresno Bee managing editor George Gruner explained why the four newsmen intend to hold firm: "The press has a commercial role to report the news.

"But beyond that, it has a public role to provide a channel for confidential sources to reveal malfeasance. If we fail to maintain confidentiality when we've promised it, then we've destroyed our public role for all time."

Since the U.S. Supreme Court recognized limits to reporters' shield privileges in a case relating to the Pentagon Papers five years ago there have been several instances of reporters threatened with jail or actually serving sentences for refusing to reveal news sources.

William Farr, a Los Angeles reporter who wrote about the Charles Manson murder case, including controversial comments by two unidentfied lawyers in the case, was jailed 46 days and still faces possible imprisonment on a contempt charge, as do reporters in Washington, D.C., and West Virginia.

California Sen. Alan Cranston, himself a former reporter, has sponsored federal legislation to protect newsmen's confidentiality in federal cases, but so far without success. He joined about 100 reporters who quietly demonstrated outside the Fresno County courthouse this week.

Lawyers for the Fresno Bee newsmen say they soon will petition the court for a hearing to show that "coercive imprisonment" will not serve the court's purpose. If granted, the four then would face up to 5 days in jail and $500 in fines for each charge, totaling 55 contempt citations as of now.

1. Should reporters be free from prosecution for withholding identification of their news sources?
YES NO NO OPINION

2. Should the contempt power of the judiciary supersede legislation by the states?
YES NO NO OPINION

3. Do you want the press to have the right to protect confidential sources who reveal malfeasance?
YES NO NO OPINION

4. Do you favor federal legislation to protect reporters' confidentiality in federal cases?
YES NO NO OPINION

Census figures are poor measure of U.S. poverty

By Harry Schwartz

1 Has the United States abolished, or almost abolished, poverty and just failed to realize that fact?

2 The official recorder of poverty, the Bureau of the Census, doesn't think so. Late last month it reported that there are almost 26 million poor people in this country, an increase of 2.5 million or almost 11% during 1975.

3 How can anyone talk about the abolition of poverty in the face of such seemingly precise data?

4 Yet there are respected observers who argue, explicitly or implicitly, that the Bureau of the Census is badly misleading the public, that we are dealing here with a situation that leads to the old aphorism about there being three kinds of lies: "lies, damn lies and statistics."

5 For example there is the recent comment by Prof. Sar A. Levitan, director of the Center for Social Policy Studies at George Washington University:

6 "If poverty is a lack of basic needs, we have almost eliminated poverty in the United States. We should be proud of this accomplishment; we should sing 'Hallelujah!' Instead, we hide the facts because of administration policy."

7 Levitan is not alone. In a recent article in the magazine, the Public Interest, Prof. Edgar K. Browning of the University of Virginia wrote:

8 " . . . The average poor family in 1973 had an income that was approximately 30% *above* the poverty line. In terms of the average income of officially poor families, there is practically no poverty — statistically speaking — in the United States today, and indeed there has not been for several years."

9 The Census Bureau says there are almost 26 million poor people in this country. Levitan and Browning, working entirely independently, seem to be arguing that we've at least broken the back of the poverty problem and that our public perception of the matter is much gloomier than the reality. Who's right?

10 The difference turns out to be a matter of definition. The Census Bureau's definition of poverty is such as to maximize the number of people in the poverty statistics. But a more realistic definition gives a brighter picture.

11 The Census Bureau defines poverty in terms of money income alone. Thus a non-farm family of four in 1975 was "poor" if its money income was $5,500 or less.

12 What the critics are pointing out, however, is that the people the Census Bureau considers poor are the prime beneficiaries of many types of important non-money income — food stamps, housing subsidies and Medicaid, to name but three. These receipts are nonexistent as far as the Census Bureau data are concerned.

13 A poor family that gets $1,000 in food stamps will find them useful in the grocery store and at meal time, but the census statistics pretend they don't exist. Such benefits in kind rather than in money have been increasing rapidly in recent years.

14 A census expert, defending his bureau's data, pointed out that "We don't know how to value income in kind."

15 But other people seem to be able to do it.

16 The Rand Corp., for example, recently made a study of New York City's welfare population, and it seemed to have no trouble taking account of Medicaid, food stamps and day-care services. As a result Rand reported that New York's welfare families receive cash, goods and services that lift 80% to 90% of them above the poverty line.

17 The Rand study reported that in 1974 an average 3.3-person welfare family in New York City received the equivalent of $6,000, or roughly $1,000 above the then four-person family poverty level of about $5,000.

18 If the Rand Corp can take account of different types of income a welfare family receives — in money and in kind — why can't the Bureau of the Census?

19 The issue is more than a statistical quibble. The problem of poverty is a serious one that deserves the highest level of rational analysis and discussion.

20 For the U.S. government to issue data on this matter that are as incomplete and, for most people, as misleading as the census data are is to perform a disservice, and to hinder and to prejudice the informed discussion that is needed.

21 This problem of incomplete statistics leading to misleading conclusions is not confined to the poverty field. In the debate over national health insurance, for example, some people like to cite statistics about tens of millions of Americans without private health insurance.

22 Such citations easily lead the unsophisticated reader to suppose that these people have no financial aid to receive medical care. But it is precisely to help many millions of underprivileged persons that Medicaid exists and spends many billions of dollars annually, a fact that too often gets lost in some debates.

Schwartz is a member of the New York Times editorial board.

EXERCISE 2. Interpreting Statistical Data

Directions: Find information in the article to answer the following questions. Then record the number of the paragraph (or paragraphs) where the information is found in the blank in front of each question.

____ 1. What number of persons did the U.S. Bureau of the Census report as "poor people" during 1975?

____ 2. How does the Census Bureau define poverty?

____ 3. What non-money income received by the poor is not counted in the Census Bureau data?

____ 4. What reason does a Census Bureau expert give for not counting non-money income as part of the income of the poor?

____ 5. What corporation seemed to have no trouble in determining the value of Medicaid, food stamps, and day-care services received by New York City's welfare population?

____ 6. What percentage of New York's welfare families were lifted above the poverty line when non-money income was counted?

____ 7. What does Prof. Edgar K. Browning say about the income of the average poor family in 1973?

____ 8. How does Prof. Sar A. Levitan define poverty?

____ 9. Is there a problem of incomplete statistics in the debate over national health insurance?

____10. In which paragraph (or paragraphs) do you find the most convincing evidence that the reader must question conclusions drawn from statistics?

New perils for future national forests?

Critics say bills now in Congress favor timber industry

By Harry B. Ellis
Staff correspondent of
The Christian Science Monitor

Washington

Americans of the future would inherit national forests greatly changed – for the worse, conservationists claim – by legislation rapidly approaching passage in Congress.

The bills, among other things, would not prohibit clear cutting (leveling of all trees in an area), species conversion (hardwoods to softwoods), and other practices urged by the timber industry.

Some lawmakers, including Sen. Hubert H. Humphrey (D) of Minnesota, argue that the U.S. Forest Service stands between the logging industry and abuse of the nation's forests.

But three recent court rulings – in West Virginia, Alaska, and Texas – have found the U.S. Forest Service in violation of existing law designed to preserve the nation's 155 national forests.

The Forest Service, whose appropriations from Congress are comparatively low, gets most of its money from selling timber-cutting rights in the national forests.

Existing law criticized

Timber interests, stalled by the court decisions and stressing the nation's rapidly growing consumption of wood, urge a redefinition of timber law.

All sources agree that existing law, beginning with the National Forest Organic Law of 1897, needs updating. The question: in whose interests?

"The [pending] House bill," said a congressional source, "contains nothing that the [timber] industry opposes. The bill passed by the Senate has only two provisions potentially troublesome to lumbermen. Neither bill restricts clear cutting – either in size of tract or area of the country."

Conservation efforts in both houses, led by Sen. Jennings Randolph (D) of West Virginia and Rep. George E. Brown Jr. (D) of California, failed to stave off bills favored by powerful industry lobbies.

Two changes made

Senator Randolph, said an aide, was able to insert two "positive" provisions in the Senate version – a requirement for "sustained yield, even-flow" cutting and the elimination of "marginal lands" from U.S. Forest Service sales. The pending House bill lacks even these restrictions.

The full House is scheduled to debate its committee-passed bill next week. If passed, House and Senate versions would go to conference, with supporters of the bills aiming at passage into law before Congress adjourns for the election campaign early in October.

The resulting law, if based on the present House and Senate versions, would – in the view of Randolph Brown adherents – fail to prevent the following "current forestry abuses":

- Over-use of, and too large, clear cutting in national forests. The size of clear cutting in Western fir forests is said to be too large, "causing rapid soil and nutrient loss on steep slopes."
- Clear cutting in Eastern mixed hardwood forests, "for which," said a congressional aide, "there is no rationale" except from the industry's point of view. "Clear cutting in these forests is bad for the watershed, and leads to erosion."

This practice, leading to the replacement of hardwoods with faster-growing pine trees, in time would alter the nature of some Eastern forests.

Senator Randolph, claiming "Congress has failed to face up to the [forestry] issue," predicts further litigation in the courts if present bills become law, with Congress ultimately having to revise the legislation once again.

KEEPING TRACK OF BILLS IN CONGRESS

You will find it easier to keep track of bills going through Congress if you have a clear understanding of the steps every bill must go through.

After a bill is introduced, it is referred to a committee. Before it can become a law, it must go through the following steps in both the House of Representatives and the Senate:

1. Hearings in committee.
2. Reported out of committee. This means that a majority of the committee voted to send the bill to the floor for consideration by all members of that body.
3. Debated on the floor.
4. Voted on by all the members of that body, and either passed or rejected.

Any bill passed *in exactly the same form* by both the House and Senate is sent to the President. If the President signs the bill, it becomes a law. If the bill is vetoed, it is returned to the House in which it originated. It does not become a law unless two-thirds of the House and two-thirds of the Senate vote to override the President's veto.

However, major legislation is seldom passed in exactly the same form by both houses of Congress. Before the bill can be sent to the President, the two houses must agree on a compromise form of the bill. This action requires three additional steps:

1. Rewriting of the bill by a conference committee.
2. Action on the conference proposal by the House.
3. Action on the conference proposal by the Senate.

EXERCISE 3. Charting a Bill's Progress

Directions: Read the article "New perils for future national forests?" and then answer the following questions.

1. What phrase in the first paragraph tells you that the bill has already gone through many of the required steps?

____

2. What word in the second paragraph alerts you to the fact that the House and Senate are considering different versions of the bill?

____

3. How many steps have been completed by the House? ______
4. How many steps have been completed by the Senate? ______
5. What steps must the bill go through before it can be sent to the President?______________________________

Erasing reams of federal forms

FHA forms needed to buy home — By R. Norman Matheny, staff photographer

Snipping federal paperwork — successful?

Paperwork to be trimmed without cutting any corners

By Lucia Mouat
Staff correspondent of The Christian Science Monitor

Washington

If the Commission on Federal Paperwork (CFP) does not somehow stem Washington's steady outflow of forms for individuals and businesses to fill in, it will not be for lack of good ideas.

In its one-year existence, CFP has heard an earful of complaints from Americans. Thirteen geographically scattered hearings already have been held. Another 12 are scheduled before the group's final recommendations are due to the President and Congress in October, 1977.

This week, in looking for solutions to this barrage of public complaints, the commission took the unusual step of calling on 110 top federal management experts for help.

In a two-day "brainstorming" session these government bureaucrats – all of whom have won federal awards for cost-saving management ideas – offered several strong suggestions for change.

One recommendation on which virtually all of the government workers agreed was tapping of a central federal agency to serve as a clearinghouse in collecting and controlling data-gathering. Only then, reasoned the government workers, could a close eye be kept on how many forms from different agencies duplicate each other, and how much of the information sought really is necessary to carrying out the intent of Congress' laws.

Other suggestions included much greater standardization of forms, publication of government sources of information (so citizens would know where to turn for what data), more congressional attention to the problem in legislation itself, and swifter disposal of government records.

One government discussion group, which adopted the motto of "Not Retention But Disposal," suggested that holding periods for existing federal records be reduced 50 percent over the next five years, and that until then there be a moratorium on additional filing equipment and space.

Consumer leader Esther Peterson, a member of the Paperwork Commission, termed the workers' recommendations "tough" and a "courageous" contribution.

Most impressive to FPC Deputy Director Michael McGinn was the fact most of the government workers present said they thought a 30 percent cut in government paper a distinct possibility if their recommendations were followed.

"To me that's dramatic," notes Mr. McGinn. "After all, this isn't a group of harassed businessmen – these are the users [of the gathered information]."

Estimates are that the federal government currently turns out some 10 billion pieces of paper a year with a resulting toll on the nation's economy of $40 billion.

Between last October and the end of June, in response to a direct plea from President Ford, executive branch agencies managed to whittle the number of federal forms by 12.5 percent rather than his requested 10 percent. However, the President was the first to concede many of the discarded items were minor while the most intricate, time-consuming forms often remained.

USING PUBLIC HEARINGS TO INFLUENCE GOVERNMENT

Each year Congress and the administrative agencies it has created hold many public hearings. Individuals and representatives of business, labor, and consumer groups have an opportunity to present their views.

By studying newspaper reports of testimony given at these hearings, readers can often learn vital information in time to support or oppose a proposal that is before Congress.

EXERCISE 4. Following Public Hearings

Directions: Read the article "Erasing reams of federal forms." Imagine that you are the president of a small business firm subjected to many governmental forms. Put a check in the blank in front of those things you might do after reading this article.

____1. Write to your Representative for information about the location of the twelve hearings still to be held.

____2. Request permission to appear before one of these hearings.

____3. Enlist support of other business leaders in your community and suggest that they attend the hearings and tell their views.

____4. Prepare a news release for publication in your local newspaper telling what you are going to present at the hearings.

EXERCISE 5. Using Information from a News Article

Directions: Reread the article "Erasing reams of federal forms." List below several statements from the article which you might work into your press release.

____

____

____

USE OF CONSUMER POWER

In recent years, consumers have become increasingly active in politics and government. Read the two articles "U.S. challenged on meat rule" and "Consumer group pleased" to discover some of the ways consumer organizations are trying to influence government officials and voters. Then use the exercises to help you evaluate the use of consumer power described in these articles.

> **U.S. challenged on meat rule**
>
> **United Press International**
>
> WASHINGTON — Consumer groups on Friday demanded that the Agriculture Department retract a regulation that allows finely ground bone to be blended into hot dogs and other processed meats.
>
> The consumer coalition says that the presence of ground bone in processed meats might pose a serious health hazard.
>
> **THE AGRICULTURE** Department regulations allows meat processors to use "mechanically deboned" meat in such products as hot dogs and bologna. The mechanical process rescues meat lost in deboning by hand, but it also leaves a small percentage of finely ground bone. An Agriculture Department official said the bone residue is "so fine it would not be detectable by sight, taste or feel," and it estimated mechanical deboning could add nearly 1-billion pounds of meat to the nation's food supply each year.

United Press International

EXERCISE 6. Analyzing Consumer Power

Directions: Read the statements below. Scan the article "U.S. challenged on meat rule" again, and think about what is said and what is not said. Think about what you know from personal experience. Then circle YES if you agree with each statement, NO if you do not agree, and UNDECIDED if you are not sure.

1. The consumer coalition presented proof that the presence of ground bone in processed meat was a serious health hazard.
YES NO UNDECIDED

2. The Agriculture Department agreed to change its regulation allowing meat processors to use "mechanical deboned" meat in hot dogs and bologna.
YES NO UNDECIDED

3. An Agriculture Department official proved that the bone residue is "so fine it would not be detectable by sight, taste, or feel."
YES NO UNDECIDED

4. If the consumer coalition's demands are met, the loss of 1-billion pounds of meat will increase the cost of bologna and hot dogs.
YES NO UNDECIDED

5. Employees who have the power to make regulations, but who do not have to be reelected by the people, require a check by consumer coalitions.
YES NO UNDECIDED

Consumer group pleased

WASHINGTON (UPI)—The Consumer Federation of America, the nation's largest organized consumer group, today claimed "extreme success" in helping elect and re-elect proconsumer forces in Congress.

The 1976 election marked the organization's first entry into the political arena since changes in the tax laws made it legal for such groups to engage in political activities without losing their tax exempt status.

Of 82 House incumbents endorsed by CFA, 79 were re-elected, the group said. Of seven nonincumbents running for the House and endorsed by CFA, five were elected.

THE CFA ALSO endorsed three Democratic House members who made successful bids to become senators —Reps. Spark Matsunaga of Hawaii, Donald Riegle of Michigan and Paul Sarbanes of Maryland.

In addition, the group said it actively opposed the re-election of Sens. William Brock, R-Tenn., and Robert Taft, R-Ohio, both of whom lost.

"We are delighted by the extreme success of our first venture into candidate endorsement," said Carol Tucker Foreman, executive director of the federation of 240 consumer groups. "Consumer votes contributed to some important victories and some important defeats.

"WE BELIEVE IT is essential that members of Congress understand that their records will be made known, that we will assist our friends and that we will let consumers know who votes consistently to shut consumers out of government decision making, opposes efforts to improve product safety and protect consumers' pocketbooks," she said.

"We do not have the ability to make large campaign contributions, but we can and will make the record known to the public and urge consumers to vote to protect their health, safety and economic interests."

She said the group was "particularly distressed" by the defeat of two members—Sen. Frank Moss, D-Utah, and Rep. Edward Mezvinsky, D-Iowa, both of whom were rated proconsumer by the group.

Mrs. Foreman also noted that the CFA's low consumer rating of Sen. John Tunney, D-Calif., apparently contributed to his defeat by S.I. Hayakawa. Tunney received only a 35 per cent record based on his votes during 1976.

United Press International

EXERCISE 7. Questioning Claims

Directions: Read the article "Consumer group pleased" to understand the claims made by the Consumer Federation of America. Then check the statements below by circling YES, NO, or UNDECIDED.

1. The article convinces me that the Consumer Federation of America played an important role in the election of pro-consumer forces in Congress.
YES NO UNDECIDED

2. The article convinces me that as a voter I should give my vote to those candidates that secure the endorsement of the Consumer Federation of America.
YES NO UNDECIDED

3. The article fails to prove that the CFA endorsement was a deciding factor in the election or defeat of candidates.
YES NO UNDECIDED

A Treaty Is A Treaty

By Morris Thompson
Commissioner of Indian Affairs

Reprinted from Seattle Post-Intelligencer, Wed. Nov. 17 Issue.

One of the most controversial issues in the Northwest the past two years has been Indian fishing rights on the Columbia River and in Puget Sound and Northwestern Washington.

From statements I have read in the press and conversation I have had with people in the Northwest, it has become apparent to me that a majority of them do not understand the unique relationship Indian tribes have with the federal government and the reasons for the relationship.

Because the Belloni and Boldt decisions are the law of the land and must be implemented, I think it is very important that all people affected by them understand the treaty-making process with Indian tribes and what responsibilities the federal government has in insuring that the rights under these treaties are upheld.

I mentioned the unique relationship Indian tribes have with the federal government. What is that unique relationship and how did it come about.?

It is based on the treaties the United States signed with the tribes as sovereign nations, and as co-equal governments.

That is an important point to remember, because the relationship of the federal government to the Indian tribes is a political one and not a racial one.

I don't mean political in any partisan sense of the word, but a relationship of one political entity to another the relationship is not based on the fact that the Indian tribes now are a minority in our society, or that they are ethnically different from the dominant society, or that they are poor, or that they are red.

And the relationship is not with individual Indians, but with tribes as governments.

The federal government stopped making treaties with Indian tribes in 1871, and no treaties have been signed since that date.

When our founding fathers met to draft the Constitution 200 years ago, they recognized the need for the federal government to deal with Indian tribes and to perform necessary functions on behalft of Indians.

This was set down in the commerce clause of the Constitution which said the Congress was given the specific charge ". . . to regulate commerce with foreign nations,and among the several states, and with the Indian tribes."

And to seal the arrangement whereby the central government was made capable of performing these fuctions on behalf of the Indians, the framers provided that the Constitution, and all treaties (including treaties with Indian tribes ". . . shall be the supreme law of the land, anything in the Constitution or laws of any state to the contrary notwithstanding."

That is why the relationship of Indian tribes to the federal government is unique.

Let me give some background on the Boldt decision, and while the particulars may be a bit different from the Belloni decision, the treaty rights involved are the same.

Governor Stevens was sent to Washington Territory to secure the land for settlement. He was told to make treaties with the tribes he found there and try to get them to move to reservations.

He was successful. The treaties were made, the Indians tribes moved to reservations and the land was available for the incoming rush of settlers.

Now, remember the Constitution said a treaty is ". . . the supreme law of the land, anything in the Constitution or laws of any state to the contrary notwithstanding."

Those treaties signed by the Indian tribes and Governor Stevens on behalf of the United States government are still in effect today.

When the tribes signed these treaties, they reserved their right to fish in their "usual and accustomed places." And that meant to them both on and off the reservations.

There is another point to consider. When Indian tirbes signed treaties with the United States in most cases they relinquished title to lands wanted by the federal government and which the Indian formerly occupied.

But it was not a question of the tribes getting something from the federal government. They gave up something, and what they did not specifically give up, they reserved.

And they reserved their right, and that is an important word, to fish in their usual and accustomed places, both on and off the reservations.

The United States agreed to that.

Indian tribes, therfore, are not just another user group when it comes to fishing if they have retained that right in the treaty they signed as a co-equal government with the United States.

The United States has a treaty with Canada concerning the salmon which come into the Fraser River of British Columbia. The catch is divided between the countries according to the treaty.

No one argues the validity of that treaty or the right of Canada, or the United States, to catch the fish.

And that is exactly the situation which exists between the Indian tribes on the Columbia River and Western Washington and the federal government.

Those treaty rights were upheld in two federal district courts and the Ninth Circuit Court to hear the Boldt appeal:

The Hon. James M. Burns wrote the following words when he was sitting on the Ninth Circuit Court to hear the Boldt appeal:

"I concur, but I want add a brief comment from the viewpoint of a district judge. As was suggested at oral argument, any decision by us to affirm also involves ratification of the role of the district judge as a 'perpetual fishmaster.' Although I recognize that district judges cannot escape their Constitutional responsibilities, and continuing duties imposed upon them, I deplore situations that make it necessary for us to become enduring managers of the fisheries, forests, and highways, to say nothing of school districts, police departments, and so on. The record in this case, and the history set forth in the Puyallup and Antoine cases, among others, make it crystal clear that it has been the recalcitrance of Washington state officials (and their vocal non-Indian commerical and sports fishing allies) which produced the denial of Indian rights requiring intervention by the district court. This responsibility should neither escape notice nor be forgotten."

Let's remember that the relationship of Indian tribes to the United States is a political one. The Constitution gave the federal government and the Congress the power to deal with the Indian tribes and to sign treaties with them.

An Indian does not have a right to fish because of any recial differences. He has a right to fish because his tribe has a valid treaty with the United States giving him that right.

EXERCISE 8. Comparing Relationships

Directions: Read "A Treaty Is A Treaty" to discover the unique relationship that Indian tribes have with the federal government. Then read the following statements. Put a check in front of each statement that tells what Commissioner Thompson said.

____1. The relationship is a political one and not a racial one.

____2. The relationship is based on treaties the United States signed with the tribes as sovereign nations and as co-equal governments.

____3. The relationship is with individual Indians.

____4. The relationship resulted from the commerce clause of the United States Constitution which gave Congress power to regulate commerce with the Indian tribes.

____5. The United States Constitution states that treaties (including treaties with Indian tribes) ". . . shall be the supreme law of the land, anything in the Constitution or laws of any state to the contrary notwithstanding."

EXERCISE 9. Reading To Check Specific Details

Directions: Scan the article to see if each statement below agrees with the details given in "A Treaty Is A Treaty." If it agrees, circle YES. If it does not agree, circle NO.

1. The treaties signed by the Indian tribes and Governor Stevens on behalf of the United States government are still in effect today.
YES NO

2. The Indians reserved their right to fish in their "usual and accustomed places," both on and off the reservations.
YES NO

3. The Indians relinquished title to lands wanted by the federal government, but what they did not specifically give up, they reserved.
YES NO

4. The Indians' right to fish has been upheld in two federal district courts.
YES NO

5. The Hon. James M. Burns stated that Washington State officials have the power to decide where Indians and non-Indians can fish.
YES NO

EXERCISE 10. Reading Charts

Newspapers often report information in chart form so that readers can see relationships at a glance. Use the charts on Social Security Benefits and Social Security Taxes to answer the following questions:

1. What was the annual maximum tax paid by a worker during the years

1937–49 ____________?

1959 ____________?

1969–70 ____________?

1976 ____________?

1977 ____________?

2. What was the maximum monthly benefit for a worker retiring at age 65 during the years

1940 ____________?

1959 ____________?

1970 ____________?

1976 ____________?

3. What was the annual maximum tax paid by a self-employed worker in

1951–53 ____________?

1959 ____________?

1976 ____________?

1977 ____________?

4. What is the difference between the annual maximum tax paid by a self-employed worker in 1977 and the tax paid by a worker who is not self-employed? ____________

5. What is the difference between the annual maximum tax paid by a self-employed worker in 1976 and the combined tax paid by an employee and employer during that year? ____________

Social Security benefits—How they have grown

	Maximum monthly benefit for worker retiring at 65
1940	$ 41.20
1951	68.50
1953	85.00
1955	98.50
1959	116.00
1962	121.00
1966	132.70
1968	156.00
1970	189.80
1972	216.10
1973	266.10
1974	304.90
1975	330.30
1976	387.30
1977	422.16*

***estimate; the exact amount depends on average wage increase and cost of living increase for 1976.**

Social Security taxes—How they have grown

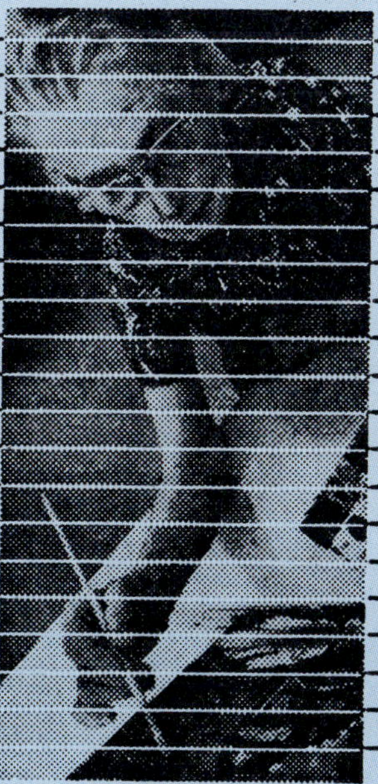

	Annual maximum tax paid by worker; matched by employer	Annual maximum tax paid by self-employed
1937-49	$ 30.00	$ **
1950	45.00	**
1951-1953	54.00	81.00
1954	72.00	108.00
1955-56	84.00	126.00
1957-58	94.50	141.75
1959	120.00	180.00
1960-61	144.00	216.00
1962	150.00	225.60
1963-65	174.00	259.20
1966	277.20	405.90
1967	290.40	422.40
1968	343.20	499.20
1969-1970	374.40	538.20
1971	405.60	585.00
1972	468.00	675.00
1973	631.80	864.00
1974	772.20	1,042.80
1975	824.85	1,113.90
1976	895.05	1,208.70
1977	965.25	1,303.50

The *Chicago Daily News*

Congress Set to Act on Budget

Committees Propose $2 Billion Increase in Stimulus Package

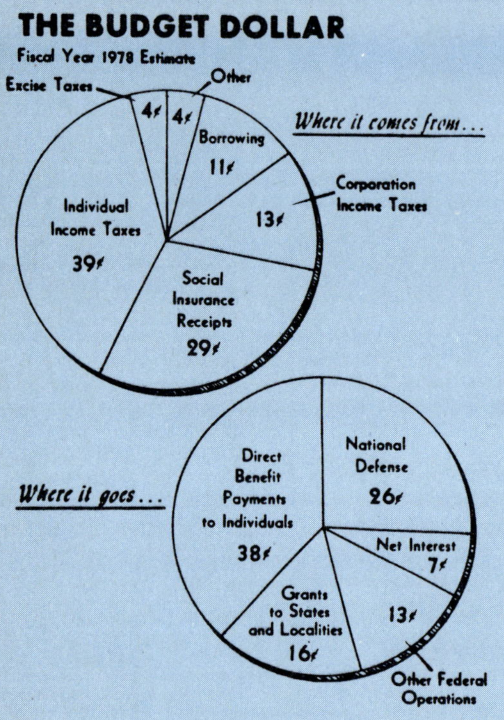

The House and Senate Budget Committees have approved an economic stimulus package in excess of President Carter's request. The Senate package totaling $17.2 billion for the next eight months and the House package totaling $17.3 billion exceed the President's spending and tax reduction proposal by nearly $2 billion.

Both Houses approved a tax reduction proposal which was part of the stimulus package. The House Ways and Means Committee will begin mark-up immediately on legislation to determine exactly how the $13.8 billion reduction in taxes approved by the Budget Committee will be achieved. Proposals include a $50 rebate to all individuals, an increase in the standard deduction, and cuts in business taxes. The AFL-CIO opposed the tax proposals in the Budget Committee on the basis that such cuts would reduce needed revenue for more jobs.

Action to approve the Committees' proposals in both the House and Senate will be taken the week of February 21st. If approved in their present forms, both the House and Senate Commiteee proposals would provide for approximately one million jobs.

From *American Teacher,* February, 1977, page 10.

EXERCISE 11. Reading Circle Graphs

Directions: Use the circle graphs in the box above to answer these questions about The Budget Dollar:

1. What amount comes from Individual Income Taxes? ______.

2. What amount comes from Corporation Income Taxes? ______.

3. What amount comes from Borrowing? ______.

4. What amount comes from Social Insurance Receipts? ______.

5. What amount is spent for National Defense? ______.

6. What amount goes to Direct Benefit Payments to Individuals? ______.

7. What amount is spent for Net Interest? ______.

8. What amount is returned in Grants to States and Localities. ______.

PRACTICE IN YOUR LOCAL NEWSPAPER

PRACTICE 1. Collect articles containing statistics. Underline conclusions drawn by the writer. Do you feel the data justifies the generalizations? Look for other interpretations of the same statistics.

PRACTICE 2. If Congress is in session, clip several articles about legislation that is now before Congress and analyze how many steps remain in the legislative process. Keep in mind that it takes months and sometimes years to get a bill enacted into law.

PRACTICE 3. Check papers to see how your representatives in Congress voted on legislation.

PRACTICE 4. Keep a file of articles that are helpful to consumers. Try to locate regular features dealing with consumer problems.

PRACTICE 5. Look for charts and graphs that clarify statistical data.

PRACTICE 6. Keep track of decisions handed down by the Supreme Court. See if any deal with freedom of the press or treaty rights of Indians.

CHAPTER 17
ENTERTAINMENT IDEAS IN NEWS AND ADS

You check the newspaper to see what's on TV tonight.

You check the newspaper to see where that new science-fiction movic is playing.

You check the newspaper to see when your team's next home game is going to be.

You check the newspaper to find out when the skating rink opens.

This is one of the ways in which you use your newspaper for what-to-do help—you have an idea of what you want to do, and you use the newspaper to find out how and where to do it.

Now try another way to find what-to-do help in the newspaper.

Don't make up your mind about what you want to do. Just look through the paper. As you read news stories and ads, keep asking yourself these questions:

Can I go and watch this?
Can I take part in this instead of just watching?

EXERCISE 1. Finding Things to Do

Directions: Each of the ads and news stories on the next page has a number. Fill in the blanks with the proper numbers to complete each of the following six statements:

Example: Number ___6___ tells where you can get tickets for the high school wrestling tournament.

1. Did you ever watch a high school wrestling match?
Number __________ tells where you can buy tickets for one.

2. Did you ever bicycle through the park on a sunny Saturday?
Number __________ tells where to phone for information on renting a bike.

3. Did you know that you can baby sit and have fun too?
Number __________ tells where you can take your kid sister for free entertainment.

4. Did you know two can go to the movie almost as cheaply as one?
Number __________ tells when girls can go to the movies for 90¢.

5. Do you like to see kids beat adults at their own game?
Number __________ tells where you can go to see science projects made by high school students.

6. Do you wonder what it's like not to sit in the last row?
Number __________ tells about a sporting event where students can live it up in the best reserved seats for half-price.

7. Would you trade two movies for a really great dance?
Number __________ tells where you can get a dance plus a show.

8. Window-shopping is fun in new stores in new neighborhoods.
Number __________ starts you on your way to the Intergalactic Trading Post.

9. Don't forget to plan some fun for your dog.
Number __________ tells you where you can take him to watch well-trained dogs show off.

(1)

2 Negroes Recalled

OLYMPIA — During February ... Capitol Museum ... ing a case with re... reminders of two p... Negro families of the are...

Some relate to ... Bush and ... were amo... ly arrivals ... in 1845. ... what is stil... prairie, sout...

Bush and ... excellent far... erous ...

(2)

103 POUNDS

UPPER BRACKET — Greg Maestas, Adams City, vs. Joe Montoya, Greeley Central; Fred Hicks, Cherry Creek, vs. Tim Kenny, Bear Creek; or Loui Guillen, Grand Junction, vs. John Stei... mark, Arvada West; ... Pueblo South; Pete Chavez, Palmer, vs. Frank Lopez, West Denver, or Bill Aragon, ... Lincoln.

LOWER BRACKET — Jerry Barba, ... South Denver, vs. Ken Ham... ilton, ... Mike Rasmussen, ... or Carl Gallegos, ... Alan ... Greeley West, vs. Modesto Gal... Grand Junction Central; Neil Bert... Art Buan, Harrison, ... Widefield; Roy Her... vs. Steve Abeyta, ... Ranum.

...ears Upset

(3)

Viking Cagers, Matmen Schedule Key Contests

Action is highly concentrated for Portland State teams this week.

The Viking basketball team has only one game on the slate — the gigantic at Seattle Pacific Saturday.

Portland State wrestlers ...e to the ... twice — both ...es at h... important ... me... ...ingt... n S...

...into Saturday's clash with near identical win-loss records.

In addition, the Viks and Falcons are one-up so far this season. The Less Habegger-coached Seattle five dumped PSC, 109-90 in the consolation game of Tacoma's Daffodil Classic early in the season. The Viks came back to whip SPC in Portland, 95-86, a week ...

... Howard Westcott's ...ill be seeking re... ...n they take on the ...

(4)

Today's Events

These events and meetings are open to the general public:

East Meadow

Alcoholics Anonymous, open meeting, 9 PM, Methodist Church, Newbridge Avenue.

... teen recreation evening ... theatre, ball games, golf, swimming, dances, judo, ...des 8-12 as of September ... Meadow H.S., Carman ...

...own

...rkshop, men and ... 7:30-9:30 PM, $2, ... Lane.

...Park

...es, regular meet... ...hall, Front Street.

New Hyde Park

... junior-senior high ...

(5)

***Intergalactic* Trading Post**

17 ST. MARK'S PL. U.S.A.

Wholesale & Retail

677-3780

(6)

Division 1 Wrestling Ticket Sale Starts

Reserved seat tickets for the Division I Colorado state high school wrestling tournament are on sale at the May-D&F box office through Friday.

Reserved seat tickets also can be purchased at the Arena box office after 4 p.m. Thursday and ...day ... and noon Saturday.

(7)

(8)

Pete's on the Beam to Science Fai...

By JOHN STOLFUS

...convert the electronic equipment of an old TV set ...into a model of a laser beam. Yet, Peter ... he turned the trick. To prove ... of the NEWS-sponso...

It takes a bit of doi... glass tubing and assorted ... a New York City high s... entering his homemade ... Science Fair this weeke...

The public is invited to v... five fairs on Friday fro... a.m. to 3 p.m., and on S... from 9:30 a.m. to noon ... sion is free. Here are ... tions:

Manhattan: Joan of ... 154 W. 93d St.

Bronx: Castle Hill...

Brooklyn: Leffe... Empire Blvd.

Queens: Franci... 58-20 Utopia Pkwy...

Richmond: N... Clawson St. and I...

(9)

For Children

THE AMERICAN MUSEUM OF NATURAL HISTORY, exhibits (free); AMERICAN MUSEUM—HAYDEN PLANETARIUM, sky shows and exhibits, Central Park West at 81st Street (60c-$1.80, TR 3-1300).

BROOKLYN MUSEUM, treasure hunts on Fridays from 1-3 p. m. for ages 7-12, (free).

"Sleeping Beauty," presented by the Pickwick Puppets on Tuesday, August 8, at 10:30 a. m. and 2 p. m. at 92nd Street YM-YWHA, Lexington Avenue, FI 8-1500 (60c);

"A Very Special Clown," presented by Salvatore Guida on Saturdays at 1 and 2:30 p. m. Sundays at 1 p. m., at Theatre 80 St. Mark's, 80 St. Marks' Place, AL 4-9740 ($2);

Films, "The Golden Fish," "The Stonecutter," presented on Friday, August 4, at 4 p. m. at New York Public Library, Hamilton Fish Park Branch, 415 East Houston Street (free);

Story telling, by Diane Wolkstein ... the Department of ... August 3, at ... Drive ...

(10)

Plan Many Activities At Harlem Branch Y

The Harlem Branch YMCA, 180 W. 135th St., in keeping with its accent on Total Community Envolvement announces a series of up and coming events:

1) The annual ...

...ranging from $50 savin... to surprise awards presented on Sunday Feb. 4.

(11)

American League

...ringfield 4, Providence 2
...ochester 7, Cleveland 3

HOCKEY

SPEED·ACTION·THRILLS

You Can Bet On The Bucks

PORTLAND BUCKAROOS vs. SAN DIEGO GULLS

...unday Night At 7 P.M.

February 11

...ORIAL COLISEUM

Prices

...eral Admission $1.50 ...d $2.00, $2.50, $3.00

Students through High School Half price in any category

...Tickets On Sale

(12)

Ski Reports

TIMBERLINE — Temperature 31, no new snow, 60 inches total, roads clear.

MULTORPOR SKI BOWL — Tempera...ture 26 degrees, no new snow, 18 inches total.

MOUNT HOOD MEADOWS — Temperature 32, no new snow, 88 inches total.

BATCHELOR BUTTE — Temperature ... no new snow, 71 inches total, high... ...vs clear.

...OODOO SKI BOWL — Temperature ... no new snow, 56 inches total, night ...ng.

...ILLAMETTE PASS — Temperature ... trace new snow, 48 inches ... clear.

MOUNT ASHLAND — Temp... 70 inches total, road mostly ba... spot...

(13)

TAKE A TRIP by Bike

Tuesday Night Special

Open til 11 pm

Central Park Bike Shop TR 7-2584

104 West 81 St. Reg Hrs: 8-8 pm daily

(14)

DOG CLUBS SCHEDULE SIX WEEKEND EVENTS

The Obedience Club of San Diego licensed trial will be Sunday at Balboa Park, Torrance.

(15)

'Iolanthe' on Mall

A free performance of Gilbert and Sullivan's "Iolanthe" will be presented by the New York City Opera on Wednesday, August 9, at 8 p. m. on the Central Park Mall at 72nd Street.

(16)

Jazz Interactions Mo...

Jazz Interactions, afte... lengthy residence at the ... Spot, will move its Sunday ... noon jazz sessions to ... home, The Red Garter at ... 4th Street, on August ... the Roland Kirk Ense... another prominent grou... featured. The Sunda... take place from 5 t... Admission is $2.

(17)

A.I.T.

MONDAY NIGHT IS LADIES NIGHT! LADIES ADMISSION— 90¢ EXCEPT AT THEATRES WITH *

PLAYHOUSE BEDFORD AVE. Bellmore SU·5·7479

ROCK HUDSON · GEORGE PEPPARD **TOBRUK** ALSO George Maharis **A COVENANT WITH DEATH**

OCEANSIDE LONG BEACH RD. * RO·6·8010

NORTH MASSAPEQUA HICKSVILLE RD. PY·9·8282

ACADEMY AWARD WINNER! **The FORTUNE COOKIE** ALSO "THE RUSSIANS ARE COMING"

Those Magnificent Men in their Flying Machines & STAGECOACH

AMITY CARMANS RD. S. Farmingdale MY·1·0200

(18)

To Theatre

Mighty Midgets Club, under direction of Mrs. ...n, is planning an afte... theatre. The club, ... between the age... ...ping to see the mus... 'Curly McDimple'' ...heeler Theatre. ...d number of fr... available. A... ...ersons are invite... ...rs. Dodson during ...an. 15-19.

...rtha McPhereson ...ssie Washington ...th annual Baby ...others may enter ...tots by contacting Mrs. Dodson at the YMCA. Awards ...

EXERCISE 2. Analyzing the Ads for Specific Information

There is some basic information you need before you can make up your mind to go to something. Ads and news stories give you some of the information to help you decide whether or not you want to go and how to prepare.

Directions: Look at the ad for the Daytona '500' and then answer the questions. Put a check in front of the phrase which best completes the statement.

WHAT IS IT?

1. This event is a

____a. race of 500 cars.

____b. stock car race.

____c. automobile sales show.

The Oregonian

2. It is called the Daytona '500' because

____a. the cars will race a total of 500 miles.

____b. 500 cars are in the race.

____c. first prize is $500.00.

3. You will see
____a. a TV broadcast of the race.
____b. the actual cars racing.
____c. a movie of the race.

WHERE DO YOU HAVE TO GO?

4. You will see the show at
____a. home.
____b. Daytona.
____c. County Expo. Center, Portland.

HOW DO YOU GET THERE?

5. If you can't go by car, the ad says
____a. take a stock car
____b. nothing about how to get there.
____c. phone Stevens Jeweler for bus information.

HOW MUCH DOES IT COST?

6. The cheapest ticket costs
____a. $5.00
____b. $3.50
____c. 70¢

7. Some seats are cheaper because
____a. they are side view and not reserved.
____b. they are in the balcony.
____c. they are on the main floor and reserved.

WHEN IS IT?

8. The day and time of the race is
____a. Feb. 11 at 8 A.M.
____b. Sunday at 9 A.M.
____c. Feb. 25 at 9 A.M.

WHERE AND WHEN CAN YOU GET TICKETS?

9. You can buy tickets
____a. now at the stores listed.
____b. only at Northwest Location, Feb. 25.
____c. It doesn't say.

HOW LONG WILL THE EVENT LAST?

10. You will get out of the event about

____a. 7 P.M.

____b. 9 A.M.

____c. The ad doesn't say.

EXERCISE 3. Filling in the Answers

Not all what-to-do information is handed to you on a silver platter. It's up to you to notice what information is missing and figure out how to track it down.

Directions: Read "Oregonian Tourney Deadline Near . . . " Each line in the article is numbered. Pretend that you want to enter the bowling tournaments. Then look at the list of "Things I Need to Know." Fill in the blank with the number of the line that answers the question. If the answer is not given, fill in an "0." The first two are done for you as an example.

Oregonian Tourney Deadline Near . . .

Tournament notes: Today (Sunday) is the final day to enter The Oregonian singles and mixed doubles handicap tournaments being conducted in five Portland-Vancouver, Wash., houses (Amato Lanes, 20th Century Lanes, Milwaukie Bowl, Valley Lanes and Crosley Bowl in Vancouver).

Winner of each tourney is guaranteed $500 cash. House eliminations are scheduled next weekend (Feb. 17-18); tournament finals are set for Feb. 24-25 at Milwaukie Bowl for singles and at 20th Century for mixed doubles . . .

The Oregonian

THINGS I NEED TO KNOW

1. ____2____ What kind of event is it?

2. ____4, 5____ Where do I have to go?

3. ________ How do I get there?

4. ________ How much does it cost?

5. ________ What day do I have to enter?

6. ________ What time do I have to enter?

7. ________ How long will it take?

8. ________ Am I eligible to enter?

There's a lot of information you didn't get from the story. How can you find out? Get ready for a discussion of ways to get the information you need.

EXERCISE 4. Finding the Right Ad for the Right Trip

Don't knock it if you haven't tried it. And don't *not* try it because you "know" it costs too much or is too hard to manage.

So don't knock a day on a fishing boat. Do the ads say how much it costs? No. Is it only for millionaires? It can't cost more than a dime or so to phone and find out. And what you may find out is that it costs $7.00 a person for a 7 A.M.–2 P.M. trip. Even less if you get a group together. And less than that if your class, or your club, or your school charters a whole boat.

Now that you are in the market for a fishing boat, study the ads to find the answers to these important questions.

Directions: Each of these ads has a letter beside it. Fill in the blank with the letter of the ad that answers each of these questions.

____1. Will girls feel welcome on a fishing boat?

____2. Is it all right for beginning fisherman to go?

____3. Can you get near the boat basins by bus or train?

____4. What's the latest time of day a fishing boat sails?

____5. What's the earliest time of day a fishing boat sails?

____6. Can you rent fishing poles and equipment?

EXERCISE 5. Finding More About Things You Can Do Yourself

News articles often tell you about events you may be eligible to enter. Suppose you are a boy and you are interested in entering the Golden Gloves. Can you find out from this news article whether you are eligible?

Directions: Put a check in front of the phrase that gives the right answer.

1. The youngest you can be in this group seems to be

____a. 17

____b. 16

____c. 15

126, 135, 147 Lb. Glovers Well Seasoned for Finals

(This is the second in a series of sketches on the 34 Golden Glove Finalists. They'll compete for the championships Friday night at Madison Square Garden.)

By Jack Smith

Strong, speedy and well-conditioned, contenders from the 126, 135 and 147-pound divisions may supply the fastest action on the program for the Golden Gloves Finals Friday night at Madison Square Garden. They have been the busiest fighters in the tournament, totaling 44 bouts, and have proven themselves in the long schedule of preliminaries, Quarterfinals and semifinals.

They range in age from 16 to 20 and come from Bronx, Brooklyn, Manhattan, Queens, Jersey

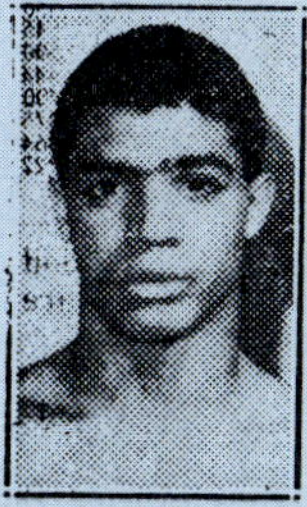

Jose Saldana

Adolfo Viruet

City and Pelham. Among them are factory clerks, a Job Corps trainee and hospital worker. Six are high school students. Here they are:

126 lb. Sub-Novice

JOSE SALDANA, 17, Parks Department, of 320 E. 156th St., Bronx. Celebrates 17th birthday today. A junior at DeWitt Clinton High. Tournament record: four decisions.

ADOLFO VIRUET, 16, Leatherpushers AC, of 203 W. 107th St. Attends PS 185. His brother, Eddie, fights for the 108-pound Sub-Novice title. Tournament record: one knockout, two decisions, one bye.

126 lb. Open

CHU CHU MALAVE, PAL, 17, of 496 E. 189th St. Bronx. In third year at Fashion Industries High. A good student, hopes to become custom tailor. Fights his brother for the title. Tournament record: two knockouts, two decisions.

VINCENT MALAVE, PAL, 18, of 496 E. 189th St., Bronx. Works as stock clerk in department store. Attended Brandeis High. Aims to beat his brother for the championship. Tournament record: three decisions, one bye.

135 lb. Sub-Novice

TOM COLALUCA, 16, Cage Recreation Center, of 2296 Bathgate Ave., Bronx. A junior at Roosevelt High. Father and brother also fought in Gloves. Tournament record: three knockouts, one decision, one bye.

Tix at Garden

All remaining tickets for Friday night's Golden Gloves Finals at Madison Square Garden are available now ONLY at the Garden box office. The office, at 7th Ave. between 31st and 33d Sts., is open from 10 to 7 daily. Tickets are not available at THE NEWS Ticket Office.

JOSE TORO, PAL, 20, of 687 Stone Ave., Brooklyn. Born and schooled in Santurce, P.R. Works for baby carriage manufacturer. Tournament record: one knockout, four decisions.

135 lb. Open

WILLIAM ARMSTEAD, PAL, 20, of 319 Kingsboro Walk, Brooklyn. Married, one youngster, Lisa, 8 months. Works as a porter. Fourth year in Golden Gloves, first time in Finals. Tournament record: three decisions, one bye.

ROLAND TROTMAN, 19,

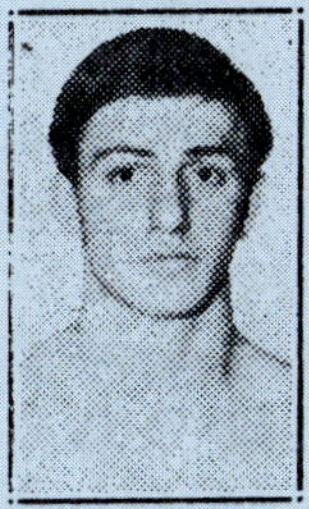

Tom Colaluca

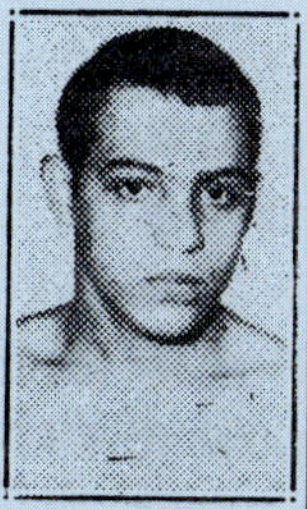

Jose Toro

Wagner Center, of 57 E. 117th St. Defending champ. Senior at Benjamin Franklin High. His father and five uncles are ex-Glovers. Defeated West German champ in international bouts last summer. Tournament record: four decisions.

147 lb. Sub-Novice

RUBEN MELENDEZ, Wagner Center, 19, unemployed factory hand, of 687 Saratoga Ave., Brooklyn. Born and schooled in

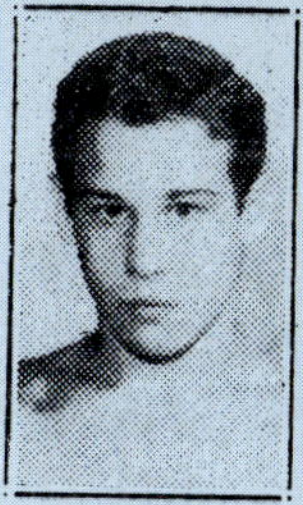

Chu Chu Malave

Vincent Malave

Vieques, P. R. Brother, Dave, won 147-Open title in '66. Tournament record: three knockouts, two decisions, one bye.

THOMAS O'MEARA, unattached, 17, of 125 Fifth Ave., Pelham. Born in Ireland, now attends Pelham High. Has part time job in ice cream parlor. Tournament record: one knockout, four decisions, one bye.

147 lb. Open

ROBERT MIDDLEBROOKS, Parks Dept., 20, of 163-30 Phroane Ave., Jamaica, Queens.

William Armstead

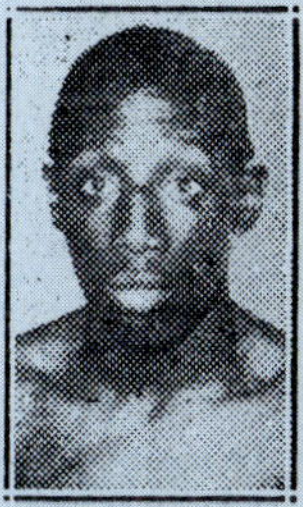

Roland Trotman

Works at auto-service center. Graduate of Jamaica High. Earned letters in track. First year in Gloves. Tournament record: one knockout, one decision, two byes.

JEFFREY HOLMES, Jersey City Recreation Dept., with Liberty Park Job Corps in Jersey City. First time in Gloves. Hopes to make Olympic team. Tournament record: two knockouts, two byes.

2. You can be in the Golden Gloves only if you live in

____a. Manhattan.
____b. Bronx.
____c. It doesn't seem to matter where you live.

3. You can be in the Golden Gloves if you belong to

____a. no group at all.
____b. a PAL (Police Athletic League) club only.
____c. any kind of athletic club or recreation center.

4. Your occupation can be

____a. anything—it doesn't matter.
____b. student.
____c. dropout only.

EXERCISE 6. Finding Movie Information Quickly

If you want to get all the what-to-do information your local paper gives, it will help if you understand the way the paper presents it.

Directions: Get a copy of your local paper. Use it to find the answers to these questions. Circle either YES or NO.

Example: Does your newspaper carry movie ads? YES NO

1. Is there a movie timetable? YES NO

2. What section of the paper is it in? (Write the number or letter.) __________

3. Are drive-ins listed separately, like this? YES NO

The Miami Herald

DRIVE-INS

ARROW (W. Hollywood) — Marylane, 7.00, 10:15, Sadismo, 8:50
BOULEVARD — Ulysses, 7:00, 11:10, Circle Love, 9:15
BREEZEWAY (Homestead) — Don't Make Waves, 7:15, 11:00, Pussycat, 9:10
CORAL WAY — Casino Royale, 7:00, 11:00, Luv, 9:25

RKO THEATERS

COLISEUM—"The Learning Tree," ★★★ – 12, 2, 4, 6, 8, 10.

FORDHAM—"The Learning Tree," ★★★–12, 2, 4, 6, 8, 10.

WHITE PLAINS—"The Learning Tree, ★★★–1:30, 3:40, 5:50, 8, 10.

4. Are theaters listed alphabetically by name like this? YES NO

AMITYVILLE—Mon. ★★ How to Succeed in Business Without Really Trying, 2:00, 7:00, 9:05. **Tues.** ★★ How to Succeed in Business Without Really Trying, 2:00, 4:00, 6:00, 8:00, 10:00.

BABYLON—Mon. The Shaggy Dog, 3:35, 7:00, 10:20; ●The Absent Minded Professor, 2:00, 8:40. **Tues.** The Shaggy Dog, 3:35, 6:55, 10:10; ●The Absent Minded Professor, 2:00, 5:20, 8:40.

BAY SHORE—Mon. ★★ How to Succeed in Business Without Really Trying, 2:00, 7:00, 9:00. **Tues.** ★★ **How** to Succeed in Business **Without Really Trying, 2:15 4:30, 6:45, 9:05.**

5. Are theaters listed under the name of the community or part of town they are in, like this? YES NO

6. Does the timetable give the names of movies and the times, like this? YES NO

7. Does it give some other information, like this? YES NO

FILM RATING GUIDE
For Parents and Their Children

G GENERAL AUDIENCES All Ages Admitted	**R** RESTRICTED Under 17 requires accompanying Parent or Adult Guardian
PG PARENTAL GUIDANCE SUGGESTED Some Material May Not Be Suitable For Pre-Teenagers	**X** NO ONE UNDER 17 ADMITTED (Age limit may vary in certain areas)

The *Chicago Sun-Times*

WBAP-TV (Channel 5)

5:00 **Truth or Consequences** C
5:30 **Huntley-Brinkley** C-NBC
6:00 **News, Weather, Sports** C
6:30 **I Dream of Jeannie** C-NBC
Jeannie still locked in the moon safe (conclusion)
7:00 **Jerry Lewis Show** C-NBC
Guests Ernest Borgnine, Baja Marimba Band,
7:30 Donnie Osmond
8:00 **Tuesday Night Movie** NBC
"McHale's Navy Joins the Air Force." C
8:30 Tim Conway, Joe Flynn, Bob Hastings, Ted Bissell, Tom Tully. Navy ensign
9:00 poses as an Air Force fighter pilot and rises in rank as he is forced to carry
9:30 out one frantic combat incident after another
10:00 **News, Weather, Sports** C

Fort Worth Star-Telegram

EXERCISE 7. Breaking the TV Schedule Code

Get ready for a class discussion of the TV schedule. You will need the entertainment section of your local paper. Try to find the reason for every little initial or symbol. Use these questions for a starter:

1. Color programs here are marked with a C. How are color programs marked in your paper?

____

____

____

2. Of course your paper tells you when a program *begins*. This one makes it easy to see when it *ends*, too. Is your TV schedule set up so that you can tell how long a program is?

YES NO If yes, how? ____________________

____

8	:00 :15 :30 :45	w/James Drury Diane Baker Doug McClure C. Bickford	Perry Mason (R) "Posthumous" drama Perry Mason (R)
9	:00 :15 :30 :45	Bob Hope Presents (C, R) "Wipeout" Tom Tryon	Untouchables (R) "The King of Champagne" Untouchables (R)
10	:00 :15 :30 :45	I Spy (C, R) w/Bob Culp Bill Cosby Zohra Lampert	10 O'Clock News WTTG Team (C) Alfred Hitchcock Mystery

Ken Harter, *The Washington Post*

3. Movies are set off here by putting edges like movie-film on either side. Are movies marked a special way in your newspaper?

YES NO If yes, how? ____________________

____

9	:00 :15 :30 :45	Leave It To Beaver (R) Today w/Inga (C) w/Kathy Keegan	Bozo's Big Top (C) The Big Movie "Those
10	:00 :15 :30 :45	Snap Judgment (C) w/Ed McMahon Concentration (C) w/Hugh Downs	Endearing Young Charms" (1945) stars
11	:00 :15 :30 :45	Personality (C) w/Larry Blyden The Hollywood Squares (C)	Robt. Young Loraine Day Bold Journey "The Amazon"

Ken Harter, *The Washington Post*

4. R means re-run—a repeated show. Does your paper mark re-runs?

YES NO If yes, how? ____________________

____

6	:00 :15 :30 :45	News 4 Washington (C) Huntley-Brinkley Report (C)	Outer Limits (R) "The Man With the Power" Outer Limits (R)
7	:00 :15 :30 :45	News 4 Washingron (C) The Virginian (C, R) "Linda"	Twilight Zone (R) "Walter Jameson" Truth or Consequences (C)

Ken Harter, © *The Washington Post.*

5. The Times marks selected or special programs with a "bullet." Does your paper mark best-bet programs?

YES NO If yes, how? ____________________

____

9:00 (2) ● MOVIE: "The Guns of Navarone" (1961), part two, Gregory Peck, David Niven, Anthony Quinn and others. Allied rain on Nazi-held Aegean fortress. Big, scenic and bombastic with super-heroics (C)
(4) Here Come the Brides: "A Far Cry From Yesterday," adventure and comedy. Robert Brown, Joan Blondell and others (C) (season premiere)
(31) Sight and Sound
(41) Duelo de Pasiones

6. (1956) shows the year the picture was first shown. Does your paper tell you how old TV movies are?

YES NO If yes, how? ____________________

____

7. This paper tells you what it thinks of the movie. Does your paper rate TV movies in any way?

YES NO If yes, how? ____________________

____

—4:00 P.M.—
(2)—Flipper (C), (rerun)
3—Batman (C)
(4)—The Flintstones (C)
(7)—11-13—Dark Shadows (C)
(9)—French Chef, "Le Marquis Au Chocolat"
10—Mike Douglas (C)
(32)—Meet Mr. Mitch (C)

San Francisco Examiner

8. The numbers bordered like TV screens are San Francisco channels. The other numbers are out-of-town channels. Does your paper mark out-of-town channels?
YES NO If yes, how? ______________________

____

Does it mark UHF channels?
YES NO If yes, how? ______________________

____

PRACTICE IN YOUR LOCAL NEWSPAPER

PRACTICE 1. Each student in your class is going to look for what-to-do ideas in one or more pages of your local paper. Write down the numbers of the pages you are supposed to check:____. Color-mark one, two, or three activities you think class members would enjoy. Bring the pages to class.

PRACTICE 2. The class will choose three things to do from the paper—for example, a free concert, talent contest, and auto show. The class will discuss what you need to know before you do it. And the class will talk about how to get the information.

PRACTICE 3. Study the TV schedule. Pick out a regular program you have never watched. Watch the program for at least 10 minutes. Then fill in these blanks:

Name of program ______________________

Day ________ Time ________ Channel ________

What is the program about? (in one sentence)

____

____

Did you like it or not? Why?

____

____

CHAPTER 18
THE FINANCIAL PAGE:
SHOULD A PAPER BOY BUY STOCK?

A paper boy gets experience in running his own business by taking care of his paper route. "Regional Airlines Can Be Erratic" tells how one paper boy also gets experience in investing his business profits. Read the newspaper clipping; then work Exercise 1 to see if you understand the advice the columnist gives the paper boy.

EXERCISE 1. Learning How to Select the Right Stock

Directions: Read the statements below. Circle YES if the statement is what Mr. Spear told the paper boy he should do. Circle NO if the statement is not what Mr. Spear tells the paper boy to do.

YES NO 1. Mr. Spear advises the paper boy to sell his shares in Mohawk Airlines.

YES NO 2. Mr. Spear suggests the paper boy add to his Minnesota Mining and Mfg. stock.

Investing

Regional airlines can be erratic

By Roger E. Spear

Q. I am 12 and a paperboy for a paper that arries your column. I am trying to save enough money to go to college. I will not need this money until I am 18 and would like to see it grow. Within the last month I bought Minnesota Mining & Mfg. and Mohawk Airlines. I have $300 to invest. What do you think of buying more Mohawk, or should I put the money in the bank?—D. J.

Spear

A. I do not advise you to buy more Mohawk Airlines. This is a regional carrier serving the Northeast and I believe that most such situations show an erratic earnings picture rather than a growth pattern. These stocks have fallen out of favor, including even Pacific Southwest, one of the most ably managed and best situated of the group, in my opinion. Your 3M is satisfactory and you might well add to this holding. If you wish to diversify, I suggest you use your present funds to buy Transamerica, which appears relatively undervalued. Ordinarily, I would advise a savings account as a backlog to any stock list. But you have parents to take care of contingencies and I do not feel that it is necessary in your situation.

Roger Spear's 48-page Guide to Successful Investing is available for $1, from Roger E. Spear, care of The Chicago Daily News, Box 1618, Grand Central Station, New York, N. Y. 10017.

YES NO 3. Mr. Spear suggests that the paper boy should open a savings account as a backlog to his stock list.

YES NO 4. Mr. Spear suggests that if the paper boy wishes to diversify, he should buy Transamerica stock.

EXERCISE 2. "Don't Put All Your Eggs in One Basket"

Mr. Spear suggests that the paper boy might want to "diversify." This means to buy several stocks in several different kinds of businesses rather than buy all his stocks in the same business.

What is the advantage of investing in three shares each of ten different kinds of businesses, instead of thirty shares of one business? Write your answer below:

____

____

____

____

____

____

WHY DO PEOPLE BUY STOCK?

When you buy a share of stock, you buy a little part of an incorporated business. The corporation uses your money to help run or expand its business. If the corporation makes a profit, it sends you a check for your *share* of the profits—say, $1.00 for each share of stock. This money is called a *dividend*. If the corporation makes a very big profit, it may decide to make the dividend bigger, say $2.00 for each share of stock, and you get more money back even though the amount you invested is the same. But, if the corporation doesn't make a profit, your share of nothing is nothing.

If your stock keeps paying good dividends, people will want that stock so much that you can sell it for more than you paid for it. But if the stock never pays a dividend, few people will want to buy it. If you can sell it at all, you will get much less money than you paid for it.

Let's pretend you have some extra money, and you decide to buy some stock. When you want to buy a house, you go to a real estate agent; when you want to buy a car, you go to a car salesman. If you want to buy stock in a company, you go to a *stock-broker*. He will buy the stock for you by going to a *stock exchange*. A stock exchange is a central market place where stockbrokers meet to buy and sell stocks and bonds.

Before you buy stock, someone who owns shares must want to sell. The price of stock changes from day to day.

The stockbroker charges you a commission or fee for buying and selling stock. Usually, the fee is about one percent of the cost of the stock.

People who own stock want to know whether the price is going up or down, how many shares were sold during the day, how big a dividend the company paid on each share of stock, etc. They get all this information quickly by reading the tables newspapers publish, showing the stock market transactions for the day. An example is printed on the opposite page.

You can bet that the paper boy doesn't skip the stock market page when he reads the paper. He watches his Mohawk Airlines, because if he sells, he wants to sell when it's up. He watches to see how many shares were traded, to get an idea of how much of a market there is for Mohawk stock. He'll read the stock market quotations to see what Transamerica is doing, too, before he decides whether or not to buy it. A news story about a new product to compete with 3M's Scotch Tape would also get his attention.

You don't need to own stock to enjoy reading the exciting stories told by the dull-looking figures of the stock market tables. You do need to know how to read and interpret these tables. In a way, it's like learning another language.

HOW TO READ THE STOCK MARKET TABLES

The tables usually show all of the transactions for the New York Stock Exchange and the American Stock Exchange, which are both in New York. Many papers carry tables of the Midwest Exchange located in Chicago and the Pacific Coast Stock Exchange in San Francisco. Some carry partial listings of less important exchanges in other cities. If you do not find the stock you are looking for listed on the New York Stock Exchange, look at the tables for other exchanges.

Newspapers may use different symbols, but if you learn to read one table, you will be able to read another. The symbols are usually explained in footnotes at the end of the tables or in a box at one side.

Study this clipping of a small part of a stock market table. These transactions were reported in the Wall Street Journal on February 19, 1968. Notice that the stocks are listed alphabetically.

30 **THE WALL STREET JOURNAL,**
Tuesday, February 20, 1968

Monday's Volume, 7,270,000 Shares

Volume since Jan. 1:	1968	1967	1966
Total sales	379,357,188	341,582,530	315,188,670

MOST ACTIVE STOCKS

	Open	High	Low	Close	Chg.	Volume
Auto Spriklr	40⅜	40⅜	37¼	37¼	−3⅛	166,300
Benguet	13½	13½	12⅞	13	− ⅝	136,100
Beth Steel	30	30⅛	29¼	29¾	− ½	128,200
Control Dat	117¼	122½	115	120⅜	+2⅛	127,800
McDonnD	49	51⅝	49	50⅜	+2¾	84,400
Gen Time	36½	37⅛	36½	36½	+3¼	75,100
Gulf Wn In	48⅜	48¾	47¼	47⅜	− ⅞	71,600
Teledyne	105¼	108⅝	105¼	108¼	+ 3	64,500
Talon Inc	33	33¼	32⅞	32⅞	− ⅛	64,100
East Air Lin	35¼	36½	35	35½	+ ⅛	59,300
Glen Ald	14⅜	14⅜	14⅛	14¼	.....	59,300

Average closing price of most active stocks: 47.77.

A-B-C-D

−1967-68− High	Low	Stocks	Div.	Sales in 100s	Open	High	Low	Close	Net Chg.
17⅞	13	Abacus	.70f	4	16	16⅛	16	16⅛	− ⅛
53⅞	41	Abbott Lab	1	35	43⅛	44	43	44	+1
34⅞	27⅞	Abex Cp	1.60	12	29⅞	29⅞	29¾	29⅞	....
58¼	38⅛	ACF Ind	2.20	97	42⅝	42⅝	41¾	42¼	− ⅜
46¾	32	Acme Mkt	2b	29	37½	38	37½	38	+ ½
34	27	AdamE	2.50e	17	31⅝	31⅝	31	31	− ⅜
87¼	14½	AdMillis	.40a	42	43¼	44⅞	43¼	44⅝	+ ⅜
80½	46⅞	Address	1.40	124	62⅝	64	62½	63⅝	+1¼
38	16½	Admiral		39	16⅞	17⅜	16⅞	17	.....
69⅛	35	Aeroquip	1b	23	55¼	55¼	54⅝	54⅝	− ⅞
46¼	31⅝	Air Prod	.20b	42	36½	37¼	36½	36¾	+ ¼
44⅞	31⅜	AirRedtn	1.50	142	31½	31⅝	30¾	31	− ¾
12⅝	3½	AJ Industries		84	10⅛	10¼	10⅛	10¼	+ ⅛
19½	17¾	Ala Gas	.96	12	18⅛	18⅜	18⅛	18⅜	+ ¼
43⅞	16¾	Alberto C	.20	17	36¾	37	36⅝	36⅝	+ ⅛
33¾	23	AlcanAlum	1	96	23⅞	24	23¾	24	+ ⅛
17⅞	7⅞	Alleg Cp	.20g	83	14⅝	14¾	14¼	14½	+ ⅛
79¼	55⅛	AllegLud	2.40	4	66¾	67	66¾	67	.....
79	69¼	AllegLud	pf 3	1	71½	71½	71½	71½	.....
27¾	21	Alleg Pw	1.20	22	23	23⅛	22⅞	22⅞	− ¼
107	91	Alleg&West	6	z20	100	100	100	100	+1
31⅞	21½	AllenInd	1.40	4	26⅝	26⅞	26⅝	26⅞	+ ½
46⅞	33¼	AlliedCh	1.90	200	36½	37½	36	36	− ½
33¼	15¼	Allied Kid	1	6	26⅝	27	26⅝	27	+ ½
63¾	26½	Allied Pd	.60	35	52½	53	52¼	53	+ ¼
114	102½	AlliedPd	pf 3	1	104	104	104	104	+ ½
41½	22⅛	AlliedStr	1.40	47	36¾	36¾	36⅝	36¾	+ ⅛
77¾	64	AlliedSt	pf 4	z20	66½	66½	66½	66½	.....
24	11	AlliedSup	.60	61	17⅞	18⅜	17¾	18⅛	+ ¼
44	21⅝	Allis Chal	1	297	32	32½	31⅞	32⅜	+ ¼
14⅞	7¾	Alpha P Cem		16	13	13⅛	13	13	.....
15¼	5¾	Alside	.20	8	11⅞	11⅞	11½	11½	− ¼
93⅞	67¼	Alcoa	1.80	96	70⅞	72½	70⅞	72¼	+2¼
33	20⅜	AmalSug	1.40	2	30¾	30¾	30⅝	30⅝	+ ⅛

The first stock listed is Abacus. The first two columns at the left show the highest price ($17\frac{7}{8}$ or $\$17.87\frac{1}{2}$) and the lowest price (13 or \$13.00) at which the stock sold during 1967 and to date in 1968. These two columns are not always given.

The third column from the left gives the name of the stock followed by the dividend rate of .70. This means that a dividend of 70 cents per share was declared for the year. Dividends are usually paid out four times a year—at the end of each quarter-year—so this would mean $17\frac{1}{2}$ cents per share per quarter. (The f refers to a footnote appearing at the end of the tables, giving more information about the dividend. This is very technical information which you do not need to understand now.)

The fourth column reports the sales in hundreds. It tells how many shares of the stock were traded on the exchange that day. The 4 means 4×100 or 400 shares.

The fifth column, which is headed "Open" refers to the opening price (first-sale). The first sale was of 16—\$16.00 per share.

The sixth column shows the highest price at which the stock was sold during the day. It was $16\frac{1}{8}$, which means sixteen and one-eighth dollars or $\$16.12\frac{1}{2}$. The seventh column shows the lowest price for the day. It was 16 or \$16.00.

The eighth column, headed "Close," gives the price of the last transaction of the day. The closing price was $16\frac{1}{8}$ or $\$16.12\frac{1}{2}$.

The last column gives the net change from the price at which the stock closed the day before. In this net change, $-\frac{1}{8}$ means that the stock sold for one-eighth of a dollar less—$12\frac{1}{2}$ cents less—than it did at the end of the last trading day.

EXERCISE 3. How to Read Tables

Directions: Use the table on page 241 to answer the following questions. Use the fractions as given in the table without changing them to dollars and cents.

1. What was the highest price paid for Abbott Laboratories during 1967–68? ______________________________.

2. What was the lowest price paid for Abbott Laboratories during 1967–68? ______________________________.

3. How much will the quarterly dividend be? ______________.

   (Hint: Remember that the *1* after the name of a stock stands for $1.00 annual dividend, since it has no footnote explaining otherwise.)

4. How many shares of Abbott stock were traded on this day? ______.

5. What was the opening price of Abbott stock? ______________.

6. What was the closing price of Abbott stock? ______________.

7. What was the highest price at which Abbott stock was sold on this day? ______________________________.

8. What was the lowest price at which Abbott stock was sold on this day? ______________________________.

EXERCISE 4. How to Figure Dividends

Directions: Pretend that you own the stock described in each question below. First look up the name of the stock in the table. Find the annual dividend per share. Then multiply the dividend by the number of shares you own to see how much your dividends will be. The first one is done for you.

1. You own 100 shares of Ala Gas. Look up the dividend in the table and you will see it is .96. Multiply this .96 by the number of shares you own like this:

.96 per-share dividend

×100 number of shares you own

$96.00 annual dividends you will receive

2. You own 50 shares of Alberto C.

____per-share dividend
____number of shares you own
____annual dividends you will receive

3. You own 20 shares of Address.

____per-share dividend
____number of shares you own
____annual dividends you will receive

4. You own 25 shares of Admiral.

____per-share dividend
____number shares you own
____annual dividends you will receive

HOW THE NEWS AFFECTS THE STOCK MARKET

People who own stock soon learn that what happens in the world may cause their stocks to go up or down in price. News of the assassination of a world leader, rumblings of discontent in foreign countries, new legislation in Congress, discoveries of natural resources, and so on, will all be reflected on the financial pages. A good example of this is the story about how the stock market reacted to news of the Viet Nam War peace talks on April 3, 1968.

Peace News Powers Stocks to Peak Trade; Price Advance Pared

Statistics on what stocks did are on page 16.

BY WILLIAM CLARK
[Financial Editor]

North Viet Nam's "We'll talk" response to President Johnson's peace gesture yesterday triggered the heaviest stock trading volume in history. Despite selling by profit-takers which reduced early price advances, a big majority of issues traded on the New York Stock exchange and elsewhere ended the day with net gains.

At 2:03 p. m. Chicago time, with 27 minutes yet to go in the session, the number of shares changing hands on the New York Stock exchange moved past the old one-day record of 17,730,000, set only two days earlier on the strength of the President's Sunday night order to curb bombing as a prelude to negotiations. From that point, trading went on to reach an unprecedented total of 19,290,000 shares at the closing bell.

Tape Gap a Record

The frantic pace of trading caused the Big Board's high speed tape to lag as much as 46 minutes in its recording of individual transactions. That gap, which prevailed around 11 a. m. Chicago time, also was a record.

Back on March 10, 1967, the first trading day after President Johnson said he would try to restore the 7 per cent tax credit for new corporate investment in productive facilities, the tape was 27 minutes late. That stood as its maximum tardiness until yesterday.

At its best level of the session, Dow-Jones industrial average stood 13.12 points above its Tuesday close. That was at 12:30 Chicago time. From that point, the profit-takers whittled away, the popular average settling for a net gain for the day of 5.15, or 0.59 per cent, to 869.11—its highest close since Jan. 22.

The New York Stock exchange's composite index finished at 51.84, up 0.46. The average price of a share of stock on the exchange advanced 44 cents. Advances outnumbered declines 887 to 452.

Standard & Poor's 500-stock index rose 0.83 to 93.47.

Cites Institutional Investors

There was little doubt this time, as there was to some extent Monday, that institutional investors—mutual funds, pension trusts, insurance companies, etc.—contributed to the massive wave of buying that swept the exchanges yesterday morning.

The lateness of the tape, the result of the enormous amount of activity in the morning, was itself a factor in the slowing of the pace around the middle of the day.

Investors said they felt as tho they were trading in the dark, not knowing what price trends might have set in the three-quarters of an hour between the sale showing at the moment on the tape and the last actual transaction.

Another Peace Rally

It was again, as it was on Monday, a "peace rally." Opening prices were mixed and the pace of trading unspectacular until news wires carried the first word of Hanoi's willingness to talk with United States envoys. That opened the gates, even tho it later appeared that the talks to which Hanoi agreed would only cover the conditions under which further discussion might be held.

There is wide agreement among analysts that a satisfactory end to the fighting in Viet Nam would speed progress toward solution of such other problems as the gold drain and the balance of payments, and would clear the way for expansion of consumer-oriented business on the home front—all to the benefit of the stock market.

ESTIMATES 18 MILLIONS IN COMMISSIONS

New York, April 3 (AP)—Record trading on the New York Stock exchange today resulted in commissions to brokerage houses of more than 18 million dollars, a Wall street authority estimated. He said the estimate was based on the trading of 19,290,000 shares at an average price of $49 per share and an average commission charge of 1 per cent. The estimate of 18 million dollars was "an educated guess, as close as you can get."

Reprinted, courtesy of the *Chicago Tribune*

The Dow Jones industrial average, which showed a gain

DOW JONES AVERAGES
New York(AP)Final Dow-Jones averages
STOCKS

	Open	High	Low	Close	Net
30 Ind	941.70	946.65	932.93	938.59	— 1.61
20 RR	271.96	273.80	270.42	272.36	+ 0.38
15 Utl	135.58	137.14	134.71	135.77	+ 0.32
65 Stk	34026	342.57	337.68	339.95	+ 0.27

Transactions in stocks used in averages:
Indus 663,300
Rails 149,300
Utils .. 136,000
65 Stk 948,600

exceeding a point at the start, closed with a loss of 1.61 at 938.59.

The Oregonian

EXERCISE 5. Using the Averages

Directions: Imagine that you own 100 shares of stock in the Santa Fe Railroad. Check the Dow Jones Averages on the right. Then answer these questions:

1. What was the High for the 20 Railroad stocks (RR)? ____________.

2. What was the Low for the 20 Railroad stocks? ____________.

WORDS TO HELP YOU

Profit-takers—share owners who buy stock not as a long-term investment, but just long enough for the price to go up so they can sell and make a profit
majority-of-issues—majority of stocks
Big Board—New York Stock Exchange
Market Averages and **Indexes** (or Market Indicators)—measuring devices used to keep a record of the over-all ups and downs in stock market prices over a long period of time. The most important Market Indicators are described below:

Dow-Jones Averages are based on statistics compiled on 65 important stocks, divided into 30 industrial common stocks, 20 railroad stocks, and 15 public utility common stocks. These are important, well-established companies which are the foundation of our national economy.

New York Stock Exchange Index is based on statistics compiled on about 1,270 stocks chosen to represent the industries and services that are leading the U.S. economy.

Standard & Poor's Index is based on 500 stocks selected by Standard & Poor Corporation, a statistical organization which compiled market averages for many years.

3. What was the Close for the 20 Railroad stocks? ___________.

4. What was the change for the 20 Railroad stocks from the day before?

___________.

5. Look up the same information for the 30 Industrials (Ind) and write your figures here:

High___________Low___________Close___________Change

___________.

6. Look up the same information for the 15 Utilities (Utl) and write your figures here:

High___________Low___________Close___________Change

___________.

7. On the basis of what you have discovered in writing down these averages, do you think railroads are as good an investment as Industrial Corporations or Utilities? ____Yes____No

BULLS, BEARS, CATS, AND DOGS ON WALL STREET

No, they have not suddenly opened a zoo in the financial center of New York City! The financial world has a slang of its own. Read this column by Sylvia Porter to discover the meanings of some of the most frequently used expressions.

DON'T GET 'HUNG UP' ON 'PUP'

A New Language Flourishes Among The Wall Street Set

Hard to Tell What's Going On Without Unique Dictionary

BY SYLVIA PORTER

"That guy is no lamb at this game, and right now he's a bull on a lot of cats and dogs I'd never suggest you own. He doesn't get hung up in many pups, though, and some of his hot issues in recent years have been real yo-yos."

What nutty bafflegab is this? It is the day-to-day lingo of Wall Street—and I excerpted it from a long, gossipy conversation I had a couple of days ago about the activities of one of New York's successful brokers.

I have just been thumbing through the first dictionary ever to be published devoted exclusively to "Stock Market Terms" and every slang word in the above paragraph is defined in it. The dictionary, with 1,200 entries, was compiled by Peter Wyckoff, a Wall Street research analyst, and will be published by Prentice-Hall Sept. 24. To translate:

SYLVIA PORTER

LAMB: A beginner at speculation. He follows the flock, buying or selling blindly on tips and rumors.

BULL: An optimist—in Wall Street it would mean a bull on the stock market generally or on certain individual stocks. The term originated on the London Stock Exchange. The reason the term is linked with those who buy for an uplift in prices may be the tendency of a bull to lift and throw up an object with his horns.

CATS AND DOGS: Wall Street slang meaning highly speculative and usually low-priced stocks which do not pay dividends.

HOT ISSUE: A security which meets a heavy demand on being sold publicly for the first time. The price of the issue usually rises sharply as soon as it is placed on the market and the original buyers can, if they want, turn a quick profit.

YO-YO STOCKS: Volatile, high-priced specialty issues which fluctuate over a wide trading range.

HUNG UP: The plight of an investor who has capital tied up in a stock which has slumped below his purchase price and who, therefore, can't dispose of the security without taking a loss.

PUPS: Low priced, inactive stocks.

The man we were gossiping about thus is an experienced, shrewd Wall Street operator who has made big-time money in recent years in both low-priced speculative stocks and high-priced new issues and who is nimble enough to avoid getting caught in low-priced stocks which have inactive markets.

Every profession and business has its own special language and the vernacular of the stock market is as full and rich as any I know. Just as a physician will use words when talking to another physician way over the heads of most of us, so a Wall Street pro will talk to other pros in a jargon peculiar to his activities.

Some of the talk of the ticker is easy to figure out. For instance, when a broker tells you the stock market is "falling out of bed" it means that prices are in a sudden, sharp decline.

Some of it is defiantly befuddling. For instance, when a broker tells you a "head and shoulders pattern on a point and figure chart" forecasts a break in the price of a stock, it means this is his technical interpretation of a series of price changes in a specific stock which he has charted on a piece of graph paper.

MY FAMILY owns blue chip stocks with a high degree of liquidity. In commonplace language, we own the stocks of leading, well-established and well-managed corporations in essential industries and which we can readily convert into cash when and as we wish.

PRACTICE IN YOUR LOCAL NEWSPAPER

PRACTICE 1. Skim the financial pages of your newspaper and try to find at least five examples of the "day-to-day lingo of Wall Street." Circle the words and bring the clippings to class. Think about these questions: Are the words or phrases in the dictionary? If they are, do you think the articles you have clipped out use any of the dictionary meanings? Can you guess, from the articles, what the words or phrases mean? Your teacher may assign a student to look up some of the special words in the public library's copy of *Stock Market Terms* by Peter Wyckoff.

PRACTICE 2. Select a stock you think you would like to buy. Try to find news notes on the business pages to guide you. It will be more fun if you buy a stock in a company you know is marketing a new food product, or merging with another company, or drilling for off-shore oil in Papua. Every day for four weeks look up the stock market transactions for the stock you have selected in the market tables. Make a graph like the sample graph headed "Stock Prices Keep Changing." Draw in lines to show how the closing price of your stock fluctuates (changes) from day to day.

PRACTICE 3. Figure the cost of 10 shares of the stock you have selected, based on the lowest price given for that day. Find the commission your broker might charge by taking 1 percent of the total you pay for the 10 shares. If this figure is less than $6.00, substitute $6.00 because that is the minimum commission most brokers would charge. Add the commission to the cost of the stock to find your *capital outlay* (total cost).

Example: Suppose you bought 10 shares of American Hospital stock at the lowest price on Feb. 19. You would have paid $77.50 per share.

	$77.50	per share
	× 10	shares
	775.00	cost of stock
plus	7.75	1% broker's commission (To find 1% of a figure, just move the decimal point two places to the left.)
	$782.75	Capital outlay for 10 shares—Total Cost

STOCK PRICES KEEP CHANGING

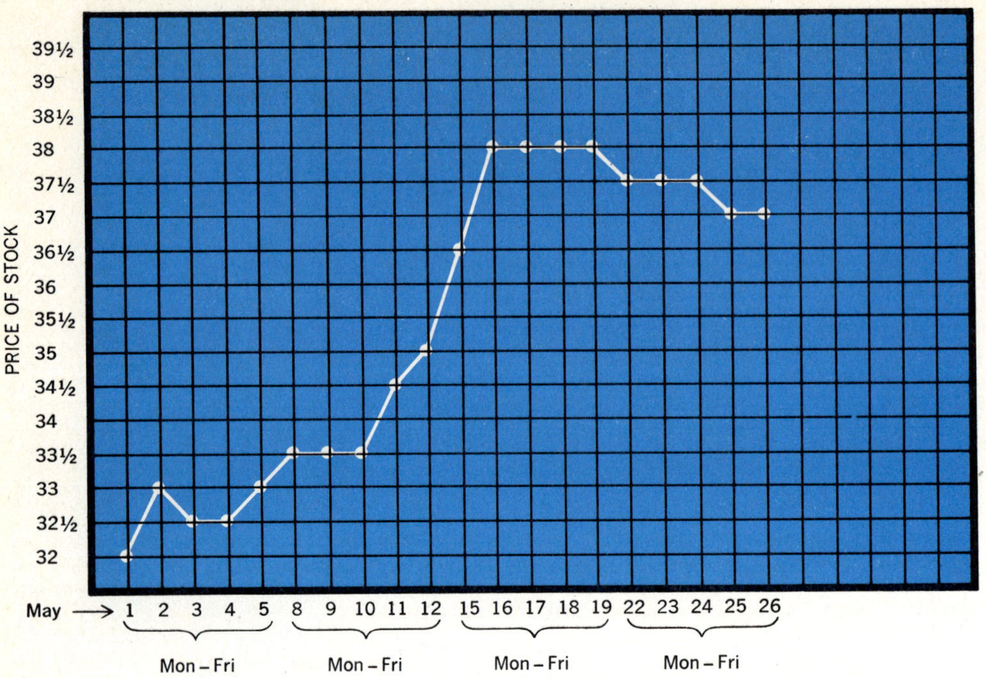

The closing price of the stock has been rounded off to the nearest half point. For example, closing price for May 1 was 32¼. This is graphed at 32. May 16 closing price was 37⅞. This is graphed at 38.

PRACTICE IN YOUR LOCAL NEWSPAPER

PRACTICE 4. At the end of four weeks sell the stock at the highest price quoted on that day's stock market. Pay your broker 1% commission on the total sale price. Subtract the commission from the sale price. Now do you have a profit? Or a loss? (Hint: If sale price minus commission is more than capital outlay, you have a *profit*. If it is less than capital outlay, you have a *loss*.)

Example: If the price of American Hospital went up to $80.25 per share on the day you sold, you would figure your profit as follows:

$80.25	per share	802.50
× 10	shares	.01
802.50	sale price of stock	$ 8.025∅
−8.03	commission ←——(Round off to $8.03)	
794.47	net price	
−782.75	Capital outlay (Total cost)	
$11.72	Total Profit	

If you sold your stock for less than you paid for it, you would figure your loss as follows:

Price at which stock is sold times number of shares, minus commission. Then subtract that figure from the capital outlay. If the price of American Hospital went down to $75.00 per share on the day you sold, you would figure your loss as follows:

$75.00	per share
× 10	shares
750.00	sale price of stock
−7.50	commission
742.50	net price
−782.75	Capital outlay (Total cost)
40.25	Total Loss

PRACTICE 5. Have a profit-making contest. Each student will pretend to buy $1,000 worth of any one stock he chooses, and then keep track of its value. See whose stock is worth the most after 4 weeks, 8 weeks, and 16 weeks.

PRACTICE 6. Another way to have fun following the market is to organize the whole class into an investment club. Pretend each member is putting up $1,000. The class will follow stock trends, read the advice given by experts, and study business news. Perhaps each student can watch a particular stock and report to the rest of the class about its fluctuations. On the basis of the student reports, the club can vote on the five different stocks it wants to invest its money in. Now your club has a stock portfolio. Once a week decide which stocks to buy or sell. After 10 weeks, sell all the stock at that day's closing prices, and have an accounting committee figure out what profit (or loss) each person has made on his $1,000 investment.

CHAPTER 19
READING THE COMICS

Maybe you thought it was crazy when the teacher said you need to learn how to read the newspaper. Well, now you are going to learn how to read the funnies! You say that you've been reading the funnies since before you could read, so you must know them inside out—right? Well, you may be surprised at some of the things you don't know about them.

EXERCISE 1. How Much Do You Know About the Funnies?

Here is a list of statements. Circle the T or F in front of each statement. The first one is done for you as an example. This is just a self check to see what you do and do not know about the funnies.

T F 1. Most comic strip characters never grow old.

T F 2. Comic strips use only easy words.

T F 3. All comic strips are meant to make you laugh.

T F 4. All comic strips tell a continued story.

T F 5. Comic strip people's words are always in a balloon.

T F 6. The comic strip story is told using only pictures and the characters' words.

T F 7. A comic strip always has four picture panels.

T F 8. All picture panels are the same width.

T F 9. Comic strips show closeups, long shots, unusual angles, and dramatic lighting, just like TV or movies.

T F 10. Politics is kept out of comic strips.

EXERCISE 2. Using Comic Strip Reminders

Here are the ten statements repeated with a cartoon panel used to illustrate each point. This time look at the cartoon panel with each statement before you circle your answer.

T F 1. Comic strip characters never grow older.

Answer: T Most comic strip heroes stay the same age. Gasoline Alley is almost the only strip where characters grow older.
Snuffy Smith—Jughaid hasn't aged in 20 years.
Gasoline Alley—Skeezix grew up, married, and had children.

T F 2. Comic strips use only easy words.

intellect
senile
grasp
advanced
theories
potential
legitimate
donning
taunted
baring
saunters
alleged
subterranean
complex
heretic

top, *Pittsburgh Post-Gazette;* upper left, JUDGE PARKER by Harold Le Doux. © Field Enterprises, Inc. Courtesy of Field Newspaper Syndicate; lower left and upper right, Dick Tracy created by Chester Gould © Chicago Tribune-New York Daily News Syndicate; bottom, Reprint from the comic strip STEVE CANYON 1967. © Field Enterprises, 1977. lower right, © 1967 King Features Syndicate, Inc.

Answer: F. Sometimes comic strips use very difficult words as you can see by these few examples.

T F 3. All comic strips are meant to make you laugh.

Answer: F. Does this panel make you laugh?

T F 4. All comic strips tell a continued story.

Answer: F. This strip is complete.

T F 5. Comic strip people's words are always in balloons.

Answer: F. No balloons here.

T F 6. The comic strip story is told using only pictures and the character's words.

Answer: F. Parts of a story are often written down. They are the words of the storyteller, not a character.

T F 7. A comic strip always has four panels.

MISS PEACH by Mell Lazarus. Courtesy of Mell Lazarus and Field Newspaper Syndicate.

Answer: F. Miss Peach likes to use just one. Count the number of panels in your local newspaper strips. You'll find 2, 3, 4, and even 5 or 6.

T F 8. All picture panels are the same width.

© by Walt Kelly. Reprinted by permission

Answer: F. Artists have little enough room in a strip as it is. They don't want to have set panel sizes, too. Sometimes they even break the walls between the panels as in Pogo.

T F 9. Comic strips show closeups, long shots, unusual angles, camera angles, and dramatic lighting similar to TV or movies.

TIFFANY JONES by Pat Tourret and Jenny Butterworth. TM ® Field Newspaper Syndicate. Associated Newspapers Ltd. 1969. Courtesy of Field Newspaper Syndicate.

Answer: T. A comic strip is often like a movie film—a series of still shots using closeups, long shots, a variety of angles, and dramatic lighting.

T F 10. Opinions on politics and government policies are kept out of comics.

Answer: F. We sometimes forget that one of the freedoms we enjoy in this country is "freedom of the press." Cartoonists often use their comic strips to poke fun at politics or government policies.

Compare your answers to Exercise 1 with your answers to Exercise 2. Have you learned more about the funnies?

The point is, you can get more pleasure out of any kind of entertainment when you know what to look for.

Take basketball. Ramon brings Kathy to her first basketball game. All she sees is a lot of tall fellows running madly back and forth with a big ball. Ramon explains some of the rules players have to use in guarding, passing, rebounding, etc. Then Kathy can begin to appreciate a good play.

The funnies follow some rules, too.

EXERCISE 3. What Rules Do Cartoonists Follow?

Look back at the panels used in Exercise 2. Guess at some of the rules the artist is following. Make notes next to cartoon panels to remind you of what you want to say.

Example: How do you know which character speaks first? Look at this Pogo panel.

How do you know which character speaks first? Well, the artist knows people read from left to right, or from top to bottom. That means he usually has to set up his picture so that the person who speaks first is on the left. Check some other strips to see if this is so. Try to find a panel where the first person who speaks is *not* on the left. What has the artist done to help you know who is speaking?

EXERCISE 4. Learning the Cartoon "Sign Language"

Another rule of the funnies is that the artist has to tell his story in pictures as much as possible. The funnies have a "sign language" that you know very well.

Directions: Fill in the letter of the phrase that best completes the statement. Three letters will be left over. The first statement is completed for you as an example.

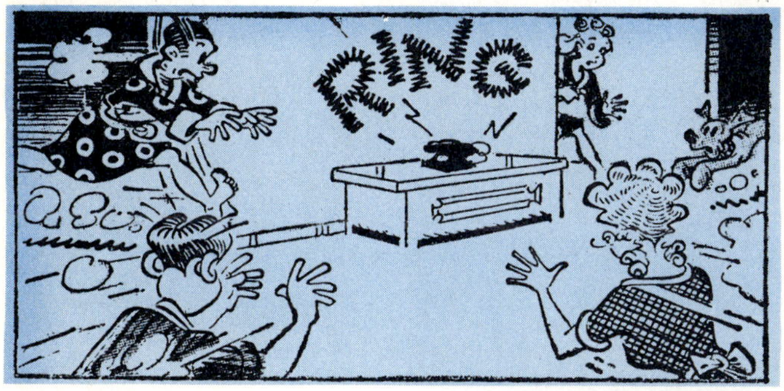

Phrases

a. He left a cloud of dust.
b. He is scratching his head.
c. His hat flew off and his hair is standing on end.
d. His balloon is connected to him by bubbles.
e. He is sweating and shaking.
f. His words are not in balloons.
g. He is smiling.

1. We know Dagwood is moving fast because __a__.

2. We know Tiny Tim is puzzled because ____.

3. We know Beetle Bailey's sergeant is startled because ____.

4. We know Yogi Bear is scared because ____.

CHAPTER 20
HOW TO BE A CRITIC

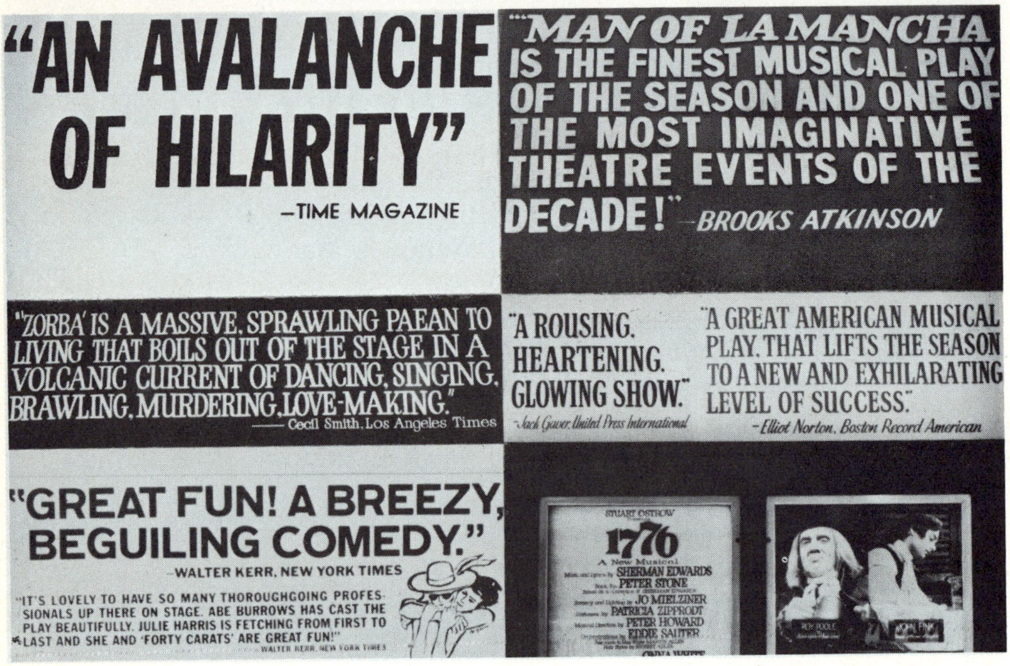

Criticizing does *not* mean complaining about something.

Criticizing *does* mean deciding the value of something, based on your own knowledge and understanding.

Why should you learn to criticize? Because then you learn to develop certain standards for yourself. You learn to tell what will please you, so you can go after it. And you learn what will not please you, so you can skip it.

The newspapers can help you. Read newspaper stories of TV shows, movies, plays, art exhibits, and books. You will learn more about these subjects, so that you can appreciate them more. If you read carefully and *critically,* you can find out what the reviewers' standards are. Then you can decide if they are standards you want to use when you judge for yourself.

WORDS TO HELP YOU

criterion—a standard on which a decision or judgment may be based. Do you know swimming is no fun for you when the water temperature drops below 55? Then your criterion for fun-swimming is water temperature of 55 or above. Others might be: a sandy beach, sunshine, and maybe friends you enjoy being with.

critic—someone with knowledge and understanding of the subject, who gives a judgment of its value.

review—an article, generally written by a critic, which makes a judgment of the value of a movie, play, concert, art exhibit, or whatever.

reviewer—another word for critic.

EXERCISE 1. Finding a Critic's Criteria

Here are some quotes from newspaper reviews of TV shows, movies, and plays. Each quote shows something about the critic's criteria. He has reasons for judging something to be good or bad. There are two statements after each quotation. Circle the letter of the statement which you think best expresses the critic's criteria for judgment.

Example: "This apple is terrible. It tastes like soap." The critic's criterion would be:

a. Apples are terrible.

(b.) A good apple should not taste like soap.

1. "This TV play is in a class by itself—and a high class it is. The author . . . does not preach, or indulge in obvious moralizing; he allows the viewer to draw his own conclusions. . . ."

The reviewer's criterion is:

a. A good TV play does not preach. It lets you make up your own mind.

b. A good TV play spells out the moral of the play for you.

2. "The switches back and forth in time and place are sometimes a little hard to follow."

The reviewer's criterion is:

a. Switches back and forth in time should be easy to follow.

b. Plays shouldn't switch back and forth in time and place.

3. "Perhaps there is some basis in fact for this plot. No matter. It remains improbable. . . . There's nothing wrong with this picture that a better, more sensible story would not have cured."

The reviewer's criterion is:

a. It should be easy to believe that a story really happened.

b. If a story is really true, it doesn't matter if it is hard to believe it happened.

4. "It wasn't a bad musical; it was genuinely awful. . . . The tunes were labored and derivative . . . and the spoken dialogue moved relentlessly from one trite line to the next."

The reviewer's criterion is:

a. It's easier to enjoy a musical that has familiar tunes and ideas.

b. A good musical has new tunes and ideas.

5. "Only a few of the many basic facts and opinions about The Fabulous Funnies could have been packed into a TV hour in any event. But the producers wasted precious time in superfluous matters. . . . The skit by two comics was irrelevant."

The reviewer's criterion is:

a. Facts and opinions are irrelevant in a show about the funnies.

b. Irrelevant or unimportant material should not be put in a show if it means leaving out basic facts.

EXERCISE 2. Finding Your Own Criterion

Get ready for a discussion of criteria for good detective programs on TV. Make notes in the space below to remind you of what you want to say.

Example of a criterion: "You shouldn't be able to guess how the story will end. I like it when I change my mind two or three times about who the murderer is."

Example of a note to remind you of your criterion: "Suspense. . . . Who dunnit?"

Here are some things you might have opinions about:

Choice of actor ______________________________

Background . . . costumes ______________________________

Believable actions ______________________________

Coincidences ______________________________

Motive . . . bad guys ______________________________

Motive . . . other people ______________________________

Music ______________________________

Love scenes ____________________

Violence ____________________

Fights, other violence ____________________

Clues ____________________

EXERCISE 3. Writing a TV Review

Name two or three shows most of the class have seen recently. Choose one to review and fill in as much of the outline below as you can.

Example:

The name of the show I am reviewing is: Teen-Rock Bandstand

One thing I like about the show is: the girl's dresses. I like to see how other girls dress and fix their hair.

Another thing I like about the show is: the dancing. I can pick up new steps and practice them with the TV group.

One thing I don't like about the show is: the MC. He thinks he talks like us, but he's a couple of years behind.

Another thing I don't like about the show is: ____________________

____

YOUR OUTLINE FOR A TV REVIEW

The name of the show I am reviewing is: ____________________

I think the show is (tell how good, or bad you think the show is:)

____

One thing I like about the show is: ____________________

____

Another thing I like about the show is: ____________________

____

One thing I don't like about the show is: ____________________

____

Another thing I don't like about the show is: ____________________

____

Other comments: ____________________

____

EXERCISE 4. Analyzing an Art Review

A reviewer can help you look at things in a new way. When you have read this review of an art show, you may have a new way of looking at automobiles and even street signs.

Directions: Read " 'West Coast Now' Show Reflects Contemporary Society." Some paragraphs have been pulled out and reproduced separately. Mark the statements in front of each paragraph by circling T for true or F for false.

T F 1. Artists love cars.

T F 2. Cars have a big part in our society; landscapes and horses do not.

> Artists are people, too, and they love cars, maybe even more than most and their art shows it. This is exactly what we should expect, if we believe that our art is a reflection of the society in which we live.
>
> To expect the artist to continue making idyllic landscapes or bronze horsemen would be like insisting on driving a horse and buggy or seeing only silent black and white movies.

T F 3. Machines make most things better than people.

T F 4. Mass-manufactured tin cans are durable.

> We are so used to the mass-manufactured product, that we have few unique handmade objects in our possession. In almost every instance the industry can do it better (did you ever try to make your own noodles or tin can?), and our concepts of quality and beauty deeply reflects this conditioning.

T F 5. We can look at a lacquer surface and tell whether there is wood or steel under it.

T F 6. We enjoy a perfect surface in cars and in sculptures.

> We admire the perfect surface of the car, with its impeccable high-gloss lacquer finish. This is a surface without identity. The handcrafted objects were immediately identifiable as made of wood or steel; the surface showed it as well as the forms, and we responded to it in terms of hardness or softness, weight, and strength. The lacquer surface tells nothing about what is under it: it isolates the characteristics of form and APPARENT mass.

16 * * THE SUNDAY OREGONIAN, FEBRUARY 11, 1968

'West Coast Now' Show Reflects Contemporary Society

MOLDED FIBERGLASS 'SACTO MEANDER,' BY RICHARD RANDELL

DETAIL from photograph of 1968 Buick, which Erik Gronborg wanted to accompany photos of work in "West Coast Now" exhibition at Portland Art Museum as illustration for the article he has written on the exhibition for this page.

UNTITLED SCULPTURE OF FIBERGLASS REINFORCED PLASTIC BY DE WAIN VALENTINE

The following is the first of two articles by Erik Gronborg concerning the "West Coast Now" exhibition which opened last Friday at Portland Art Museum. This, which Gronborg has titled "The car, our artistic consciousness," will be followed next week by "The story teller: representational art." Gronborg is a sculptor and assistant professor of art at Reed College.

By ERIK GRONBORG

No object is purchased by us with greater consideration of its looks than our car. No object is loved more, and of no other object do we have firmer opinions of what looks good or bad. The car is the supreme example of how our environment shapes our attitudes and ways of seeing and hearing.

Artists are people, too, and they love cars, maybe even more than most and their art shows it. This is exactly what we should expect, if we believe that our art is a reflection of the society in which we live.

To expect the artist to continue making idyllic landscapes or bronze horsemen would be like insisting on driving a horse and buggy or seeing only silent black and white movies.

The art of previous centuries, and even most of this, was handcrafted, and the materials and tools used were those of all the other crafts: stone, wood, clay, and in the cities also steel and bronze. Artists are always using the materials and techniques they are familiar with and which seem most suited to create the effects and images which are exciting in the artist's experience of our environment.

By image I do not mean whether it looks like a man or a tree, but the overall character which gives you the feeling that all the parts naturally belong to one object, just like all the parts, the wheels, bumpers, windows, make a car which looks complete.

The handcrafted object is no longer the best, the most durable, the most delicate or shiny and we recognize that.

We are so used to the mass-manufactured product, that we have few unique handmade objects in our possession. In almost every instance the industry can do it better (did you ever try to make your own noodles or tin can?), and our concepts of quality and beauty deeply reflects this conditioning.

We admire the perfect surface of the car, with its impeccable high-gloss lacquer finish. This is a surface without identity. The handcrafted objects were immediately identifiable as made of wood or steel; the surface showed it as well as the forms, and we responded to it in terms of hardness or softness, weight, and strength. The lacquer surface tells nothing about what is under it: it isolates the characteristics of form and APPARENT mass.

The car is made of thin steel sheets and still has an appearance of mass and solidity and function — until you get a fender smashed a little and the whole illusion is gone like a busted balloon.

A considerable number of sculptures in the "West Coast Now" exhibition at Portland Art Museum are finished with a high-gloss paint to create the same responses, appeal to our delight in the absolutely even, perfect shape and surface, the character of our industrial genius. These sculptures are constructed of a number of materials: steel, plywood, clay, fiberglas, wood, anything which will give a shape to be polished and sprayed with lacquer or enamel.

To walk through "West Coast Now" at the museum is like walking through your local market, or driving down the main street; everywhere color — bright clean colors. Sculpture in marble and bronze, and paintings in the sombre browns, greens, yellows belong to a time when we were near to nature. We live in a world of chaotic exploding colors, all competing for our attention. The sculpture shows it.

See the red and blue undulating wave by Randell or the pure red, white, blue by Edge, or the rainbow painting by Simpson. Numerous artists are creating with color alone, using fluorescent light neon light, ordinary light bulbs. As seen in the museum, in the works of Geise and Prentiss, the real work of art is not the solid object, the box and mirror and light bulb, but the visual light image. Turn off the light and the art is gone.

If we look at the car again, we see how the technology of manufacturing in sheet steel imposes certain characteristics on the forms. To give strength to the thin sheets it is necessary to curve and bend the steel. This mechanical necessity is exploited visually to create the beautifully sensuous curves and ruler-straight edges which in the best instances create a natural flow of forms out of the car body. These absolutely arbitrary, or call them abstract forms have no relationship to the objects they cover. The body is a shell, and through the forms alone the designer can emphasize solidity, bulk, length, speed, youthful exuberance, or staid dignity.

In the "good old days" a fast race horse looked fast, and a strong man looked strong. Through our technology we can make an object look light or heavy, big or small, solid or fragile, etc., IRRESPECTIVE of the real nature of that object.

These are the tools with which many artists create today. But it is important to understand that these effects in cars are used separately and often for purposes other than artistic (it improves sales to have a car look fast or sturdy.)

By the artists, they are used to create a unified image, without any superfluous elements. Where else in our environment can we see, for example, a perfect cube or cylinder, defined only in terms of size and color, without the obstructing presence of function and purpose, material and method of manufacture?

Another important lesson from our cars is that certain forms are the result of a specific process, and can be achieved only that way. The forms express that. The swelling curves of the car body were formed under thousands of tons of pressure from flat steel sheets in seconds. No handcrafting could produce those forms. Only the machines could produce all the exactly identical pieces, the wheels, the pattern of the grille.

Only with great difficulty can the artists achieve results of such natural grace and perfection, and often they have to use elements from the industry, such as the various steel parts of Arlo Acton's sculpture.

Why are all these objects at the art musem, and why are cars not? The works at the museum share in an insistence of being, without reason or function; once there, they affect the whole space around them, orient and give scale and character to the floor, the walls, the other objects, people. They share in the mystery of presence of all art.

The Oregonian

T F 7. A designer can make something look heavy even if it is not heavy.

T F 8. A designer can make a slow car look fast.

In the "good old days" a fast race horse looked fast, and a strong man looked strong. Through our technology we can make an object look light or heavy, big or small, solid or fragile, etc., IRRESPECTIVE of the real nature of that object.

T F 9. We live with loud, bright colors.

T F 10. The colors at the "West Coast Now" exhibit are the colors of nature.

To walk through "West Coast Now" at the museum is like walking through your local market, or driving down the main street; everywhere color — bright clean colors. Sculpture in marble and bronze, and paintings in the sombre browns, greens, yellows belong to a time when we were near to nature. We live in a world of chaotic exploding colors, all competing for our attention. The sculpture shows it.

PRACTICE IN YOUR LOCAL NEWSPAPER

PRACTICE 1. Write a couple of paragraphs reviewing the comic strips in your local paper. Which do you like best? Why? Compare two strips (perhaps the ones you like best and least). How are they different? Are they alike in any way?

PRACTICE 2. Cut out the funnies page from your local paper. See if you can find at least one strip that is like each of these:

Find a joke strip: like "Peanuts"
Find an adventure story: like "Steve Canyon"
Find a romantic psychological drama (a soap opera): like "Mary Worth"

PRACTICE 3. Bring in an example of one of these from your local paper. In each, mark a section that shows a criterion:

a. A book review.
b. A movie review.
c. A review of an art show, an automobile show, a concert, or any other kind of display or performance.

PRACTICE 4. Make your own TV rating sheet. Get the TV schedule from your local paper. Take an ink stick or ball-point pen and cross out any show you have never watched and all news programs. Now, you be the critic. Put a mark in front of each remaining program to show how you would rate it. Use this rating system:

o o Great, I try not to miss it.
o Good, I liked it.
-- Okay, if there's nothing better to do.
X Forget it. You'd have to pay me to watch it.

Here is an example of a TV schedule marked up:

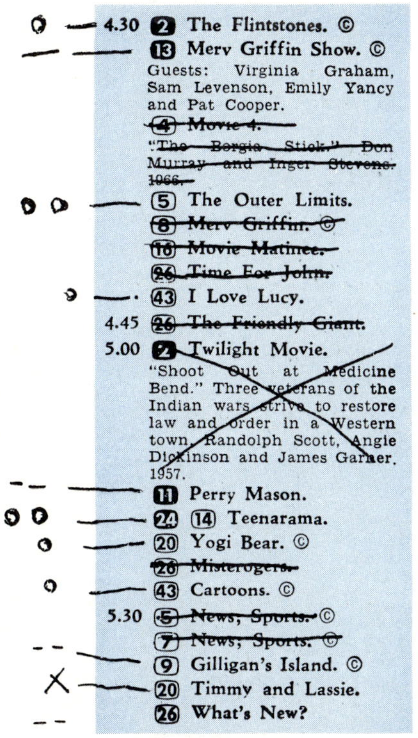
4.30 (2) The Flintstones. ©
(13) Merv Griffin Show. © Guests: Virginia Graham, Sam Levenson, Emily Yancy and Pat Cooper.
~~(4) Movie 4. "The Borgia Stick." Don Murray and Inger Stevens. 1966.~~
(5) The Outer Limits.
~~(8) Merv Griffin. ©~~
~~(18) Movie Matinee.~~
~~(26) Time For John.~~
(43) I Love Lucy.
4.45 ~~(26) The Friendly Giant.~~
5.00 (2) Twilight Movie. "Shoot Out at Medicine Bend." Three veterans of the Indian wars strive to restore law and order in a Western town. Randolph Scott, Angie Dickinson and James Garner. 1957.
(11) Perry Mason.
(24) (14) Teenarama.
(20) Yogi Bear. ©
~~(26) Misterogers.~~
(43) Cartoons. ©
5.30 ~~(5) News, Sports.~~ ©
~~(7) News, Sports. ©~~
(9) Gilligan's Island. ©
(20) Timmy and Lassie.
(26) What's New?

The Sun, Baltimore

PRACTICE 5. Your teacher may make tackboard space available for student reviews of movies, TV shows, and other local entertainment events. After you have gone to a movie or other event, write a short review and post it on the board. Be guided by the form on page 261—tell *why* you liked or disliked the performance. Check the board every day to see what other students think. If you disagree with the opinion another student has posted, write a paragraph explaining why, and post it under the opinion you are reacting to.

CHAPTER 21
YOU AND THE FREE PRESS

WHAT A FREE PRESS MEANS TO YOU

As a citizen of the United States, you live in a land which guarantees a free press. The daily newspaper is open to everyone. In its columns, opposing forces wage a never-ending battle for your attention.

In your study of how to read your newspaper, you have learned how important it is to separate fact from opinion, to find out WHO is making the statement, to examine arguments for misleading conclusions, to read more than one account of a story, to use news analyses and background stories to help you understand complex subjects. Are you also aware of the importance of keeping our press both free and responsible?

You can gain insight into this question by reading the article by John S. Knight on page 268 and completing the exercises. Some of the terms he uses are defined for you. Study them first.

WORDS TO HELP YOU

arbitary—(misprint of arbitrary in the article) unreasonable.

sedition—action or language arousing discontent or rebellion against the government.

phantasmagoria—a shifting series of illusions or deceptive appearances as in a dream.

scrutiny—searching examination or investigation.

Man in Charge—Lyndon B. Johnson, President of the United States at the time this article was published.

credibility gap between press and the President—lessened confidence in the truthfulness of White House statements.

distortion of fact—twisting of truth.

EXERCISE 1. Defining a "Free Responsible Press"

Mr. Knight's definition of the American press might be described as telling it "like it really is." Use the questions in this exercise to gain historical perspective on the problem of "managed news," the causes of the "credibility gap," and other important aspects of the struggle to keep our press both free and responsible.

Directions: Scan the article to find the answer to each of the following questions. Write in the number of the paragraph in which the question is answered. The first one is done for you.

__/__ 1. How did Andrew Hamilton define freedom of the press in his defense of John Peter Zenger?

____ 2. For what offense are newspapermen still subject to imprisonment upon conviction?

____ 3. How much money does our government spend on public relations and information programs?

____ 4. How long has "management of news" existed?

____ 5. In what way does Mr. Knight compare television with printed material in newspapers?

____ 6. Does Mr. Knight indicate that readers should be aware that some syndicated columnists may slant their material to support their own views?

____ 7. Does Mr. Knight say that the United States no longer has a political press which slants news?

John S. Knight

The struggle for a free. responsible press

John S. Knight, publisher of the Knight newspapers and former publisher of The Chicago Daily News, today receives the John Peter Zenger award "for meritorious service in the cause of the press and the people's right to know." The award, presented by the University of Arizona's School of Journalism, is named after the colonial printer whose trial established truth as a defense to libel, thus freeing the American press to report news that displeased the government. This column is taken from Knight's acceptance remarks.

(1) The struggle in behalf of a free and responsible press, as indicated by the name of the award itself, is a never-ending battle. It is, as Andrew Hamilton said in his defense of John Peter Zenger, a cause to secure "the liberty both of exposing and opposing arbitary power by speaking and writing the truth."

(2) Today's newspapermen — at least in this country—do not face the governmental dangers of John Peter Zenger. He was tried for sedition. But newspapermen since, and to this present day, are found guilty of contempt of court for refusal to divulge the name of a news source and, like Zenger, are subject to imprisonment upon conviction.

(3) Further, the difficulties of their assignments are infinitely greater. A 24-hour budget of news is overwhelming; more perhaps than the human mind can comprehend.

(4) **THE WASHINGTON** correspondent, whose responsibility it is to examine the workings of the Great Society, must also produce a news report that makes this phantasmagoria capable of being understood.

(5) According to the Associated Press, our government's public relations and information programs cost taxpayers about $425,000,000 a year. This is more than is spent annually by the Congress and the judiciary.

(6) And more than double the combined outlay for newsgathering by the two major U.S. news services, the three major television networks and the 10 largest American newspapers.

(7) So when the White House complains about adverse stories in our press—notably about Vietnam — let us remember that the press carries five times as much of the government's views as are presented by the administration's critics.

(8) **MOREOVER,** as James Reston pointed out to you four years ago, this nation is undergoing a set of social revolutions, each one as significant to the future as the Industrial Revolution itself.

(9) All of these revolutions are meeting in the cities, where the technologically unemployed farmer, the Negro demanding his fair place in the affluent society and the youngster are competing for jobs for which they are largely unprepared.

• •

(10) Possibly because of the growing importance of news, we in this business find ourselves being subjected to detailed scrutiny.

(11) We have been weighed and found wanting by everyone from the Man in Charge, who finds us high in calories and low in conscience, as Arthur Krock put it a few years ago, to the man in the street, who wonders why there is such a credibility gap between the press and the President.

(12) And he wonders, when he is told hard and unpleasant facts about America's involvement with Vietnam, why he has not heard these facts before.

(13) The blame, I suggest, lies both with the press and with the President.

(14) The press as well as the public is too inclined to forget, so long as all is going well, that, as Rep. John Moss said a few years ago, "Management of the news has always existed in government at all levels, just as it exists in every private business. Everybody wants to put out information in a way to show his actions in the best possible light."

(15) **BUT WE** of the now-aroused press must object when, in his efforts to put himself in the best possible light, the President forgets his responsibility to the people. They are the ones who hired him.

(16) It is one thing to hide vital facts which Hanoi, Peking or the Viet Cong don't know, and another thing entirely to misinform the people• when it serves no security purpose.

(17) And it is totally inexcusable to lie to the people about matters which are of their utmost concern, and about which the enemy already knows.

(18) Upon entering this fateful year, the role of newspapers is more important than ever.

(19) As the politician uses his purchased air for his understandably one-sided argument, the importance of print grows. We need the permanence of print for reference.

(20) This is merely age-old "instant replay," recently discovered by television. But the second time around it drifts off into the air just like the first, while print remains.

(21) Our obligation is to provide the voters with fair, honest all-sided, clear presentation of campaign news. They need the sharp illumination of your own editorials and the pungent, uninhibited viewpoints of your readers.

(22) If it is possible to put labels on syndicated columnists, the reader would benefit if warned of their political or other persuasions. These journalists are now choosing up sides and the number of "house columnists" is—sad to relate—increasing in number.

(23) How well will we do our job in 1968? Certainly, we have improved over the years. There is no longer a political press in the sense of slanted news, although we still catch hell from all sides.

WHO IS RESPONSIBLE FOR THE STORY?

As you read newspapers, keep in mind what John S. Knight states about how news is "managed" by both government and private business. Develop the habit of asking yourself: Who is responsible for this story—who gave out the information? Is it a department of government, a tax-free foundation, a spokesman for labor, industry, education, or some other group? What is the purpose of the story? What idea does it want to leave with you, and why?

Keep an open mind as you read. Search for related articles which may present other facts or interpretations. Remember that it is up to each reader to study all sides of a question, to exercise critical judgment, to form his own opinions.

EXERCISE 2. Is News Mostly "Government Issue"?

Directions: Go through several pages of the news section of your local newspaper to see who is responsible for each story. When you find one from any agency of the government, mark it with a G. Count the number of G stories and compare the number with the total number of stories on the pages marked. What do you discover about the proportion of stories issued by the government?

______________________________ Total marked G

______________________________ Total of all stories

______________________________ Percentage of G Issue

____

____

____

PRO AND CON VIEWS

In recent years newspapers have presented many different views on how to protect the consumer. The following two articles are typical examples. Ask yourself who is responsible for each story? Use the exercises with each article to help you get the facts, to make judgments about them, and to form tentative opinions.

EXERCISE 3. What Does Betty Furness Really Say?

Directions: Read the questions given below. Then skim the article. When you find a statement which answers a question, write in the number of the paragraph in which the question is answered. If the article does not answer the question, mark X in the blank.

____1. What did Betty Furness urge a Senate sub-committee to do?

____2. What information did she give about the cost of operating refrigerators?

____3. What did she say about appliance warranties?

____4. Did Miss Furness endorse a bill for the establishment of a Cabinet-level Department of Consumer Affairs?

____5. Under what departments of government would Miss Furness *not* place a consumer-protection agency?

____6. What office does she think should administer a consumer-protection agency?

____7. What information is given about the cost of having the government run a consumer-protection agency?

____8. How successful has the government's "truth-in-packaging" law been in protecting the consumer?

____9. What was the reaction of the committee to her remarks?

____10. Does Betty Furness say that TV advertisers are underestimating the intelligence of the American people?

Associated Press

18-A—THE DETROIT NEWS—Thursday, March 20, 1969

—AP Wirephoto

Betty Furness slaps TV commercials

Betty Furness blasts TV ads—her own included

(1) WASHINGTON —(AP) —Betty Furness had some harsh things to say yesterday about television commercials —including those she used to give on behalf of refrigerators.

(2) And she questioned the dedication of such agencies as the Agriculture and Commerce departments to the cause of consumer protection, a field in which she also served.

(3) Miss Furness, who was a special adviser on consumer affairs to former President Johnson, urged a Senate subcommittee to approve a tougher federal role in protecting buyers from being cheated.

(4) **THESE WERE** among her observations:

Refrigerators: "I used to sell those things. I didn't know one cost more to run than the other. I'm sorry. I'm stupid. I never went to college. It costs more to operate a frost-free refrigerator than to defrost it yourself, a good deal more to operate one with an ice cube maker. You get the thrill of discovery when you get the bill."

(5) On reading appliance warranties: "You give up. You feel like a fool. You can't understand it . . . A warranty won't tell you what a product will do. It tells you what it won't do."

(6) The new truth-in-packaging law—"It's been helpful only in a minor way. You still have to do a lot of figuring in supermarkets."

(7) Television commercials: "They offer sex appeal, youth and blond hair in addition to the product. It must be a bitter disappointment for a lot of people who buy a product to find the girl didn't come with it."

(8) Do advertisers underestimate the intelligence of the American people? "They may be underestimating the extent to which people are getting tired of girls in white hats."

(9) **WHILE URGING** stronger protection for consumers, Miss Furness stopped short of endorsing a bill the subcommittee is considering for establishment of a Cabinet-level Department of Consumer Affairs.

(10) She recommended more study about specific programs before such a step is taken.

(11) Meanwhile, Miss Furness favored establishing a consumer-protection agency as a part of the President's office.

(12) She opposed placing it under either the Agriculture or Commerce departments.

EXERCISE 4. What Do *You* Think?

Directions: Complete each statement below with your own ideas:

1. I think TV advertising needs to be ______________________________

____

____

2. I think a consumer-protection agency would ____________________

____

____

THE AD MAN'S VIEW

Now read "Advertising restrictions weighed" on the following page for a different view on consumer protection. Once again ask yourself who is responsible for the story and what is the purpose of its release?

1. Who is responsible for the story?____________________________

2. What is the purpose? ______________________________________

EXERCISE 5. What Do the Ad Executives Really Say?

Directions: Read the questions. Then skim the article. When you find a statement which answers a question, write in the number of the paragraph in which the answer appears. If the article does not answer the question, mark X in the blank.

____1. How may restrictions on advertising endanger the American economy?

____2. What would a computer center do?

____3. What sources would the computer center use to gather information on manufactured products?

____4. Would the information gathered include opinions by users of products similar to that given in advertising?

Advertising restrictions weighed

By Shurei Hirozawa
Business and Labor Editor

(1) Two advertising industry executives expressed concern here today that restrictions being built up around advertising by consumerism will stifle the competition that built up the American economy.

(2) Walter E. Terry, chairman, and Howard H. Bell, president, of the American Advertising Federation, spoke at the Advertising Recognition Week luncheon today at the Ilikai Hotel.

(3) Sponsor of the event is the Honolulu Advertising Club.

(4) CONSUMER protection has become a strong movement in this country, with a truth in packaging bill having passed Congress last year and the truth in lending bill this year, Terry said.

(5) Sen. Philip A. Hart, Democrat of Michigan, told a recent AAF Government Affairs Conference that he is thinking about introducing a bill that in effect will set up a consumers council.

(6) A computer center would compile information on manufactured products and feed this information to centers in communities around the country.

(7) A coin-operated machine would give a housewife all the information on a product she may want to purchase.

(8) "There's nothing wrong with truth, information and facts," said Terry, "because that is what advertising is about."

(9) THE CONCERN of advertising is that such a system wouldn't protect the consumer, but limit choices.

(10) Such computerized information, to be gathered from manufacturers, government sources and independent laboratories, probably won't say what the product would do for the consumer, or excite him, says Terry.

(11) "How would such a system get people excited about a garbage disposal?" he asked. Sales would suffer and the whole economy could fall apart.

(12) The American Advertising Federation, made up of 178 advertising clubs, advertisers, advertising agencies, radio and TV stations, newspapers, and related enterprises, wants to see the emphasis on consumer education instead, Bell said.

(13) IN CHICAGO, a group using a mobile exhibit, is helping Spanish-speaking people understand the many products they use.

(14) Other advertising clubs, through which the federation works, are being encouraged to initiate similar programs of education, he said.

(15) On the Federal Communications Commission proposal to ban tobacco advertising from TV, Bell said the federation feels Congress should deal with this problem instead.

(16) Congress passed the Cigarette Labeling Act three years ago that requires a warning on each package, and said no further action should be taken beyond this.

(17) THIS MORATORIUM ends next June 30, and unless Congress acts before that, the FCC or FTC would put their proposals into effect. The two feel that Congress will act in time.

(18) The trend of legislative control of business activities has made advertising the main target. In Iowa, a tax on advertising was passed, and it is being appealed to the Supreme Court.

(19) The appeal is based on the fact that the law infringes on interstate commerce, which is illegal, Bell said.

(20) A radio broadcast would be heard in other states, for example.

(21) And an Iowa newspaper would be forced to collect the tax from an advertiser in New York, which is a violation of free speech.

(22) Terry and Bell are also making arrangements for the American Advertising Federation convention, to be held in Honolulu in 1971, with 2,000 delegates expected. The Honolulu Advertising Club will be the host.

Honolulu Star-Bulletin

____5. Would part of the cost of gathering this information be passed on to the consumer?

____6. How much would it cost the consumers' council to set up and run a computer center?

____7. Does advertising think a computerized system would limit choices of manufactured articles?

____8. Does the article describe the membership of the American Advertising Federation?

____9. Does the federation prefer regulation of tobacco advertising by Congress or by the Federal Communications Center?

____10. What action is being taken against a tax on advertising passed by the legislature in Iowa?

EXERCISE 6. What Do *You* Think?

Directions: Complete each statement below with your own ideas.

1. I think the best way to protect the consumer is ______________________

____

____

2. I think a computer center would ______________________

____

____

3. I think advertising ______________________

____

____

EXERCISE 7. How "Free and Responsible" Is Your Local Newspaper?

Directions: Use the check list below to help you rate your local newspaper or another paper of your choice.

Name of paper ______________________

1. Is the paper politically independent, pro-Democrat, or pro-Republican?

____

2. How can you tell? Do you think one political party gets more news coverage than another? Does the editorial obviously favor one side over another? Explain your reasoning here: ______________________

____

3. Can you tell if the paper is pro-labor or anti-labor? ____________

If yes, how do you know? ______________________________

____

4. Do you think the paper gives certain racial, social, or ethnic groups special attention?——If so, describe the group and your reasons for thinking so.

____

____

5. Which of the paper's features do you think are most popular with readers and why?

____

____

____

6. Does the newspaper sometimes criticize local, state, and national government?——Does it sometimes criticize business?——Can you give some examples to back up your opinion?

____

____

____

7. Does the newspaper ever "crusade," or keep printing stories on programs and policies it believes in until results are achieved?——Can you give examples?

____

____

____

8. Is your newspaper very active in community affairs? That is, does it report school board meetings, citizen action, zoning hearings, etc.?

____

____

RATING YOURSELF AS A CRITICAL READER

Critical readers help keep the press free and responsible. Check your own role as a responsible reader with the statements below:

1. A critical reader asks who is responsible for a particular news story.
2. A critical reader looks for the purpose behind the news release.
3. A critical reader looks for more than one account of an important news story.
4. A critical reader tries to discover if information given in the story is true by comparing it with what he knows, or by checking it in reliable sources.
5. A critical reader weighs the qualifications of the writer of the article.
6. A critical reader recognizes devices of propaganda and slanted writing.
7. A critical reader learns the political affiliations of the newspaper he reads.

EXERCISE 8. Check Out a Big Story by Using Multimedia

Learn to use one media to check up on another. If you see a big news story on TV, follow up by reading about the incident in the newspapers. Choose a current story and use the exercise below to get a picture of how well you utilize multimedia to check out a big story.

Directions: Answer the questions below to give a picture of what you do.

1. What is the story about? ______________________________

____

____

2. Where did you first learn about the story—newspaper, radio, TV, or other sources? ______________________________

3. Try to find the story in more than one newspaper. List the papers and the dates of stories:

____

____

4. Do the accounts vary? ______________ How? ______________

___

___

___

5. Read any editorials on the subject. Describe briefly, telling whether they are for or against.

___

___

___

___

6. Is the story discussed by syndicated columnists? ___ Which ones?

___

7. Check the letters to the editor for comments relating to the story. Are they for or against or both? ______________

___

8. Check the TV and radio programs for documentaries on the topic, or to see if any of the persons involved in the story were to be guests on panel or other talk shows.

What did you find? ______________

___

___

9. Read any weekly magazines such as *Time* or *Newsweek* to see how they treated the story. If so, what did you discover? ______________

___

___

___

10. Do you need to consult encyclopedias or other reference works to gain background material? ______________________________

____

____

11. Discuss the story with friends, parents, or teachers. Did what they say change your opinions in any way? ____ If so, how? ______________

____

____

12. Watch for new developments in this story and keep a file.

RATING YOURSELF AS AN INFORMED CITIZEN

In discussing the importance of newspapers to the success of democratic government, Thomas Jefferson wrote: "When the press is free and every man able to read—all is safe." Each of us has a responsibility to use the free press to become an informed citizen. Complete the exercises below to test your citizenship I.Q.

EXERCISE 9. Arbitrary Power Exposed and Opposed

Directions: List below examples of arbitrary power which the newspapers you read have exposed or opposed recently.

____

____

____

____

EXERCISE 10. Major Legislation

Directions: Describe briefly a bill before Congress or your state legislature which you have been following. What has happened so far? Are your own representatives mentioned in connection with this legislation? ______________________________

EXERCISE 11. Supreme Court Decisions

Directions: Describe briefly one or more Supreme Court decisions which you have read about. Does the decision affect you personally?

EXERCISE 12. Local Government

Directions: Complete the statements below by filling in the blanks with the required information.

1. The city government is in control of the ________ party. (Democratic or Republican)
2. The chief executive officer is ________
3. The laws (ordinances) of the city are passed by the ________
4. The name of my representative in this body is ________
5. The name of the Chief of Police is ________
6. The most important official in public schools is ________
7. The person who usually speaks for the city on transit problems is ________

8. Major problems facing the city are ______________________________

____

____

____

CAREERS UNLIMITED

Have you learned how to use the newspaper to discover career opportunities? Use the check list in the exercise below to help you answer the question.

EXERCISE 13. Surveying Job Opportunities

Directions: Place a check mark in front of each thing you are doing. (Those you have not done offer possibilities for further study of career opportunities.)

____1. I read news stories and features about successful people.

____2. I study special supplements put out on colleges and careers.

____3. I read an article by a specialist in a field of interest to me (for example, science, religion, advertising and marketing).

____4. I study the business and financial page to gain insight into where the jobs will be tomorrow.

____5. I study classified employment ads to learn about available jobs, salaries, working conditions, qualifications.

____6. I study stories about scholarships and other awards.

____7. I watch for announcements about federally funded job training.

____8. I keep a mini morgue on careers and ideas related to them.

EXERCISE 14. Most Helpful in Finding a Career

Directions: Describe briefly any regular newspaper features which have been helpful to you in deciding on a career or how to acquire the education it will require. ______________________________

YOU AS A NEWSPAPER READER

EXERCISE 15. Yesterday

Directions: Describe in a few sentences how you read newspapers before studying *How to Read Your Newspaper*.

EXERCISE 16. Today

Dircctions: Describe in a few sentences what you do now that is different from the way you used to read newspapers. For example, do you read sections you didn't before? Have you discovered a reporter or columnist you like and always read now? Do you clip articles for a morgue? If so, on what subject or subjects are you collecting material?

PRACTICE IN YOUR LOCAL NEWSPAPER

PRACTICE 1. Choose a big controversial story. Check each article to see who is responsible for its release. When you find groups identified by vague words such as "independent," "study," or "concerned" clip out the story. After you have several samples of stories released from a group, try to determine for yourself what the true purpose of the group is. Does the "independent" group endorse members of one political party more than another? What can you find out about individuals in the group? How long has the group been in existence? Is it an open or closed membership? What is the source of the group's income? Is it a non-profit foundation exempt from taxation? A community action group seeking funds? If you cannot discover from the releases, call the Better Business Bureau or write to the newspaper for information.

PRACTICE 2. Collect the columns written by one or more syndicated political writers for a month. Make a list of the subjects discussed by each columnist. Try to decide for yourself if his writing is slanted or objective.

PRACTICE 3. Keep a morgue of articles dealing with freedom of the press. Watch for stories about curbs on press coverage of trials; about suppression of news by government officials; about Supreme Court rulings which restrict mergers of papers and joint ownership of TV stations and papers; about rulings by regulatory agencies such as the Federal Trade Commission or the Federal Communications Commission.

ANSWER KEY

CHAPTER 1.

Ex. 1 (p. 5)	1. YES 2. NO 3. NO 4. YES 5. YES
Ex. 2 (p. 6)	Self Check
Ex. 3 (p. 7)	1. YES 2. YES 3. NO 4. ? 5. YES 6. ? 7. YES 8. YES
Ex. 4 (p. 10)	See Instructor
Ex. 5 (p. 10)	1. 3 2. 1, 4 3. 4 4. 2 5. 2 & 5 6. 1, 3, 4 7. 4 8. 2 9. 3 10. 1
Ex. 6 (p. 10)	See Instructor

CHAPTER 2.

Ex. 1 (p. 15)	1. E 2. O 3. M & E 4. O 5. E 6. E 7. E 8. M 9. M & E 10. E
Ex. 2 (p. 20)	(A) 1. 2 2. 1 3. 3 (B) 1. 4 2. 11 3. 12 (C) 1. Nearby 2. 2 3. 3 4. 4 5. Washington (D) 1. 5 2. 3 3. 4 4. Qualified 5. Salt Lake City (AP) (E) 1. 4 2. 11 3. 10 4. 2

CHAPTER 3.

Ex. 1 (p. 26)	1. 1 2. 2 3. 5 4. 3 5. 4
Ex. 2 (p. 28)	1. Arthur J. Snider 2. Paul Staples 3. Albert Jedlicka 4. John McDermott 5. Marvin Miles 6. Jack McCurdy
Ex. 3 (p. 30)	1. NO 2. NO 3. YES
Ex. 4 (p. 39)	See Instructor
Ex. 5 (p. 39)	See Instructor

CHAPTER 4.

Ex. 1 (p. 44)	See Instructor
Ex. 2 (p. 48)	See Instructor
Ex. 3 (p. 48)	1. 1 2. 5 3. 8

Ex. 4 (p. 50) through Ex. 6 (p. 54) See Instructor

Ex. 7 (p. 54)	1. **X** 2. **X** 3. **X** 4. — 5. –

CHAPTER 5.

Ex. 1 (p. 58)	1. truck 2. spilled bombs 3. early this morning 4. Chicago area 5. it turned over 6. missed turn

Ex. 2 (p. 61) through Ex. 4 (p. 63) See Instructor

CHAPTER 6.

Ex. 1 (p. 65)	1. S 2. S 3. S 4. D 5. D 6. D 7. S

Ex. 2 (p. 66) through Ex. 10 (p. 77) See Instructor

CHAPTER 7.

Ex. 1 (p. 80) through Ex. 6 (p. 85) See Instructor

Ex. 7 (p. 86)	1. YES 2. ? 3. YES 4. NO 5. YES 6. ?
Ex. 8 (p. 86)	See Instructor
Ex. 9 (p. 87)	4. BD 3. BD 9. A 8. D 7. D 5. BD 6. D 10. A 13. A 14. A 11. A 1. B 12. A 2. B
Ex. 10 (p. 88)	Self Check

CHAPTER 8.

Ex. 1 (p. 90)	1. 3 2. 1 3. 9 4. 5, 7 5. 8
Ex. 2 (p. 92)	1. 3 2. 3 3. 3 4. 4 5. 11 6. 11 7. 11 8. 11
Ex. 3 (p. 92)	1. A 2. E 3. B 4. B 5. B 6. C 7. D
Ex. 4 (p. 93)	1. South Shore 2. Dennis Perdue 3. 2 sec. to 3 min. 4. good throw 5. 3, 3, 10
Ex. 5 (p. 94)	1. YES 2. YES 3. NO 4. YES 5. NO
Ex. 6 (p. 94)	1. 14 2. 9 3. 1 4. 280 5. 40 6. 4 7. 231 8. 77 9. 14th 10. Add total number of points for each team.
Ex. 7 (p. 96)	1. T 2. T 3. F 4. I 5. T 6. T 7. F 8. F 9. T 10. I
Ex. 8 (p. 97)	1. 5 2. 6 3. 6 4. 9
Ex. 9 (p. 98)	1. 4 2. 9 3. 8 4. 4
Ex. 10 (p. 98)	1. 10 2. 6 3. 8 4. 6 5. 11
Ex. 11 (p. 99)	$\frac{69.0000}{123} = .5609+$ or .561
Ex. 12 (p. 100)	1. Pierre de Couvertin 2. an olive branch 3. Aethlios 4. cease hostilities 5. Self Check
Ex. 13 (p. 102)	1. Delphi 2. Olympia 3. Olympia 4. Athens 5. legend
Ex. 14 (p. 102)	1. a 2. b 3. c 4. b 5. b 6. Self Check
Ex. 15 (p. 103)	Self Check

CHAPTER 9.

Ex. 1 (p. 106)	1. 19 2. 6 3. 5 4. 11
Ex. 2 (p. 108)	1. 4 & 5 2. 31 3. 34 4. 26 5. 24
Ex. 3 (p. 108)	1. 7 2. 24 3. 32 4. 30 5. 27 6. 35
Ex. 4 (p. 110)	1. 4 2. 2 3. 6 4. 7
Ex. 5 (p. 110)	$1536.00 128 weeks $20.00 11 weeks
Ex. 6 (p. 112)	Self Check
Ex. 7 (p. 113)	1. B = $3199.00 A to B = $349.00 2. B = $499.00 A to B = $299.00 3. B = $2700.00 A to B = $50.00 4. B = $73.09 A to B = $11.26 5. B = 48 A to B = 12 6. B = $3508.32 A to B = $201.48 7. B = $4007.32 A to B = $97.52 8. B = $808.32 A to B = $251.48 9. B = 13.51% A to B = .61%
Ex. 8 (p. 114)	See Instructor
Ex. 9 (p. 114)	1. 1 2. 17 3. Information not given 4. 21 5. 19 6. 23
Ex. 10 (p. 117)	1. 41 2. 23 3. 22
Ex. 11 (p. 118)	1. a 2. a 3. c
Ex. 12 (p. 119)	1. 3 2. 4 3. 6 4. 14 5. 16
Ex. 13 (p. 119)	1. 1 2. 2 3. 13 4. 14
Ex. 14 (p. 120)	Self Check
Ex. 15 (p. 122)	1. loan-sharking 2. 25% 3. 700% 4. 6 for 5
Ex. 16 (p. 122)	1. Drop 2. Drop 3. Keep
Ex. 17 (p. 122)	See Instructor
Ex. 18 (p. 123)	1. 6 2. 3 3. 5 4. 12 5. 17
Ex. 19 (p. 124)	1. 5 2. Discuss
Ex. 20 (p. 125)	1. 8 or 12 2. 8 3. 1, 12, or 13
Ex. 21 (p. 126)	See Instructor
Ex. 22 (p. 126)	See Instructor
Ex. 23 (p. 127)	Self Check

CHAPTER 10.

Ex. 1 (p. 129)	1. WE-9-1968 2. Mr. Summers 3. YES 4. April 5. one of the ISES offices 6. in the phone book 7. car washer, gas station attendent 8. library aide
Ex. 2 (p. 131)	1. YES 2. YES 3. YES 4. NO
Ex. 3 (p. 132)	1. 230 2. 170 3. 210 4. 220 5. 175 6. 160 7. 215 8. 225 9. 240 10. 245
Ex. 4 (p. 134)	Ad 1—1. YES 2. YES 3. YES 4. YES 5. YES Ad 2—1. YES 2. YES 3. NO 4. NO 5. YES Ad 3—1. YES 2. YES 3. YES 4. YES 5. NO Ad 4—1. NO 2. NO 3. YES 4. YES 5. YES

Ex. 5 (p. 136) through Ex. 6 (p. 140) Self Check

CHAPTER 11.

Ex. 1 (p. 147)	1. a 2. a 3. c 4. b
Ex. 2 (p. 150)	The coliseum management wants to charge $2.
Ex. 3 (p. 150)	c
Ex. 4 (p. 150)	1. a 2. b 3. a 4. c
Ex. 5 (p. 151)	a. certainly b. mess d. dearly f. unfair advantage g. attractive j. long overdue

Ex. 6 (p. 152) through Ex. 7 (p. 155) Self Check

CHAPTER 12.

Ex. *1* (*p. 160*) See Instructor

Ex. *2* (*p. 161*) *1.* c *2.* c *3.* b

Ex. *3* (*p. 163*) *through* Ex. *4* (*p. 164*) Self Check

CHAPTER 13.

Ex. *1* (*p. 167*) *1.* 2 or 13 *2.* 10 *3.* 9 or 15 *4.* 6 *5.* 11 *6.* 12 *7.* 5 or 15 *8.* 8

Ex. *2* (*p. 169*) *1.* T *2.* T *3.* T *4.* F *5.* F

Ex. *3* (*p. 170*) 2

Ex. *4* (*p. 170*) *1.* F *2.* T *3.* F

Ex. *5* (*p. 171*) *1.* T *2.* F *3.* T *4.* T *5.* F *6.* T

Ex. *6* (*p. 171*) *1.* T *2.* T *3.* F

Ex. *7* (*p. 172*) grated simmer shortening sauté serving

Ex. *8* (*p. 174*) *1.* a

Ex. *9* (*p. 174*) Self Check

Ex. *10* (*p. 175*) *1.* 8 *2.* 1, 6, 12 *3.* 8 *4.* 7 *5.* 6 *6.* 7 *7.* 1 *8.* 12

Ex. *11* (*p. 176*) Self Check

CHAPTER 14.

Ex. *1* (*p. 180*) *1.* Cape Town, S.A. *2.* Groote Schuur *3.* Sunday *4.* Louis Washkansky *5.* Denise Ann Darvall *6.* auto crash *7.* Washkansky was dying *8.* Prof. Chris Barnard *9.* See Instructor

Ex. *2* (*p. 181*) See Instructor

Ex. *3* (*p. 181*) *1.* b *2.* c *3.* c *4.* b *5.* a *6.* a *7.* b *8.* b

Ex. *4* (*p. 182*) 2

Ex. *5* (*p. 182*) *through* Ex. *10* (*p. 189*) See Instructor

Ex. *11* (*p. 190*) *1.* c *2.* a *3.* a

CHAPTER 15.

Ex. *1* (*p. 198*) *1.* b *2.* c *3.* b *4.* a/c

Ex. *2* (*p. 199*) *through* Ex. *4* (*p. 201*) See Instructor

Ex. *5* (*p. 202*) Self Check

Ex. *6* (*p. 203*) *1.* b *2.* a *3.* b

Ex. *7* (*p. 204*) *1.* 12.67, 24.37 *2.* 30, 119.95, 3598.50, 2500.00, 6098.50, 4850.00, 1248.50 *3.* 9-3/4 *4.* insurance, maintenance

Ex. *8* (*p. 205*) *1.* 274, 758 *2.* 1-B, 6-B, 8 *3.* "there is/is not an operator 65 or over" *4.* 1-B, 310, 2A-1, 543

Ex. *9* (*p. 206*) *1.* a *2.* b *3.* a *4.* c *5.* b

CHAPTER 16.

Ex. *1* (*p. 210*) Self Check

Ex. *2* (*p. 213*) *1.* 2 *2.* 11 *3.* 12 *4.* 14 *5.* 16 *6.* 16 *7.* 8 *8.* 6 *9.* 21 *10.* 12, 22

Ex. *3* (*p. 215*) *1.* rapidly approaching passage *2.* bills *3.* 2 *4.* 4 *5.* debate by House, passage by House, rewriting by conference committee, passage by House, passage by Senate

Ex. *4* (*p. 217*) 1, 2, 3, 4

Ex. *5* (*p. 217*) Self Check

Ex. *6* (*p. 218*) *1.* NO *2.* NO *3.* UNDECIDED *4.* UNDECIDED *5.* YES

Ex. *7* (*p. 219*) Self Check

Ex. *8* (*p. 221*) *1.* **X** *2.* **X** *3.* — *4.* **X** *5.* **X**

Ex. *9* (*p. 221*) *1.* YES *2.* YES *3.* YES *4.* YES *5.* NO

Ex. *10* (*p. 222*) *1.* $30.00, $120.00, $374.40, $895.05, $965.25 *2.* $41.20, $116.00, $189.80, $387.30 *3.* $81.00, $180.00, $1208.70, $1303.50 *4.* $338.25 *5.* $581.40

Ex. *11* (*p. 224*) *1.* 39¢ *2.* 13¢ *3.* 11¢ *4.* 29¢ *5.* 26¢ *6.* 38¢ *7.* 7¢ *8.* 16¢

CHAPTER 17.

Ex. *1* (*p. 227*) *1.* 6 *2.* 13 *3.* 9 *4.* 14 *5.* 8 *6.* 11 *7.* 7 *8.* 5 *9.* 14

Ex. *2* (*p. 229*) *1.* b *2.* a *3.* a *4.* c *5.* b *6.* b *7.* a *8.* b *9.* a *10.* c

Ex. *3* (*p. 231*) *1.* 2/3 *2.* 4/5 *3.* 0 *4.* 0 *5.* 1/2 *6.* 0 *7.* 0 *8.* 0

Ex. *4* (*p. 232*) *1.* F *2.* F *3.* C/E *4.* E *5.* A *6.* G

Ex. *5* (*p. 232*) *1.* b *2.* c *3.* a *4.* a

Ex. *6* (*p. 234*) *through* Ex. *7* (*p. 235*) Self Check

CHAPTER 18.

Ex. *1* (*p. 238*) *1.* NO *2.* YES *3.* NO *4.* YES

Ex. *2* (*p. 239*) See Instructor

Ex. *3* (*p. 242*) *1.* 53 7/8 *2.* 41 *3.* $.25 *4.* 3,500 *5.* 43 1/8 *6.* 44 *7.* 44 *8.* 43

Ex. *4* (*p. 242*) *2.* $ .20 *3.* $ 1.40 *4.* 0
50 20 25
$10.00 $28.00 0

Ex. *5* (*p. 244*) *1.* 273.80 *2.* 270.42 *3.* 272.36 *4.* +0.88 *5.* High *946.85* Low *932.93* Close *938.59* Change *−1.61* *6.* High *137.14* Low *134.71* Close *135.77* Change *+.32* *7.* Opinion

CHAPTER 19.

Ex. *1* (*p. 250*) Answers in text

Ex. *2* (*p. 251*) Answers in text

Ex. *3* (*p. 256*) See Instructor

Ex. *4* (*p. 257*) *1.* a *2.* b *3.* c *4.* e

CHAPTER 20.

Ex. *1* (*p. 259*) *1.* a *2.* a *3.* a *4.* b *5.* b

Ex. *2* (*p. 260*) See Instructor

Ex. *3* (*p. 261*) Self Check

Ex. *4* (*p. 262*) *1.* T *2.* T *3.* T *4.* F *5.* F *6.* T *7.* T *8.* T *9.* T *10.* F

CHAPTER 21.

Ex. *1* (*p. 267*) *1.* 1 *2.* 2 *3.* 5 *4.* 14 *5.* 19 *6.* 22 *7.* 23

Ex. *2* (*p. 269*) Self Check

Ex. *3* (*p. 270*) *1.* 3 *2.* 4 *3.* 5 *4.* 9 *5.* 12 *6.* 11 *7.* X *8.* 6 *9.* X *10.* 8

Ex. *4* (*p. 271*) Self Check

Ex. *5* (*p. 271*) *1.* 1 *2.* 6 *3.* 10 *4.* X *5.* 7 *6.* X *7.* 9 *8.* 12 *9.* 15 *10.* 18

Ex. *6* (*p. 273*) *through* Ex. *16* (*p. 280*) Self Check

SKILLS CHECKLIST

(For additional skills and more detailed suggestions, see the Teacher's Manual.)

SKILL	WHERE IT CAN BE FOUND
1. Analyzing emotional appeals	Pages 36, 37, 38, 39, 68, 69, 73, 74, 75–76, 77, 136–137, 189–191.
2. Analyzing points of view	Pages 65–67, 74, 122–123, 127, 143, 159–165, 186–187, 188–191, 220–221, 269–273.
3. Assessing the role of the press and other media	Pages 144, 159–160, 162–165, 225, 256, 258, 266–269, 273–277, 281.
4. Decoding acronyms, abbreviations, affixes, pronouns, synonyms	Pages 2, 32, 60–62, 64, 86, 92–93, 95, 102–103, 112, 113, 119–120, 130, 134–137, 200, 202, 204, 206, 235, 272.
5. Determining cause and effect relationships	Pages 46, 48, 50, 58, 88, 108, 110, 112, 119, 120–121, 171, 180, 239–240, 243–244.
6. Determining if facts support a generalization	Pages 39, 71–73, 78–79, 148–149, 150–152, 160–161, 171–172, 212–213, 218–219, 220–221, 225, 271–272.
7. Developing ability to think critically	Pages 71–73, 79–88, 108–112, 118–123, 127, 136–138, 144–158, 160–164, 183–184, 186–187, 197–199, 202–204, 210–211, 218–219, 220–221, 259–265, 269–279.
8. Distinguishing source and evaluating authority	Pages 56–64, 68–69, 82–86, 150, 160–161, 171, 172, 174, 176, 179, 181, 188, 189, 194–195, 196–199, 203, 210, 212–213, 218–219, 220–221, 239, 268–269, 271–274.
9. Expressing ideas in writing	Pages 49, 50, 51, 53, 66–67, 71, 74, 82–83, 88, 101, 103, 120, 127, 136, 140–141, 142, 143, 153, 155–158, 163, 164, 165, 176, 183–184, 187, 193, 199, 209, 217, 237, 239, 260–262, 264–265, 269, 271, 274, 275–280.
10. Expressing ideas orally (other than general discussion)	Pages 63, 128, 163, 174, 177, 201, 260–261.
11. Getting meaning from context	Pages 90, 92, 108–109, 122, 183–184, 212–213, 220–221, 252, 258–260, 267–268.
12. Identifying relationships of time	Pages 45, 51, 54, 58, 67, 73, 87–88, 99–101, 102–103, 174, 180, 201, 214–215, 222–223.
13. Identifying the main idea	Pages 41–50, 80, 81, 82, 84, 88, 114–115, 118, 124, 150, 160, 161, 162, 171–172, 180–181, 182, 220–221.
14. Improving computational skills	Pages 6, 7, 8, 10, 11, 12, 70, 87–88, 94–96, 97, 98–99, 102–103, 110, 112, 113, 118–128, 143, 204, 205, 206, 212–213, 222–223, 224–225, 239–245, 247–249.
15. Interpreting figurative language	Pages 50, 108–109, 121, 142, 198, 207, 208.
16. Interpreting symbols, charts, tables, graphs, pictures, and cartoons	Pages 54, 55, 73, 78, 94–96, 97–98, 104, 107, 132–133, 145–146, 154–156, 173, 184, 192, 205, 222–223, 224, 235–237, 241–245, 247, 248, 249, 250–257, 263, 265.
17. Learning specialized terms	Pages 1–4, 16–18, 24–25, 26, 30, 32–33, 36, 39, 41, 65–75, 92, 108–111, 113, 118–125, 172–173, 183, 186, 204–205, 206, 211, 212–213, 214, 215, 239–241, 246–247.
18. Locating information in newspapers (indexes, sections, numbering systems, format)	Pages 4–13, 78, 92, 132–133, 166, 226–237, 240–241, 250–257, 258.
19. Making inferences, drawing conclusions, predicting outcomes	Pages 15–16, 30, 39, 46–47, 71–73, 77–78, 80–81, 90–91, 108, 110, 114–117, 131, 136–137, 140–142, 148–149, 154–156, 170, 172, 181–182, 183–184, 193–194, 198–199, 203, 229–231, 233–234, 259–260.
20. Recognizing and evaluating opinion	Pages 71–73, 86–87, 122, 150–151, 152–153, 154–158, 159–165, 174, 189, 210–211, 218–219, 258–265, 270–273.
21. Scanning and skimming for specific details	Pages 20–22, 26, 39, 40, 54, 58, 81, 87, 89, 90–91, 92, 100–101, 129–131, 167–169, 175, 181, 205, 218, 221, 227, 247.
22. Understanding punctuation	Pages 17, 18–19, 60–63, 84–85, 90, 92.
23. Using a glossary and dictionary	Pages 101, 185, 190, 245, 259, 267.
24. Using newspapers to find career opportunities and to become alert consumers	Pages 68, 105–128, 129–143, 166–177, 196–209, 218–219, 222–223, 225, 226–237, 238–249, 258–265, 269–281.
25. Using reference material	Pages 103, 139, 172, 183, 184, 246, 247, 276, 277, 281.